**DO NOT REMOVE
CARDS FROM POCKET**

International Herald Tribune

Doing Business in Today's Western Europe

Alan Tillier

NTC Business Books
a division of *NTC Publishing Group* • Lincolnwood, Illinois USA

Library of Congress Cataloging-in-Publication Data

Tillier, Alan.
    International Herald Tribune : doing business in today's Western Europe /
Alan Tillier.
      p.   cm.
    ISBN 0-8442-3387-0 (hardcover)
    1. Investments, Foreign—European Economic Community countries.
2. European Economic Community countries—Commerce. 3. European
Economic Community countries—Industries. I. Title.
HG5430.5.T55   1991
332.6′73′094—dc20
                                                                91-9011
                                                                CIP

Published by NTC Business Books, a division of NTC Publishing Group
4255 West Touhy Avenue
Lincolnwood (Chicago), Illinois 60646-1975, U.S.A.
© 1992 by International Herald Tribune s.a. All rights reserved.
No part of this book may be reproduced, stored in a retrieval system, or transmitted in any form
or by any means, electronic, mechanical, photocopying, recording or otherwise, without the prior permission
of NTC Publishing Group.

Manufactured in the United States of America.

2 3 4 5 6 7 8 9 BC 9 8 7 6 5 4 3 2 1

CONTENTS

FOREWORD

THIS NEW BOOK FROM THE *INTERNATIONAL HERALD TRIBUNE* IS THE latest in a series of titles designed to complement the business news published in the IHT. The newspaper's daily business coverage has been extended substantially through the years as readership of the IHT in the business community has mushroomed. But IHT books such as the annual *French Company Handbook* and the *Guide to Business Travel* series, covering Europe and Asia, add detail beyond that which is possible for the daily paper.

We hope this IHT guide, *Doing Business in Today's Western Europe* will prove a practical tool for business people already active within the European Community and for those about to enter what will be, after January 1, 1993, the world's largest single market, with its 340 million people.

Founded in Paris in 1887, the IHT circulates from eleven international print centers to nearly half a million readers each day in 164 countries. No longer are most of these readers American—most of them are international business executives.

Doing Business in Today's Western Europe does not, of course, deal with the fine detail of the European Community's 1992 Single Market program. These efforts evolve week to week, as the EC Commission in Brussels and the 12 member governments work to harmonize laws and regulations and to further the cause of a more unified Europe, on both the economic and the political fronts. A fuller accounting of the technical detail involved in these processes can be obtained from the EC's information centers which have now been established in most sizeable European cities.

In this volume, Alan Tillier, a distinguished international journalist, looks at some of the most important areas of cooperative European action, such as mergers and acquisitions policy, the social or workers charter, technical standardization, public procurement policies, and aviation and telecommunications policies. In addition, the book presents a country-by-country analysis of governmental and economic realities, opportunities for investors and exporters, the commercial real estate scene, labor and management relations, foreign business success stories, and regional development. And we are pleased, as we know the reader will be, by the care which the author has taken in including telephone numbers and other data which can help unlock further information and contacts.

The author has drawn upon a wide array of sources in preparing this book, from government and EC officials to factory floor workers. His efforts to cover all 12 member countries and, at the same time, to present an appropriate overview of Europe's movement towards greater federalism have proved daunting and fascinating tasks.

We hope this book will both instruct and entertain. It does not seek to be a definitive "Eurobook"—for Europe's "quiet revolution," to use Jacques Delors' phrase, is moving too fast. But it does provide, in our view, a very helpful handbook, an interesting background study and a useful reference tool on an ever-changing subject of enormous significance.

Lee W. Huebner
Publisher
International Herald Tribune

ACKNOWLEDGMENTS

A WIDE RANGE OF OFFICIALS AND BUSINESSPEOPLE GAVE GENEROUSLY of their time during the preparation of this book. The author wishes to thank them and to acknowledge his special debt to the following journalistic colleagues: Belgium, Brooks Tigner; Germany, Clive Freeman, Peggy Salz Trautman, and Richard Smith; Greece, Stephen Stafford; Italy, David Lane; Luxembourg, David Turner; Netherlands, Mark Fuller; Portugal, Patrick Blum and Peter Wise; Spain, Jane Monahan. Any errors and omissions are the fault of the author and not of the aforementioned men and women who interrupted their busy daily schedules covering the Single Market to offer advice and help.

Part One

THE EUROPEAN COMMUNITY

How Real Is Europe's
Single Market?

THE COUNTDOWN TO EUROPE'S SINGLE MARKET DEADLINE MUST now be measured in days rather than years. How much of the EC's grand strategy for streamlining itself into a U.S.-style marketplace is likely to have been achieved?

When midnight finally tolls on December 31, 1992 it will mark the end of an eight-year race against the clock. During that time the rules and conditions that have governed the way business is done in Europe have been radically changed.

The main change is that the many national ways of doing business in Europe have been transformed into an EC way. In areas like company law, anti-trust rules, environmental protection, consumer safeguards and financial services, the confusing patchwork of national practices is coming to an end.

The EC's timetable for removing national restrictions and replacing them with Community-wide rules and standards has been respected much more closely than many experts predicted back in the mid-1980s. In the early years of the 1992 program, progress did indeed seem disappointingly slow. But by the late 1980s a surge of agreements on knotty problems like technical harmonization, government purchasing and employment rules on employee rights enabled the EC Commission in Brussels to announce that the Single Market drive had passed the point of no return.

That is undoubtedly the case. There can be no return for the European Community to the days before the 1992 strategy was launched. The EC arguably marked time in the period between 1973 and 1984 and it seems unlikely that those doldrums will ever be revisited. The Community will either go forward to economic, monetary, and political union of some sort or it will founder and then become a different kind of grouping.

Hence the repeated calls by Jacques Delors, the president of the EC Commission, for countries to move faster towards union without waiting for economic convergence in an ideal Europe. In fact, convergence is underway and the approach of the Single Market is seeing inflation-plagued countries, such as Britain, Italy and, above all, Greece beginning to put their houses in order. While several inter-governmental discussions prepared the timetable of economic and monetary union with its goal of a single currency and also the shape of political union, Europe's companies were engaged in a new round of cross-border mergers and partnerships. Polls, too, show that the majority of Europe's citizens favor a European currency.

How cut and dried is the transition to Europe's Single Market? Although Europe's politicians and EC officialdom presented the 1992 program as a neat package of 282 measures that would iron out the key national differences, the truth is that bringing age-old business methods and traditions into line has proved a much more messy process.

For a variety of reasons, it is hard to click a stopwatch and say how far the 1992 program has progressed at any given moment. To begin with, the European Commission keeps on adding new proposals. More than 40 measures have been tacked on to the original ones because on closer examination it was found that a subject proved more complex than was at first anticipated. At the same time, about 20 of the original measures were withdrawn for similar reasons.

A second reason why it is hard to measure progress exactly is the variety of stages through which each measure must pass. When Single Market proposals are put to the EC governments there are several different shades of acceptance, ranging from final adoption to partial adoption to common positions through to "awaiting adoption." Sounds complicated? Enough, certainly, to make counting tricky.

In broad terms, about two-thirds of the Single Market measures had been agreed by all twelve EC states at the midpoint of 1991. That was only half the story, though, as national parliaments in the EC countries had not kept up with the speed of adoption by governments. The upshot was that only about ten percent of the Single Market measures had been transposed onto the national statute books of all the member states.

More worrying is that a number of crucial liberalizations are unlikely to go through. A Community-wide system of indirect taxation, notably in the use of common VAT rates, is not fully in place because countries like Britain seek exceptions. Yet the 1992 strategy was based on the idea that national customs officials could only be put out of business if there were no longer tax differences for them to collect. Still, efforts continue to harmonize the rates—not easy when each VAT point represents some $4 billion dollars for national treasuries.

Other issues still defying agreement include the free movement of people—another fundamental plank in the unification of Europe—and a host of technical standards, particularly in the area of farm livestock. Again, the persistence of these national barriers is an embarrassing reminder that the Single Market is far from complete.

It is unlikely that the freedoms and harmonizations now achieved will unravel. Perhaps the most encouraging point to be made is that Europeans no longer feel themselves constrained by the 1992 deadline, so the effort to iron out all the remaining national divergences will continue during the 1990s. As a canny Scottish banker put it: "1992 began yesterday and is the starting line not the finishing post." The hope is that progress towards greater political union (and with it a post-Gulf security policy) and a single European currency will itself resolve the Single Market's unfinished business. Maybe the immediate business boom will not match earlier predictions, but few doubt that it will come. The huge costs of crossing borders will dwindle and thousands of nationally-oriented regulations and standards will disappear resulting in savings of hundreds of billions of dollars.

Seen from the outside, the Community is a highly-desirable club to which to belong. The six countries of the rival European Free Trade Association (Austria, Finland, Iceland, Norway, Sweden, and Switzerland), plus tiny Liechtenstein, have formed a European Economic Area with the EC. Austria and Sweden are seeking membership of the EC as are Cyprus, Malta, and Turkey. The new Area, from the Arctic to the Mediterranean, will also act as an extra spur to the East European countries as they look westwards for their economic recovery. Czechoslovakia, Hungary, and Poland all have reached their desired free trading arrangements with the EC for the near future. Their long term goal is membership by the end of the decade. So at a time of economic problems and nationalist tensions, the Single Market stands as a beacon of hope.

Giles Merritt,
International Herald Tribune columnist
Alan Tillier

THE EUROPEAN COMMUNITY AT A GLANCE

::::::: EVOLUTION OF THE EUROPEAN ::::::: COMMUNITY

1950: A step towards a form of post-war cooperation in Europe proposed by Frenchman Jean Monnet is taken, when Monnet's fellow Frenchman, foreign minister Robert Schuman, opens negotiations with neighboring countries.

1951: Belgium, France, Germany, Italy, Luxembourg, and the Netherlands (the Six) sign the Paris Treaty creating the supranational European Coal and Steel Community.

1957: The Six gather again—this time in Rome—to sign the treaty establishing the European Economic Community. Their goal—a "common market" with the unhampered circulation of goods, capital and workers. The long-term aim is the union of the peoples of Europe.

1960: The European Social Fund, forerunner of other community-wide funds, is set up to aid employment and vocational training.

1962: Substantial help is granted the community's farmers via a common agricultural policy guaranteeing minimum prices. Later comes joint community action on energy, research, the environment, consumer protection, and fishing.

1967: Value added taxes (VATs) on goods and services are introduced in all six countries and come to provide the community with 60 percent of its budgetary resources.

1968: A customs union is created with the six abolishing duties at their own borders and setting a common tariff for imports from non-EEC countries.

1973: Britain, earlier victim of its own vacillation and General de Gaulle's veto, joins the "club" along with Denmark and Ireland.

1975: The signing of the Lomé Convention under which the European Development Fund grants aid to 46 (later 66) African, Pacific, and Caribbean countries.

1975: The creation of the European Regional Development Fund to assist those areas lagging behind the leaders.

1979: The creation of the European Monetary System to help currency stability. The main feature becomes the exchange rate mechanism (ERM). Under this, members (by 1991 all EC states, except Greece and Portugal) agree to maintain their exchange rates 2.25 or 6 percent above or below their central exchange rates against other ERM currencies.

1979 sees the arrival, too, of the fledging European currency unit or Ecu, later used for community accounting, but not yet in the hands of citizens.

1979: The European Parliament elected by direct vote for the first time. It now has 518 members, known as MEPs, grouped by party affiliation and not by nationality.

1981: Greece joins the community to bring the total of nations to ten.

1985: Jacques Delors, former French finance minister, becomes president of the Brussels-based European Commission, which sends policy proposals to the council of ministers. He provides new impetus towards the goal of European unity after years of bickering and bureaucratic stagnation. Following the adoption of the Single European Act, Commissioner Lord Cockfield has the task of drawing up a list of measures for a true Single Market by the end of 1992. The 282 measures, or "directives," form the 1992 program of economic integration. Specific proposals include the following.

> *Harmonization of standards, testing and certificating*
> Simple pressure vessels; toys, automobiles, trucks and motorcycles and their emissions; telecommunications; construction products; personal protection equipment; machine safety; measuring instruments; medical devices; gas appliances; agricultural and forestry tractors; cosmetics; quick frozen foods; flavorings; food emulsifiers; extraction solvents; food preservatives; infant formula; jams; modified starches; fruit juices; food inspection; definition of spirited beverages and aromatised

wines; coffee and chicory extracts; food additives; materials and articles in contact with food; noise of tower cranes; noise of household appliances; tire pressure gauges; noise of hydraulic diggers; detergents; liquid fertilizers and secondary fertilizers; noise of lawnmowers; medical products and medical specialties; radio interferences; earthmoving equipment; and lifting and loading equipment.

New rules for harmonizing packing, labelling and processing requirements
Ingredients for food and beverages; irradiation; extraction solvents; nutritional labelling; classification, packaging and labelling of dangerous preparations, and food labelling.

Harmonization of regulations for the health industry, including marketing
Medical specialties; pharmaceuticals; veterinary medicinal products; high technology medicines; implantable electromedical devices; disposable single-use devices, and in-vitro diagnostics.

Changes in government procurement regulations
Coordination of procedures for the award of public works and supply contracts; extension of EC law to telecommunications, utilities and transport services.

Harmonization of regulation of services
Banking; mutual funds; broadcasting; tourism; road passenger transport; railways; information services; life and non-life insurance; securities; maritime transport; air transport; electronic payment cards. Liberalization of capital movements: Long-term capital, stocks; short-term capital.

Consumer protection regulations
Misleading definition of products; indication of prices.

Harmonization of laws regulating company behavior
Mergers and acquisitions; trademarks; copyrights; cross-border mergers; accountancy operations across borders; bankruptcy; protection of computer programs; transaction taxes; company law.

Harmonization of taxation
Value added taxes; excise taxes on alcohol, tobacco, and other addictive products.

Harmonization of veterinary and phytosanitary controls:
Antibiotic residues; bovine animals and meat; porcine animals and meat; plant health; fish and fish products; live poultry, poultry meat and hatching eggs; pesticide residues in fruit and vegetables.

Elimination and simplification of national transit documents and procedures for intra-EC trade
Introduction of a single administrative document; abolition of customs presentation charges; elimination of customs formalities, introduction of common border posts.

Harmonization of rules on the free movement of labor and the professions within the EC
Mutual recognition of higher educational diplomas; comparability of vocational training qualifications; specific training in general medical practice; training of engineers; activities in pharmacy; activities related to commercial agents; income taxation provisions; elimination of burdensome requirements for residence permits.

1986: Spain and Portugal join the community to bring the total of nations to the current 12.

1987: The Single European Act comes into force after ratification by the 12 national parliaments. The new treaty brings the community into line with the needs of the 1990s and provides the contours for the world's largest, frontierless internal market. The Act extends qualified majority voting in the council of ministers ("sensitive" areas, such as taxation, movement of people, and workers' rights, remain subject to unanimous agreement). The administrative power of the Commission is strengthened, the Parliament becomes more involved in decision making, the European Court of Justice is empowered to consider actions brought by individuals. An impetus is given to achieving longer-term goals: economic and monetary union and a common foreign policy.

1990: New negotiations open with the countries of the European Free Trade Association (EFTA), the "other" Europe, comprising Austria, Finland, Iceland, Norway, Sweden, and Switzerland. This is the Community's largest trading partner, and the objective is to create a European Economic Area by extending most of the Single Market to cover EFTA. The 12 also seek closer relations via associate membership with the reborn countries of Eastern Europe and to coordinate aid measures for the Soviet Union.

1990: Rome summit sees Mrs. Thatcher vigorously opposing a future single currency in Europe. Her stalling tactics contribute later to her "overthrow." A second Rome summit sees the launching of two ongoing intergovernmental conferences. One concerns monetary union and the establishment of a European central bank. The other is devoted to political union, common foreign and defense policies strengthening the European Parliament and extending majority voting by ministers. The Gulf War gives an impetus to discussion of joint security and military policies.

1990: Belgium, France, Germany, Luxembourg and the Netherlands sign the Schengen Convention abolishing border controls for travelers between the five countries from the beginning of 1992, a year ahead of the Single Market (Italy, Spain, and Portugal join the five). Controls will continue for travelers and commercial visitors from outside the EC. The Convention is seen as a "laboratory" for the Single Market.

1991: The Luxembourg Presidency of the EC attempts to bring value added taxes into line in the 12 countries before the full removal of border controls. Differences are narrowed. Britain opposes the Social Charter, claiming it would mean centralized control of industry.

1991: The European Bank for Reconstruction and Development, a bridge to the East, begins operations in London.

1991: Commission President Jacques Delors proposes a compromise to overcome British opposition to a future single currency—Britain could sign a treaty on economic and monetary union while reserving the right to opt out later.

1991: European automakers (and computer and electronics firms) voice new fears over Japanese penetration, particularly via Britain.

1991: The summit in Maastrich, Netherlands, saw Britain still opposing the word "federal" in a new EC treaty. Earlier, progress had been made on extending the powers of the Parliament and the European court. Members of the summit agreed on a single currency and central bank by 1999 at the latest, but allowed Britain to have second thoughts on the common currency, the Ecu, and to stand aside from harmonization by the 11 others on social policy and labor laws.

THE COMMISSION

The Commission in Brussels proposes Community policy and legislation to the Council of Ministers, executes the Council's decisions, and supervises the day-to-day running of the Community, ensuring that member states comply with the rules. There are 17 commissioners, two each from Britain, France, Germany, Italy, and Spain and one each from the other members—Belgium, Denmark, Greece, Ireland, Luxembourg, Netherlands, and Portugal.

President: Jacques Delors. Special responsibilities include monetary affairs, press relations.

Vice-presidents:
Frans Andriessen (external relations and trade policy, cooperation with other European countries);
Martin Bangemann (internal market and industrial affairs, relations with the European Parliament);
Sir Leon Brittan (competition policy, financial institutions);
Henning Christophersen (economic and financial affairs, coordination of structural/aid funds, statistics);
Manuel Marin Gonzalez (cooperation and development, fisheries), and Filippo Maria Pandolfi (science, R & D, telecommunications, information industries, joint research center).

Other commissioners:
Jean Dondelinger (audiovisual and cultural affairs);
Antonio Cardoso e Cunha (personnel, energy, and small and medium sized enterprises);
Ray MacSharry (agriculture);
Abel Matutes (Mediterranean policy, Latin America, Asia, north-south relations);
Bruce Millan (regional policy);
Vassa Papandreou (employment, industrial relations and social affairs);
Carlo Ripa di Meana (environment);
Peter M. Schmidhuber (budget);
Christiane Scrivener (taxation and customs union);
Karel Van Miert (tranport).

DIRECTORATES GENERAL

The Commission's Wednesday meetings on the 13th floor of the Berlaymont building in Brussels are prepared by the commissioners' heads of staff or *chefs de cabinet*. They work with the heads of the directorates general, a bad translation from the French that now is firmly embedded in the language of the Community. In fact, the directorates general are the departments of the 14,000-strong European civil service and are referred to as "DGs." Of the 23, perhaps the most important for businesspeople are:

DG I: A kind of European State Department or Foreign Office that handles external relations. It is sub-divided into sections covering all corners of the globe. Directorate B covers North America and its key officials are Graham Avery, John Richardson, and Agne Pantelouri. Here also is the Poland-Hungary taskforce and officials dealing with the future links between the Community and other European countries, West and East;

DG III: Internal market and industrial affairs;

DG IV: Competition;

DG V: Employment, social affairs and education;

DG VI: Agriculture;

DG VII: Transport;

DG XI: Environment, consumer protection, and nuclear safety;

DG XII: Science and research and development;

DG XIII: Telecommunications, information industries and innovation;

DG XV: Financial institutions, company law;

DG XVII: Energy;

DG XXI: Customs union, indirect taxation;

DG XXIII: Enterprise policy, distributive trades, tourism, and cooperatives. DG XXIII's special brief is to improve the regulatory environment for businesses in Europe, particularly small and medium-sized enterprises. The directorate welcomes queries as it operates the EC's *fiche d'impact* under which Commission proposals must be accompanied by an assessment of the impact on business. DG XXIII is at 80 Rue d'Arlon, 1040 Brussels, close to Community headquarters. Tel: 32-2-236-1676.

THE COUNCIL

The council is the Community's ministerial decision-making body. Most measures for Europe's upcoming Single Market are subject to majority voting in the Council. Each member state has votes based on population. Until now, this system has meant Britain, France, Germany, and Italy each having ten votes, with eight votes for Spain, five each for Belgium, Greece, Portugal, and the Netherlands, three each for Denmark and Ireland, and two for Luxembourg. Total votes number 76, but the qualified majority has been set at 54. M. Delors has predicted that within the decade some 80 percent of the 12 countries' policies will be affected by decisions made in Brussels. A contrary notion has gained support. Known as "subsidiarity," it proposed that the 12 transfer to EC bodies only those responsibilities that are better carried out in Brussels. The need now is to define precisely the scope of subsidiarity in energy, defense, foreign affairs, culture and education, the environment, research and development, taxation, and social policy. In other words, the Community needs to decide how much pooling of sovereignty is feasible. The most important meetings are those of the European Council, six monthly gatherings of heads of state or government to discuss broad policy. During the Community's lifetime, specialist councils have been created: agriculture, finance, industry, research, internal market, budget, transportation, environment, labor, and social affairs. The foreign affairs council has the coordinating role over the activities of the specialist councils. It prepares the European Councils and deals with external trade. The emphasis now is on reaching successful conclusions at the two intergovernmental "conferences," or ongoing negotiations on economics and politics.

Councils are attended by relevant ministers from member states and by the Commission's representatives. The latter do not vote. Meetings are chaired by the state holding the EC presidency, which rotates every six months in alphabetical order. Britain will occupy the chair during the last six months of 1992.

How does the voting really work? The former unanimous—or veto—system of voting is not extinct. The big five states have 48 votes, the seven smaller countries 28. Negotiation tactics by a nation unhappy with a proposal revolve around putting together a minority block of 23 votes. The council has currently approved more than 200 of the 282 *directives,* binding on member states but which have to be approved by national parliaments. There are other forms of community legislation handled by the council and the commission: *regulations,* which are directly applicable in all states and which do not have to be confirmed by national parliaments to be legal. The regulation prevails over national law; *decisions,* which are binding for states, companies or individuals. Decisions imposing financial obligations are enforceable in national courts; and *recommendations* and *opinions* which have no binding force.

EUROPEAN PARLIAMENT

The European Parliament is a directly-elected body of 518 members, meeting principally in Strasbourg, but also in Luxembourg. Committee meetings are held sometimes in Brussels. Under EC treaties, the Parliament's formal opinion is required on many proposals before they can be adopted by the council of ministers. Most Single Market proposals are subject to the "cooperation procedure," under which the Parliament gives a first opinion when the commission makes a proposal, and then a second opinion after the council has reached a decision. The Parliament has "parties," or groups, which are multinational. The powers of the Strasbourg assembly are—for the moment—limited in comparison with national parliaments but they are steadily expanding. The European Single Act does grant Parliament powers of amendment, thus influencing European law. Parliament can even force the resignation of the commission (a two-thirds majority is required) and has some control over the EC budget. The Parliament is of particular interest to lobbyists who find the bars, restaurants, and corridors of Strasbourg useful for meeting not only European members of Parliament, but also senior EC officials up to the rank of commissioner. There is much question of increasing Parliament's powers beyond the "second reading" right granted it by the European Single Act. A stronger parliament would take action on the so-called "democratic deficit," by which is meant the extent of democratic control or the lack of it.

:::::::: EUROPEAN COURT OF JUSTICE ::::::::

The European Court of Justice, sitting in Luxembourg, rules on the interpretation and application of Community laws. The court comprises 13 judges and six advocates-general who are appointed for six year terms. The judges may request the modification of national decisions and legislation incompatible with EC treaties. It can rule in cases submitted by national courts when litigation involves Community law. However, as with the Parliament, the court lacks some teeth. However, the Court will be able to fine member states that refuse to implement EC law. This will provide a better operating environment for the EC.

::::::::::::::::::: EC OFFICES :::::::::::::::::::

EC Commission
Rue de la Loi 200
1049 Brussels
Tel: 32-2-235-1111
(1991–1992, the Commission
moves to a series of temporary
buildings while awaiting a new
headquarters).

Belgium
Rue Archimede 73
1040 Brussels
Tel: 32-2-235-3844
Fax: 32-2-235-0166.

Britain
8 Storey's Gate
London SW1P 3AT
Tel: 44-71-222-8122
Fax: 44-71-222-0900.

Denmark
Ostergade 61
PO Box 144
1004 Copenhagen K
Tel: 45-33-144140
Fax: 45-33-111203.

France
288 bd St. Germain
75007 Paris
Tel: 33-1-4063-3800
Fax: 33-1-4556-9417.

Germany
Zitelmannstrasse 22
5300 Bonn
Tel: 49-228-530090
Fax: 49-228-530-0950.

Greece
2 Vassilissis Sofias
Case Postale 11002
Athens 10674
Tel: 30-1-724-3982
Fax: 30-1-724-4620.

Ireland
39 Molesworth Street
Dublin 2.
Tel: 353-1-712244
Fax: 353-1-712657.

Italy
Via Poli 29
00187 Rome
Tel: 39-6-678-9722
Fax: 39-6-679-1658.

Luxembourg
Batiment Jean Monnet
Rue Alcide de Gasperi
352-2920 Luxembourg
Tel: 352-43011
Fax: 352-4301-4433.

Netherlands
Korte Vijverberg 5
2513 AB
The Hague
Tel: 31-70-469326
Fax: 31-70-646619.

Portugal
Centro Europeu Jean Monnet
Largo Jean Monnet 1-10
1200 Lisbon
Tel: 351-1-154-1144;
Fax: 351-1-155-4397.

Spain
Calle de Serrano 41
5a Planta
Madrid 1
Tel: 34-1-435-1700
Fax: 34-1-276-0387.

United States
2100 M Street
Suite 700
Washington, D.C. 20037
Tel: 202-862-9500
Fax: 202-429-1766

EUROPEAN PARLIAMENT

Palais de l'Europe
BP 1024
Strasbourg, France
Tel: 33-8817-4001

Plateau de Kirchberg
2929 Luxembourg
Tel: 352-43001
89-91 rue Belliard,
1040 Brussels, Belgium
Tel: 32-2-284-2111

Information offices:

Belgium
89-91 rue Belliard
1040 Brussels
Tel: 32-2-284-2111

Britain
2 Queen Anne's Gate
London SW1H 9AA
Tel: 44-71-222-0411

Denmark
Borsen DK 1217
Copenhagen K
Tel: 45-33-143377

France
288 Bd St Germain
75007 Paris
Tel: 33-1-4063-4000

Germany
Bonn Center
Bundeskanzlerplatz
5300 Bonn 1
Tel: 49-228-223091

Greece
2 Vassilissis Sofias
Athens 10674
Tel: 30-1-723-3421

Ireland
43 Molesworth Street
Dublin 2
Tel: 353-1-719100

Italy
Via 1V Novembre 149
00187 Rome
Tel: 39-6-679-0618

Luxembourg
1 Rue du Fort Thüngen
2929 Luxembourg
Tel: 352-4300-2597

Netherlands
Korte Vijverberg 6
2513 AB
The Hague
Tel: 31-70-362-4941

Portugal
Centro Europeu Jean Monnet
Largo Jean Monnet 1
1200 Lisbon
Tel: 351-1-578031

Spain
Fernanflor 4
28014 Madrid
Tel: 34-1-429-3352

DATABASES

Info 92. A database established by the European Commission and accessed through Eurobases. A tool for seeing how Single Market legislation will affect companies.

Eurobases
200 Rue de la Loi
B-1049

Brussels
Tel: 32-2-235-0001.

Plant Location International. A long-established service used by US multinationals. It has links with US databases and is considered by many to be the finest service in Europe.

Industrial Research Park
Avenue de Tyras
111,1120 Brussels
Tel: 32-2-268-0030.

Euro Information Services. A new Commission service, often linked with chambers of commerce and business consultants. Services are established in nearly 200 cities and towns across the Community. These mini-versions of the EC offices in the 12 capitals supply information, help with contacts with EC representatives, and advise on customs problems. They also assist conferences and run both BC-Net, an advice support network for small and medium businesses, and the Business Cooperation Center (BCC) of the Commission, designed specifically to arrange and assist joint ventures. Requests for partners are matched with data right across the Community. For access, contact EC offices in Europe, the US, Japan, and elsewhere.

Echo A reverse charge call to Luxembourg 08003456 connects with the desk offering advice on technology matters, EC programs, accessing EC databases and Max, Echo's talking computer. Also call Echo on: Belgium 11456; Denmark 80010756; Germany 0130823456; Netherlands 060223156; UK 0800899256.

Mead Data Central. US number (800) 227-4908, offers **CELEX,** the database of EC legislation, through its Lexis/Nexis service and also **Rapid,** produced by the EC Commission's Spokesman's service and updated daily. This contains press releases, news items, memos, speeches, and gives basic summaries and explanations of Commission proposals and decisions, detailed background notes, selected speeches by Commissioners; **Ted,** or Tenders Electronic Daily, with invitations to tender for public supply and works contracts (particularly in electrical and mechanical engineering, construction, printing, supply of fuels) from the EC, GATT members, ACP states, Japan, Sweden, and the U.S.

COMMON INTERESTS
AND AMBITIONS

Jacques Delors, President, European Commission

THE CHALLENGE IS, OF COURSE, POLITICAL, BUT ALSO MORAL AND spiritual, and it is what awaits the Community in the period immediately following the completion of the internal market scheduled for December 31, 1992. Two points in particular are worth dwelling on in response to this challenge.

The first is the question of the future relationship between the European Community and the United States in the context of a changing Atlantic alliance. In December 1989, in Berlin, US Secretary of State, James Baker, asked the right questions, to which the Community has still to articulate responses. Of course, it is true that our relationship with the US has intensified, but we have to pose the basic question of the nature of tomorrow's partnership. It must be one of equals, as political thinkers on both sides of the Atlantic have affirmed frequently, and one which corresponds to the vision of Jean Monnet, the intellectual father of the New Europe. Up to now, we have not posed this question for one simple reason: Among the 12 member states there are some who, nostalgia being what it is, still dream of being able to act alone.

Such an attitude involves a considerable overestimation of the maneuvering room of even the large member states. Only a united Community can have room to maneuver, can acquire the necessary capacity for reflection, influence, and action, and can assume its rightful role in the new world taking shape.

Such questions cannot wait for a new institutional reform of the Community, and indeed our reflections on them may have a significant practical consequence on the prospects of such reforms. As I have often said, because history is accelerating, the Community must also move faster to fulfill its task and to introduce indispensable reforms.

A common European home? A confederation? An enlarged Community? There are many different options, combinations, and possibilities. I propose two criteria to guide such discussions and to keep them rooted in practical consideration. First, how can we define the essential interests common to all European countries today? Second, what is the extent of our economic, social, and political ambitions within the Community framework? If we pose these two questions simultaneously, and if the Community can reply that it is ambitious, then the commitments of future membership will be more binding and this will clarify the issue of the future model of the Community.

The question of essential common interests is extremely important, because it is a way to avoid disputes between those who say, for example, that they support speaking with a single voice on foreign policy, and those who say that this is impossible. Essential common interests have brought about earlier progress in European construction, and conversely, no progress was ever made without the recognition of such an essential common interest.

An obvious example from recent history is the Single Market of 1992, which was founded on this essential common interest. It was a qualitative leap in the face of threatened economic decline and Europe's inability to find a way out of its "crisis," as we called it then. The Single Market was to act also as a catalytic force in an increasingly competitive world economy.

Once the single-market decision was made, we put in place the Single European Act and reviewed and adapted our common policies. At the same time, we reinforced those policies in order to create and solidify the Community's internal market. However, a balanced and durable market cannot be created just by abolishing internal frontiers and assuring complete freedom of movement for people, goods, services, and capital. We also needed a series of flanking political measures corresponding to another essential common interest: that of assisting countries lagging behind. These countries can then see in the Community's policies support for their own development efforts. The longer-run interests of the more developed countries are also served as they gain the opportunity to expand their trade and further strengthen their economies.

Completing the internal market has been followed by moves toward the realization of economic and monetary union as decided by the EC member states at the Madrid European Council in June 1989. The process began on July 1, 1990, and has been accepted not just for economic reasons but as an essential contribution to Europe as a political entity. This is a point that was already made in 1970 in the Werner Report, which in response to a request from the heads of state and government meeting in the Hague produced a plan for the realization, by stages, of economic and monetary union.

A step forward was made in 1979 with the European Monetary System (EMS), but this was to a large extent only a response, however positive, to currency fluctuations. Today, we have updated and revised the Werner report and have begun the process of economic and monetary union (EMU). We could not free capital movements and respond adequately to the instability that such liberalization might provoke without a common monetary policy. Moreover, the people of Europe were asking how a political Europe was possible without a single currency. EMU is the political response, and the Dublin European Council agreed that the negotiations on the necessary treaty changes would begin in December 1990, with the objective of ratification by the member states before the end of 1992.

So, at a key moment, common interest prevailed. Tomorrow it will be necessary to find these essential common interests to reinforce cooperation in foreign policy, thus overcoming the contradictions inherent in traditions and geopolitical situations that are perceived as very different. It may well follow from this process that the EC has to give more attention to security issues in the broad sense, including military security, because this will also be a matter of common interest. The first criterion, therefore, is to decide who shares these essential common interests. Some countries now outside the Community will certainly want to say that they do. But others will refuse a concerted foreign policy, and, *a fortiori* a defense policy, through a posture of neutrality or through maintenance of different views.

The second criterion is the level of our common ambitions. This is surely the basic point we must put to our friends in other countries who want to become part of the EC, albeit on their own terms. Our response will be along these lines: Is it not reasonable that our group of countries, while willing to cooperate with you, want to go further? How can this be denied, especially since it forms the *affectio societatis,* the social pact between us?

The level of our ambitions is associated with two fundamental ideas. The first is the realization that the Community has international responsibilities, and the resulting awareness that its margin for maneuver can only be maximized by speaking with a single voice and acting in unison. The second ambition, which already divides us (but by a margin of eleven-to-one rather than seven-to-five) is our conception of political democracy and social organization. These factors determine the level of our ambition and explain why the Community does not intend to dilute itself into a feeble entity that has renounced its responsibilities and ambitions, a view with which I concur fully.

Regarding the second ambition, one thing can be said without any fear of contradiction: There is a European model of society that is accepted by the vast majority in the Community and that is considered worth defending. This European model of society is distinct from (not necessarily better than but different from) the American and Japanese models.

The people of Europe want to keep this model. In all the efforts and sacrifices that have gone into adapting the Community's economy, an accent has always been put on what the Germans call the Sozialmarktwirtschaft, the social market economy. So it is these two elements, our essential common interests and the level of our ambitions, that should serve as our guide for the future.

Whenever I am asked about tomorrow's great European construction I draw from these two elements one simple idea: The European Community is not simply a fruit of the Cold War, and so must not die with the Cold War's end. It is the fruit of an ideal that was alive even in the last century, that was carried forward by a growing minority of politicians, that found institutional expression after the war, and that remains very much alive today. Were it not alive we would never have made such progress in the face of so many pessimistic predictions.

The countries of Europe can cooperate in several ways, even though the level of ambition and the search for essential common interests are not viewed in the same way by every country. Similarly, several forms of cooperation are possible with and within the other regional groupings in the world. The growth of these groupings, which are motivated by the same type of issues that inspired and necessitated the EC, shows that the world is in a process of reorganization.

Only through sharing the burden can global problems be addressed and can the EC itself continue to gain influence. This will be done primarily through the reorganization of the world economy. And as long as the member states of the European Community do not agree on the direction of this reorganization, progress will be stalled. Whatever progress has been made in recent years, the world economic system is still unjust, and therefore inefficient.

Certain problems can only be solved with the emergence of new forms of cooperation at a global and not simply a European level. One example is the vital question of the environment, with its ethical aspects and the need for a planetwide response. Even with the many conferences on the environment, no one has yet proposed or dared propose reinforcing the United Nations Environment Program, which is the only one directed at all parties in the world.

In the Community, we have agreed on setting up a European Environment Agency to try to have a permanent "check up" on nature. We hope that it will become a full-fledged international agency, and when that day comes Europe will not adopt a proprietorial attitude! The same goes for the fight against the other great threats facing the world such as cancer, narcotics, and AIDS.

Such efforts show that while the Community must reinforce itself, it must not hesitate, if necessary, to propose various other forms of cooperation at regional, global, or other levels, including the pan-European. Other examples include the new relationship we are trying to forge with the European Free Trade Association countries; the Community's new association agreements with the East European countries, which have a strong political component; and the common actions we could undertake in the framework of strengthening the Conference on Security and Cooperation in Europe. These relations are within our grasp, but all this must not deter thinking about the Community's future, be it only as an instrument for tackling problems on a world scale. Thus the organization of the EC, in particular its federal structure, remains an idea full of possibilities.

A federal community is not an idea of the past, but of the future. It is perfectly compatible with accepting the global responsibilities I mentioned.

History has not rendered it obsolete. After all, the Community was not simply a product of the Cold War; and the federal approach has demonstrated its value, as seen in the efficiency of the Community's organization in comparison to organizations established purely on an intergovernmental basis. The Community's experience has shown that it can reconcile the union of people and the closer association of nations. Jean Monnet used to say that it was a question above all of uniting people. Today, with the perspective of realism, I would add, "and of bringing nations together."

Up to now the federal approach has allowed us to reconcile these elements in a subtle institutional balance. Preserving this balance is vital in order to assure action on common interests, to respect patriotism and national interests where necessary, and to put an end to the battle for supremacy between the intergovernmental and the supranational. In this context, recognizing our essential common interests, heads of state agreed to set up a second negotiation on the treaty changes necessary for political union in the European Community. These negotiations opened and concluded within the same time frame as the negotiations on EMU.

Until now, it has been possible to reconcile the intergovernmental, which reflects our roots and our histories, and the supranational. But it is not clear that this will always be possible. This is why I favor a federal approach, which has the merit of transparency and clarity. Each member state knows what it must do, and beyond which point it may not go.

This federal approach can also play a vital inspirational role. The difficulty in moving toward political union is that, although this step comes at the right time to keep up with the pace of change, it also comes as some very wide differences of opinion between countries and schools of thought remain. We will not escape from these difficulties unless we know what we owe to the past, and what we owe to the future.

Thus, the Community once again faces the same choices as it did in the 1950s and the 1980s: rapid progress or gradual disintegration. If we opt for the second path, disintegration will be so slow that without realizing it we will again sink into decline and neglect our global responsibilities. This would satisfy all those politicians who think only of themselves. But what will the verdict be in 20 years, or even in 10?

We hear too many self-satisfied speeches on what is happening in the Community or in Europe generally. But too much self-satisfaction leads to complacency and stagnation, which is the last thing we need. Instead, we need lucidity, vigilance, and courage to meet the new challenges thrown down by history.

THE NEW EUROPE—AN ALTERNATIVE VIEW

Dr. David Owen, Former British Foreign Secretary

THE ROLE OF THE NATION STATE INTO THE 21ST CENTURY IS THE KEY political question of our time. It is paradoxical that at a time when the USSR has been breaking up and moving towards 15 separate nations, some want the European Community to merge its 12 nations into one superstate.

Hitherto the unique strength of the European Community has been that its design has allowed us to develop its inner unity, while respecting the nationhood of its member states.

Though the initial six started with strong overtones of developing into one nation, France could always be relied on to limit the federal dream of the founding fathers. It used to be inconceivable that any French President, not just Charles de Gaulle, would create a European Community that had a directly elected President with a Cabinet of European Ministers answerable to a European Parliament.

Today, there is no such certainty in the European Community. Now the so-called "democratic deficit" is used as an argument for the merging of our nations on democratic grounds. The economic grounds, the so-called "economies of scale," have always been in the background as an argument for greater integration.

The intention is a United States of Europe though it rarely speaks its name. Yet all experience shows that the larger the democratic unit of government, the less it is answerable to the people it controls. The nation state has lasted over so many centuries in Europe because in the main it reflected a geographical area with which people could identify and broadly control.

It is no accident that it was the new democrats in the USSR who argued for independence for its 12 Republics and for independence for the three Baltic States that were invaded in 1940 and which we in the West never accepted as being part of the USSR. It was the bureaucrats and old style Leninists who wanted to keep the Empire in existence. They had to accept that they could no longer keep down the satellite nations but they wanted to retain the boundaries of the USSR. It has always been a notable characteristic of the debate within the European Community that the bureaucrats have been to the fore in arguing for the merging of our nations and decrying the virtues of nationhood. It is, of course, superficially tidier to bring all the 12 nations together but I will never be convinced that it will be more democratic. It is an old aphorism that the price of democracy is a little untidiness.

We have seen in the last two years in Central Europe the flowering of nationhood, a period of history reminiscent of 1848. The Soviet Empire collapsed because it had overreached itself and Communism did not work. The defeat in Afghanistan was the outward and visible sign. The collapsing economy only became apparent later. We are still discovering how rotten was the East German economy and yet for years we believed that this was one of the most successful of the Communist economies. Even now our political leaders in the West still find it hard to understand how broken down is the Soviet economy. It is the independence of nationhood which will eventually ensure that the benefits of a democratic system and a market economy extend to all those people who have lived under Communist rule.

The democratic imperative for the European Community is to extend the certainty of membership to Poland, Czechoslovakia and Hungary by the year 2000, just as we extended the certainty of membership to Greece, Spain and Portugal when they returned to the democratic fold. Today we hear the same dire economic predictions about enlargement to the North as we heard 15 years ago about enlargement to the South. We used to be told how damaging it would be for the Community to embrace the Spanish economy and yet Spain is now one of the most rapidly growing and prosperous members of the European Community. Greece has taken longer than many of us hoped to adapt fully to the Community. I am optimistic that adaptation will now proceed faster than hitherto.

With the three Baltic States, Latvia, Estonia, and Lithuania, now finally free, then Norway, Sweden, and Finland can give them the same sort of help to buttress their democracy and develop a market economy as the Community should do for Poland, Hungary, and Czechoslovakia. But we will never succeed in the transformation of these nations if we spread our financial, managerial, and technical skills so as to embrace the whole of the old USSR, Bulgaria, Rumania, Yugoslavia, and Albania.

Far better to ensure true democracy and a viable market economy for those countries closest geographically to us. We can be reasonably certain that this will profoundly influence their neighbors and that slowly the whole process of transformation will gather momentum. The best economic help we in the West can give is to move as fast as the Soviets want in balanced reductions of military spending, manpower and hardware. Of course, we can add to this some technical help and general goodwill but to pour money out as we did with Poland in the 1980s would be folly.

The achievable is the enlargement of the European Community from 12-plus (East) Germany to 16, with Austria becoming a member in the next few years and helping particularly Hungary to make the transition to full membership by the end of this Century and all of us helping Poland and Czechoslovakia. I know that a strong case can be made for Yugoslavia joining the Community. We all know that Turkey feels that it should be a member and after its courageous stance towards Iraq there will be more arguing its case. But to all the many other applicants, the European Community will have to say that experience shows that enlargement can only take place at a manageable rate. Norway is probably a special case in that only their referendum halted membership. But even so it would be preferable if Norway, Sweden, and Finland formed a Community with the Baltic States as part of a transition to full membership.

The problem in talking of enlargement is that there are many voices, particularly in Brussels, that want to stick with the existing 12. In part they fear enlargement because it might weaken the Community in the short term but in the main their opposition stems from their determination to merge the 12 nations into one.

The argument against enlargement of the European Community is essentially an argument about the United States of Europe and the merging of nationhood. It is very necessary that responsible voices are raised within the Community in support of a Community of nations to forge greater unity and further integration and not a United States of Europe.

Greece is the cradle of democracy. Greece has a long history of independence. It is, like the UK, a maritime nation and a nation with a strong cultural identity. I find it hard to believe that the Greece I knew well as a student and the Greece that I encouraged as Foreign Secretary to become a member of the European Community to buttress the restoration of its democracy, will lightly dismantle the essentials of its nationhood.

In the UK, I believe it is the settled will and widespread conviction of most people to retain our nationhood albeit within a more unified Community.

The essentials of nationhood change over time. They are nevertheless tangible, one knows a nation when one sees it. Nationhood is not something which can be lost or subsumed without it soon becoming all too apparent. The problem about flirting with a United States of Europe is that it is a flirtation that could end in an unwanted marriage.

At the start of this century, few would have believed that a structure like NATO would have been compatible with independent nationhood. Yet NATO was able to accept a Supreme Allied Commander and the pooling of the defense effort of 16 nations while retaining their separate national commands and national identity. NATO was able to match and face down the might of the Warsaw Pact in the 1960s and 70s where the Soviet Union dominated to an extent that was never the case with the US.

There is no doubt, particularly after the inability of the European Community to respond quickly and unitedly to the Iraqi invasion of Kuwait, that we should transform the Western European Union (WEU) into a Community defense organization. That would mean all its member states being automatic signatories to the Treaty of Brussels, while respecting the neutrality of Ireland, and Austria when it becomes a member as I fully expect it to do in the next few years. NATO would still exist as a wider organization of 16 countries, crucially linking Europe with North America. But the Community, already necessarily involved in security and disarmament questions, would gain an inner core of competence and knowledge which it currently lacks and without which its political cooperation in foreign affairs will lack coherence and clout. This is a development that the US should welcome, not fear.

Neither NATO nor a transformed WEU require the abandonment of the unfettered right of a nation state to call on its own armed forces to defend its own territory or to use its own armed forces outside its own territory and that of its alliances to protect its own perception of its national interests. NATO achieved progressively greater unity without challenging the essential sovereignty of its member states.

At the start of this century it was assumed that control of one's own currency was the hallmark of a nation. Only after the Bretton Woods Agreement in 1946 did it become apparent that one could join a collective arrangement for the stability of one's currency without foregoing the essential financial freedoms of an independent nation. A free-floating currency is not the hallmark of a nation. With the relative success of the European Monetary System it is understandable that particularly those members within the Exchange Rate Mechanism should be considering the advantages of statutory fixed exchange rates and a single currency.

We should have a European System of Central Banks and we should move towards a common currency and even ensure broadly the same levels of indirect taxation within the member states. None of those challenges essential economic rights of nationhood. But it is very hard to see how the level of redistribution of income and rates of direct personal taxation can be taken away from the member states without there being a fundamental erosion of nationhood. It is not at all certain that maintaining that freedom is compatible with maintaining a single currency where there can be no national change, even in extremis, of the exchange rate. Time alone will tell whether the Community can develop sufficient economic convergence and political consensus that it would be ready to live with the internal discipline of a totally fixed exchange rate. If one wants a United States of Europe, a single currency presents no problems and it is again characteristic of those people who are heading the rush towards a single currency that in their heart of hearts they already want a marriage of nations within the European Community.

Another reason for doubting the virtue of a bloc-on-bloc world where only large nations can survive is that we are possibly on the threshold of making the United Nations the international body that the founding fathers envisaged in 1945. The UN Charter is designed for a world of many diverse nations. Large nations and small nations all working within a structure which will, I hope, start to reflect the concept of Common Security that the Palme Commission started to develop in its report published nearly a decade ago. In such a world, which respects nationhood, it may be possible to develop the mechanisms for achieving a better ordering of our natural resources and our wealth. A world where national ambitions are curbed by the recognition of existing boundaries and the capacity to enforce that recognition.

There is no doubt that the European Community, if it is successful in developing a Community of nations, will contribute positively to such a new world order for we will have shown that democratic countries can combine together at a very high level of integration without abandoning their national identity, culture, individuality or pride.

MERGER AND
ACQUISITIONS POLICY

by Brooks Tigner

AFTER 17 YEARS OF DEBATE, THE EUROPEAN COMMUNITY HAS THE authority to regulate large, cross-border mergers and acquisitions (M&As) in the EC. The issue has taken so long to resolve because it represents a significant transfer of control over a key area of decision-making from national capitals to the Commission in Brussels.

The new law establishes a procedure that allows the Commission to decide in advance of a proposed merger undertaking whether it is compatible with EC competition rules. The process is basically an anti-trust review and applies to all companies—regardless of their nationality—that join forces in the Community, assuming certain specific, prior conditions come into play.

The legal instrument that went into force September 21, 1990 is known in Community lingo as the "merger regulation." However, this is a misnomer since cross-border acquisitions, raids and joint-ventures are also covered. European business and industry supports the idea of such a regulation in order to harmonize the legal operating environment within the EC. But there are worries that the new law may not operate as smoothly as Commission authorities have so reassuringly declared. Only time—and probably more than a few cases before the EC's Court of Justice—will tell.

The regulation is designed to provide business and industry with a single or "one-stop" merger review by transferring control of big M&As from national authorities across the EC to the Commission. Technically, this affects only Britain, Germany, and France, since no other member states have formal anti-trust authorities.

Only the very largest cross-border mergers are affected: those where aggregate worldwide turnover of the companies involved is more than five billion ECUs (+ $6.5 billion) *and* where at least two of the companies involved generate an aggregate *EC-wide turnover* exceeding 250m ECUs. Only those mergers whose turnovers are inferior to either of these two thresholds will fall to national anti-trust bodies to decide. However, there are certain provisos operating in favor of the latter.

If two-thirds of the turnover of each company occurs in one and the same EC member state, then Brussels has no say. That is, if a majority of each potential partner's sales turnover is generated overwhelmingly in one "home" market, then the linkage is not judged to have a sufficiently "Communitywide" dimension and should be left to the national authorities involved to rule.

Neither can the Commission automatically review M&As where "prudential" rules are involved, i.e. questions of national security or maintaining plurality of the media. But, in these cases, a member-state authority may, if it chooses, refer a given "excluded" case to the Commission for advise or even an actual ruling.

Otherwise, companies that are fused in "a Communitywide dimension" will have to submit detailed information to the Commission within a week of a publicly announced merger, acquisition or joint venture. The nature of this data is set out in the regulation's annex in the form of specific questions about a company's size, market share, product range, R&D activity, and so on. All information supplied will be handled confidentially by the Commission's competition authority, DG-IV, which has set up a new computerized security system to guard against leaks or abuses of company files.

DG-IV, says it has already assembled a taskforce of 50 to handle the expected 40–50 mergers annually falling within the regulation's scope. At the end of four years (late 1994), the task force will number 85. By this time the annual caseload should also rise to approximately 150 as the regulation's upper threshold "floor" falls to two billion ECUs for worldwide turnover.

The Commission has one month to decide on a merger following notification. If cleared, then the affair is over and the merger parties can get on with their undertaking. If Brussels has competitive doubts, however, then all merger activity is frozen for four months during which the Commission must gather its evidence and give a definitive ruling.

Companies which fail to notify Brussels or supply insufficient or false information can be penalized with fines ranging from 1000 ECUs up to 50,000 ECUs. Those refusing to abide by a (negative) merger ruling can be fined up to 10 percent of their aggregate turnover. So far, the maximum fine imposed by the Commission for breach of competition policy has been around 15m ECUs.

Although corporate lawyers complain about the regulation's complex reporting requirement, their real worries center on whether or not the new EC law really will function as a "one-stop" review mechanism for cross-border mergers. Observers fear, for instance, that the line between national and EC jurisdiction for a given merger is still unclear and might give rise to a double review, first by national and then by EC authorities.

They have other concerns, too. What about those mergers with total worldwide turnover of less than five billion ECUs but with more than 250m ECUs of EC sales? What if a proposed merger between companies in two different member states raises national security questions for one national government but not for the other? Will the former's merger authority rule or should Brussels step in as a disinterested outsider?

Moreover, how will the Commission reconcile its new merger-review powers with the EC's existing competition laws, namely Articles 85 and 86 of the Community's founding Treaty of Rome constitution? These two articles lay down strictures, respectively, against cartels and abuses of a company's dominant position within a given industry or sector. DG-IV officials say they will use the same statistical and theoretical yardsticks to measure anti-competitive behavior under Articles 85/86 as they will to judge whether a proposed merger will promote or hinder competitive conditions in the internal market. Nevertheless, merger lawyers worry that a merger might initially be approved under the new regulation and then subsequently be rescinded under Article 85 or 86 as the new entity restructures its activities.

Thus, while it is much too early to make any predictions about how, or whether, the regulatory gray area between DG-IV and the EC's national antitrust bodies will be eliminated, no one doubts the regulation's power to shape Europe's industrial landscape as the continent's major corporate players stake out their territory in the run-up to the Single Market and beyond. In the end, the EC's Court of Justice in Luxembourg will probably play a central role as companies challenge DG-IV rulings and, moreover, as national merger bodies struggle with Brussels for jurisdiction over a section of corporate law vital to the EC's economic future.

TECHNICAL STANDARDIZATION

ONE OF THE MOST LETHAL ADMINISTRATIVE TRAPS LYING IN WAIT FOR the 12 European Community states is technical standardization. Not only does the longterm success of the Single Market depend on Community-wide norms, but there is great fear among the EC's trade partners that technical standards will be used to keep out their goods.

The EC knows the issue is a potential time bomb and has taken measures to avoid it. Whether it succeeds won't become evident, however, until well after the 1992 internal market deadline has been passed: reforming the way countries define and test their technical standards necessarily requires years of laborious effort.

As in the USA, setting standards in Europe has by tradition been a voluntary effort involving a wide range of industry groups, government organs, and professional institutes. While efficiently organized along national lines, it has led to chaos on the pan-EC scale: 12 different approaches to setting technical standards and 12 sets of product testing, inspection and certification rules. Try fitting an English plug into a Spanish socket.

Brussels is imposing order in three ways. First, in 1985 the EC created its "new approach" to standardization. Instead of laying down highly detailed specifications for individual items as it did in the past—a failed attempt at total harmonization—the EC laws base themselves on two novel ideas. One requires simply that new products for circulation in the Single Market meet "essential safety requirements." These spell out broad guidelines for the manufacturer concerning a product's toxicity, inflammability, wear-and-tear limits, electrical configuration and so on—basic consumer safety features, in other words. The other innovation is administrative. Once a company's product is vetted as safe for the general public in its own country, it receives an "EC Mark" of approval that automatically entitles the company to sell its goods in all other member states with no further red tape. The new "home rule" approach has already been applied, for example, to construction products, pressure valves, handheld tools and machinery and toys. It will gradually spread to most other product areas as well. And it offers the same benefits to non-EC companies as for domestic firms.

The second big change is a new role for the three pan-European organizations responsible for setting technical standards. Two are based in Brussels. Each known by its French acronym, CENELEC deals with the electrotechnical field, while CEN handles all other industrial sectors except telecommunications standards. The latter is managed by the newly created European Telecommunications Standards Institute (ETSI), headquartered in southern France. Separately, CEN, CENELEC and ETSI operate as independent umbrella groups representing their respective national standards-setting institutes in 18 countries: the EC states plus EFTA member states Switzerland, Austria, Sweden, Finland, Norway, and Iceland. But together the three comprise what is known as the Joint European Standards Institution, (JESI).

Until recently, JESI waited for the member states to propose standards. That was the "bottom up" approach: a request originated from an individual industry association or national standards body which then notified one of the JESI bodies. The latter then put out a notice to all its members to halt standards work in that area until the new norm was approved.

The new method is "top down," with CEN, CENELEC and ETSI taking a more aggressive role. Acting on mandates from the Commission, they now have responsibility for drawing up an increasing number of broadly worded pan-European technical standards, such as those for construction products. As for ETSI, its standards are very precise and often binding since the EC views its telecoms and information technology sectors as vital to the Community's economic future.

The three groups are also playing a pivotal role in a soon-to-be-created EC body for conformity assessment, which leads us to the third leg of Brussels' strategy. The European Organization for Testing and Certification (EOTC) should come into existence soon and is of vital interest to all businesses that export into and across the EC. Based in Brussels, EOTC's membership will draw on a wide spectrum of European society: consumer organizations, trade unions, industry associations, standards bodies of the member states, and the Commission. Its primary task will be to herd the EC's 10,000 test laboratories—each of which has a different legal status and reputation—into using the same internationally recognized operating rules.

Similar to JESI's duties vis-à-vis technical standards, the Commission expects EOTC to streamline product certification methods in the EC. This calls for application of the "home rule" principle in this area, too. That means if a product is approved under the certification rules of one member state, then it earns immediate market access to all the others, thus reducing cost and delay to business and industry. US exporters will enjoy the same privileges.

Impressive as this all seems, however, JESI will not resemble anything like a monolith, at least not in the medium term. Public and private national bodies across the 12 member states will continue to carry out the nuts-and-bolts of defining standards and testing/certifying products. JESI's primary duty is the coordination and speeding up of what those national bodies do. Fullscale control and harmonization of conformity assessment rules, as well as the setting of technical norms at the European level are feasible only in the longterm.

Making sense of this process is not easy and it has led to political misunderstandings on both sides of the Atlantic. The EC stresses that, whenever possible, its technical norms take those of the International Standards Organization (ISO) as a first, identical reference. But JESI also reminds outsiders that the EC is not dragging itself through this whole exercise merely to recreate a mini-ISO structure in Europe. As one official put it: "In view of our goal of economic unification, the needs of European industry must come first."

Nevertheless, business and industry circles outside the EC do exercise varying influence over EC technical standards. For instance, the EFTA countries signed several agreements in 1989 with the EC to strengthen relations between their standardization bodies. Two provide for financial support from EFTA to CEN, CENELEC, and ETSI, while the third calls for the bilateral exchange of technical information between their electronic databases. One of these, known as Integrated Standardization Information System (ISIS), should come on-line in 1991–92. It offers data on existing standards and those under review for future approval or revision.

US firms have no formal say in the drafting of EC norms, although their subsidiaries operating in Europe may exercise some influence if they are members of a standards-setting group within a national industry. Brussels has assured Washington that it will receive advance notice of all public technical review sessions, while JESI says it welcomes well-researched suggestions from US industry on technical matters. But suggestions will remain just that, with no obligation to act on them.

More encouraging is the EC's intention to negotiate with its main trade partners for the mutual recognition of testing, inspection, and certification methods. This would enable approved products carrying the official "EC" label to circulate freely in other markets and vice versa, provided non-EC products have been approved by their national authorities first or, ideally, in foreign labs designated by the EC to carry out its technical requirements.

The only hitch is getting each side to recognize and, if necessary, alter the other's laboratory-and-testing procedures. No need to stay glued to your seat: it will be a long-running dialogue.

PUBLIC PROCUREMENT POLICY

ASIDE FROM TAXES, THERE IS NO AREA THAT WILL TEST THE VIABILITY of the Single Market as much as public procurement. The challenge of throwing open national, state, and local contracts to cross-border bidding in the EC transcends mere questions of legal competition. On the one hand, it implies shattering the cosy relationships that public contracting authorities have established over the years with local suppliers. On the other, it requires an even-handed approach to the bidding process itself—rules, in other words, that are applied fairly to all who want to participate. Neither aim will be easy to achieve, no matter how many laws are promulgated in Brussels.

The stakes are huge: the estimated value of contracts for goods, services, and construction projects that are farmed out by public authorities in the EC is some 350 billion ECUs ($460 billion) or approximately 10 percent of the Community's global GNP. If defense and other non-tradeable goods are thrown in, the value rises to 530 billion ECUs—a sum larger, in fact, than total trade between the 12 member states.

Public contracting bodies in an EC state, as elsewhere, are extremely reluctant to disburse the taxpayer's money to foreign firms, especially if the latter's workforce, plant or expertise reside outside its territory. Moreover, there are often hidden factors that influence a contract's final award: informal ties with local firms, political pressure in favor of corporate "national champions," etc.

Government bodies have devised myriad techniques over the years—some blatant, some hard to detect—to ensure that contracts go to favored bidders. Either a contract-awarder ignores publication rules or he delays publication of a tender to the last minute so that foreign bidders have too little time to respond. A large part of the problem lies in the traditional reluctance of injured bidders, including disadvantaged local companies, to protest for fear of jeopardizing the few contracts they do manage to secure.

Brussels figures the Community loses 21 billion ECUs ($27 billion) each year, or 0.06 of total GNP as a result of national fractured markets. The loss arises from such things as outdated supplies, over-priced goods and services, and the sheer inefficiency of relying on contractees who've always had a guaranteed market.

Though EC states have long complained about the injustices they do to each other in this sector, foot-dragging has been chronic. Until very recently, they were content to tinker with a mildly liberal EC directive dating back some 15 years—so mild that it has had no effect on the market.

The drive toward the Single Market has finally spurred corrective action, however. Based on recent EC laws, the 12 member states are now laying down new competitive conditions, not only for bidders across the Community but beyond as well.

The sector's liberalization rests on five legislative initiatives. The first three, already voted into law, come into effect by 1993 and concern contracts for public works and supplies. Two define bidding conditions and the third lays down an appeals procedure when unfair tender practices are suspected.

The supplies directive establishes a minimum contract value of 200,000 ECUs as the "threshold" for mandatory, advance publication of tenders. For public works (construction and civil engineering projects and their related design, managerial, and financing services), all contracts exceeding a value of five million ECUs must be publicly notified.

"Notification" means transmitting to Brussels within a fixed period all necessary information relevant to a public contract—name of tendering authority, description of work required, closing date for bids. Once in hand, the Commission will then publish the tender in the Community's record of publication, the *Official Journal*.

Together, the three directives aim to close several, notorious loopholes in the EC's previous approach to cross-border bidding rules. First, they cover all public authorities across the 12 member states: direct government branches and agencies at the local, state and national levels *as well as* semi-public and wholly private intermediaries that act on behalf of public bodies. These include, for example, independent state-owned companies or private firms that have monopoly status—either as contractor or contractee.

Secondly, they compel public authorities to specify or make reference to European technical standards whenever possible. This was a favorite device for excluding foreign bidders who were not tooled up for national technical norms.

Finally, the new laws give Brussels the right to monitor public authorities that flaunt their obligation to notify tenders. Investigations will be speeded up and, if necessary, lead to legal actions before the Court of Justice in Luxembourg. However, the Commission's enforcement powers stop short of the right to review and enforce tender procedures: it has no power to intervene in national legal proceedings or suspend an award.

The remaining two proposals pertain to public works and supplies contracts in the EC's "excluded" sectors of telecommunications, water, transport, and energy. As with the other initiatives, one deals with bidding and threshold conditions while the other lays down enforcement and rules of appeal.

Liberalization has come last to these excluded areas because they are by far the most lucrative source of public contracts, especially in telecommunications and energy. By no coincidence either, bidding has been restricted almost exclusively to large, national companies.

The directives lay down the following publication thresholds: 600,000 ECUs for supplies in telecommunications; 400,000 ECUs for supply contracts in the other sectors, and five million ECUs for all works contracts.

However, there are certain provisos. For example, in the water sector only drinking water is covered. Similarly, supplies of energy to power plants are excluded as are contracts covering hydrocarbon exploration. That means a large part of the public market for energy supplies is still closed to cross-border competition.

For US and other non-EC countries competing for EC tenders there are additional conditions. Their bids can be rejected if they contain less than 50 percent of EC products or if a non-EC bid's price differential is less than three percent compared to other bids. Washington has branded the caveats as protectionist, but Brussels says the exclusions will only be withdrawn if "equivalent and fair" access to US public markets is guaranteed to EC bidders.

Taken together the five directives make a good swipe at national barriers but, in the end, real progress will depend on the goodwill of the 12 member-state governments. And on whether bidders themselves are prepared to blow the whistle on recalcitrant contracting authorities. History shows there is great reluctance to do this, but that may change as companies feel more confident about complaining.

Bouygues, France's giant engineering company, for example, complained last year (1990) about losing a construction bid as part of the work on a giant bridge in Denmark to connect two of the country's peninsulas. The Commission investigated the case. The French group still lost out to local Danish firms but at least it recouped its bidding costs. Not much compared to a contract, but a start.

AVIATION POLICY

THE EC STANDS AT THE EDGE OF A NEW ERA IN CIVIL AVIATION AS IT peers into the 1990s. The trend established with its first "air package" of deregulatory measures in December 1987 has led to a steadily accelerating flight toward more competition between airlines, lower prices, and a dismantling of the protectionist measures EC countries traditionally use in favor of their national "flag" carriers.

Don't confuse this with the USA's rip-roaring deregulation of 10 years ago, however. Competition between EC airlines has increased— but in measured terms and primarily between the very biggest, state-owned companies; market access for small and newcomer airlines is still difficult. Prices have dropped a bit, but not uniformly across the EC and by no means as much as they did following US liberalization. Finally, there are still numerous non-tariff technical barriers at the national level that must be eliminated before the 12 member states can claim they have a "single" aviation market.

That said, 1990 produced more legislative initiatives affecting more aspects of EC civil aviation than in any single year of the previous decade. We have seen, for example, new flexibility in pricing rules, further dismantling of "capacity-sharing" privileges between flag carriers, new "fifth-freedom" rights, more air cargo liberalization, new EC-wide negotiations with third-countries and, finally, expanding anti-cartel investigations. Moreover, Brussels is widening its influence over such auxiliary areas as air-traffic control, duty free sales, on-ground passenger-flow regulations, "slot" allocation at Community airports and EC funding for new materials in aviations and aeronautics research.

Nonetheless, the EC Commission's deregulatory approach to civil aviation is gradualist. It will unfold in carefully controlled steps to at least the mid-1990s, if not a few years beyond. Indeed, the EC's big state-owned airlines still form a powerful bloc to disruptive change. Moreover, Brussels realizes that certain practices that currently favor EC consumers—such as "interlining," which allows the automatic transfer of business class tickets from one airline to another—would disappear with wholesale deregulation.

THE 1991–93 TRANSITION

Since January 1990 the Commission has brought forth seven legislative proposals affecting everything from overbooking rules to new airfreight freedoms to strictures against predatory pricing. The most important step, however, was taken in June 1990 when EC air transport ministers approved their second "package" of deregulation measures, whose staggered effects began in November. The new deal lays down the following measures:

- More routes open to competition. The threshold for routes that must offer "multiple-designation" (i.e. official recognition) of foreign carriers by a government falls to either 100,000 passengers or 600 round-trips per year after January 1, 1992.

- Elimination of the "single-disapproval" mechanism whereby only one government at either end of a bilateral route can refuse a change in ticket prices. Beginning in 1993, tariff changes by designated airlines will have to be refused by both governments, i.e. double disapproval.

- More flexibility for "deep-discount" ticket pricing.

- Sharp restriction of bilateral capacity-sharing deals. Sharing—now fixed at 40 percent of a route's passengers—will fall annually in stages to only 25 percent by 1992, to be wholly eliminated in 1993. In other words: flag carriers will no longer enjoy a guaranteed slice of passenger volume on each route.

- Starting in 1993: more cabotage, the practice of allowing a foreign airline to pick up and set down passengers wholly within the territory of another member state.

A complementary set of measures to the air package will emerge in the next two years (1991–93). These include, for example, reforming the slot-allocation rules that determine an airline's take-off and landing schedule at each airport or restricting the ways flag carriers coordinate flights between themselves. Other EC proposals will lay down uniform airline-licensing rules and a Communitywide code of conduct for travel agents.

Elsewhere, Brussels hopes in the long-run to fuse the continent's 42 myriad air traffic control systems (ATC) into a single structure. The first step is to get all national aviation authorities in the EC to join the

Brussels-based air navigation group, Eurocontrol. Only nine EC countries belong now. The second is to make them all use the same ATC equipment—radar systems and communications—and the same operating rules.

:::::::::::::COMPETITION POLICY :::::::::::::

The Commission's competition authority, DG-IV, has strongly condemned recent moves by EC airlines to bolster their monopoly market shares before full liberalization occurs in 1993. Early in 1990, for example, Lufthansa tried to deny interlining privileges to a small carrier that refused to abide by bilateral (price-fixing) tariff agreements with Lufthansa. That prompted a ruling that forces EC flag carriers to extend interlining privileges to all players—big or small, public or private—whatever the commercial conditions.

DG-IV must also decide how it will react to attempts by the big carriers to consolidate and/or extend their market dominance before the mature competitive conditions of 1993 come into play. Air France, for example, has already taken over France's biggest domestic carrier, Air Inter, and the country's only other internationally-oriented airline, UTA. But it had to relinquish its grip on several domestic routes in order to gain Brussels' blessing. In addition, Brussels will closely monitor how Air France exploits its new market position. In the meantime, the EC's small private carriers such as Belgium's TEA airline or RyanAir of Ireland are worried. They fear that they'll simply be squeezed or priced out of the market.

EC Competition Commissioner, Leon Brittan, says he will keep close tabs on events if EC carriers try to carve up markets to their advantage. Indeed, he has repeatedly raised the red warning flag against market abuses in other Single Market industries. Whether he'll achieve his "level playing field"—or in this case, level landing strip—in the face of so much posturing by the aviation sector's biggest players, however, remains to be seen: The DG-4 division has already struck down a three-way alliance among KLM, Sabena, and British Airways, but now talks are underway again between the latter two.

SOCIAL CHARTER

THE SINGLE MARKET WAS CHAMPIONED BY AND FOR EUROPEAN business and industry. The 1992 plan was drawn up by then Commissioner Lord Cockfield working closely with the European Round Table of Industrialists. While it has the open, if cautious, support of labor groups, they are concerned, too, that the dropping of borders across the EC will eat away their hard-won labor rights and working conditions of the last 50 years. Their greatest fear (still only a theoretical one) is "social dumping," the corporate practice of shutting down operations in a high labor-cost country, such as Germany, and reopening them in the less rigorous—and cheaper—labor markets of Portugal, Greece, and Spain.

That said, foreign investors should understand that, Britain aside, business and industry in Europe is somewhat more socially conscious than their US or Japanese counterparts. This is exemplified by a well-established body of labor law in most EC countries guaranteeing specific rights to all employees—white and blue collar—as well as by the general consensus in Europe that business and labor relations must be collaborative rather than confrontational. However, those relations will be put under real strains as the two sides attempt to define their respective obligations and rights within the context of the EC's "Social Charter."

Adopted in December 1989 by all but one of the 12 member states, the Social Charter is a declaration of political will and, as such, complementary to the Single Market. It represents an unprecedented attempt to produce a set of laws defining basic labor rights across the EC after 1992. It is wholly opposed by the UK, which refused to sign the document.

The Social Charter means the Commission will have to make proposals, via yearly "action programs" for some 50 laws, voluntary guidelines, and administrative instruments during the next three years on specific labor issues: part-time and temporary work rights, industrial relations, worker consultation procedures. Drafting these proposals won't be easy and neither will their adoption by member states.

Labor rules, for instance, vary considerably from one EC state to the next as do industrial relations, making uniform laws next to impossible. Moreover, as long as labor laws at the EC level require unanimous approval by the 12 member states, which is the case today, then the UK can always hold up progress with its dissenting position, though this voting structure may change. Finally, the Social Charter's two "partners"—unions and industry—are each, of course, determined to bend the Charter's proposals as much to their own advantage as possible.

Indeed, progress across all fronts of the Charter has been slow. The 1990 action program, for example, should have included: three directives describing "atypical" work contracts (part-time, casual, and fixed-term) and the legal mechanisms for defining working relationships between employee and employer; two instruments regulating labor rights for work subcontracted across borders and worker-participation rights for floating labor; and, finally, a Commission "communication" on working and living conditions for cross-border workers. All are either still in the draft stage or are being substantially revised.

So, too, are initiatives for the later action program. These include stock-option rights for workers in pan-EC companies, labor rights for employment arising from public contracts and access to vocational training.

In all, the Social Charter aims for about a dozen basic pan-EC labor rights, but the real crux of the whole program will lie in two crucial objectives. On the one hand are the provisions for formal bargaining between labor and management (industrial relations) and, on the other, the Charter's formulas for union influence (worker participation) in major corporate decisions: co-management rights, in other words. Both are highly controversial.

European labor, of course, wants to consolidate its bargaining position on as wide an EC-basis as possible via negotiations by sectoral pan-EC unions, which do not yet exist. This is steadfastly opposed by EC business and industry—especially in Britain—which prefers to continue bargaining on a national basis with each union. So far, progress in fleshing out the structure of these bargaining details has been nil.

As for worker participation, the Social Charter proposes three models, varying from actual board representation for labor unions and their "co-determination" with management on vital business decisions (as in Germany today) down to the more classic arrangement of simple union representation on the shop floor. Many EC countries can live with this three-pronged approach, which would allow each member state to choose the model that best fits its labor traditions.

A test case for future European legislation on social matters will probably hinge on two of the Commission's first Charter proposals, unveiled in summer 1990. One suggests that part-time workers have the same rights and benefits, on a pro-rata basis, as their fulltime colleagues. The other lays down minimum rest periods for workers across the Community.

Although EC Commissioner for Social Affairs, Vasso Papandreou, is determined to see the Social Charter through before the end of 1992, she has met difficulties in rallying support even from her fellow Commissioners for the part-time rights proposal. And she has already been forced to dilute the proposal on rest periods in order to appease Britain. Papandreou now says the latter proposal's goals "could be" achieved through conventional collective bargaining, thus avoiding statutory legislation. That concession may lead to the eventual composition of other Social Charter initiatives.

Indeed, European business and industry would rather work out their own mutual terms of endearment with employees rather than have them imposed by bureaucratic fiat, an ideological approach opposed by much of European labor. At any rate, flexibility and choice of options will probably be the keys to any Social Charter that is acceptable to both sides.

TELECOMMUNICATIONS

REGULATORS ARE LIKELY TO TAKE A STERN LINE WITH PUBLIC telecom operators which do not begin to liberalize their services and so allow private companies to supply data communications, mobile telephones, and satellite links. Under the agreement, signed by the 12 EC telecommunications ministers in July 1990, and which came into force at the beginning of 1991, telecom operators are obliged to end their monopolies over many non-voice services, a valuable end of the market. The overall market is expanding very fast and is estimated now at $120 billion a year. It will most likely account for seven percent of the Community's gross domestic product at the end of the decade, double the current figure.

In many countries around the EC, governments have already taken steps to liberalize the markets for terminal equipment, such as handsets and facsimile machines, and so ease telecom management out of direct ministerial control.

But the latest step of allowing private operators to supply the services which run along the network infrastructure and into the terminal is only now taking effect. Introduction of this step may well come with teething troubles.

The EC states divide fairly evenly between those that believe more US-style liberalization is the way ahead and those that wish to protect their often inefficient operators or manufacturers from external competition. On the liberal wing are the UK, the Netherlands, Denmark, and Germany. On the protectionist side are France, Italy, Belgium, and Spain.

The UK is well ahead in these free market stakes and is currently considering its next round of reform allowing further entrants should be allowed to compete with British Telecom and Mercury on providing voice lines.

The Netherlands is still well behind and is not in favor of a second operator building a network. It believes that huge investment on cabling and exchanges is unrealistic for a country with a population of only 16 million.

Germany has radically changed its view on telecoms policy after years of protectionism that infuriated US suppliers. It is introducing mobile competitors and may do the same for land-based voice in a larger unified German market.

France, despite some world-beating telecom developments, blows hot and cold on liberalization. It led the way in letting private companies supply terminals such as handsets and facsimile machines, but is only just loosening control on France Telecom.

Italy and Belgium are more traditional protectionists. Italy is slowly overhauling its interlocking operators, while Belgium after a tide of complaints from multinational customers ought shortly to introduce private-style management.

These attitudes to liberalization so far will determine the success of the next stage and the opening up of service markets, such as data communications, to the likes of IBM and General Electric Information Services. Both US companies will start taking advantage of the latest EC rules and the Commission will begin vetting the way operators offer leased lines for sale to see whether they restrict the resale of capacity.

These lines will provide the permanent networks over which IBM and GEISCO will run their value-added data services. They are value added because they must incorporate along the way an additional element of data processing. So far, these data services have found a limited market in the financial sector. Now the EC wants to encourage their wider use with the sending of more commercial data computer-to-computer instead of by mail.

Under the EC's July 1990 agreement, governments can only restrict free access and use of these leased lines for data up until the end of 1992 by which time a Commission-vetted licensing system has to be in place in each country. Greece, Spain and Portugal, have until 1996 to meet these conditions, before private operators can resell data services to companies. However, the July 1990 agreement came with a further set of conditions on the way leased lines and data services should be provided. Some fear that these open network provision rules could be used to protect state telecom operators (PTTs).

De-regulation of sales of satellite dishes and access to transmitters is also being tackled by the EC. The present state hold over use of two-way dishes may be ended in exchange for a monopoly over satellite use.

Emphasis in the telecoms field will shift to mobile communications with trials of a European cellular telephone system to be put in cars or carried by hand and which works in more than one country with the same equipment.

Another development may be a growth in a new generation of cordless telephones and with it the introduction of Telepoint terminals across Europe. These handsets would only work within a short distance of a Telepoint. This technology is being tried in the UK but has yet to take off. Other countries, including France and Germany, are interested but may yet choose alternative systems to the UK, more geared to the office and with cordless private exchanges.

Another perennial telecom technology likely to figure in new products is ISDN—digital—systems. France, Germany, Belgium, and the UK are already selling this system to business customers in limited numbers. But ISDN, with its computer-like signals, may only be a step to a bigger revolution in telecoms when TV comes down a high capacity optical cable. That revolution is still in the research labs and some years from installation.

Part Two

THE MEMBER NATIONS

Facts on Belgium

. . . .

Capital Brussels
Flanders Region Ghent
Wallonia Region Namur
Population 9.9m
Unemployment 10.2%
GNP Growth 1988: 4.1%; 1989: 4.5%; 1990:
   3.8%; 1991 (est.): 3.2%
GDP per Capita 1988: $15,369; 1989: $16,807
Inflation 1988: 1.2%; 1989: 3.1%; 1990: 3.9%
Corporate Investment 1988: +15.9%; 1989:
   +14.5%; 1990: +7%
Foreign Trade 1988: −BF11b; 1989:
   +BF20b; 1990: +BF30b
Current Account 1989: +BF130b; 1990:
   +BF140b (Belgium–Luxembourg Union for
   all trade figures)
Belgium–US trade (1988)
   Exports to US (FOB): $4.6b
   Imports from US (CIF): $3.87b
   ($1 = BF35)

. . . .

Belgium

*"Belgium is a nation of excellent shopkeepers... our franc is even
stronger than the deutschmark." Brussels newspaper editor*

THE CAPITAL, BRUSSELS, PROVIDES THE STAGE FOR THE DAILY DRAMA
of European economic, monetary, and political union. It plays in its
35th year—far longer than Chorus Line—to packed houses of politicians, civil servants, and the world's press corps, which has clamored
for seats to the point of becoming second in size to the Washington
foreign press. The media, however, play a key role in interpreting the
often byzantine maneuverings in the corridors of the two main EC
buildings—the Berlaymont with its policy-initiating European Commission, and the adjacent Charlemagne, where the ministers of the 12
deliberate till late at night and sometimes announce their decisions
amid euphoria-cum-pandemonium. One such memorably hectic
scene in 1990 was when the German Helmut Kohl stated that progress
toward union was as relentless as the Rhine. "It only flows in one direction and I have never found anyone to make it flow in the other.
Nobody can dam it, and so it is with Europe." Perhaps he was forget-
ting the impressive waterfalls near the river's source, or Dutch complaints that the Rhine flows into their flatlands in a highly-polluted
state. So Europe "just keeps rolling" but at variable speeds and conditions. Beware, if you are new to Europe, the month of August. Then,
the Northern Europeans turn Latin, take the month off, and close up
Europe. Host country Belgium now figures among the activists of the
12, as if its own move to a confederal state had convinced it of the need
for fast federalism elsewhere. Anyway, the Belgians have done well financially out of the presence of the EC decision machine and the
multinationals attracted to Belgium since the 1950s and 1960s. It holds
its own, despite competition from London, Paris, Amsterdam, Frankfurt, and now Berlin. A very recent study by the French showed that
of some 803 American and 147 Japanese companies with sizeable European headquarters, about a third had chosen Britain, but a good
fifth had gone to Belgium—with Paris way back. It can hardly be otherwise. The 280 directives, and the rules and regulations of the Single

Market need to be comprehended, particularly by American and Japanese companies, and it's certainly not by accident that American law firms are hanging out their shingles by the dozen, that international consultants are tapping a research market, worth by itself several hundred million dollars, and that the lobbyists are wining and dining. Lobbying is not new in Brussels, but hitherto has been more European in style—offices of industry associations, employers' federations, trade unions, and consumer groups. Often one-man operations. That is changing as the big Washington law firms throw receptions. The Japanese, by now, have a vast information-gathering network for their machinery makers and consumer goods companies. Oldtimers, like the American multinational 3M with its well-oiled European headquarters in Brussels and four decades of manufacturing across Europe, are taking the approach of the Single Market in their stride. Others, though, need help to influence the more important of the 14,000 civil servants and the 518 members of the European Parliament, many of whom are seeking a way of moving from Strasbourg, France, to Brussels.

Aside from the jargon of the European Community, the second semantic problem in Brussels is understanding what the Belgians themselves mean when they refer to "government," "region," "language community," "commune," and the like. Belgian domestic politics are dominated by issues of language and region. There are now three regional governments, and it's significant that King Baudouin is King of the Belgians, not of Belgium. With its layers of administration, Brussels is highly-confusing, but despite this the economy has been booming. The Belgians, along with their Dutch neighbors, have long been the most international of the nations of the 12. They regularly export 60 percent of their production, most of it to the European Community. They also sell diamonds, chemicals, petroleum, transport equipment, tractors, and bicycles to the US. All indicators shine: a strong Belgian franc, a trade surplus, rising investment by industry, inflation more or less under control, and falling unemployment. The openness of the Belgian economy means that most traders are optimistic about the barrier-free market. The banks, in general, are also outward looking. Société Générale de Belgique, the country's largest banking and industrial company, has been shaken up and made more profitable since the French Suez bank took control. Sabena, the troubled national airline, is reorganizing and is readying itself to play a key role in transforming Brussels airport into a more prominent European hub.

The Channel Tunnel will most likely bring special benefits to Belgium, with Brussels becoming a more strategic railway junction. Belgium has strong trade links with Spain and Portugal and the removal of customs barriers in the Iberian Peninsula is expected to boost Bel-

THE MAIN EUROPEAN TECHNOLOGICAL PROGRAMS
(1987–1991)
Budget in millions of ecu (1 ecu = $1.20)

ESPRIT
information technology *1,600*

RACE
telecommunication *550*

STAR
telecom for the regions *750*

SPRINT
technological applications MKB *90*

BRITE/EURAM
new materials/production techniques *500*

AERONAUTICS
aerospace technology *35*

DRIVE
traffic and transport technology *60*

BRIDGE
biotechnology *100*

ECLAIR
biotechnology for agriculture *105*

FLAIR
nutrition technology *25*

DELTA
new educational techniques *20*

JET
thermonuclear fusion technology *611*

JESSI
development and production of chips *4,000*
(estimate)

EUREKA
European cooperation in high-tech *1,000*
(a year)

(Source: European Commission)

gian exports. A frequently debated point is whether Belgium's many small and medium-sized firms will be sufficiently dynamic to survive in the new era of European competition. The odds could favor them, for the Belgians, devoid of their own raw materials, are specialists at fashioning imported materials and then exporting them as semi-finished goods. Successful exports include chemicals, plastics, and various forms of energy, as well as minerals, with the smaller firms serving the bigger exporters, such as Solvay and Fina. In addition, the traditional steel and textiles sectors have been modernized and relaunched. The corporate tax burden has been reduced to 41 percent, soon to 39 percent, boosting business confidence. There are many special situations, loopholes, concessions, and advantages for foreigners investing in the country, although takeovers and mergers often run up against tightly-controlled blocks of shares. To prevent any takeover of the economy, the government has sought a say in any bid over $85 million or involving 20 percent of voting stock. One aim is to protect utilities.

MARKET OPPORTUNITIES

Multinationals have been attracted to Belgium because of its special corporate tax rules for "coordination centers." The government is offering tax breaks to lure multinationals looking for a regional headquarters or a financing vehicle. By the end of 1990, well over 200 centers had been approved and fifty more companies were knocking on the door. Companies must have consolidated world turnover of $300 million and employ at least ten Belgians at the center. They must also be involved in any one or more of these activities: publicity, advertising, and sales promotion; gathering and dissemination of information; insurance and reinsurance; scientific research; liaison with national and international bodies; accounting, administrative, and data processing; financial management, such as currency hedging, factoring, re-invoicing between group leasing, or other related activities.

Development or centralization of activities qualified companies for such benefits as cost-plus taxation; exemption from withholding taxes for dividends, interest and royalties; exemption from capital tax; increased tax breaks for foreign executives—and more. Tax benefits have been lowered slightly but these moves have not noticeably slowed the rush of companies heading towards Belgium. In this area, the country has an edge over other EC countries.

Belgium is also offering deals for companies considering new EC distribution centers. Herman Verwilst, senior official at the economics ministry, says "Belgium gives prior ruling on tax concessions and sticks by that ruling."

S P O T L I G H T

• *Investment Subsidies* •

Belgium has had a panoply of tax breaks for investors, be they companies setting up in re-conversion areas, so-called innovation companies involved in high-tech, or coordination centers which, as their name implies, centralized the activities of companies of the same group. The European Commission's policy of promoting economic equality throughout the region covered by the 12 EC states has obliged Belgium and some other EC countries to reduce subsidies. In Belgium's case, it meant that 1991 was the cut-off date for the creation of new innovation and reconversion companies, while other aids have been redefined—downwards. Coordination centers live on, but the advantages are not quite what they were. The new EC rules, says Sir Leon Brittan, commissioner for competition policy, "should enhance the ability of the weakest regions to compete for investment."

COMPUTER HARDWARE

Almost all hardware for the $1.2 billion annual market is imported and growth is forecast at 20 percent a year, into the early 1990s. The US dominates the mainframe sector and also non-UNIX minis, but European makers are selling more and more micros. Micro clones from the Far East have also made inroads. The commercial section of the US Embassy in Brussels, which monitors this and other markets very closely, estimates that the market for mainframes has reached saturation point and that the future here is in replacements. Mini-computers, with 60 percent of the total installed base, offer most promise, together with workstations. Personal computers are selling well as prices drop and because they offer a way into computerization for the many thousands of small and medium-sized firms that form the backbone of Belgian industry and commerce. US makers face stiff competition in the micro sector, with the lower end taken over by clone developers from the Far East. The best outlets, by all accounts, for US companies are in desktop publishing systems, local area networks, laser printers, portable communicating terminals, laptop computers, and workstations. All these sectors are destined for sharp growth. Small or medium-sized exporters to Belgium should go for industrial automation, CAD/CAM, or communications.

COMPUTER SOFTWARE/SERVICES

Here growth is very fast—at around 18 percent a year—and this kind of expansion will double the size of the market from $1.25 billion in 1988–89 to $2.5 billion, in 1992. Packaged software is strongest and could well account for almost half of software and service sales in 1992. Application tools are responsible for most of the growth, with greatest Belgian interest in fourth generation languages, query languages, and distributed relational database management systems. The professional services market is now worth more than $300 million, with strong demand for "custom solutions." The processing services market, which includes value-added services such as E-mail, managed data networks, and EDI, could well grow to $700 million in two to three years. Some seven Belgians out of ten are now in the service sector.

AUTOMOTIVE

Automobile manufacturing has seen massive investments in the past two to three years by the multinationals—there are no purely Belgian manufacturers. Belgium now ranks sixth among European car producers after Germany, France, Italy, Spain, and Britain—there is a small, but interesting motor show at the world fairgrounds next to Brussels. Nine vehicles out of ten are exported, representing 15 percent of the exports of the Belgium–Luxembourg Economic Union, a mini forerunner of the EC. Ford and General Motors have joined Renault, Volkswagen, and Volvo in building assembly plants turning out 1.3 million cars a year. Ford also produces tractors and agricultural machinery in Flanders. The aftermarket is around two billion dollars—$600 million in parts, $175 million in accessories and maintenance products, and the rest in services. The national system of checkups boosts sales. Champion Sparkplugs and Monroe Shock Absorbers, both of the US, have built manufacturing plants. Johnson Matthey, the British precious metals group, has opened a plant near Brussels to prepare for the surge in demand for catalytic converters when new controls within the EC come into force. These controls probably will mean a demand for 20 million auto-catalysts a year. For the moment, there is no requirement for local content in the automotive parts field, but this could change. A local plant or a local partner are answers to this possible threat.

FRANCHISING

Franchising continues to grow strongly in Belgium, whereas retail sales have been lackluster. This growth has been put at between 11 and 15 percent and indicates a sector worth $3.4 billion by the time of the Single Market. A new EC directive creates the legal framework for franchising on an EC-wide basis. This will provide a further boost. Meanwhile, Belgium offers good opportunities because franchise sales amount to only five percent of retail sales, half that in France or the Netherlands, the two neighboring countries that have similar consumer retail patterns.

BIOTECHNOLOGY

With an $18 million annual turnover—a tenth in pharmaceuticals—the Belgian chemical industry is a pillar of the national economy. Biotechnology is an important component. There are many industries and R & D centers in biotechnology, and American drug companies are the big boys. Collaboration with universities is good, as are the resultant exports. In fact, in this area, Belgium is proving to be an interesting test market. The US Embassy offers a tip: Entering the market can be done through Fechmie, the industry association, which sends foreign business proposals to its several thousand members, large and small. The Single Market means a drug approved in one member state will automatically be approved in all other member states—a strong argument for producing in biotechnologically-friendly Belgium.

MEDICAL EQUIPMENT

A sophisticated market for exporters, innovative, up-market medical equipment is a growth area. The best prospects are in miniaturized-digitalized radiology, ultrasound, and other noninvasive, electronic analysis and diagnostic equipment and related software. It is not a huge market, perhaps $200 million dollars or just over a year, but it is largely dependent on supplies from abroad. Belgium is a health-conscious country with a comprehensive social security system. There are no tariff or other barriers and, compared to the US, approval procedures are relatively easy.

TELECOMMUNICATIONS

Belgium, like other European countries, has ended the telecommunications monopoly with a new company with diminished scope replacing the old RTT company. It continues to handle basic services—from telephone to the future ISDN—but has to compete with the private sector for value added and information services, and for the sale, installation, and service of terminal equipment. There's a separate body for type-approval for interfacing. The Belgian telecommunications industry has done well out of the old RTT. Foreign, particularly US suppliers should benefit from the opening up of the terminal equipment market.

S P O T L I G H T

• *The European Machine* •

Eurocrats, the European civil servants at EC headquarters, initiate the paperwork and policies of the European "machine." It takes initiated insiders to understand all. Ministers themselves have been known to be baffled. The best help comes from the American Chamber of Commerce—Amcham—in Brussels:

50 Avenue des Arts
Tel: 32-2-513-6892/513-6770
Fax: 32-2-513-7928.

Amcham has an EC committee and, more importantly, an EC Affairs Office which publishes indispensable guides to the EC maze. One is the *EC Information Handbook,* packed with facts, information, and names of the people who count in the EC Commission, the 23 special departments or Directorates General, the European Parliament, and the many satellite organizations in Brussels. It also has an explanation of the Single European Act, bedrock of a future federal Europe. Another booklet, *Business Guide to EC Initiatives,* goes into the details of EC proposals and considers their relevant importance for the business world. A quarterly publication, *Countdown 92,* tracks the progress, or lack of it, of the ratification of European directives in the 12 national parliaments. The spotlight has been turned on those countries lagging behind. A mid-1991 report stated that the Single Market program was behind schedule in such important areas as taxation, trademarkets, and a free market in automobiles. Elsewhere, Price Waterhouse's Brussels office publishes a dictionary of EC terms. Tel: 32-2-773-1411. It defines such terms as *minimal harmonization* and a current

continued

favorite *subsidiarity*, or—more simply put—power should only accrue to the Brussels center where necessary with national governments retaining control over areas that they can administer more efficiently. Unfortunately, subsidiarity is often ignored. Eurospeak is no joke in reality.

TRANSPORTATION AND COMMUNICATIONS

The density of highways, railways, and waterways, plus the proximity of large markets in Britain, France, and Germany are strong arguments in Belgium's favor in the competition for plant investment and warehousing in the Single Market. The country's logistical center is the vast port of Antwerp, which challenges nearby Rotterdam in the Netherlands as *the* distribution point for bulk cargo, parts, foodstuffs, and consumer goods. It aims to serve not only Belgium, but also Germany, the Netherlands, and northern France, the industrial heart of the Single Market. Antwerp's extensive warehousing facilities are being extended to the left bank of the River Schelde where large tracts of land are available for development. In addition to railways, two manmade waterways, the Albert and ABC canals, provide links to the area around Belgium, which contains a large proportion of the population of the Single Market. Ghent and Zeebrugge ports in Flanders have traditional trade links with Britain. The highways with their American-style "spaghetti bowls" are among the best in Europe and are lit at night, an unusual feature which eases the strain on truckers and, apparently, provides a distraction for astronauts who can spot the Belgian lights as they can the Great Wall of China.

Belgium, however, needs to improve its air and rail infrastructure. Until now, the main airport, Brussels' Zavantem, has not been up to scratch. Some one billion dollars are being thrown at the problem with the aim of extending annual capacity from 7 million to 9.5 million passengers by 1993, as well as boosting the cargo side. With the extensive, but rundown rail network, the stimulus is coming from the plan to extend the French TGV (train à grande vitesse) system northwards and so help create a truly European highspeed rail network. The TGV Nord will pass through Belgium on its way to the Netherlands, expanding passenger traffic and economic zones. Belgian government spending of $500 million a year is envisaged over the next two decades to ensure that the country does not miss out on rail's share of a boom in goods movement in the Single Market. Regional disputes over new high-speed lines are being settled, albeit with difficulty.

The post office has been criticized for poor customer relations, as well as for lack of capacity, particularly in Brussels, for new lines and value-added services. Partial privatization of the State monopoly should improve customer service, while modernization during the 1990s will move the whole system from analogue to digital technology.

MANAGEMENT AND WORKFORCE

Belgian workers place higher priority upon job security and generous social benefits than extravagant pay claims. It is difficult to fire a Belgian worker and Belgian trade unions, while not militant compared to some, seek further protection, afforded by the EC's proposed Social Charter. The inward investor also finds that social security costs for employers can add a third or more to the whole range of salaries. Yet, actual pay rises have been limited in recent years and the bi-annual pay bargaining, involving national and regional government, industry, and the unions has been reasonably smooth. Increases have been held below the national growth of 3.5 percent. It is hoped that this arrangement will hold during any period of lower growth. Belgian employers have been happy with increased productivity, while investors from the US are returning. Hundreds of US companies set up in the 1960s, but many had left by the 1980s because of high taxes.

Incoming management will be impressed by the Belgian way of safeguarding competitiveness. The Conseil Central de'Economie (CCE), composed of employer federations and unions, periodically reviews the national competitive position. Criteria include six variables: export performance, wage costs, financial costs, energy costs, the trend of gross fixed business investment (this has been rising sharply), and R & D expenditure as a percentage of GNP. Belgium's performance is thus compared constantly with that of its main trading partners—Germany, France, Britain, Italy, the Netherlands, the US and Japan. An Act of Parliament stipulates that competitiveness is threatened if there is a deterioration in export performance and in at least one other of the six sectors. The Council is required to take action within one month if Belgium's position is under such threat. It can do this through collective wage agreements or by recommending that the government undertake cost-related measures, such as curbs on incomes, measures to ease the tax burden and financial costs of business, and investment and R & D incentives. Simultaneously, the corporate tax rate is falling (from 43 percent in 1989, to 41 percent in 1990 and 39 percent in 1991), while abnormally high income taxes have also edged down.

A managerial revolution in major companies has been spurred by the French Suez group which acquired a majority interest in Société Générale, Belgium's biggest holding company with its vast banking and industrial interests. The French now run the Brussels head office of the conglomerate with a staff of only 100. Leveraged buyouts, mergers, and acquisitions are also the order of the day. The year 1990 saw a continuation of a trend begun the previous year when more than 60 Belgian companies were acquired by foreign firms, particularly by the French. France's national employers' federation, the Patronat, has a new Brussels office.

However, smaller companies, often family-owned, remain the backbone of the economy. Companies with at least 50 staff must have a workers' council for health and safety, and those with one hundred employees or more must have a council with broader rights over financial information. In practice, managers rule in these companies. There are fears about the quality of management at this level in handling the opportunities and problems of the Single Market. So far, however, these "small" Belgian managers have acquitted themselves very well.

Across the country, with the exception of some public service sectors, the Belgian formula of "a good day's work for a good day's pay" has held up. Strikes have been limited mainly to teachers and railwaymen, although telephone workers may follow as many jobs are threatened by plans to overhaul the inefficient national telecoms network. Stability and productivity encouraged both Ford and Volvo to expand production in Flanders. Ford preferred to invest in Genk than at Dagenham in England, while Volvo's nearby plants have been producing as much as 23 percent of the Swedish group's world automobile output and more than 40 percent of trucks. Investors have the advantage also of a labor force that speaks French, Dutch, German, and English.

The downside, perhaps, for an American company is the insistence on generous vacations and national holidays, a strictly delimited working day, and perks such as luncheon vouchers. Set against this is the awareness on all sides of the chances of the Single Market.

REAL ESTATE

Rents everywhere have soared, in the manner of the ugly office towers that disfigure parts of Brussels. They have doubled in just five years. Residential property has followed the office sector, although it remains, for the moment at least, the best bargain in Europe. The rises are the price paid for becoming Europe's administrative "capital." Yet, office space remains remarkably cheap when compared with the other European business centers, from ultra-expensive London at the top of the list (five times Brussels), down through Paris, Milan, Madrid, Frankfurt, Barcelona, and Lisbon. The British property specialists, Jones Lang Wootton, who dominate the letting market, charted 1990 prices as they went through the BF7500 per square meter per annum "barrier" in 1990, while down went the vacancy rate to three percent. Until recent years, Brussels was the cheapest of all West European capitals, but this enviable state of affairs began to change with the arrival of Spain and Portugal as new EC members in 1986, the launching of the Single Market program, and the general excitement, investment, and movement of decision makers created by the runup to the Single Market. The asbestos-riddled Berlaymont building, headquarters of the Commission, is to be torn down and replaced by something grander—and safer. Amsterdam has since become the least expensive center. In the Brussels-Capital Region, every additional EC job generates a new, non-EC job, usually in the service sector, and this, in turn, creates the demand for offices rather than factories. And, then, Belgian political devolution has not prevented the new regions putting up large offices in the capital. Strangely, the non-EC Swedes have led the latest wave of speculative buying, the biggest since the

British wave of the 1970s. Now that they are able to export capital, the Swedes have invested a staggering BF60 billion in Brussels and Antwerp, obliging Scandic Hotels to open Swedish hostelries so that exhausted Scandinavian wheeler-dealers can rest their heads in familiar surroundings. Other big buyers came from the Far East, notably Hong Kong millionaires, and even Australians with faith in the EC, and presumably in global warming. The Dutch have upped their stakes, as have the French. New office development, says the regional executive, must include some new housing and make a contribution to the city's services and infrastructure. There will be no more skyscraper blocks, except in the area of the existing World Trade Center towers near the North Station. In 1990, available office space was down to a mere 200,000 square meters. This will exert new pressure on rents in an area about the size of Washington, DC, and which is already experiencing the same spill-over. The fastest-developing areas are toward the outer orbital highway, the airport at Zaventeem, the town of Leuven, in fact all over the central Brabant province, be it the Dutch-speaking region in the north or the French-speaking region in the south. Road and rail connections are excellent and Antwerp and Brussels are within easy commuting distance, linked by not one, but two highways. Antwerp rents touched BF4000 per square meter in 1990, with higher prices for new, smart buildings. Future office costs in Brussels will depend on the extent of the strengthening, or deepening, of the EC. The number of civil servants—already 15,000 or more—the links between the Western and Eastern halves of the European continent, and relations with the EFTA trading bloc are all factors which will determine the number of additional international institutions and firms. Office space will also be needed for extra law firms and lobbyists (notably American), accountants, consultants, real estate specialists, advertising agents, media and translation bureaus, and all the other players in Europe's *de facto* capital.

• *Getting To Know the Capital* •

Brussels has no clearly defined center—no equivalent of the Champs-Elysées in Paris, Picca-

dilly Circus in London, or the Plaza de Mayor in Madrid, from which streets lead out as from a hub (even if the spokes are usually far from straight). For most visitors, the handiest reference point is the Grand' Place, with its magnificent Hôtel de Ville (city hall) and gilded medieval and renaissance buildings. Around the Grand' Place is a maze of narrow streets, many of them now reserved for pedestrians, with a delightfully bewildering selection of shops and restaurants. In this section of the city, too, is the Théâtre Royal de la Monnaie, a small, elegant opera house with performances so good that it draws audiences from as far away as Paris. Close by is the *bourse* (stock exchange), housed in a pillared, ornate building.

Neither does Brussels have a compact business center. Bank and corporate offices are strung out along the Avenue des Arts, the Avenue de la Loi, the Avenue Louise, and the Rue Royale, which leads from the grand park fronting the Royal Palace. As the American banks cut back, the Japanese arrive in force. New corporate buildings have sprung up around the Gare du Nord and, increasingly, companies are moving to air conditioned offices set in landscaped gardens in the suburbs. But nowhere is very far

from anywhere else: "a bunch of suburbs in search of a city" Brussels may be, but it's no Los Angeles, to which that quip was first applied.

The Berlaymont, the European Commission's headquarters until a new building is completed; the Charlemagne, where the Council of Ministers meets; and the offices of the 12 national "permanent representatives" (permreps) are all close to the Parc Cinquantenaire which, with its victory arch, celebrates the 50th anniversary of Belgium's independence in 1830. Close to this cluster of buildings are the offices of the many trade associations and other lobbying groups that seek to influence the Eurocrats as they formulate policies and recommendations for the Council of Ministers.

Brussels is host city also to NATO; its headquarters are on the main highway to the airport.

The capital has good bus, subway, and streetcar systems: fast, clean, and relatively inexpensive. Don't be surprised when streetcars plunge into tunnels, because some double as subway trains. Taxis are plentiful, but not cheap; however, the metered fare includes the tip.

:::::::::::::EUROCITY ANTWERP :::::::::::::

Brussels has become a city of service industries, but Belgium's second city, Antwerp, is heavily involved in trade through its port and in manufacturing. It is a "Eurocity," partly because its influence spreads far beyond its immediate borders, partly because it seeks closer ties with other major European cities. The typical Antwerper is a docker or is in some way connected with the port. Another "typical" Antwerper is the Hasidic Jewish diamond trader. The authorities say the great inland port along the River Scheldt is number three in the world, after Rotterdam and Singapore. The international qualification, in Antwerp's eyes, excludes Japanese and US ports devoted to national traffic, and so-called oil ports, such as France's Marseilles. Forty percent of Antwerp's 96 million annual tons is general cargo, and most of this is transit cargo to the Ruhr and destinations outside Belgium. International? Well, there are 300 regular lines using the port, 100 flags, and links with 800 other ports around the globe. There's heavy traffic in cereals. Container trade grows. The port specializes in moving iron and steel and has benefitted from the boom in these products. Swedish iron ore comes in via Narvik, Norway, and more ore is shipped from Australia, Brazil, and Mauritania in huge freighters. General Motors assembles in Antwerp and exports via the port, while car carriers bring in Japanese and South Korean vehicles. Antwerp competes with the big ports of North West Europe and, like them, seeks constantly to reduce loading and unloading times. It claims to be able to fill railway ore wagons at the dockside, shunt them through the Ardennes to Luxembourg mills, or those in northeast France, and be back in 22 hours. Antwerp's dockers say they are the quickest in the world, at 2.7 tons the man hour, but it's best to stay out of discussion of this delicate topic if Rotterdamers are around. Likewise, who will benefit most from the opening of the Channel Tunnel which, aside from its freight tonnage between Britain and her Continental cousins, will also influence the siting of European distribution centers? Antwerpers say their more southerly position will give them the edge. This is certainly the view of the *naties,* the firms handling everything in the port. Downtown, in the shadow of the massive central station, the air is filled with *mazel und broche* (luck and blessings), as diamond traders in the 18,000-strong Jewish community pursue their secretive business—cleaving, sawing, polishing, and selling 60 percent of the world's diamond production. These little streets are said to be the richest after Wall Street. The Dutch-speaking Flemish are the business success story of postwar Belgium. The area has attracted a sizeable amount of foreign investment. Aside from GM, the big names include Alcatel, Upjohn, Ford (tractors), and Daf (trucks), as well as Belgian names, such as Agfa-Gevaert and Bekaert (steel wire). But the port remains the key, with 75,000 of the half a million population working there as dockers, railwaymen, civil servants, customs officials, bankers, insurers, forwarders, and laborers.

Antwerp is not all work. It was home in the past to Rubens, Dürer, Van Dyck, and Erasmus, and this heritage will be honored when the city becomes the official cultural capital of Europe for 1993.

OPPORTUNITIES IN THE REGIONS

Investors should think local, not national, when seeking advice—and grants. Authorities handling regional development and incentives have gone to the regions, which is logical, but which has been dictated by the new federal composition of power. Brussels, the capital, is now officially also a region, a capital-region. It is one of the three largely autonomous regions that emerged, or more exactly re-emerged in different form, from the 1989 constitutional reform. Belgium is officially bilingual. Flanders, in the north, speaks Dutch; Wallonia, in the south, speaks French; and Brussels, a super enclave in the middle, is supposed to be bilingual but in practice is mainly French-speaking. Wallonia was the economic leader during most of the 160-year history of Belgium. With the decline of steel, metal-working, and coal mining from the 1960s onwards, it was Flanders turn to become the national economic motor, and gateway, with considerable foreign investment around Antwerp and the arrival of high-tech industries attracted by motivated, multilingual workers and, of course, the coastline. The redistribution of economic wealth and population led to years of tension between the two communities and the fall of several coalition governments. Just one collapse occurred over the refusal of the French-speaking Mayor of a small border village to speak Dutch. Premier Wilfried Martens, a center right Flemish Christian Democrat, who has dominated Belgian politics for a decade putting together governments of different hues, was largely responsible for the new devolution which will give the regions what they have been seeking and allow them "to get on with things." Neither side can any longer blame the other or block spending bills. The buck now stops in Ghent, the prosperous port and car assembly city that is the official capital of Flanders (Antwerp being the *de facto* center) and in Namur, the picturesque capital of Wallonia. Conscious of their new responsibilities, the Flemish rulers have ignored loud protests and closed the remaining coal mines; the Walloon executive has cracked the whip over Wallonia's largest city, Liège, which had spent itself into bankruptcy and which has been forced to reduce its featherbedded, pumped-up municipal workforce in exchange for help from the banks. Some 40 percent of the national budget has been handed over to Flanders, Wallonia, and Brussels. The trio is now responsible for foreign trade, transport (except the national airline and railway system), public works, roads and ports, and industrial, environmental, and energy policies. In all, it is a dramatic change which will be spread over another eight years. Premier Martens aims for what he calls "dynamic federalism." There could well be new problems, over the route and payment of new roads, and high-speed train lines. Will there be a Flemish franc and a Walloon franc? National government, which retains responsibility for foreign affairs, defense, monetary policy, and social security, will have emergency powers over regional spending programs and taxation—just in case. In addition, special tribunals will hear disputes between regions. On the face of things, Brussels looks to be a complicated case, with a regional government structure added to the existing city government, two linguistic institutions, and 19 communal councils. An investor interested in Flanders, for example, may well have to go to Ghent, to Antwerp, to Brussels, where the Flanders government has a big new setup, or talk to the national finance minister.

Confusion is sure to arise at home and abroad. Professor Marcel de Merleir, the noted Belgian adviser on where best to build a factory in Europe, recalls the tragi-comic episode when Premier Martens was in Japan at the same time as the chief ministers of Flanders and Wallonia. The Japanese could not understand why Belgium seemingly had three prime ministers, and this feeling is shared by some investors stepping off the plane at Brussels. The new layers of authority in Belgium can only be understood by having a local adviser—or one of the many US lawyers or lobbyists in town. Select one who has been there for a while. M. Martens has spoken of the regional reform as "the most important the country has known," and he hopes that the new dynamism of Europe will enable Belgians to see the future in broad, rather than parochial, terms.

FLANDERS

The five provinces in the Dutch-speaking north are West Flanders, East Flanders, Antwerp, Flemish Brabant, and Limburg; they have proved the strongest magnet for foreign investors. It's estimated that most of the 1,000 sizeable foreign firms that have chosen Belgium since the war have settled in the formerly agricultural north where growth has consistently outstripped the south. The north is also responsible for the largest part of Belgian exports, important in a country which has the highest export figure per capita in the world. Manufacturing is highly diversified, notably in metals, food, paper, textiles, and, more recently, in automobiles. Elsewhere, some 400 firms work in basic chemicals, pharmaceuticals, processing, and trading. One calculation puts recent and ongoing investment by multinationals in northern Belgium at around three billion dollars. Flanders has the advantage of three ports, Antwerp, Ghent, and Zeebrugge. The workforce is multilingual because of history and geography, and school-leavers speak Dutch, French, English, and, in many cases, German.

A number of foreign firms have taken advantage of the 25 business centers, or industrial complexes, which are subsidized by local government and which group offices, depots, and production areas under one roof. These centers are useful first stops for companies anxious to canvas the market or rent facilities before building their own premises. All five development authorities in Flanders, known by the acronym GOM, have supported these centers and one is to be found at Zaventem, next to Brussels airport. Moving in and out of the centers is relatively easy, with only two months notice required before departure. In Ghent, the Flanders Technology International fair is held every two years and it claims to be one of the largest in the world.

West Flanders

The E17 highway, which crosses Europe from north to south, passes through Kortrijk, the major industrial center of West Flanders.

There's also the E40, running from the port of Ostend to the ancient city of Brugge and on to Germany. Ostend and Zeebrugge, the province's other main port, are the outlets for the export-oriented production in the province. Zeebrugge, in recent years, has grown to handle more than 20 million tons of cargo, most of it roll-on/roll-off container traffic. A network of waterways links the two ports to inland industrial sites. However, the area is threatened by the Channel Tunnel which will take freight from the ships plying the routes to Britain. International, long distance container traffic will not be affected. The main activities in West Flanders are metalworking, electronics, and textiles. The province has attracted units of Siemens, Philips, Ford New Holland, Outboard Marine, Grace, Bayer, BASF, Samsonite, United Biscuits, and Trellborg.

East Flanders

East Flanders has the country's second port, Ghent, linked to the North Sea by sea canal. There's also direct access to the European inland waterway network, including the Rhine. A modern marshalling station has been built for rail traffic, while the port has easy access to the E17 and E40 transcontinental highways. Ghent is the site of a big Volvo plant, while Japanese carmakers use it as an entry point for the European market. Sidmar steel is located in the port area as are FMC Food and Machinery (tooling and engineering) and Mannesmann Carnoy (metalworking). The textile sector is much smaller than it was before the Second World War, but what remains has been modernized and includes UCO, Santens, Beaulieu, and Lee Europe. One of the most famous local firms is the biotechnology leader, Plants Genetic Systems. Newcomers include micro-electronics and computer firms, such as Alcatel, Mietec, Sprague, Siemens, and others. Not surprisingly, most of the major investments have been made near the Ghent canal, with its flow of iron and steel, general cargo—and fruitjuice, for here is the largest European terminal for frozen, concentrated juice.

Antwerp

The province generates one fifth of Belgium's GNP. Aside from the port activities, the striking feature has been the growth of the car assembly industry, turning out some 400,000 vehicles a year. The diamond cutting and selling business has held its world lead, despite competition from South East Asia. The chemical and pharmaceutical industries have grown to employ 35,000 people. The region is wealthy and the local "good life" includes exclusive riding, and golf and tennis clubs—one tournament offers the winner a diamond-studded racket. In the exclusive residential areas by Nachtegalen (Nightingale) Park, on the edge of Antwerp, "expat" Hong Kong and Indian millionaires live next to comfortably-off Belgians—and Germans.

Flemish Brabant

Flemish Brabant curves around Brussels. The area provides vital economic links with Brussels—the airport, the highways, the cordon of multinationals. The one way foreigners are affected is schooling, namely the lack of French-speaking establishments in many suburban areas. The airport has built Brucargo, an ambitious freight, courier, and postal hub, which it hopes one day will rival Amsterdam's Schiphol. The European Mail System operates at Brucargo, sorting and forwarding from one country to another. Federal Express leads the courier services which take advantage of permitted night flying. The airport itself has been privatized and improved—to a degree. One still expects something better in Europe's "capital." However, the province is at the crossroads of seven European highways and stands to profit from the northern extension of the French TGV (train à grande vitesse) express train network. The province lures increasing numbers of companies from crowded Brussels with its escalating real estate prices. Links to industry have been woven by three universities—Leuven Catholic University, Brussels Free University and Imec, the inter-university micro-electronics center. Private and government venture capital funds exist. One forecast heard in Brussels is that government and regional subsidies to investors will decline to 20 percent or less. Well, this province will give you, in some cases, up to 40 percent.

Limburg

Limburg province in the east of Belgium has seen its coal mines close one by one, and the last remaining mines are set to go out of business. The authorities faced a serious problem of unemployment among the young—42 percent of the population is under 25—and were forced to look energetically for outside investors. Incentives to invest in the province are now among the best, if not the best, in the country. Foreign and multinational enterprises account for 60 percent of industrial jobs. Among them are Ford, ITT, Dow Chemical, Hercules, Philips Petroleum, Quaker Oats, Pittsburg Corning, Union Electric Steel, Philips, Siemens, Hoechst, Klockner, Volvo, and DSM. The Japanese have arrived—Toyota, Matsushita, Chiyoda, Nitto, and Amano. The regional development authority has plenty of sites, matches partners for joint ventures, and works with other development agencies in Flanders in promoting subcontracting.

WALLONIA

A degree of optimism has returned to Wallonia, the southern and French-speaking part of Belgium, after many years of industrial decline brought on by the closing of coal mines and the end of an era during which the steel industry was a source of guaranteed employment. Wallonia's provinces are still adapting to changed circumstances, but the feeling now is that the tide has turned. Chemical, metal, and paper companies have invested, resulting in an upswing of industrial production following the low point of 1986. The region's in-

---

S P O T L I G H T

• *Investment* •

Wallonia, which sees itself as a natural distribution point within the Single Market, is determined that the future European high-speed rail network will also run through its territory, hence the regional government's fight to have a "branch line" of the TGV (*Train à Grande Vitesse*). The Walloon authorities, headquartered in Namur, want a line to run eastwards via the principal Walloon city of Liège to Cologne, Germany, and for work on this line to proceed simultaneously with the northwards extension of the Paris–Lille Channel Tunnel line towards Brussels, Antwerp and the Netherlands. Disputes over the routes for the Belgian section of the TGV will mean delay. It had been hoped to "include" Belgium in time for the Channel Tunnel opening in 1993. Wallonia has good roads, but is now doing something to upgrade its two main airports, Charleroi–Gosselies and Liège–Bierset. The first is a budding international airport for southern Brussels, whereas the second serves the Meuse–Rhine "Euroregion" with its population of 2.5 million.

Wallonia offers a variety of aid for investors with the level of assistance reaching some 21 percent. The region offers cheap land for investors and runs a number of high-tech promotion schemes (Athena and Elan). Some 750 companies benefit from foreign investment. The region exports over half its output and export-oriented companies receive special aid. Investors should contact:

Ministry for the Walloon Region
7 Avenue Prince de Liege
5100 Jambes/Namur
Tel: 32-81-321211
Fax: 32-81-306434 or

Regional Investment Bank (SRIW)
19 Place Josephine Charlotte
5100 Jambes/Namur
Tel: 32-81-322211
Fax: 32-81-306424.

dustrial heritage is equalled by few in Europe. Earlier in the century Walloon factories were producing heavy machinery, tramways, and electrical equipment. Today, traces of the earlier period are still visible but the highways are excellent, the universities dynamic, the countryside dotted with inns renowned for their gastronomy. An early sign of recovery was the revival of the massive steel company, Cockerill Sambre at Liège. This was the very symbol of regional might, but in the 1970s it was close to complete collapse. Since then, its workforce has been drastically slimmed and the emphasis placed on higher-value-added steel products. Cockerill is slowly traveling the road back. In general, relations are quieter on the labor front than they were at the time of the recession. Re-conversion subsidies, research grants, and tax breaks are generous. Moreover, solutions now are a matter for the Walloons themselves, following regionalization.

Year One was how a politician described 1989. Fred Vossen, director of Plant Location International which, with its Eurosite database, advises on the best investment sites across Europe, pinpoints Wallonia's advantage in the 1990s. He sees companies grouping their European distribution centers, or EDCs, as they are known. Wallonia's geography, in this respect, is even more "central" in Western Europe than that of the Netherlands. "It is amusing to hear everyone in Europe say they are at the heart of the continent. Austria, France, Switzerland, even Denmark, make such claims. But the map shows that Belgium is the real center." New trans-European highways and high-speed rail lines will also enhance Wallonia's chances for a second industrial revolution. Wages, benefits and employer contributions to the social security system are high, but M. Vossen maintains that the "reality" is different, and that the difference between what you officially are charged and what you pay can be substantial—after deductions.

Liège

Liège province shares boundaries with Germany, Luxembourg, and the Netherlands. It is particularly well-served, with highways to Maastricht and Amsterdam, to Cologne and Frankfurt, to Basle and many other important Eurocities. It will be on the future TGV line. Already, the new industrial base is formed of electronics, aircraft engineering, computers, engineering, astro-physics, biotechnology, fibre glass, fibre optics, and carbon fibers. The Société Provinciale d'Industrialisation has created more than 35 industrial, trading, and service areas, including a science park adjacent to Liège University. The city, as recently as the winter of 1989–90, faced a financial crisis, but has since begun to learn to live in a more disciplined way. Federalism and the advent of the Single Market are exercising salutary influences.

:::::::::::::::SUCCESS STORY— :::::::::::::::
JOHNSON MATTHEY

The modern plant of Britain's Johnson Matthey company, built at a cost of $30 million in the Evere industrial park, just east of Brussels, is aiming for annual production of five million autocatalysts a year to meet a third of EC needs from 1993.

Single Market directives, similar to US clean air measures of the 1970s, will make it obligatory for all new cars to be fitted with these environment-friendly devices. Austria, Norway, Sweden and Switzerland have earlier introduced standards equivalent of those in the US. Germany, Greece, and the Netherlands offered tax breaks to motorists prepared to fit control equipment voluntarily. Now, exhaust control is going to be law across the EC.

Following US and Australian legislation, Johnson Matthey opened plants in Pennsylvania and in Sydney. It was ahead of legislation in Europe. The size of the European market—for which 12 to 13 million automobiles are produced a year—was too big for Johnson Matthey's plant at Royston, north of London, which is capable of making one million autocatalysts a year. Today, the Evere plant is moving towards 24-hour, three-shift production totalling 4.5 million units a year.

The EC has adopted three-way autocatalysts that neutralize carbon monoxide, nitrogen oxide, and unburned hydrocarbons. The new British-owned plant and others across Europe are designed to make the EC self-sufficient in this particular technology and so satisfy Carlo Ripa di Meana, the EC environment commissioner, who has stated: "The environment will occupy the community's stage more and more as we approach the Single Market." Stricter testing and stricter standards are on the way.

Johnson Matthey, the world leader in autocatalysts, has been a highly successful company, but did not say "no" to Belgium's aid, tailored to be generous to high-tech companies employing around 100 people. High-tech investment qualifies for aid on three-quarters of cost; lower-tech on two-thirds. In this case, the Brussels regional development and investment authorities were keen to strengthen the ring of high-tech industries around the capital. The favored sites are the industrial parks with links to the main universities. John Matthey worked with the banks to receive interest rate subsidies. As chairman

David Davies said: "We came to Evere because of its central position in our European market, but also because of the help and support from the Brussels authorities."

Autocatalysts and other Johnson Matthey products are now being made in a chain of plants stretching from Britain to Italy via Belgium. When the British and Belgian engineers drive to work they pass their neighbors, who include Alfa-Laval, Honeywell, Institut Merieux, Neste Chemicals, SKF, Texas Instruments, and Unisys.

• *Eyewitness* •

Richard Hill, Consultant

History in the form of the Romans, the Spaniards, the Austrians, the French, and the Dutch (plus more recent invading Germans) has, perhaps surprisingly, taught the Belgians to be tolerant toward others. They allow the expatriate to live comfortably in their country, on the understanding that foreigners let them live comfortably, too (comfortable living being number one in the Belgian value system). Some expatriates would say that their hosts choose to go on living as if they weren't there: an invitation to a Belgian home is the exception rather than the rule. In that respect, Belgium is not much different from many other European countries.

Despite its byzantine political structure, Belgium still lends itself to comfortable living. Brussels is probably the most amenable capital city of Europe, although the growth of the European institutions is putting enormous demands on its powers of digestion. Being pragmatic people, the Belgians always find a solution, probably a compromise which in the short term satisfies everyone except the environmentalists and the conservationists. Apart from pragmatism, Belgium is short on -*isms*.

"Amenable" means accessible, too. As a business and administrative center, Brussels offers rapid communications with other capitals. The airport is somewhat folkloric, but big plans are afoot, and the telecommunications system needs upgrading fast. But for physical access and egress—by rail, by road over the superb motorway network, or even by air—Belgium cannot be bettered.

Communications includes languages, a discipline in which most educated Belgians excel. With exceptions, they make intelligent and industrious employees. Being naturally cosmopolitan, they smooth the process of conducting affairs at the European level. Despite their internecine quarrels, they show none of the egocentric attitudes of the British, the French, or even, clandestinely, the Germans.

Belgium has another, underrated feature: the variety and the beauty of its countryside, ranging from the art cities of Flanders to the heathlands of Limburg and the forests of the Ardennes. Add to that, excellent educational facilities in and around Brussels, and a very rich cultural offering for a city of its size. And then, of course, there's the cooking. . . .

THE LEADERS

TOP 20 COMPANIES (1989)

		Sales	(BFm) Profits
(1)	Petrofina	577,673	22,445
(2)	Delhaize Le Leon	259,962	6,357
(3)	Solvay	256,796	16,712
(4)	Electrabel	219,308	21,014
(5)	GIB	195,129	2,613
(6)	Cockerill-Sambre	187,951	15,367
(7)	Ford Belgium	178,600	492
(8)	Acec–Union Miniere	175,547	19,872
(9)	Exxon Chemical	133,991	6,048
(10)	Volvo Belgium	99,453	3,952
(11)	Wagons-Lits	96,439	1,588
(12)	Bayer Belgium	87,917	6,342
(13)	RTT	84,703	7,862
(14)	Philips Belgium	72,584	. . . . . .
(15)	Renault Belgium	69,200	445
(16)	BASF Belgium	65,790	2,874
(17)	BP Belgium	63,535	5,382

		(BFm)	
		Sales	*Profits*
(18)	Bekaert	61,199	3,668
(19)	Sidmar	60,292	7,339
(20)	Volkswagen Belgium	59,628	1,724
	($1 = BF35)		

Source: Federation des Enterprises de Belgique

1990 Results

Falls
Bekaert − BF454m (− 113 percent); Acec-UM Miniere BF3.4b (− 60 percent); Société Générale BF12-2b (− 40 percent); Solvay BF 15-9b (− 5 percent).

Gains
Generale de Banque BF8.04b (+ 8 percent);
GIB BF2.98b (+ 14 percent); Bruxelles Lambert BF5-71b (+ 33.5 percent).

TOP 20 BANKS (1989)

		(BFm) Balance Sheet *(unconsolidated)*	*Profits*
(1)	Generale de Banque	2243289	2600
(2)	Bruxelles Lambert	1752001	4046
(3)	Credit Communal	1645229	2294
(4)	Kredietbank	1403983	4980
(5)	Credit Lyonnais	792960 (1988)	92 (1988)
(6)	Sanwa	702671	101
(7)	Sumitomo	533080	174
(8)	Paribas	324900	1057
(9)	Mitsui	264446	150
(10)	Morgan Guaranty	261344	2149
(11)	BNP	187337	93
(12)	Fuji	170913	6
(13)	Citibank	168323	120

		(BFm) Balance Sheet (unconsolidated)	Profits
(14)	Credit General	118113	432
(15)	Taiyo Kobe	108398	36
(16)	Barclays	102000	9
(17)	Deutsche	99935	−14
(18)	Mitsubishi	92299	108
(19)	International Westminster	85167	3
(20)	Bank of Tokyo	84809	98

Source: Association Belge des Banques)

KEY CONTACTS

USEFUL BRUSSELS TELEPHONE NUMBERS

Trade and Commercial Information

EC Commission: 32-2-235-1111
Belgian Foreign Trade Office: 32-2-219-4450
Belgian Standards: 32-2-734-9205
Confederation of British Industry: 32-2-231-0465
Permreps (Permanent Representatives of the 12 EC Member States):

Belgium: 32-2-230-9900
Britain: 32-2-230-6205
Denmark: 32-2-233-0811
France: 32-2-511-4955
Germany: 32-2-513-4500
Greece: 32-2-735-8085

Ireland: 32-2-218-0605
Italy: 32-2-230-8170
Luxembourg: 32-2-735-8085
Netherlands: 32-2-513-7775
Portugal: 32-2-211-1211
Spain: 32-2-509-8611

Chambers of Commerce

Member Nations
Belgium–Germany: 32-2-218-5040
Belgium–Greece: 32-2-647-3495
Belgium–Italy: 32-2-230-1123

The Netherlands: 32-2-219-1174
Portugal: 32-2-647-7846
Spain: 32-2-230-2240

Others
Belgium–Africa: 32-2-512-4100
Belgium–Canada: 32-2-511-5227

Brussels: 32-2-648-5002
Swiss: 32-2-217-5543

Embassies

Member Nations
Britain: 32-2-217-9000
Denmark: 32-2-648-2525
France: 32-2-512-1715
Germany: 32-2-770-5830
Greece: 32-2-648-1730
Ireland: 32-2-513-6633
Italy: 32-2-649-9700
Luxembourg: 32-2-733-9977

Netherlands: 32-2-230-3020
Portugal: 32-2-539-3691
Spain (TK)

Others
Canada: 32-2-735-6040
Japan: 32-2-513-9200
United States: 32-2-513-3830

US STATE OFFICES

Arkansas
Ave Louise 437, Bte 4,
B-1050 Brussels
Tel: 32-2-649-6024
Fax: 32-2-649-4807

Florida (Europe Office)
Rue Arm. Campenhout 63,
B-1050 Brussels
Tel: 32-2-537-2900
Fax: 32-2-537-5938

Georgia (Dept. Industry/Trade)
Ave Louise 380,
B-1050 Brussels
Tel: 32-2-647-7825
Fax: 32-2-640-6813

Illinois (Europe Office)
28.30 Bld de la Cambre
Bte 2
B-1050 Brussels
Tel: 32-2-646-5730
Fax: 32-2-646-5511

Kentucky
149 Ave Louise, Box 15,
B-1050 Brussels
Tel: 32-2-534-1730
Fax: 32-2-534-1845

Maryland (Europe Office)
Ave Louise 222, Bte 7,
B-1050 Brussels
Tel: 32-2-647-5367
Fax: 32-2-647-5700

Michigan (Export Development)
Rue Ducale 41,
B-1000 Brussels
Tel: 32-2-511-0732
Fax: 32-2-514-3617

Ohio
51 B Chaussee de Charleroig
B-1060 Brussels
Tel: 32-2-534-4920
Fax: 32-2-534-4662

Pennsylvania
Rue Montoyer 31, Bte 4,
B-1040 Brussels
Tel: 32-2-513-7796
Fax: 32-2-514-2351

Utah
19 Rue du Planeur
B-1140 Brussels
Tel: 32-2-727-2946
Fax: 32-2-727-2949

Virginia
Ave Louise 479, Bte 55,
B-1050 Brussels
Tel: 32-2-648-6179
Fax: 32-2-648-0698

PORT AUTHORITIES

Illinois/Chicago
Place du Champs de Mars 5,
Bte 14,
B-1050 Brussels
Tel: 32-2-512-0105
Fax: 32-2-512-5809

Maryland (Baltimore)
Ave Louise 222, Bte 1,
B-1050 Brussels
Tel: 32-2-648-9390
Fax: 32-2-647-5700

Virginia
Ave Louise 479, Bte 55,
B-1050 Brussels
Tel: 32-2-648-8072
Fax: 32-2-646-3554

Facts on Britain

· ·

Capital London
Population 57.2m
Working Population 28m
Unemployment 8%
GDP Growth 1989: 2%; 1990: 0.5%; 1991
  (est.) 0.5%
GDP per Capita $11,720
Inflation 5%
Manufacturing (% of GDP) 24%
Services (% of GDP) 58%
Current Account − $27b
British–US Trade
  US exports 1989: $20.866m
  UK exports 1989: $18.242m
Direct Investment
  UK in US: $110b
  US in UK: $54b

· ·

BRITAIN

"The popularity of Britain as a target nation is not only a result of the ease with which foreigners can bid for British companies. Their interest extends well into the private market implying that a strong underlying motivation exists to own British companies." Mark Dixon, Translink's European Deal Review

BRITAIN, STILL FAR AND AWAY THE MOST POPULAR COUNTRY AMONG US, Japanese, and other investors looking at Europe, is a case study in how a country's fortunes can swing in the relatively short period of two years. Britain boomed for eight years in the 1980s because the welcome mat, language, and lifestyle attracted foreign investors, while Mrs. Thatcher's new spirit of enterprise took hold. The end of the 1980s and the beginning of the 1990s proved more difficult, as prices and wages spun out of control and interest rates soared. Britain switched from being one of the fastest to one of the slowest-growth economies in Europe and among the industrialized nations in general. In late 1990, Margaret Thatcher, in one of her last acts as Prime Minister, decided to accept a degree of European control over the value of her currency in the hope that restraint and discipline would halve the double-digit inflation rate and permit a relaunching of the economy through cheaper money. Her successor, John Major, went further. Without giving a commitment to a future single currency in Europe, saying this was for the Westminster parliament to decide, he pledged greater cooperation with the other EC states. The key phrase, before a German audience which heard him praise their country's "exemplary record" on inflation, was, "I want us to be where we belong—at the very heart of Europe." Most observers believed this heralded a substantive change, not just one of style. Britain's picture did look somewhat better in 1991 with the inflation figure down to the region of six percent and with four points or more off interest rates, but the economy remained in a state of recession.

Two contrasting statements sum up Britain's dilemma as it approaches the Single Market and the greater competitiveness across Europe that will come in its wake. A government communique when things were still rosy declared: "Since 1980, the economy has grown faster than that of any other major EC country. Prospects are buoyant; further growth is forecast, particularly in manufacturing." True, but the decade ended on a much sourer note, with investment, manufacturing output and corporate profits down, and with unemployment, which had been reduced to six percent, rising to two million. Headlines provided the contrast, for at the end of 1990 they blazoned, "Britain hits recession." This was confirmed when company profits fell and experts predicted a year "of demanning, falling investment, dividend cuts, and destocking."

Ministers, economists, industrialists and trade unionists argued over how to halt a spiral of wages and inflation, running two to three times higher than in Germany, France, and other competitors. Britain's long-debated entry into the exchange rate mechanism (ERM) of the European Monetary System, hopefully will provide the discipline, albeit painful, required to restore competitiveness and reduce the current account deficit from the region of $22 billion a year. Admittedly, the increase in the cost of living looks somewhat better when calculated on the official retail price index, but Britain's level still outstripped that of France and Germany. The new Chancellor of the Exchequer (finance minister) Norman Lamont stubbornly said he would drive inflation down to four percent by the beginning of 1992, and government policy revolves around that objective before the next election.

What to do to return Britain to the sustained growth and low inflation of the mid-1980s, before the government loosened the economic reins and everyone went on a credit-fueled spending spree? Professor Douglas McWilliams, chief economic adviser to the Confederation of British Industry, said the goal should be an inflation level of three percent within five years (by the mid-1990s). He pointed to the real danger. "Unless we change our inflationary habits, UK wages will overtake German wages by 1995 with disastrous consequences on the ability of British firms to compete in world markets."

Britain had already been shaken by Italian claims to have overtaken it to become the world's fifth economy. There followed a study by the National Economic Development Council, chaired by the Chancellor, which said Britain was lagging a decade behind France as well as Germany in living standards and output per employee. Recession was not the word used by this leading body of experts, who spoke instead of a "pause" while inflation was squeezed from the economy. The study said it was unfortunate that the "pause" came when the task of raising British production and output per worker to European standards was only half-complete.

A lot of Britons were looking at the "evidence" of the success of policies in mainland Europe where car ownership, consumption of such items as steel and electricity, and the availability of telephones and television sets in homes were much higher. Economic commentator David Smith had this cross-Channel view: "The French experience offers a guide to the type of adjustment the British could have to undergo in the next few years. France entered the exchange rate mechanism at its inception in March, 1979, but for the first few years refused to accept the disciplines of ERM membership. The franc was devalued five times between 1979 and January, 1987. Then four years ago, the government embarked on the strong currency or *franc fort* policy. Instead of resorting to devaluation, France would accept the discipline of adjusting to low, West German-style inflation, and maintaining a fixed exchange rate for the franc against Europe's strongest currency, the D-mark."

The message was clear for Premier John Major on the eve of a coming general election. Inflation before and after the Gulf crisis dominated the political debate. The industry confederation, in a detailed analysis of the problem which was sent to all parties as they geared up for an election, said there was no "one big explanation," tempting as it was to look for one. Britain's leading business group offered plenty of suggestions—a reform of the very system of calculation of statistics to bring British methods in line with other Europeans; a rein on government spending and borrowing; an export drive; and even income tax increases, saying it would be wrong to avoid even these on political grounds. The last suggestion would prove a difficult pill for the Conservatives, whose former leader reduced the basic rate of personal income tax to 25 percent along with launching her "enterprise culture" through privatization of much of the public sector—British Airways, British Telecom, British gas, electricity and water, Rolls Royce aero engines, Rover cars and more.

Both giant firms and small companies were hurting badly in 1991, after starting the previous year in a more confident mood. Europe-wide surveys, based on company margins (pre-tax profits as a percentage of sales) and return on total assets, had shown that 28 of the 50 top-performing companies were British. Heading this corporate table at the time was Glaxo pharmaceuticals, followed by RTZ mining, with four other British companies in the top ten (Tarmac construction, British Telecom, Guinness, and the BTR conglomerate). Beecham foods, retailers Great Universal Stores and Marks & Spencer were in the leading 16, along with BAT industries, tobacco and financial services, and ICI chemicals. One survey showed that although industrial performance in depth was lacking, the British engineering sector had made something of a comeback and was poised to play its part in reducing the horrendous balance of payments in manufactured goods which rose to close to $25 billion.

The picture changed as company profits fell, notably at ICI, the country's biggest industrial company, BTR, and various building and engineering companies, as well as at a diverse range of non-industrial companies. The fashion group Laura Ashley was just one example. Automobile makers warned of steep falls in sales. The high interest rate squeeze increased the number of insolvencies among smaller fry (property, retailing, textiles) by two or three times. It all resulted in unemployment edging up 50,000 to 1.65 million before hitting two million, with more jobs under threat from the "recession," or slowdown, as the government preferred to call it. Growth, which had been running at 2.3 percent began to slide.

Mr. Major, whose deadline for a new General Election is 1992, had his immediate economic problems compounded by think tank forecasts of 200,000 jobs threatened, mainly in manufacturing as Europe's barriers come down. The polls consistently had the opposition Labor Party in the lead. The new Prime Minister, naturally, hit back at those talking up the recession, saying 1992 would see the recovery.

Britain remains a favorite location for US, Japanese and French investment. Nissan, Toyota and Honda have all chosen the country as a relatively cheap base for attacking the European market as a whole. US companies have flocked to areas near Heathrow airport and to Scotland. US Department of Commerce figures show that Britain's share of US investment in the EC rose from 38 percent to 41 percent by 1990. Some 116 projects were recorded by the Invest in Britain Bureau in a 15-month period.

US investment confirms a long-established trend. Altogether, more than 2,000 US companies have invested in Britain, including 96 of Fortune magazine's Top 100. In all, US investment is equal to the total

US investment in the former West Germany, France, Ireland, and Spain combined. Corporate tax, now reduced to 33 percent, and basic personal tax at 25 percent (with a single higher rate of 40 percent) have maintained Britain's appeal, along with its improved labor relations and a level of wage settlements that is now declining. Britain also is one of the EC's largest markets with the 22 million households normally spending between $500–$600 billion a year on goods and services.

The nation's lifestyle, which combines history, culture and a degree of familiarity, is as important in attracting US companies which account for some 12 percent of the gross domestic product and which employ more than half a million British men and women.

Britain is also the most favored European country among Japanese investors. Since YKK opened the way in 1972, some 120 Japanese concerns have made substantial investments. The Nomura Research Institute says Japanese investment could rise from the current $4.5 billion to $12 billion by the end of the decade—unless something goes wrong seriously in Japan. At this rate, Japan could account for a tenth of Britain's manufacturing production by the year 2000, although Japan has a long way to go before it reaches the US investment level. The Japanese will hesitate before choosing neighboring France as an alternative, for the new French Premier, Edith Cresson, is not on "their side."

Among Britain's European partners, Germany and France have poured deutschmarks and francs into manufacturing and services in Britain. The automobile industry has attracted the Germans as well as the Japanese. Leading automobile components firms, notably Robert Bosch (compact alternators), Ina Bearings (tension pulleys), Kabelwerke Reinshagen (wiring harnesses), and Keiper Recaro (car seats) have invested recently to join other German firms engaged in a wide variety of activities from electrical components to roof racks. Major French water companies have bought into Britain following the privatization of the water industry, Peugeot has been one of the biggest success stories in automobile manufacturing, while dynamic, medium-sized companies from France, such as Plastic Omnium (plastics for industry, city refuse collectors, and other uses) have made profitable inroads into Britain, as have construction, food and advertising firms. These broad-based investments by foreign firms indicate that Britain's basic appeal could well survive current economic problems.

SPOTLIGHT

· *John Major* ·

John who? At first, many people outside Britain could not place Mrs. Thatcher's successor. John Major had been in her shadow, although as Chancellor of the Exchequer he had ranked No. 2. Certainly, the new 47 year old Prime Minister was created politically by the lady who seemed to have a permanent lease on Number Ten Downing Street, before her anti-European stance and the Conservatives' slump in the polls forced her resignation. Major was not the early frontrunner, but his camp ran the slickest campaign to win the support of Conservative Members of Parliament (MPs). As the *London Times* said: "They transformed the image of the Chancellor from a greyish, little-known political technician to that of a thrustful politician with a sense of mission for the Britain of the 1990s." Resolve (and success) in the Gulf War boosted his popularity. Mrs. Thatcher's father was a grocer, but Major claims equally humble origins. Dad was a music hall artist who toured Britain and the U.S. Later, financial problems in the family garden gnomes business forced the Majors to leave a house in a pleasant London suburb for a rundown, two-room flat with the gas ring on the landing and the toilet three floors below. The future Prime Minister said: "It was a good environment to be brought up in," showing the self-deprecating side the British like. He seemed destined for failure. Upon quitting school at 16, he worked as a laborer, was once "on the dole" (unemployed) and was turned down by a bus company for weakness in arithmetic. He popped up at the Standard Chartered Bank in Nigeria and then as press officer for the boss, a former Chancellor. Elected an MP as recently as 1979, he came under Mrs. Thatcher's wing. She appreciated Major as the perfect, quick-witted, self-made man of the Thatcher years.

Major is not just Britain's Mr. Nice Guy. He stood firmly by the U.S. during the Gulf War and shrewdly set out to charm and influence other European leaders—and so end Britain's relative isolation. He has made a special effort with the Germans, and as this extract from a major speech shows, he is either extremely adroit—or has a new speechwriter far removed from Mrs. Thatcher's "No, no, no" (to Europe).

We are bringing our own ideas to the (EC) intergovernmental conferences on economic and monetary union and political union. And a willingness to discuss both our own ideas and the ideas of our partners, openly and positively. Britain will relish the debate and the argument. That is the essence of doing business in today's Community. And, we want to arrive at solutions which will enable us to move forward more united, not less. That is why we think it better that change in the Community should be of an evolutionary rather than a revolutionary kind. It would be a tragedy if Europe tried to move so that in the cause of unity it provoked disunity.

There are many things we can and must do in common with our European partners. At the same time, Europe is made up of nation states; their vitality and diversity are sources of strength. The important thing is to strike the right balance between closer cooperation and a proper respect for national institutions and traditions. The British agenda—first, price stability must be the prime objective of monetary policy. Whether or not it is sensible to use the same money, surely we can all agree on the need for sound money. As finance minister, I took sterling into the (European) exchange rate mechanism because I knew membership would help drive inflation down....Second, economic and monetary union must be based on free and open markets. Stage One (of the European Monetary and Economic Union) still has a long way to go before we can proclaim that Europe is truly open for finance....Third,

continued

> the development of monetary cooperation must depend on much greater progress towards economic convergence between member states. The gaps at present are simply too wide....A common foreign and security policy requires consensus. Another necessary condition is recognition of the vital need to keep Atlantic ties strong. As we look at the wider world, the pivotal role of the United States is clear...the Community must get its relationship with North America right.
>
> Style or substance? Sir Leon Brittan, a British EC Commissioner, said: "Often style is substance in the Community." He meant that change of tone is most important.

MARKET OPPORTUNITIES

COMPUTERS AND PERIPHERALS

A ten billion dollar-plus market that has been growing at double digit rate (mainframe installations at 25 percent, minicomputer-based systems at 12 percent, and microcomputers at 42 percent). The PC market has been dominated by IBM and IBM-clones, with other makers going after specialized, niche markets. Sales of peripherals and board level expansion products held up in 1990, but the whole computer sector, as well as others, could well be affected by a slowdown into 1991. US products account for around 21 percent of the total computer and peripheral market.

COMPUTER SOFTWARE AND SERVICES

Although difficult to measure, consensus is that software and services have been growing at 25 percent, equal to that of the equipment sector. The market was estimated at $4.5 billion, with US imports accounting for two-thirds of the total market.

ELECTRONIC COMPONENTS

The market rose to $5.5 billion in 1989–1990, up from $4.8 billion the previous year. Estimated US imports in 1989 were $420 million, rising at a rate of 12 percent annually. The US import figure is deceptively low, since a substantial proportion of local production capacity is owned by American firms, and half of other imports are from plants owned by or contracted to US companies.

TELECOMMUNICATIONS EQUIPMENT

The privatized telecommunications market is largely self-sufficient in switching and transmission equipment, but takes a large volume of components, sub-systems, and subscriber apparatus from foreign sources. US companies have a significant share of the import sector, and can look to meeting increasing demand for intelligent networks and attachments. The total market in this sector was $4.2 billion. US imports had 5 percent, but could well grow by 15 percent a year.

BIOTECHNOLOGY

This has evolved from a research-based industry to a product-based industry. The market of $2.3 billion represented research spending, license fees, and physical product imports. US imports were one-tenth of the total market, but an early 1990 estimate was that these could grow by 11 percent a year. Again, much depends on the 1991 recovery, or otherwise, of the economy. Actual products, such as pharmaceuticals and seeds, will be traded increasingly.

SAFETY AND SECURITY EQUIPMENT

Demand continued to grow for electronic surveillance, access control and fire alarm/detection systems. The market was estimated at $1.8 billion. US companies have done well to date (six percent of the market and a quarter of imports). Top of British shopping lists have been such items as electronic equipment, intruder alarms, locks, and safety and rescue equipment.

Which nations acquired in United Kingdom?

	First Six Months 1990		Full year 1989	
Acquiring nations	*Number of deals*	*Ecu value (Millions)*	*Number of deals*	*Ecu value (Millions)*
Sweden	23.0	3791.9	23.2	587.5
France	26.5	2513.1	41.0	3974.8
United States	30.8	1766.7	68.0	10097.6
West Germany	15.0	787.3	15.6	3465.0
Japan	11.0	597.7	21.5	753.0
Norway	3.0	208.4	4.3	39.9
Switzerland	7.0	157.5	13.5	83.9
The Netherlands	11.0	305.0	7.5	401.9
Denmark	5.0	120.5	7.1	230.7
Ireland	5.0	87.9	15.6	250.3
Belgium	2.0	4.5	4.4	579.3
Spain	2.0	2.7	5.0	81.1
Total (with others)	146.5	10636.9	237.7	20832.5

Source: Adapted from Translink's European Deal Review

SCIENTIFIC/LABORATORY INSTRUMENTS

The market for these, specialized computerized laboratory data management systems and associated software reached $1.7 billion. Until that time, the market had grown 13 percent annually, with software increasing at a rate of 46 percent. Britain is one of the major world markets for this kind of equipment and US imports have been winning 11 percent of the market. The best sales opportunities are for high-tech products incorporating a high-level of precision engineering and advanced electronics, particularly spectrophotometers, electronic recorders/loggers, chromatographs, and portable instruments in all product categories.

MEDICAL EQUIPMENT

Most healthcare is provided by the National Health Service, but administrative changes within the NHS will offer more opportunities to suppliers. Another factor is official encouragement of private sector healthcare. Nearly six million people, a tenth of the population, are now eligible for at least some treatment within the private sector, which has more than 200 hospitals carrying out a sixth of all major operations. The total market in 1989 was close to $1 billion, with US imports supplying 20 percent.

SPORTING GOODS

Adult participation in sports throughout Britain grew sharply in the 1980s with 10 percent more men and 20 percent more women taking part. US suppliers have a strong presence (there are now more than 200 American football league teams and many non-league teams). The sporting goods market totalled some $680 million.

POLLUTION CONTROL

Both air and water pollution control and monitoring equipment offer big opportunities for exporters as the electrical generating industry goes private. The air pollution control equipment market has topped $700 million a year with some $125 million being spent on desulphurization equipment for power plants. Both Britain and the European Community are enacting new, more stringent legislation which will expand the market for both air and water pollution control equipment. The water pollution control equipment and instrumentation market has grown to some $760 million. Detailed information for US suppliers is available from the UK desk officer at the Commerce Department, Washington, Tel: 202-377-3748.

TRANSPORTATION AND COMMUNICATIONS

Britain's aging road and railway networks are being repatched, but although the government's financial contribution to improving freight and passenger flows has risen, the state declines to throw public money at infrastructure in the French manner. The best example is the government's refusal to pay for a £4 billion high-speed rail link between London and the British end of the Channel Tunnel, set to open in mid-1993. Government support for British Rail and London's creaking underground system in the three years from 1990 to 1992 has been set at £6 billion. The French are spending £20 billion on their TGVs (high-speed trains), notably to their end of the tunnel. Britain's trains in the Single Market will be running 50 to 100 miles per hour slower than their French and German counterparts. Britain also lacks a nationwide, high-speed network. Fortunately, the freight truck fleet is large and competitive.

The Department of Transport says it will spend £15 billion over ten years on roads—the same figure that the Confederation of British Industry, estimates that deficient transport adds annually to the costs of doing business. Snarled London traffic results in 30 percent higher distribution charges, or £1000 in lost productivity annually per employee. There will be a flurry of spending over the next three years and this outlay could account for half the allocation for the decade. However, much of the work on roads will consist of widening motorways from six to eight lanes rather than building brand new roads. There have been initial steps toward the kind of toll-roads which have been built in France, in many cases, by consortiums working with government-guaranteed loans. All British highways are currently toll-free. New roads are needed across the south and southwest of England to bring goods more speedily to the Channel Tunnel. Police traffic experts have warned that severe bottlenecks could occur when the tunnel pours the equivalent of a two-lane highway at full capacity into the southwest county of Kent for 24 hours a day. The M20 link to the tunnel could be ready in 1991, but the M2 backup is now scheduled for 1997. By 1993, an estimated 640,000 heavy trucks, 172,000 buses, and 2.5 million cars will pass through the tunnel into Kent. Cross-channel traffic could double within 15 years. It seems inevitable that the government will have to act on rail and road in this crowded southwestern corridor, linking Britain to the rest of Europe. Road connections up the eastern side of England also need to be modernized. The vital M25 ring road around the capital is saturated and provides daily material for comedians and BBC traffic flashes: "Traffic is back to normal—or what passes for normal."

Many seaports have been privatized and modernized over the past decade. They handle more than 500 million tons of bulk freight. Firms investing anywhere in Britain will find there is a port within 75 miles—Dover, Southampton, Felixstowe, Harwich, Hull, or Liverpool.

Associated British Ports Holdings, the former state-owned operator, was privatized in 1983 and the featherbedding, dock labor scheme scrapped in 1989. Other ports, so called "trust" ports, have also recently gone over to the private sector meaning that everywhere ports can reduce their total labor force and become more efficient.

The government's new concern for protecting the environment in a relatively small land is another factor that will hinder major infrastructure projects, including the provision of new runways at the three London airports, Heathrow, Gatwick, and Stansted. One consequence will be improved regional airports and the expansion of London City airport, an innovative, private undertaking.

The government has pursued a deregulation policy opening up Heathrow to all comers. American and United were first to take advantage. Gatwick and newly-expanded Stansted, east of the capital, will be hit in the short run, but forecasts are for annual growth over 15 years of 3.5 percent to 5.8 percent, confirming London's airports as *the* hub in Europe.

Until 1991, Britain was the only EC country with two competing and privately-owned telecommunications companies—the dominant British Telecom (BT) with more than 90 percent of the market and the smaller Mercury network. Service compared favorably with the rest of Europe for direct dialing and specialized voice, data, text, and visual communications, plus high-speed satellite services around the world. Cellnet and Vodaphone became European leaders in mobile communications. But the prices were just too high. A 1991 government report, a white paper entitled "Competition and Choice: Telecommunications Policy for the 1990s," moved telecommunications deregulation firmly to stage two. The government promised it would open up the sector to unfettered competition, local and foreign, in order to reduce the price of local calls, the highest in any major industrialized country, and to reduce the cost of international calls—ten percent at the beginning and more later. AT&T has already made a small systems investment, as have Pactel and US West. A new trend will be the marriage of cable TV and telecoms as in the US. BT will continue to dominate the market, but if it abuses its position it could be broken up—just as AT&T was in the US.

::::::MANAGEMENT AND WORKFORCE ::::::

Britain's age-old labor problems—excessive trade union power, strikes and low productivity—seem on the mend. Wage increases of ten percent or more outstripped gains in productivity of four percent in the manufacturing sector at the very start of the 1990s, but there were signs by 1992 of increases close to six percent. Ford, the automobile maker, which sets the pace in pay matters, agreed to pay its workforce increases calculated on an inflation rate plus 2.5 percent. This meant a European record of close to 13 percent. At the same time, the company began switching some of its production to Germany, Belgium, and Spain. High interest rates, the scourge of the British economy, reduced corporate profits across the board and began to lead to lay-offs. The recession pushed the unemployment figure higher after the earlier fall to two million, or seven percent. There were fears that it could go much higher.

Progress had been achieved on this front during the Thatcher decade, notably the slashing of the 3.1 million total of the jobless, reached in the mid-1980s. Although jobs in the main manufacturing industries had fallen by 2.9 million since 1959 to the current 4.9 million, the slack had been taken up by a booming services sector, the creation of thousands of small businesses, the rise in the self-employed to 2.8 million, and government-supported training programs which kept half a million off the unemployment registers. However, red lights flash in all these areas in 1992.

Total days lost from strikes during 1990 was well below the 1989 figure, an exceptional year with numerous stoppages in the public sector. Unofficial strikes on North Sea oil rigs were troublesome, as were labor-employer relations at Ford plants. The US company, claiming that strikes had cost it £800 million in lost production, moved some engine production to Cologne, and the assembly of its Sierra model to Genk, Belgium, and reduced its main Dagenham, Essex, plant to just one model, the Fiesta. Despite this bleak picture, George Bain, principal of the London Business School, is of the opinion that many companies have taken "a more strategic approach to the whole area of human resource management and begun to invest in their people." Yet, he and other labor-relations experts wonder whether training and human-resource budgets will be the first to be cut in the event of a sustained decline in the economy. The Department of Employment has a wide range of assistance schemes for smaller firms and for the young, first-time job-seekers, but is under pressure from the Treasury to cut back. This would be a pity as only 38 percent of the workforce in Britain has skilled vocational training, compared with 56 percent in Spain, 67 percent in Germany and 80 percent in France. This skills shortage has led to the persistence of the productivity gap between Britain and other major EC countries—output per hour among French manufacturing employees was 22 percent above Britain's with larger gaps in the cases of Germany and the Netherlands. On the other hand, many Japanese companies have been satisfied with the way in which they achieved high productivity in the plants they have established in Scotland, the North-East and Wales.

Investment decisions and associated employment by foreign-owned companies in 1989/90 (15-month period)

Country of origin	No. of projects	Jobs created	Jobs safeguarded
USA	116	14,721	8,622
FRG	67	5,067	3,673
Japan	50	10,771	6,527
Irish Republic	11	401	97
France	19	1,516	2,028
Sweden	14	927	522
Canada	10	627	7,900
Netherlands	7	130	303
Italy	8	278	359
Switzerland	14	435	482
Denmark	6	127	293
Norway	6	461	0
Rest of Europe	8	71	1,015
Rest of World	10	2,219	300
Total	346	37,751	32,121

(Source: Invest in Britain)

The new realism of the British trade unions has been influenced by falling membership and hopes centered on the EC's Social Charter which offers harmonization of social benefits across the EC, but which is opposed by the Conservative government. Organized labor, which has lost much of its power as a result of Conservative legislation, has become pro-EC. In all, the Single Market poses problems for Britain's under-equipped workforce. Amin Rajan, author of the Industrial Society's study, *1992: A Zero Sum Game,* warns that 200,000 jobs could be lost in Britain if "vulnerable" areas—and he cites financial services, the food and drink sector, telecommunications, and high-tech companies—do not take remedial action. "Modern technology and better work skills are going to be the key factors that separate winners from losers. That is because streamlined capacity post-1992 will demand enormous flexibility from machines and workforce alike to meet diverse customer needs across the 12 member states." Professor Rajan's study also argues that the "social dimension" of 1992 must be taken into account by the government, otherwise inevitable industrial restructuring could produce "social discord in the short term and negligible economic progress in the long term."

Another factor that will influence Britain will be the desire of countries with "advanced" social benefits (Germany, for example, with its high wages and job security) to see equal conditions throughout the 12—for competitive reasons rather than out of altruism. New Prime

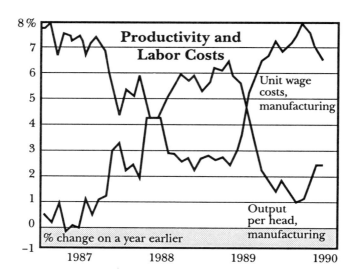

Minister Major has pronounced a more "caring society" without fully spelling out the details.

There is no legal requirement for a company in Britain to recognize a trade union. In fact, many countries, especially foreign-owned ones, have made no such arrangement. Throughout Britain, the number of employees represented by unions has fallen steadily since 1979. The union movement has lost 3.5 million members, while only 40 percent of the workforce in the services sector is unionized.

Workers these days are somewhat more skilled, but a major problem remains with teenagers leaving school. Government surveys in 1990 discovered that seven out of ten of Britain's 26 million workers left school at minimum leaving age, seven out of ten had only short initial training for their jobs, and seven out of ten had received no training since then. The government wants to make the 1990s a "skills decade" through expansion of training and enterprise councils under the Department of Employment's National Training Task Force. The aim is that every young person will go for National Vocational Qualifications. Otherwise, say experts, few of the several million new jobs that it is hoped will be created eventually by the Single Market will go Britain's way.

Under Conservative labor laws, effective legal action can be taken against any union that seeks to organize unlawful strikes. Industrial

Manufacturing productivity

% year-on-year	1986	1987	1988	1989	1990*
OUTPUT					
Official	1.2	5.2	7.3	4.3	2.0
Adjusted	1.7	5.4	7.8	4.5	2.6
LABOR INPUT					
Official	−2.6	−1.1	1.3	−0.1	−0.9
Adjusted	−2.9	−0.2	1.9	−1.3	−1.8
PRODUCTIVITY					
Official	3.4	6.2	5.5	3.7	2.5
Adjusted	4.7	5.6	5.8	5.7	4.1

Second quarter   *Source: Nomura Research Institute*

action is also unlawful if it is secondary action, or "sympathy action," taken by workers not involved in the main dispute. Unions can be restrained if they don't hold secret ballots before stopping work. Additionally, there's no statutory protection for the old-style "closed shop," or workforces composed only of union members.

Probably as many as two-thirds of foreign investors since the 1970s have recognized no union, while a fifth recognized only a single union. The latter has been the case of Nissan and other Japanese firms investing in the North-East and elsewhere. Single union deals avoid the demarcation disputes that plagued British industry in former years when multi-unionism was the norm. Many single union deals have no-strike clauses, contain new forms of arbitration and generally encourage teamwork, such as quality circles. One good sign was that increases in pay began to fall. There were more plant-by-plant negotiations and, in a few cases, pay was frozen. On one occasion, unions agreed to a 15 percent cut in pay in order to save jobs at a Scottish electronics plant.

REAL ESTATE

Rents in the City of London, the financial center, and in the capital's West End remain the highest in Europe, despite a slump reducing top rents from £60 to £50 per square foot per annum. Salomon Brothers' real estate research unit in New York is forecasting that some central London rents could drop by up to 50 percent because of oversupply. The multi-billion pound Docklands development in the East End has had teething problems, as its developers suffer from high interest rates and delays in new rail and road links. However, there's no stopping the new skyscraper city on the Thames, where the 800 ft. Canary Wharf was topped out.

The first phase of this particular Docklands development comprises 4.5 million square feet of which more than two million has been let to American Express, Texaco, the Telegraph newspapers of Canadian Conrad Black, Credit Suisse First Boston, Lehrer McGovern International, Manufacturers Hanover Bank and Morgan Stanley. The entire development will reach 11 million square feet by the end of the decade with perhaps as many as 200,000 people working there. The Canadian group, Olympia & York, is the driving force behind this multi-billion pound office and residential development, the biggest in Europe. Rents in the main tower are relatively low at around £30 the square foot, falling to £20 elsewhere, but the Docklands area as a whole needs better transport, such as improvements to the existing light railway connection and a new underground line. The year 1991 saw a glut of offices in London with more than ten percent of space vacant. High rents and staff costs, added to congestion, tended to drive some potential clients out into the regions.

As in other EC countries, rents in regional capitals are considerably cheaper—£18 per square foot per annum in Birmingham, the same in Bristol, a slighter cheaper rate of £15 in Cardiff with Edinburgh, the Scottish financial capital, recording rents at the end of 1990 of £21.

Key numbers:

Jones Lang Wootton
Chartered Surveyors
22 Hanover Square
London, W1
Tel: 44-71-493-6040

London Docklands,
Business Inquiries
Tel: 44-71-512-3000.

S P O T L I G H T

• *Science and Business Parks* •

Science and business parks have spread extensively in the past two decades. Trinity College, Cambridge University, and Heriot-Watt University, Edinburgh, launched the science park movement in

continued

1972 and have remained to the forefront. Most British universities today have an associated park. Business parks came later in the 1980s and their standards were set by US companies investing in Britain. Both kinds of park met the needs of UK-based industry as it moved from smokestacks to services.

The UK Science Parks Association has 50 members with operational parks covering 720 acres and three million square feet of buildings. New investment will add another 1.4m square feet and the amount, either spent or earmarked, has risen to £300 million. The Science Parks Association is based at:

44 Four Oaks Road
Sutton Colefield
West Midlands
England B74-2TL
Tel: 44-21-308-8815
Fax: 44-21-308-2883.

Whereas early parks were owned by their parent higher educational institutes, more recent parks are partnerships between these institutes, a local authority, a development agency, and a private sector company. Science parks have become a regional and national resource, given the way they encourage the creation and growth of high-tech companies. The tenant companies numbered some 800 (10,000 employees) at the time of the last national survey at the end of 1988. They are small, but one measure of success is that 25 percent have expanded or moved into bigger accommodation, with the failure rate a low two percent.

Most of Britain's 38 science parks were full, or almost full, by 1990 and most planned to expand by 50 percent up to and during 1991. A new wave of planned parks, including a unique medical theme park at St. Bartholomew's

Hospital, London, should raise the total to 50. A relative latecomer is Oxford University with Oxford Science Park. The Cambridge Science Park, meanwhile, has leapfrogged to Ashford, Kent, near the Channel Tunnel. Its Euro park will combine science and business. Among other leading science parks are Aston, Birmingham, center of Britain's traditional engineering area, where tenants include Delta-cam Systems, a CAD/CAM specialist, and Computer Integrated Manufacture. Surrey Research Park, near London, is in a local "Silicon Valley" with a score of companies involved in computing and software.

More than 30 large business parks have sprung up in the South-East. Probably the best-known is Stockley, near Heathrow airport, with campus-style offices covering 40 acres. It is home to Marks & Spencer, Dow Chemicals, Tandem Computers, Toshiba International, and Apple Computers. Rents are half those of London. Globe Park, Buckinghamshire, has attracted Tektronic, Rank Xerox, Lex Volvo, and SGS Thomson. Rents in business parks at Birmingham and Manchester are also half those in the capital. In fact, business parks have been opening in the north as companies, like their southern counterparts, rebel against inner city conditions and rents. In the West, Aztec Park, Bristol, has filled up with top companies such as Thorn EMI, ICL, Mercury Communications, Canon, Digital, Racal, IBM, Wang, Midland Bank, and Barclaycard. Changes in national planning regulations and the introduction of a so-called business class use have helped the growth of business parks, whose planners say that careful landscaping is more environment-friendly than some modern agricultural complexes. Some parks have taken over and beautified former industrial wasteland, notably at Newcastle where the old Vickers Armstrong site has been made "green" with science and business accommodation.

• *Getting To Know the Capital* •

For the business visitor, most of the action is in three main locations north of the Thames that are known collectively as Central London. The City, to the east, is the financial district, where the Bank of England, the Stock Exchange, and other financial institutions are concentrated. This touches the West End, a rather more vaguely defined area. It includes the theater district, raffish Soho, Piccadilly Circus, and Leicester Square; and dignified Mayfair and St. James's, where many of the finest hotels, restaurants, and shops are to be found. Westminster and Victoria are dominated by the Houses of Parliament, Westminster Abbey, Whitehall and the royal residence of Buckingham Palace. There also is Downing Street, where the prime minister and chancellor of the exchequer have their official residences, at numbers 10 and 11. Further west, and slightly north, are Knightsbridge and Kensington, with more shops, including the world-famous Harrods department store, and luxury hotels. Bordering these neighborhoods is Chelsea, once the home of artists, but now of the rich and

of trendy designers and fashionable restaurants.

Most of London wasn't planned, as Paris and New York were; and though this haphazardness has its charms, a visitor who doesn't know the territory but wants to walk or ride the bus or subway should buy a street guide. Geographers' Map Company publishes both the pocket-size *A to Z* and the larger, three-color *Master Atlas of Central London;* most newsstands and bookstores stock them.

One of London's most pleasant features is the extraordinary number and variety of parks: 387 of more than 2.5 hectares (20 acres) in Greater London. It's possible to walk all the way from Holland Park in west London to the House of Parliament, a distance of 6.4 kilometers (4 miles) exclusively in parkland, apart from a short stretch through the streets of Kensington. The parks are also useful topographical reference points when you are making your way around London.

Allow plenty of time between appointments if they're not within walking distance of each other. London is increasingly clogged, and the subway is sometimes so crowded at rush hours that you cannot get on the first train that comes along. But don't despair—most run at intervals of less than five minutes. Peak periods are 7:30 to 9:30 a.m. and 5:00 to 7:30 p.m. The big, red, double-decker buses are freed from traffic jams on some main arteries by having their own lanes, but at busy times they can be slow.

London Regional Transport publishes free, easy-to-follow bus and underground maps. Fares are charged by zone and are not cheap. There are good deals going at British tourist offices overseas, which sell Visitors' Travelcards. These are valid for three, four, or seven days, cover all zones, and include the bus to and from Heathrow. Once in London, you can also buy travel cards that cut costs. There are even cheaper cards available that you can use only during off-peak times. Deals change every now and then; check with your travel agent or the British Tourist Authority office in major U.S. cities.

As you've probably heard, traffic drives on the left in Britain. London has many one-way streets, however, and on some of them buses drive in their own lanes—which may be against the prevailing traffic. Be watchful before you step off the sidewalk.

London's black cabs (though some of them are now in other colors) are legendary for their spacious size and their drivers' familiarity with London streets, however obscure. That comes from their having been "on the knowledge"—they have spent up to two years studying the shortest routes around the capital.

::::::::::::Eurocity Birmingham::::::::::::

Birmingham, with its one million inhabitants, has been undergoing massive redevelopment backed by central and local government, the private sector, and European Community grants. In all, close to three billion dollars worth of building is either underway or planned. The investments have restored a large degree of confidence in Birmingham, which has celebrated the centenary of Queen Victoria granting it city status.

More resources, more planning and more imagination are being devoted to the current redevelopment than was the case in the 1960s when the city center was rebuilt in ugly concrete with nearby overpasses that earned the nickname of "spaghetti junction." The national slump in 1978–81 hit the West Midlands and its main city very hard and a quarter of a million jobs were lost in metalworking and distribution alone. Worse still, rioting broke out in the Handsworth area in 1985, forcing Mrs. Thatcher and the leftwing city council to work together to reverse the decline. Given the economic downturn in Britain at the start of the 1990s, problems remain for the important automobile and engineering sectors. However, Birmingham's new start as a dynamic city is symbolized by the $300 million International Convention Center and the success of the older National Exhibition Center which has confounded critics by staging around 100 shows a year, attracting four million annual visitors. Three new halls have been partly financed by the EC, which has put up $70 million towards the cost of the new center.

Birmingham has replaced London for exhibitions, helped by greater spending by British firms on this type of promotion. Even so, the British still have a way to go to match the sums spent by German and other foreign firms. The new center has 11 major halls around a central mall and has been designed for conferences of 30 to 3,000 people. Early bookings came from the International Olympic Committee and the 4,500 delegate International Conference of Genetics.

Birmingham has been aided by its position at the center of the national motorway and railway network, its proximity to London, one hour away, and by the development of its own airport. The "European Hub" terminal will handle six million passengers a year by the end of the century. BHX, as Birmingham international airport is known in aviation language, has connections to many other Eurocities.

Automobile firms such as Austin Rover, Jaguar, Peugeot, and Toyota maintain the West Midlands' long tradition in this sector. Toyota's arrival has pulled in Japanese banks, while Britain's second stock exchange has developed as a specialist center for venture capital, a century after Birmingham made its name as the source of the industrial revolution.

Just as important has been the effort to improve the quality of inner city life through the redevelopment of industrial wasteland and blighted residential areas. Britain's first private urban development agency, Birmingham Heartlands, comprises five major construction companies, Bryant, Douglas, Galliford, Tarmac, and Wimpey. And work is due to start on the $1.5 billion Midland Metro System.

OPPORTUNITIES IN THE REGIONS

Foreign-owned companies are eligible for the same incentives as local firms. Grants for investment in "problem" areas have a ceiling of 30 percent of fixed investment costs or $5,600 per job created, subject also to a ceiling.

There were complaints in 1990 that the Conservative government had put regional policy on the back burner, but as a former regional aid official stated: "Firms like to squeeze the system for what's available in the way of grants, but what is more important is the size and condition of the market, transport costs, the availability and cost of property." His argument was that companies influenced by grants were not those who should receive wads of money. Be that as it may, the Labor Party pointed out that British aid was 45 percent less than that offered by France, and 35 percent less than assistance in Germany.

There is certainly strong competition for inward investment within the EC, but Britain's attraction for Americans and Japanese is not the level of grants, but low labor costs in the regions, human resources, notably in the automobile sector, the language, and government support. This support is varied, if complex, for the government does not publish its maximum rates of aid. Ernst & Young in London has produced long studies on the question, as has Plant Location International in Brussels with its databases.

Regional incentives are available in "assisted areas" in several parts of England, Scotland, and Wales. These are divided into development areas, with aid packages of a maximum 30 percent, and intermediate areas where aid is more likely to be at 15 percent. Known officially as "regional selective assistance," this aid is now discretionary, but is theoretically open to both manufacturing and service industries. The cost of business advice in design, marketing, quality, manufacturing systems, business planning, and financial and information systems provided by independent consultants is also largely refundable.

Northern Ireland has the highest rates, including tax-free grants of half the cost of buildings and machinery, plus grants for employment, interest relief, and rent. The government also throws in research and development grants of up to 50 percent.

Often in British-assisted areas, government bodies provide factories for investors. In addition, there are 26 enterprise zones across the country, usually in urban areas (100 percent capital allowances and exemption from property taxes for ten years on industrial and commercial buildings). Then there are city grants in 50 urban areas with 20 to 50 percent assistance. Lastly, there are "Euroloans" from the European Coal and Steel Community or the European investment bank. Brussels also provides aid for regions to improve infrastructure and telecommunications. Some of the more remote British regions see the Brussels-based Eurocrats as their champions, as it is EC policy to achieve greater equality among the regions.

Britain may be coy about publishing figures for aid, but aid there is, particularly if the investment concerns new technology.

Key contacts

> Invest in Britain Bureau
> Kingsgate House
> 66-74 Victoria Street
> London SW1E 6SW
> Tel: 44-71-215-2544
> Fax: 44-71-215-8451
>
> The English unit of the Department of Trade and Industry
> Address as above
> Tel: 44-71-215-8287
> Fax: 44-71-931-0397

NORTH-EAST

Fortunately, the Japanese paid little attention to Andy Capp, the roguish, layabout cartoon character, symbol of hard times in the North-East. Or the north-south industrial—and social—divide that still exists in England. The Japanese have made substantial investments, notably in automobiles and electronics, in an area seeking a new industrial base since the closing of shipyards and engineering workshops, and the massive cutback in coal mining.

It could be said that the North-East never fully recovered from the pre-war depression. Postwar revivals that accompanied rearmament and campaigns for coal were stopped in their tracks by economic crises, notably that of the early 1980s. The scene looked sufficiently bleak for some companies, British and American, that had been lured by grants in the 1960s to pack their bags. In all, 140,000 manufacturing jobs were lost between 1979 and 1987. The decision in the mid-1980s by Nissan, Japan's second largest automaker, to build a plant near Sunderland was a turning point and was followed by Fujitsu semiconductors, Komatsu earthmoving equipment (which took over deserted Caterpillar buildings), Sanyo and Mitsumi consumer goods, NSK bearings, and a score of other Japanese companies.

ICI Chemicals, British Steel, and offshore engineering continue to form the core of local industry, along with a streamlined armaments industry building tanks and nuclear submarines. But it is the inward investors that have reduced unemployment from record levels surpassed only by Northern Ireland—the Americans such as Millicom telecommunications with its Euro-headquarters at Darlington, the Germans, Norway's Norsk Hydro, and other Scandinavians. Simultaneously, cities did something about their decaying centers and worked with development agencies to attract retailers, hoteliers, and builders of office parks and leisure complexes. Some "southern" companies have opened up in the area—and stayed. In the past, they tended to retreat when times turned bad. For one thing, the area is spacious and attractive outside of the cities and towns along the three main rivers—the Tyne, the Wear and the Tees—but urban areas themselves have been made smarter as old industrial wasteland is converted to new uses. Something good must be happening, for the North-East has the highest rate of purchases of the wickedly expensive Porsche.

Nissan is investing one billion dollars in its plant for Bluebird and Primera cars for the local and EC markets and is adding one of its European technology centers. The government contributed $160 million to start-up costs, and has granted $50 million to Fujitsu for its semiconductor plant near Durham. This is the first major electronics investment in the North-East. Fujitsu, for its part, liked the quality of local water and access to good highway links to the South. There is still too much visible decay in the North and the hope of the local development agencies is that this second Japanese giant will have the same spillover effect as the Nissan investment—the automaker turned to British suppliers for most of its parts and so gained local origin status (70 percent) in the EC's eyes, enabling it to prepare for its attack on the Single Market.

As a sign of Japanese confidence in the region, Japan's Teikyo University has established a branch at Durham University with students, professors, and 30,000 books shipped from Japan.

The North-East's selling points include available workers, housing that is very cheap compared to the South-East and good connections (50 minutes by plane to London, three hours by train). East coast ports are springboards for the rest of the EC and for Scandinavia. The problem is that the North could find itself somewhat isolated on the edge of the New Europe. Yet, if Britain is to expand its manufacturing exports, then a regenerated North will have an important role to play.

The main promotional agency is:

Northern Development Company
Great North House
Sandyford Road
Newcastle-upon-Tyne
Tyne and Wear
Tel: 44-91-261-0026
Fax: 44-91-232-9069

The NDC is the "umbrella" for local authorities, the four official enterprise zones—at Hartlepool, Middlesborough, Sunderland, and Tyneside—with their investment aids, and two urban development corporations, Tyne & Wear Development Corporation and Teeside Development Corporation. These development areas provide the highest British Government selective assistance—up to 30 percent of startup costs—and have access to cheap EC loans.

WALES

Wales, the land of song, but also that of closed pits and steel furnaces, has attracted some 300 overseas companies—American, German, and Japanese in that order—and has witnessed the emergence in a decade of assembly plants, high-tech industry, and financial services. The reasons can be found in a generally-skilled workforce and good communications—two hours by the M4 highway to London, plus the North Wales Euroroute linking incoming Irish traffic with the future Channel Tunnel. Welsh Development International, the inward investment arm of the Welsh Development Agency, is a one-stop service for foreign investors.

The Principality, Wale's official denomination, has moved from being a two-industry part of Britain to one with companies engaged in consumer electronics, motor components, food processing, engineering, chemicals and, more recently, financial services, even France's Banque Nationale de Paris.

The number one investor is the US, notably Ford with over a billion dollars going into its Bridgend engine plant and a transmission plant at Swansea, despite the partial move from Wales to Cologne. Among the 140 US concerns in Wales are Kimberley-Clark with a new mill at Flint, Kawneer, and Osicom. Amongst the Germans is Bosch, which in investing some $160 million in an alternator plant in Miskin, the largest-ever investment made by the company outside of Germany. Just as impressive has been inflow of Japanese firms, following in the steps of long-established Sony. Sharp, Brother, Matsushita, and Aiwa have set up and then expanded, while Toyota became Wale's 25th Japanese investor when it announced a $220 million investment at Deeside, North Wales.

David Waterstone, former chief executive of Welsh Development International said the Japanese, "brought a new industrial culture, and from Wales their commitment to quality, high productivity and good industrial practices has spread all over Britain. Japanese concerns in Wales are achieving levels of productivity similar to those at plants in Japan, sometimes higher."

With all this investment and the general modernization of the local economy, employment until now has been on the rise, while manufacturing production has risen a third in five years. Independent analysts, Cambridge Econometrics, reckon that Wales has been the chief beneficiary of inward investment to Britain. The sheer spread of current manufacturing, plus an educational system attuned to business needs should dampen the effect in Wales of any national turndown.

In the South, many millions in private sector money are being poured into the regeneration of Cardiff's docklands. The aim of the £2 billion development, run by the Cardiff Bay Development Corporation is to bring new life to the heart of the city. The Welsh also plan a center for the performing arts, home to the Welsh National Opera Company, a kind of Welsh "rival" to the spectacular waterside opera house in Sydney, Australia.

Key contacts

Welsh Development International
Pearl House, Cardiff
Tel: 44-222-223-666
Fax: 44-222-223-243

Cardiff Bay Development Corporation
Baltic House
Mount Stuart Square
Cardiff
Tel: 44-222-471-5576
Fax: 44-222-488-924

WEST MIDLANDS

The West Midlands, with its Black Country, birthplace of the industrial revolution, has swayed since World War II between boom and bust. Expansion came in the 1960s and early 1970s, with the growth of the British automobile industry and its components arm. Then that industry went into decline as imports rose and as the slump embraced many engineering sectors. In recent years, new greenfield sites have been offered to inward investors. Two other factors have favorably impressed Japanese and American firms—a workforce skilled in light and heavy industry, plus excellent road communications, given the proximity of several highways.

Prospects were bleak indeed in the early 1980s when British manufacturing industry, particularly the large segment in the West Midlands, near Birmingham, lost hundreds of firms and a third of the seven million jobs. Today, Jaguar cars has been saved financially by Ford, Peugeot has a profitable assembly plant at Coventry, Rover has linked with Honda, while British firms, from Rolls Royce down, have been turned around—witness Dowty at Wolverhampton where the aerospace equipment firm has increased sales per employee by 70 percent in three years. Some forecasters believe that exports will continue to grow with the elimination by the mid-1990s of trade deficits in electrical equipment and mechanical engineering.

The return of foreign investment was very evident by 1987–88 when the West Midlands took a third of all inward investment. The new town of Telford, Shropshire, has benefited from newcomers' preference for greenfield sites. Some 90 foreign firms have put down in Telford and created 10,000 jobs. Among the 15 Japanese companies, which form perhaps the biggest Japanese grouping in any British area, is NEC with a 60-acre site. Plastic Omnium and Merlin Gerin are two major French companies at Telford. The town has been following tradition by seeking manufacturing concerns.

There is still much that is black in the Black Country, but part of the current diversification and embellishment is the attractive science park at Warwick University. The Black Country Development Corporation is investing £200 million of government money until the mid-1990s in order to generate £1 billion in private investment and the creation of 20,000 jobs. The four biggest sectors in this "core region," from Oldbury to Wolverhampton, are vehicles, metal goods, mechanical engineering, and metal manufacturing which employ two out of three blue collar workers.

Key contacts

West Midlands Development Agency
Chantry House Coleshill
Warwickshire B36 9BU
Tel: 44-675-462-577
Fax: 44-675-463-026

Telford Development Corporation
New Town House
Telford
Tel: 44-952-293-131

Black Country Development Corporation
Black Country House
Rounds Green Road
Oldbury
West Midlands
B6 2D9
Tel: 44-21-511-2000
Fax: 44-21-544-5710

SCOTLAND

Scotland now has some 350 foreign-owned plants, of which 200 are American manufacturers. A high proportion of the investment has been high-tech, particularly electronics. It is concentrated in central Scotland, an area not much larger than the city of Los Angeles that has become known as Silicon Glen. Whereas the Americans, in some cases, have been in Scotland since the 1950s, the Japanese waited until the 1980s before building a strong presence, notably, NEC at Livingston with a $140 million semi-conductor plant.

Some Scots complain that, although electronics production has tripled since 1979, the multinationals use imported components in the main and regard Scotland as a low-cost offshore assembly base. Although Wang did move in and out, Digital Equipment Corporation, among others, has invested in R & D and built local microcomputers. In addition, Compaq, Sun Microsystems, and Conner Peripherals are heavily involved north of the border.

Locate in Scotland, the Government's one-stop inward investment organization, was set up in the early 1980s to combine the grant-giving powers of the Secretary of State for Scotland with the development powers of the Government-sponsored Scottish Development Agency. Since then, planned capital investment by companies locating in Scotland has amounted to more than $5 billion.

Investors have cited good productivity, a developed educational structure of universities, technical colleges and vocational institutions geared to the tertiary sector, and satisfactory communications with the rest of Britain and beyond. For example, the new town of Irvine, Firth of Clyde, part of Silicon Glen is 15 minutes drive from Prestwick Airport and its cargo services to North America.

Locate in Scotland puts together a complete development package—sites, property, project management, investment finance, and government grants. It is an initial link with suppliers as well as universities. From 1991, the Scottish Development Agency and the UK Training Agency—another government body—united under private sector leadership to promote Scotland.

Some 64 projects were secured in 1989–90, involving investment of £853 million. Some say that Scotland has the greatest concentration of artificial intelligence companies in Europe. In all, since Locate in Scotland came on the scene, some 70,000 jobs have been created or safeguarded, although Scottish unemployment at more than ten percent remains higher than England's.

British engineering industries
Forecast trade balances

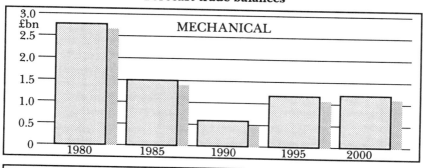

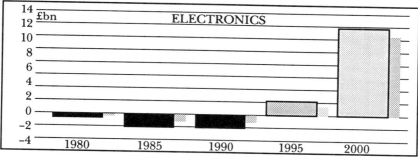

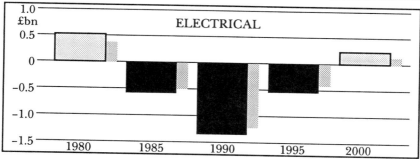

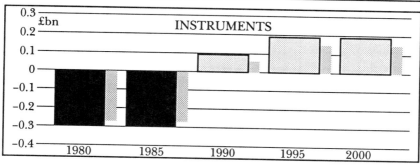

The decision of Conner Peripherals to set up in Scotland was followed by the announcement of Motorola locating its European Cellular Telephone manufacturing design and distribution headquarters in West Lothian. The American company is to spend $180 million on the new plant. IBM has a major plant at Greenock.

As for the Japanese, there are now 15 companies, engaged not only in electronics, but also in textile equipment, frozen foods based on *surimi* (minced fish), whisky, computer-controlled dyeing machinery, television cabinets, and fishing tackle. Many of these companies have introduced quality circles. Wages are often low, but the Japanese explain to the Scots that the competition is not in the neighboring glen, but in Taiwan and Korea.

According to the Secretary of State for Scotland, "Economic growth in Scotland has been less susceptible to slowdown than the rest of Britain because Scottish consumers are less heavily-borrowed than those in southern England and the healthy upturn of North Sea oil has produced higher benefits for Scotland."

Key contacts

> Scottish Development Agency/Locate in Scotland
> 120 Bothwell Street
> Glasgow
> G2 7JP
> Tel: 44-41-248-2700
> Fax: 44-41-221-3217
>
> Scottish Development Agency
> London
> Tel: 44-71-839-2117
> Fax: 44-71-839-275
>
> Irvine Development Corporation
> Tel: 44-294-214-100
> Fax: 44-294-211-467

NORTHERN IRELAND

By offering the highest startup grants within the EC (with the possible exception of Portugal), Northern Ireland, or the Province as it is known, has attracted considerable foreign investment in recent years, despite its persistent, if currently exaggerated image of a Beirut-style, strife-torn place. Investors from the US, Asia and Europe have set up in Northern Ireland. The Industrial Development Board with its $170 million budget has been able to meet half of startup costs and offer a skilled, young workforce, heirs to a long industrial tradition.

But is the place safe? One local chronicler put it this way before the late 1991 flare up of violence: "Having access to staff is fine, but raw intellectual force is only one part of the product 'mix' which encourages a company to set up across the Irish Sea in Ulster. There is surely the security aspect to be taken into account. Underlying tension is easing across Northern Ireland. Of course, diligence is required in the handful of sensitive areas that remain, but life for the ordinary member of the public continues almost as if there was nothing different about the province. Whereas five years ago, armored troops carriers were commonplace on the streets of Belfast and Londonderry, the appearance of the defence forces is now the exception." That has changed. The province has attracted some big names in textiles, notably Du Pont, whose total investment is close to $1 billion, plus auto parts and electronics services companies. The Industrial Development Board gives grants for buildings, 100% rent subsidies for factories for five years, exemption from property taxes, and help with training. It points to Japanese companies who employ 2,500 people in Ulster with its 1.5 million population compared with 3,500 people in much bigger Scotland with its five million inhabitants. The slightly heavier transport costs, says the Board, are outweighed by local manufacturing and living costs much lower than in "mainland" Britain—a $50,000 salary in Northern Ireland buys the equivalent of $130,000 in southeast England, according to more than one calculation. The year 1989–90 was a record period for inward investment with the Board promoting more than 5,100 jobs (2,000 from abroad) with commitments for $750 million of investments. The Board is located at:

64 Chichester St.
Belfast
Tel: 44-232-233-233
Fax: 44-232-231-328

Currently, there are some 209 mainland British and foreign-owned companies in Northern Ireland employing 55,000 people. The US leads—$700 million investment in the past six years bringing the total of jobs with US companies to ten percent of the workforce. Ford has a major components plant and this in turn has drawn Montupet, the French maker of aluminium cylinder heads—$160 million investment, creating 1,000 jobs. Another big newcomer is South Korea's Daewoo with a plant for VCRs for west and east Europe.

:::::::::::::::SUCCESS STORIES ::::::::::::::::

NISSAN

Peter Wickens, personnel director at the Nissan automobile plant at Sunderland admits there is no such thing as a no-strike agreement, but adds that the single union deal hammered out between Japanese management and the AEU engineering union, coupled with a company spirit based on training and commitment, has led to an efficient manufacturing unit free of "traditional" and troublesome labor problems. Nissan is one of more than 130 Japanese manufacturing companies in Britain, leading the way in new, high-investment and R&D. EC states generally have preferred to maintain their large surpluses in exported goods than build big plants in Britain in the Japanese and American way. This is changing with companies such as France's Peugeot and Germany's Bosch, but the Japanese have shown the way, with Nissan the smartest of all.

The current success of the Sunderland plant with its 1991 output of 110,000 Primera models with their 80 percent local content (and an export rate of 70 percent) can be traced back to that single union deal. As Wickens, in both conversation and his remarkable book, *The Road to Nissan,* points out:

> The eventual wording of the negotiations paragraph of the agreement was particularly precise: "The company and the union are totally committed to resolving negotiations within the company council. However, in exceptional circumstances if this is not possible, the outstanding matters will be referred to the (national) advisory, conciliation and arbitration service, or ACAS, for resolution." The key phrases are 'totally committed' and 'exceptional circumstances'... both parties agree to accept the decision of the arbitrator. During the

course of such negotiations, conciliation or arbitration, there will be no industrial action.

Mr. Wickens worked earlier on a similar, single union deal with Continental Can's investment in North Wales. Elsewhere, Coca-Cola and Schweppes made another strike-free agreement with the AEU in the bottling sector. Nissan was therefore not the first, but it has come out best because it built on its deal by providing the kind of training unheard of before, particularly in the automobile industry (one year instead of a few weeks) plus Japanese management techniques designed to raise production standards at Sunderland to Japanese levels and which are already good enough to impress German dealers. The plant walls are decorated with Skill Index Monitors for all, work is often voluntarily filmed to spot mistakes, new tools are readily available if requested. From top management to new arrivals, everyone is dressed in identical blue uniforms and everyone eats together. Promotion can be fast and the average of the workers is 24 as against 44 at a major Renault plant in France. The No. 2 Japanese automaker has poured in more than a billion dollars and will raise production to 200,000 in 1993. The European car industry, particularly the French, is worried, but Britain, which "desperately needs to regenerate its industry," (the 1991 House of Lords report, *Innovation in Manufacturing Industry,*) is delighted. Or, as Sir Julian Ridsdale, MP pointed out: "With the approach of the European Market Community, US and Japanese companies will be looking to expand business by mergers and acquisitions. We should welcome this as it could mean not only the survival and rehabilitation of existing enterprises, but their existing on a large enough scale to make increased profits." Nissan UK made a healthy profit in 1990 of £65m and opened two design centers for future automobiles to stress its commitment. In return, the plant recorded a three percent absenteeism rate while workers agreed to accept a lower-than-usual seven percent pay rise in 1992.

PLASTIC OMNIUM

Plastic Omnium, one of the outstanding industrial success stories in France among medium-sized companies, has taken on the British market with the flair that has characterized its growth at home. It makes plastic parts for the French automobile industry and those ingenious dustbins on wheels which have helped make Paris the world's most efficient city for daily refuse collection.

The company started selling its high-performance Gaflon and Teflon products, as well as its smart dustbins, in Britain in the 1970s, but by the mid-1980s, as French and international sales boomed, it plumped for a plant at Telford, West Midlands. Telford, one of the birthplaces of the 19th century Industrial Revolution, had been forced to adapt to modern times—and production. It did this by creating a new town and, above all, new industrial parks and business centers. Plastic Omnium received a government start-up grant of just under 15 percent, but altogether has invested some $20 million in providing the production lines for plastic bumpers and gas tanks for the nearby Peugeot plant in Coventry, units for companies such as Black and Decker, British Nuclear Fuels and Ford, as well as the increasingly popular plastic refuse bins which can be emptied automatically by refuse trucks and which are transforming British towns as well as Paris.

Start-up aid was just one factor for going to Telford. The proximity of Peugeot and West Midlands industry was another, as was rapidly-expanding Birmingham airport.

"Then there's the attractive Shropshire countryside nearby, so important for engineers and managers," said Paul-Henri Lemarie, son-in-law of Pierre Burelle, founder of a company which is both family-run and highly-innovative. Aside from ten plants in France, Plastic Omnium is now prominent in Holland, Germany, and Spain, plus a plastic pipe plant in Houston. It considers it is ideally situated in the West Midlands for any upturn in British manufacturing—and as a potential future supplier for the big Japanese automobile companies.

The company's success with its worldwide sales of close to $600 million has gone hand in hand with Telford's. The town still has its famous 19th century iron bridge, claimed to be the first anywhere, but the last blast furnaces closed in the 1950s, forcing a completely new start. Today Plastic Omnium has another major French company, switchgear maker Merlin Gerin, as a neighbor and 115 other foreign companies, notably the Japanese. It's the largest Japanese concentration in a town of such size, some 21 companies which include NEC, making computer printers and mobile phones, Ricoh with its copiers and Maxell with its video tapes. Inward investment has meant 9,200 new jobs for Telford. Of course, Plastic Omnium has been hit by the slowdown from which even giant Peugeot was not immune, but believes Britain will become an increasingly important market for its whole range of quality plastics for industry and for clean cities, particularly as the EC trend is towards different containers for different disposable items. Britain will also be a good market for its new line in small play parks for children.

:::::::::::::::::::: THE LEADERS :::::::::::::::::::::

INDUSTRIAL COMPANIES (1990)

		(£000s)	
		Sales	*Pre-tax profits*
(1)	British Petroleum	37,394,000	4,686,000
(2)	Shell Transport & Trading	25,912,000	3,216,000
(3)	BAT Industries	13,311,000	2,286,000
(4)	ICI	13,171,000	1,804,000
(5)	Electricity Council	12,373,800	− 726,600
(6)	British Telecom	12,315,000	3,206,000
(7)	Grand Metropolitan	9,298,000	1,042,000
(8)	British Aerospace	9,085,000	460,000
(9)	British Gas	7,983,000	1,513,000
(10)	Unilever	7,419,000	757,000
(11)	BTR	7,025,000	1,327,000
(12)	Shell UK	7,015,000	673,000
(13)	Hanson	6,998,000	1,394,000
(14)	Sainsbury	6,930,400	516,200
(15)	Ford	6,732,000	510,000
(16)	General Electric (UK)	5,878,100	816,900
(17)	Marks and Spencer	5,608,100	654,000
(18)	Tesco	5,401,900	373,100
(19)	Esso UK	5,274,900	842,400
(20)	British Steel	5,113,000	890,000
		(≠ 1 = $1.7)	

(Source: The Times, London)

1990 Results

Falls (mostly pre-tax)
ICI £977m (–33 percent); Barclays Bank £760m; NatWest £50.4m; Midland £11m; Lloyds £591m; Royal Dutch Shell £3.01b; Vickers £96m; Wimpey £43 (–66 percent); RTZ £879m (–20 percent); BAT £963m (–46 percent); Lucas £55.3m (–31 percent); Laing £20m (–65 percent).

Gains
Guinness £847 (+ 23 percent); Tesco £417m (+ 27.7 percent).

BANKS (1989–90)

		Total assets, 1989–90	(£000s) After-tax profits 1989–90	Pretax profits 1990
(1)	Barclays	127,616,000	355,000	760,000
(2)	National Westminster	116,189,000	284,000	504,000
(3)	Midland	62,479,000	– 222,000	11,000
(4)	Lloyds	57,542,000	– 586,000	591,000
(5)	Abbey National	37,149,000	323,000	
(6)	Royal Bank of Scotland	27,435,700	141,000	
(7)	TSB	25,481,000	42,000	
(8)	Standard Chartered	24,668,000	– 297,000	
(9)	Bank of Scotland	18,394,500	117,500	
(10)	S.G. Warburg	12,297,000	111,900	
(11)	Salomon Brothers Intl	9,833,067	– 2,817	
(12)	Kleinwort Benson	8,866,000	52,075	
(13)	Morgan Grenfell	6,298,000	56,303	
(14)	Union Discount	5,064,629	10,542	
(15)	ANZ Grindlays	4,597,000	58,833	
(16)	Bank of England	4,335,505	77,779	
(17)	Yorkshire Bank	4,055,876	65,776	
(18)	Cater Allen Holdings	3,965,000	5,986	
(19)	Barings	3,756,000	38,934	
(20)	Rothschilds Cont	3,626,900	21,254	

(Source: The Times)

KEY CONTACTS

USEFUL LONDON TELEPHONE NUMBERS

Trade and Commercial Information

European Business Information Center: 44-71-828-6201
Fax: 44-71-834-8416
Overseas Trade Board: 44-71-215-7877
British Library Documents Center: 44-937-546060
Central Office of Information: 44-71-928-2345
Central Statistical Office: 44-71-270-6363
Confederation British Industry: 44-71-379-7400

Government Offices

Customs & Excise: 44-71-626-1515
Department of Employment (Training Schemes): 44-71-273-6969
Department Trade & Industry: 44-71-215-7877
EC Office: 44-71-222-8122
Fax: 44-71-222-0900
East European Trade Council: 44-71-222-7622
Environment Department: 44-71-276-6645
Government EC Hotline: 44-81-200-1992
Small Firms Line: 0-800-500200
Inland Revenue: 44-71-438-6622
Institute of Directors: 44-71-839-1233
National Economic Development Office: 44-71-217-4000

Chambers of Commerce

Member Nations
Belgium: 44-71-831-3508
Denmark: 44-71-259-6795
France: 44-71-225-5250
Germany: 44-71-930-7251
Italy: 44-71-637-3153
Netherlands: 44-71-405-1358
Spain: 44-71-637-9061
Portugal: 44-71-493-9973

Other
Japan: 44-71-353-8166
United States: 44-71-493-0381
International Chamber
of Commerce
(ICC): 44-71-240-5558
London: 44-71-248-4444
California: 44-71-629-8211
Florida: 44-71-727-8388
New York: 44-71-839-5079
New Jersey: 44-71-481-8909

Embassies

Member States
Belgium: 44-71-235-5422
Denmark: 44-71-235-1255
France: 44-71-235-8080
Germany: 44-71-235-5033
Greece: 44-71-727-8040
Ireland: 44-71-235-2171
Italy: 44-71-235-9371

Luxembourg: 44-71-235-6961
Netherlands: 44-71-584-5040
Portugal: 44-71-235-5331
Spain: 44-71-235-5555

Other
United States: 44-71-499-9000

DATABASES

Spearhead: A database maintained by the Department of Trade and Industry and accessed through Profile Information, which is part of the Financial Times Group. Updated monthly, Spearhead can be accessed from overseas. It summarizes all of the EC's Single Market measures, both completed and proposed, and gives Department of Trade and Industry telephone numbers. This government service is now the most efficient of its kind in the EC, outranking the Dutch.

Profile Information
Sunbury House
79 Staines Road West
Sunbury-on-Thames
Middlesex TW16 7AH
Tel: 44-932-761444

Celex: A database established by the European Commission. Celex gives information on European legislation and is used by lobbyists and consultants.

Context Legal Systems
Grove Park Industrial Estate
Waltham Road
White Waltham
Maidenhead SL6 3LW
Tel: 44-62-882-6192

Eurobases
200 Rue de la Loi
B-1049 Brussels
Tel: 322-235-0001

British Library Document Supply Center. This is the world's largest collection of journals, reports, patents, and conference papers, as well as EC documentation. It can be accessed from overseas.

Boston Spa
Wetherby
West Yorkshire
LS23 7BQ
Tel: 44-937-546060

Applied Property Research. A database covering the 575 business parks in Britain, most of them in the southeast. It will also cover the 100 new parks coming under construction at the beginning of the 1990s.

97 St. John's Street
London EC1M 4AS

ERPC Ltd. An authoritative source on both British and European grants and incentives.

University of Strathclyde
26 Richmond Street
Glasgow G1 1XH
Tel: 44-41-552-4400

Corporate Location Europe. The leading magazine of its kind in Europe, with printed and stored facts on all EC countries drawn from a corps of correspondents.

Century House Information Ltd.
22 Towcester Road
Old Stratford
Milton Keynes MK19 6AQ
Tel: 44-908-560555
Fax: 44-908-560470

Facts on Denmark

Capital Copenhagen
Population 5.1m
Working Population 2.8m
Unemployment 10%
GDP Growth 1989: 1.1%; 1990: 1.5%; 1991
  (est.): 1.25%
GDP per Capita 1988: $19,300; 1989:
  $20,400; 1990: $21,300
Inflation 1989: 4.8%; 1990: 2.5%
Balance of Payments 1990: +9.25b kroner
($1 = 6.7 kr)

· ·

DENMARK

*"I see the Single Market and Economic and Monetary Union as ways to
ensure that Denmark will be able to influence events which would
otherwise pass by a little country like ours." Poul Schluter, Danish Prime
Minister*

AFTER TWO LEAN YEARS, A RAY OF SUNSHINE PIERCED THE ECONOMIC
gloom in Denmark. Exports rose and the domestic economy was live-
lier. Or, as one local commentator said, "It's come out of a coma."
Faith in the European Community is stronger than at any time since
Denmark became a member back in 1972. Denmark is putting its
house in order and is beginning to extricate itself from the strange situation whereby it had both one of the world's highest living standards
and one of the most crippling foreign debts per inhabitant—a staggering $7,000 per Dane.

It was only in 1989 that high salaries, generous social benefits and
an inflated public sector workforce led pessimists to predict that "in-
tervention" by the International Monetary Fund was inevitable. Since
then, the government's tight fiscal policy has led to cuts in public expenditure and taxes, notably corporate tax, and enabled the country
to enjoy one of the lowest inflation rates within the EC. The political
opposition and the unions have seen the need for a consensus in favor
of the EC's economic, monetary, and future political union, partly to
avoid Denmark being left on the edge of the Community, partly to
avoid the big neighbor, Germany going it alone. The spoken or un-
spoken fear of a Germanic Europe rather than a European Germany
is one of the factors that has spurred Denmark to double its commitment to the EC. Now that Denmark approaches the Single Market,
businessmen are becoming more confident in the country's future.
Corporation tax has been reduced from a punitive 50 percent to 40
percent. Trade unions are thinking more long-term. The public is
even more convinced than the politicians that Denmark's future lies
within the EC, and that Denmark will increasingly be the EC's natural link to Norway, Sweden and Finland, all three potential members
of the Community. It's been quite a turn-around and one that proba-

bly ensures that Premier Schluter's center-right minority government will stay in power for a while, despite a setback in late 1990 elections.

Whereas some politicians—with strong economic reasons—objected to the Brussels Commission's insistence that Denmark harmonize or reduce its high value-added tax in time for January 1, 1993, the public was telling opinion pollsters of its newfound enthusiasm for the European Community. The Danes' enthusiasm for the EC has never been so high. Past referendums—when Denmark first entered and at a time of political crisis in 1986—were touch-and-go affairs. Now, the Danes approve EC membership to the tune of 57 percent. The opposition Social Democrats are becoming pro-EC, too.

Despite the leaner, fitter economy, the Danes still have a 22 percent VAT rate and high excise taxes on many goods. When the Danish-German border opens on January 1, 1993 Danes will rush to Germany on a buying spree. So the authorities seek a deal between Brussels and Copenhagen—with the former granting a delay on the harmonization question and the latter making a serious effort to bring its tax rates into line.

The Danes also have extensive structural adjustment to make if the recent recovery is to last. Change, for example, is needed in the rigid labor market. The present generous conditions for unemployment benefit should be tightened in the opinion of many experts. The government wants the unemployment insurance system to be financed totally by employers and employees. At present central government pays about two-thirds. Taxes need to be reduced to stimulate savings and that means cutting the number of public sector employees.

The OECD in 1990 had this to say: "One cause [of slow growth] may be government or EC subsidies and regulations, which are a major factor in sectors such as housing, agriculture, transport, energy, and health. All have the benefit of tax concessions and direct or indirect subsidies, which result in the distortion of investment decisions. The Danish tax system also tends to increase the pressure for wage rises, as well as reducing incentives to work and acquire skills. It discourages private saving. Marginal tax rates may have reached the point where the extra revenue collected represents a small gain compared to the losses resulting from the distortions."

The OECD also has harsh words about the "limited internationalization" of Danish trade and Denmark's absence from fast-growing markets. Some remedies are underway, such as mergers inside Denmark to produce bigger and more aggressive companies, and increased government spending on promoting Danish goods internationally.

Among the biggest mergers was that between Novo Industri and Nordisk Gentofte, the two leading pharmaceutical firms and former competitors in the sale of insulin. The are now known as Novo-Nordisk. Three large food, sugar, and spirits companies merged to form Danisco, a company with annual sales of more than $2 billion. Den Danske Bank, now Scandinavia's largest and the 40th in Europe in terms of assets, is the result of the merger of a smaller bank of the same name, the venerable Handelsbank, and Provinsbank of Aarhus, Jutland. In addition, Privatbanken, Andelsbanken, and the savings bank SDS linked to form Unibank, which becomes Denmark's second megabank. In insurance, Baltica swapped shares with France's Compagnie Financière de Suez, while another big company in the sector, Hafnia, bought Prolific Insurance, of Britain, and swapped shares with France's Compagnie Financière de Paribas. There were further mergers between leading travel firms, in agricultural machinery, television retailing, accountancy, and food and drink.

As a possible gateway to the EC, Denmark offers a stable and well-educated workforce. The great new sea bridges—one underway, a second one between Denmark and Sweden awaiting its turn—open new vistas to a people used to going practically everywhere by boat. But relatively high wages and lack of real investment incentives remain obstacles to foreign firms. US direct investment in Denmark is a modest $1.2 billion. The good news is that inflation is down to around three percent mainly due to lower labor costs. Premier Schluter comes from southern Jutland and was a successful Copenhagen lawyer before starting his record-breaking run as leader of the government. He believes that the Nordic welfare model will influence the debate on the social dimension of the European Community, already enshrined in the EC's social charter. But he adds that the Nordic model is also changing, and that economic and technological progress within the EC will take place "in a reasonable balance with social security." Under his stewardship, there has been improvement in Denmark's seemingly eternal balance of payments and foreign debt "black holes."

Repayments in 1990 reduced the debt to $48 billion, while for the first time in many years the balance of payments swung into a healthy surplus. It has been an export-led recovery, aided by German reunification and the chances seized by Danish food and machinery firms in filling the gaps in capacity of German companies. The widespread rationalization and restructuring across the whole board of Danish manufacturing and farming have put the Danes in a stronger position to continue to exploit the larger German market. The krone is stable—more good news for Denmark as the Single Market approaches.

MARKET OPPORTUNITIES

Denmark is highly dependent on exports. Its total foreign trade in goods and services accounts for some two-thirds of gross domestic product. More than half of Denmark's trade is with the EC—Germany takes a fifth, and Britain a tenth of total trade. Trade with the Nordic neighbors, Sweden, Norway and Finland, accounts for a considerable 20 percent. The US and Japan account for six and four percent respectively. In late 1989 the government launched a 65 million kroner investment program aimed at attracting more US and Japanese high-tech investment, but the response has been slow. Despite a US takeover of a Danish insurance company in the late 1980s—a one billion kroner deal—US direct investment runs at a modest, annual rate of $80 million or less.

There are Danish hopes of a lead role in a new era of Baltic trade. In the past, trade with the old East Bloc has accounted for a mere three percent of the total, but there are plans to spend some $150 million before 1995 on bilateral programs to support economic development in the Baltic zone. The programs, for which foreign companies in Denmark are eligible, include financial support for joint ventures, energy and environmental projects, and the training of managers in Denmark. Details are available from:

Commercial Section
US Embassy
Dag Hammarskjolds Alle 24
2100 Copenhagen
Tel: 45-31-423-144.

Denmark participates in Nordic, EC, and other international support programs for the newly emerging East Europe democracies and has joined the new European Bank for Reconstruction and Development. Despite these efforts, it will probably take a number of years before Denmark reaps substantial benefits from growth in the Baltic.

A 1990 survey by the Ministry of Economic Affairs estimated that within a year's period, the expected economic upswing in the former

---

S P O T L I G H T

• *Resources* •

Oil has been extracted from the Danish sector of the North Sea since 1972, natural gas since 1984. Denmark is now Western Europe's third largest oil and gas producer, behind Britain and Norway. The level of self-sufficiency has jumped dramatically over the past decade from 10 to 67 percent. And this could rise, given the small population of just over five million. In recent years, the government has granted licenses to explore large areas for other commercially-viable oil and gas fields. Pipelines for North Sea products run to the west coast of Jutland, from where the gas is distributed through a network to industry and other consumers, and to the Swedish and German networks. The quantities produced are small when compared with the UK and Norway. The UK produced 115 million tons and Norway 56 million tons of oil equivalents from the North Sea. Yet, Denmark's 4.7 million tons for just five million people has dramatically cut the balance of payments deficit. Denmark's self-sufficiency could rise to close to 100 percent in the 1990s. Reserves exist for the next 40 years. Ironically, high government taxes mean that Danish motorists pay more than any other Europeans at the gas station.

East Germany would generate annual export earnings for Denmark of some five billion kroner ($800 million) and could help in the creation of 40,000 jobs. That is a "maximum" scenario for the future. Denmark is still largely an agricultural exporter and it continues to sell more to Britain than it does to neighboring Sweden—more than $3 billion worth of goods (meat products, including the famous bacon, general industrial machinery, fish, dairy products and furniture).

Swings in the kroner-dollar exchange rate have had a significant impact on Danish–US trade. The dollar's upswing in the mid-1980s gave Denmark surpluses as high as seven billion kroner ($1 billion). The dollar's fall gave the US a surplus in 1989 of two billion kroner. One-third of Danish imports from the US were raw materials and semi-manufactured goods for industry and agriculture. There was strong demand for aircraft and EDP equipment-plus coal. The US supplies one-third of Danish coal imports, but the latest Danish energy plan calls for a ceiling on the use of coal, and the eventual closing of large, coal-fired powerplants. Denmark is moving over to natural gas.

TELECOMMUNICATIONS

The Danish telecommunications market is gradually opening up. In 1990 restrictions were lifted in the equipment market, provided the equipment meets the standards of the Danish telecom authorities. For the moment, L.M. Ericsson and Siemens dominate the import market, but there has been an interesting development—a group of certified electricians has set up a large chain of telecommunication shops, Telepunkt A/S, aimed at competing with the telecom authorities in the newly-opened equipment and wiring market.

GOVERNMENT PROCUREMENT

New Brussels regulations will cover telecommunications, drinking water, energy, and transport services, and these will have a big impact in Denmark where total public procurement amounts to more than 50 billion kroner ($8.3 billion) annually. The US Embassy in Copenhagen estimates that purchases covering half that amount fall under the notification requirements of EC and GATT public procurement agreements. The remaining half falls outside, due to the diversified and decentralized nature of large parts of the Danish public sector. It is going to be easier for other EC companies to sell in the Danish market.

TRANSPORTATION AND COMMUNICATIONS

Kastrup, Copenhagen's user-friendly airport, has long been one of Europe's most efficient hubs for both passenger and cargo traffic. It ranks sixth within the EC and has plans to double passenger capacity to 22 million a year by just after the turn of the century. Some 80 carriers operate cargo flights, making the airport a key factor in the Danish economy and the center for airborne traffic in Scandinavia. The ground-based haulier and forwarding sectors are equally modern and make use of a highly developed road system, consisting of motorways, highways, and well-tended secondary roads on which the Danes spend a billion dollars a year. By 1993, there will be motorways from Aalborg in the north of Jutland to the German border and from northern to southern Zealand, linking with existing motorways to create what the Danes call the "Big H" network.

Aarhus and Copenhagen are the main container ports, while Fredericia handles fuels and feedstuffs. New labor legislation is stimulating competition among the other 70 ports. Bridges and ferries provide fast links for passengers and goods between the main peninsula and the numerous large and small islands. The Danes conclude that no place in their country is more than about 30 miles from the nearest port or ferry.

Normally a very high-cost country, Denmark points to an OECD report that gives it a very low rating in the important area of telecom charges. Fax charges are correspondingly low, including the airport's "credifaxephones" with keyboards for international faxes. Denmark had the second lowest score within a so-called "basket" of national business telephone charges. International calls and mobile telephone charges are well below the OECD average, so it's cheap to call home— or head office.

S   P   O   T   L   I   G   H   T

• *The Great Belt Bridge* •

The Great Belt Bridge, one of the world's largest construction projects, will solve the problem of the Great Belt waterway which slices Denmark into mainland and islands. The Belt stretch of water is a traffic bottleneck—ferries carry about 7,000 cars and 1,000 trucks each day, together with 10,000 train passengers and 6,000 tons of rail freight. According to current plans, trains will begin crossing the Belt via a combined bridge and tunnel in 1993. The elevated bridge will give road traffic a magnificent view but this will not be completed until the summer of 1996. Once the link is ready, the State operating company, Great Belt A.S., expects road and rail traffic to double. The cost: 18 billion kroner at 1988 prices, and the entire project will ultimately be paid for by toll charges. The highway section will be repaid by around 2010, the rail link by 2023.

Prior to construction, there was much international fighting to get a slice of the action, with the French company Bouygues claiming there were "buy Danish" clauses. The case went to the European Court of Justice in Luxembourg with Bouygues winning a moral victory, but little or no cash.

There are several megacontracts involved. The rail tunnel under the East side of the Belt will be built by the contracting consortium MT Group, formed by Monberg and Thorsen (Denmark), Campenon Bernard and Sogea (France), Dyckerhoff & Widmann (Germany), and Kiewit Construction (US). The west road-rail link to a mid-Belt island will be undertaken by the European Storebaelt Group, made up of Hojgaard & Schultz, Per Aarsleff, and

C.G. Jenson, all of Denmark, Holland's Ballast Neddam, Taylor Woodrow, UK and Switzerland's Losinger. Contracts for the east road bridge, the world's largest suspension bridge, will go to German, Dutch, U.S., and Italian companies.

In general, the Danes have proved themselves willing to be "good Europeans" in the handling of the contracts. They have also taken steps to protect the fragile marine environment of the Baltic Sea, during planning and construction. The project is a good test for future public procurement in Europe.

MANAGEMENT AND WORKFORCE

Most industrial growth has taken place in Jutland, which accounts for more than 54 percent of the 400,000 jobs in manufacturing industry. These jobs are provided by some 7,000 factories, of which only 100 have more than 500 employees. Three out of four have less than 50 each. These small and medium-sized companies are specialized, often working as sub-contractors for large concerns in Denmark and abroad.

The iron and metal industries (which cover everything from machinery to electronics and scientific instruments) dominate trade statistics. Next come the food, drink, and tobacco sectors, chemicals (including the growth pharmaceutical area), paper and graphic articles, textiles, clothing and leather, timber and furniture, and building materials. The building and construction sector is big, with 180,000 workers, but has yet to regain the momentum of its boom years, 1983–86. However, major infrastructure projects, such as the Great Belt bridge and power and heat projects promise further growth. The Danish merchant fleet is 20th in the world in terms of tonnage. Spending has increased because of the reflagging of Danish ships into the new Danish International Ships Register, with its relaxed rules on taxation, dues, and manning. Two-thirds of the population are in the service sector—transport, trade and tourism, and local government.

:::::::::::::::::::REAL ESTATE :::::::::::::::::::::

Favorable tax conditions in recent years have led to a surplus of new offices in the capital and its suburbs. Pension funds and insurance companies invested heavily and builders were glad of the work. There have been few takers and unoccupied space rose to 300,000 square meters. Rents for quality inner city offices remain at 1,000 kroner the square meter, but the newcomer can strike a good deal below this price. The most modern offices, in the 25,000 square meter, waterfront Nauticon complex, have been hit not only by the prices asked— 1,200 to 1,400 kroner the square meter—but also by a freeze imposed by the city authorities, who are insisting that new development should be for light industry and the EDP sector. The striking Nauticon building, close to the possible arrival point of a future bridge from Sweden, stood empty long after it should have let.

One special feature of the Danish real estate market—any tenant can go to court after one year's occupancy to seek a rent reduction. Big and small firms take advantage of this loophole which some politicians are seeking to close.

• *Getting To Know the Capital* •

For a capital that can trace its origins back to the mid-1000s, Copenhagen doesn't look particularly old. That's the result of the succession of wars and fires over the centuries. Even so, many reminders of old Copenhagen remain, most of them in stone. King Christian IV (1577–1648) was a vigorous monarch who came to the throne when he was 11 years old and grew up to have an "edifice complex." Most of Copenhagen's finest buildings date from his long reign.

Central Copenhagen is compact, bordered to the west by a series of neat, rectangular lakes that are remains of the old defensive moats, and to the east and south by inlets from the Øresund seaway. Within this area are the headquarters of many banks and corporations as well as parks; the famous Tivoli Gardens; dozens of museums, art galleries, and churches; and the royal palace of Rosenborg.

But though the center is compact, it is also confusing, a maze of winding streets with few landmarks. The first thing to do is to buy a street map, study it, and remember to take it with you when you leave your hotel for a day of appointments.

There are extensive and efficient bus and local railroad systems (harbor ferries are mainly for sightseers). For fare purposes, the metropolitan area is divided into zones, which can be confusing to the visitor. The simplest and probably cheapest solution is to buy the Copenhagen Card, a pass valid for one, two, or three days. This provides unlimited travel by bus and rail and free admission to 36 tourist attractions, including the Tivoli Gardens. You can buy the card at your hotel, railroad stations, travel agencies, or the City Tourist Office:

22 Hans Christian Andersens Boulevard
Tel: 45-3311-1325.

Taxis are expensive but fast. Tips are included in the fare.

S P O T L I G H T

• *Copenhagen's Revival* •

Copenhagen is now 900 years old and the inner city is attractive with its harbor, man-made lakes, and copper-clad steeples. However, Danny Kaye's 'wonderful' Copenhagen of the Hollywood musical has lacked luster of late. National and local governments have taken note. They are anxious to provide a better business environment prior to the Single Market. Pointing the way forward is a major property development, Nauticon, a group of four and five-storey office buildings on the waterfront. This kind of modern accommodation, it is hoped, will attract local and foreign companies who see the Baltic, once again, as a major trading artery now that East-West

continued

tensions in the area have subsided. Also, it is expected that when construction of the Great Belt bridge is complete, both trade and tourism will flow between the main islands of Funen and Zeeland. There are other multi-billion dollar bridge projects planned which could provide fixed links to Sweden and Germany. One $10 billion project linking Copenhagen and Malmo should be ready in the year 2000.

The Folketing, the Danish parliament, has been looking closely at Copenhagen's role in the Single Market. In recent years, the inner city has declined with investment going to Jutland, the mainland portion of Denmark. As important as the Great Belt bridge is the planned link to southern Sweden. Some independent studies state that fixed links with the Swedish coastal cities could place Copenhagen fifth behind London-Cambridge-Oxford, Paris, Amsterdan-Utrecht-Leiden and Bonn-Cologne-Düsseldorf in a table of European areas judged by cultural life, standard of education, communications, and research and development. Copenhagen is already the center for 70 percent of Danish research, and home to three out of four electronics companies and nearly all biotechnology firms. These companies benefit from ties to Copenhagen's Technical University, the University of Copenhagen and other research institutes.

There are also plans to open new facilities and an improved freeport at the Port of Copenhagen. Plans abound for more housing, a new congress hall, and new hotels and sports stadiums. Political divisions between the Left and Right of Danish politics have been shelved in this attempt to make the capital a more attractive city for businesspeople.

Initiativradet, the industrial development board of Copenhagen, offers free consultancy services to foreign investors on siting, financing, and marketing new companies. Although Copenhagen does not offer direct cash or tax incentives, it does offer indirect subsidies for export-oriented businesses and R & D projects. Copenhagen has the only freeport in the Nordic Union, another incentive to investors who see the Danish capital as the link between the EC and the Scandinavian countries and Eastern Europe. The development board is at:

Toldbodgade 39
DK-1253 Copenhagen
Denmark
Tel: 45-3332-4900
Fax: 45-3393-4910

EUROCITY AARHUS

The east Jutland port city of Aarhus claims several "firsts"— Denmark's first science park, the first Danish city to have its own "rep" office in Brussels, the first in Europe to have set up an EC Business Information Center. The city was once considered provincial by Copenhagers; today it is at the heart of the country's most dynamic business area.

The rich surrounding farmland has led to the presence in Aarhus of Denmark's two biggest dairy-based firms. MD Foods and Danish Turnkey Dairies. The former, maker of Lurpak butter employs 4,700 people and sells a wide range of products to the tune of more than $1.5 million a year. Danish Turnkey Dairies, owned by the British A.P.V. Baker food processing company, is smaller, but has a worldwide reach.

The agri-food sector remains the backbone of the Danish economy and it is hardly surprising that the food company, Danisco, has established an EC-financed research center in the Aarhus science park. The park with its total of 25 Danish and foreign companies takes some

of the students of Aarhus, who total a staggering 66,000, divided between Aarhus University, the School of Architecture, the School of Economics and Business Administration, the engineering college, and
quite a few others.

The city has built international high schools and staged arts festi-
vals, notably the ten-day Aarhus Festival in the summer, now one of
the biggest in Scandinavia. Add to this Denmark's largest port and the
country's second airport and you have lots of reasons for a new, if
small Eurocity. Some other big companies have moved in: Jutland Telecom; Sabroe Refrigeration (makers of industrial freezing equipment); Grinsted Products (food additives); Aarhus Oil (seed oil);
Sweden's Alfa Laval-Hoyer (turnkey ice cream plant).

"I think we've become international," said a local official.

::::::OPPORTUNITIES IN THE REGIONS ::::::

Denmark does not give special aid to foreign investors, but all investors can apply for investment grants, R & D incentives, financing for
industrial buildings, and help with export promotion. Applications for
regional development support, within this framework, are examined
by the National Agency of Industry and Trade and the Investment
Secretariat, Foreign Affairs Ministry in cooperation with the trade
promotion and development boards of the various regions.

The latest Regional Development Act states that investors may apply for government cash grants of 25 percent of the initial cost of setting up industrial and service enterprises. In the priority areas—north
Jutland, many towns in southwest Jutland, the western part of Funen
island and several smaller islands—the upper limit is 35 percent. In
most cases throughout Denmark, grants represent between 10 and 20
percent of initial costs. Investment grants are taxable, but payment
can be deferred for 10 years. If the project is a success, the Agency may
claim repayment of grants. In this event, repayment starts after five
years and is spread over the next five.

Local government authorities in regional development areas may, with the support of the National Agency of Industry and Trade, erect industrial buildings for leasing or sale to industrial firms. First year rent is 11 percent of construction costs. After that, rent consists of a four percent repayment of the investment grant plus seven percent of the remaining debt. The Ministry of Labor provides training for un-skilled workers employed by newly-established firms.

Legislation on environmental protection has been strengthened. There are detailed rules for the discharge of waste water, smoke and other nuisances, for problems of pollution arouse public passions.

NORTH JUTLAND

The county is the nearest point to the other Scandinavian markets. The city of Aalborg has the Novi science park and an airport capable of taking jumbo jets. Large roll-on roll-off ferries link the county's ports with Sweden. An integrated transport center has been created in time for the coming Jutland motorway. The county has more than its fair share of firms engaged in electronics, plus two of the world's 14 mobile telephone plants. Key contact:

Industrial Development Council of North Jutland
Tel: 45-9812-2700
Fax: 45-9812-4089.

West-central Jutland is one of the richest farming areas in Den-mark, but in recent years it has seen strong industrial growth. The port of Esbjerg in Ribe County has ferry and shipping links with Harwich and Newcastle in England. Food exports flow through Esb-jerg, but the port has also become the center of the off-shore oil and gas industry.

Southern Jutland, next to Germany, prides itself on having much lower all-round business costs than its neighbor.

Frederica on the eastern coast of Jutland has been developed into Denmark's leading port.

ZEELAND

Zeeland, the main island, has attractive counties near Copenhagen, notably Frederiksborg, a scenic area which has attracted Hewlett Packard, Digital, IBM and Nissan, among others.
Key contact:

> Industrial Development Council of Frederiksborg
> Tel: 45-4246-6600
> Fax: 45-4226-2200.

Nearby Roskilde county has Denmark's new center for advanced technology.

> Tel: 45-4236-6555
> Fax: 45-4632-0855

SUCCESS STORIES

COMMODORE COMPUTERS

Commodore established its world network systems headquarters in Denmark in late 1989. The operation reached breakeven point in less than six months, and according to a senior executive is growing into a "highly successful division." Commodore is now the second biggest supplier of professional PCs in Denmark.

Several factors came into play when the investment decision was made—the ease of finding qualified employees, the availability of warehouse space and logistical staff from the home computer side, and the "small is beautiful" philosophy as applied to Denmark. "If you put an operation of this type into Germany, or France, the whole operation can acquire a national overtone, which can affect the image of the product everywhere," said the Commodore man. "There is far less risk of that in a small country like Denmark. You don't get taken over by the country where you're based."

Commodore thinks there's a travel advantage, too, as Copenhagen can be reached faster than Frankfurt from either London or the US. "Flight delays are unusual and connections take less time. That sounds unlikely until you have tried it a few times, so Copenhagen make us rather centrally-placed."

The company's overall structure in Scandinavia has been changed. Instead of independent companies in Denmark, Norway and Sweden all reporting back to the US, activities in all three regions have been combined into a regional office, based in Copenhagen to take advantage of Denmark's EC membership and its close ties with the Scandinavian countries.

SONY SCANDINAVIA

Sony, which is now practically everywhere in Europe, set up Sony Denmark in 1978 as a marketing and sales company. Denmark since has been chosen as the base for the headquarters of Sony Scandinavia. The choice was between Stockholm and Copenhagen. "Both cities offered attractive locations, well-functioning societies, and an educated workforce," said a senior Sony man. The main argument for Sweden was the size of its market, the biggest in Scandinavia, but the choice fell to Denmark. "Denmark is part of the EC and this was the paramount decisive factor," he added. Another important factor was reliable infrastructure, including many road connections and a large number of international flights. Taastrup, just outside Copenhagen, was chosen because of the ease in commuting for employees and because of its east access for business contacts.

Sony Scandinavia has been further centralizing its Scandinavian stocks in a warehouse in Copenhagen Freeport. Stock is not only free from customs, but can be shipped easily either to EC or EFTA countries. "The planned major advantages of locating Sony Scandinavia's headquarters in Denmark have turned out to be true," said William Leedgaard, managing director.

SPOTLIGHT

• *Pharmaceuticals* •

Denmark's one billion dollar-a-year pharmaceuticals industry now ranks among the top three in the world in terms of per captia. It is most advanced in insulin, CNS products, blood products and antibiotics. The emphasis of recent research is on genetic engineering.

Following the 1989 merger of Novo Industri and Nordisk Gentofte, Novo-Nordisk has emerged as the industry's giant. The fushion was partly dictated by the need to compete with the American Eli Lilly. Together, the two former Danish rivals in the competitive insulin market will be able to invest up to $150 million a year.

Some 85 percent of Danish pharmaceuticals output is exported, with the US, the biggest customer, taking 10 percent. The EC countries as a whole buy around 40 percent, the Nordic countries 16 percent, with about the same amount going to Latin America. Asia takes 12 percent.

A major study undertaken in 1990 by Lisberg-CJ Management reveals that the industry exports more than 300 prominent drugs worldwide and spends a very high 13 percent of revenues on R&D. International scale and sales have encouraged training for pharmaceutical research, development and production. There is close cooperation with local hospitals and in one case there has been testing of a revolutionary nasal insulin spray for diabetes sufferers which in three years time could remove the need for injections. Research is lively in biochemistry, molecular biology, and internal medicine, both in the public and private sectors.

The Lisberg report says that relations between manufacturers and the supervising government authority, the National Board of Health, "display understanding" and that administrative procedures prior to the authorization of a new drug can often be completed fairly quickly.

However, Denmark is one of the few countries with special legislation restricting research into genetic engineering. This seems a handicap, but the report concludes that the industry can "live with it" and that the pharmaceutical industry sees the law as a long-term competitive advantage: it forces Danish companies to compete under conditions which other western countries have yet to introduce. Industry investments have been intense throughout the 1980s, an annual average of 12 percent of revenues. At Novo-Nordisk, much of the large sum being spent on research is designed to find ways of making the company less dependent on insulin. Novo-Nordisk is world leader in insulin and industrial enzymes, and insulin and diabetes products account for 70 percent of the company's pharmaceutical turnover. Three main areas have been selected for the new research program: CNS, diabetes and biopharmaceuticals, while there will be new research into antibiotics.

Denmark, says the Lisberg study, has internationally-recognized product authorizations, a "reasonable" legislative framework, and flexibility in pricing. Perhaps the main advantage is the high priority Denmark has given for many years to health care, and the emphasis placed upon prevention.

The Single Market will have important consequences for the industry in areas such as product legislation, labeling and advertising, patents, prices, and technology. The Danish study says the changes will mean greater competition, as well as greater consolidation of European-based companies. Certainly, in its first year as a joint enterprise, Novo-Nordisk had 16 percent higher sales and 10 percent higher pretax profits ($150 million).

:::::::::::::::::::::THE LEADERS:::::::::::::::::::::::::

TOP 10 INDUSTRIAL COMPANIES (1989)

		Sales	*($m)* Profits
(1)	FDB Coop Societies	2,868	− 4
(2)	Tank-og Ruteskibe	2,453	77
(3)	East Asiatic Company	2,441	123
(4)	Danisco	2,188	196
(5)	Postal Service	1,782	195
(6)	MD Foods	1,628	109
(7)	Carlsberg	1,413	141
(8)	Lauritzen Group	1,404	56
(9)	FLS Industries	1,300	70
(10)	ISS Int Services	1,231	36

1990 Results

Falls
Jyske Bank − Dkr202m (+ Dkr 14/1989);

Gains
Novo Nordisk Dkr760m (+ 2 percent); Dansk Olie & Naturgas
Dkr103m (− Dkr94m/1989); Superfos Grain Dkr177m (+ 55 percent);
ISS Cleaning Dkr202m (+ 35 percent).

:::::::::::::::::KEY CONTACTS :::::::::::::::::

USEFUL COPENHAGEN TELEPHONE NUMBERS

Trade and Commercial Information

Agriculture Council and Marketing Board: 45-33-145672
Bella Center: 45-32-528811
Chamber of Commerce: 45-33-912323
Customs Board: 45-33-157300
Danish Bankers Association: 45-33-120200
Danish Convention Bureau (DCB): 45-33-328601
Danish Tourist Board: 45-33-111415
Export Council: 45-31-851066
Federation of Danish Industries: 45-33-152233
Handicrafts Council: 45-33-132258
Industries Board of Trade Fairs: 45-33-144346
National Bank of Denmark: 45-33-141411
Promotion Denmark: 45-33-225222

Government Offices

Ministry of Foreign Affairs, Investment Secretariat:
Tel: 45-33-920000
Fax: 45-31-540533

Ministry of Industry: Agency for Foreign Investment
Tel: 45-86-825655
Fax: 45-86-801629

Embassies

Member Nations
Belgium: 45-31-260388
Britain: 45-31-264600
France: 45-33-155122
Germany: 45-31-261622
Greece: 45-33-114533
Ireland: 45-31-423233
Italy: 45-31-626877
Luxembourg: 45-33-121271

Netherlands: 45-33-156293
Portugal: 45-33-131301
Spain: 45-31-422266

Others
Canada: 45-33-122299
Japan: 45-33-263311
United States: 45-31-423144

Facts on France

· ·

Capital Paris
Population 56m
Working Population 24m
Unemployment 9.5%
GDP Growth 1989: 3.7%; 1990: 2.8%; 1991
   (est.): 2%
GDP per Capita 1990 (est.): $18,682
Inflation 1989: 3.6%; 1990: 3.7%; 1991
   (est.): 3%
Production Investment 1989: 7%; 1990: 5%;
   1991 (est.): 4.5%
Foreign Trade 1990: − F50b
France–US Trade (French figures) 1989:
   − F21b

· ·

▼ FRANCE

"It is necessary to bring the two powers—the power of the market and the power and duties of the state—into line to create what I have called the mixed economy society." President Mitterrand

FRANCE HAS ADDED MODERNITY TO ITS CELEBRATED MOTTO, LIBERTÉ, Egalité, Fraternité. The word has yet to be etched in stone on government buildings and schools, but it governs the way things are done. As traditional passion disappears from the political arena, be it parliament or even the boulevards, national energy is channeled into acquiring European size in manufacturing and into confirming Paris as an international financial center to rival London and Frankfurt. Mergers and acquisitions are running at a record level, both within France and between French and EC companies. Financial markets have widened and been made more transparent.

France has some world-class products, from aerospace to vaccines, but has not always been able to make them in sufficient numbers or to sell them globally. Imported machinery and techniques are needed to increase output in factories, while foreign investment is doubly welcome in terms of jobs, and as a stimulus to business in general. A high educational level, slowly improving retraining programs, and the spread of Japanese-style quality circles stand France in better stead on the eve of the Single Market. This emphasis on ideas, or "intelligence" factor has already seen France take a European lead in computer software.

Traditional France of fashion, perfume, wine and food production remains, for the world would be the poorer without it. Luxury in all forms is very big business in the 1990s. The difference is that heavier industry is no longer a dirty word among the future elite as it surveys the post-graduate scene. The best and the brightest no longer opt almost automatically for government service, as was the case a decade or two ago. Taboos surrounding money are crumbling, for when the President castigates the evils of money (a French form of political discourse) managers nod and then look for the next deal or stock option. The French way, or culture, has lost something along the way, but corporate profits rose for eight straight years until the difficulties of 1990.

153

Growth was consistently a notch above inflation. Now, as elsewhere, belts have been tightened. Wages, in the main, have been held down by an embattled Socialist government which lacks an absolute majority in the National Assembly (parliament). There were doubts about it serving out its five-year term to 1993. The French have not liked the restrictions. *Ainsi va la vie* (so goes life) runs a popular song, and the French have added pragmatism to their quick wits, their noted sense of independence, their basic conservatism. The national character has changed a little with the new entrepreneurial spirit. United Europe, too, has meant a limited surrender of national independence. Yet France retains a strong voice within the EC and the new balance seems acceptable to the French, particularly if it delays the move of Europe's epicenter to reunited Germany.

New pragmatism means new deals with foreign businessmen. The French also have been on a buying spree in the US in the manner of the British and Dutch, sometimes paying very high for a market share. A new generation of English-speaking managers is arriving on the scene. The boardrooms of the top 100 companies may still be controlled largely by the top 100 bankers, but growing cross-border alliances will inevitably change this.

The centuries-old centralized State sees its boundaries narrowing. Thirty major banks and companies, denationalized by the Conservative government of 1986–88, have not been returned to State control by the Socialists. Two major "hassles" have gone—exchange controls and the former "keep 'em on tenterhooks" attitude adopted previously towards many a foreign investor. The new message: "Go ahead if you don't hear from us in two weeks." EC, US, and Japanese investors are being wooed to stop them going to Britain—or Eastern Europe.

A senior presidential adviser said the Fifth Republic's latest symbols—grand arches, cultural palaces, and a glass pyramid in Paris—were built partly to make the country even more attractive. Maybe glory was secondary. Certainly, in today's France, new, functional business districts and centers, and science and research parks are to be found everywhere. The government actively seeks more European offices of foreign corporations. One sign of the drive for efficiency is a concrete Finance Ministry building for the civil servants who collect the taxes, moved from the regal splendors (and dust) of the Louvre palace. France today is prepared to change many of its ways. It is the number two economy in the EC and is trying hard to stay there.

Its advantages include a first-class negotiating team in Brussels, the continent's finest transport infrastructure, a famous lifestyle, and the ability to leap forward after years of hesitation. Weak points include the high level of unemployment with the rate of jobless among the young four times higher than in Germany; strains in the educational system related to job prospects in a changing market; the risk of a further decline in investment and production, notably of automobiles, and the trade deficit which has grown with the slowdown in major export markets.

The watchword for France in 1991 was "stability," both of prices and the franc. France's vigorous participation in the Gulf war strengthened the popularity of both President Francois Mitterrand and then premier Michel Rocard. But M. Rocard, who had based his stewardship on dialogue, pragmatism and market-oriented policies, ran into trouble with a restive National Assembly and the President. He was dumped in favor of Mme Edith Cresson, France's first woman premier. At home, the government reduced its spending because of the economy's slowdown after three years of rapid expansion, but promised to maintain efforts in favor of housing, education, the health service, conditions in the outskirts of Paris and the main cities, as well as the long-promised reform of France's bureaucracy. The hope is that 1992 will see an upswing in the economy, for without growth near to three percent a year France will not be able to attain its objectives. The President said his new prime minister would provide *élan;* the polls showed otherwise. The aim was to match Germany and to support fully EC intergovernmental efforts to achieve monetary, economic and eventually political union. The government is hopeful that a new impetus, has been given to both Franco-American and Euro-American cooperation following the Gulf crisis.

MARKET OPPORTUNITIES

France's national wealth, in terms of gross domestic product, has gone through the $1,000 billion a year barrier, confirming France as the world's fourth largest economy behind Japan, the US, and West Germany. The outlook is for more of the same, with a continuation of the kind of non-inflationary growth that is the envy of Britain. French ministers have taken to describing their economy as "virtuous," a poetic word indicating a state of economic purity and the fact that the French linguistic approach is, well, different. The labor front is far from quiet, despite the evident decline of the communist-led trade unions. Companies continue to invest heavily in machinery. The modernization process runs through all sectors, and France's own hardware and CAD/CAM makers are unable to meet needs. Outside suppliers are required to overcome bottlenecks in French factories. The consumer boom of the past two decades, which has stocked French homes with washing machines, television sets, upgraded bathrooms, and has packed the roads with cars, is slowing only slightly. Purchasing power has held up—don't believe the national grumbling. France's next legislative elections are set for 1993. There's no reason to expect any change in the pro-market economy. Even the large State sectors increasingly seek private dancing partners. The US Department of Commerce has taken a close and highly instructive look at market opportunities in France, with US suppliers in mind.

CAD/CAM

The market, number three in Europe after West Germany and Britain, is expected to grow at an eight percent annual rate, taking it from under $600 million in 1989 to more than $850 million in 1992. Expect a 50 percent increase in the current total of 24,000 CAD/CAM/CAE systems. French firms such as Dassault Systèmes, Cisigraph, Matra Datavision and Framatome have been emphasizing mainframe applications for several years, but the market is young and, therefore, promising. Small and medium-sized firms are buying CAD/CAM and they offer the best opportunities.

COMPUTERS/PERIPHERALS

The State subsidizes Bull, the main manufacturer, just as it does Thomson in the defense and consumer electronics fields. Loss-making Bull has thus been saved. This kind of backing (and State orders) has enabled French production of computers and peripherals to grow.

However, imports account for half of a substantial market which should reach $12 billion in 1991. The US share currently is 42 percent. Modern, "smart" offices are spurring demand. The skyscraper business city at La Defense, west Paris, the largest functioning new development of its kind in Europe, is one example, and others are the new office complexes springing up in the regions.

MEDICAL INSTRUMENTS AND SUPPLIES

The market was estimated at more than $950 million in 1988 and has been growing at a rate of 12 percent a year. Imports, which supply 80 percent of medical equipment needs, are rising 11 percent annually and should be worth $1.3 billion in 1991. American manufacturers accounted for 35 percent of imports at the end of the 1980s, and have been holding their market share. Improved medical care is having a dramatic effect on life expectancy—centenarians in the Southern city of Arles remember the painter Vincent Van Gogh. Hospitals are being modernized. Well-equipped pharmacies dot practically every boulevard, avenue, and rue in the country, and general medical expenditure is phenomenal, doubling within a ten year span to account for six percent of household budgets.

TELECOMMUNICATIONS

France now has one of the most sophisticated telecommunications systems in Europe, a far cry from the days when a standup comic could make a living berating the telephones. The market will be around $6.6 billion in 1991, with imports accounting for 14 percent of this. Other EC suppliers and those from so-called third countries have seen their sales opportunities rise since Brussels ruled that telecommunications markets should be open to competition. Already, the US share of imports is 34 percent. France is now the European leader in digitalization systems, and the French Integrated Services Digital Network will soon be nationwide. Competition is now encouraged for value-added services such as database information systems and electronic mail. Alcatel NV (CGE plus ITT) is now the number two manufacturer of equipment in the world. All equipment must meet high local operating standards. There has been a boom in answering and fax machines while mobile telephones are multiplying.

FRANCHISING

Here is the largest potential market within the EC. According to the latest overall figures, franchising generated sales of more than $15 billion, or 5.5 percent of total trade. In the past two decades, the number of trade names in use has risen from 20 to more than 700. There are now over 30,000 franchises in France, with food franchises the fastest-growing sector. Experts, including the largest fast food chain itself, said France would never succumb to this kind of food retailing. They were wrong. Services franchises still offer a major market opportunity.

FOOD PROCESSING

Processed foods are spreading in the land of a hundred sauces, hence an increased demand for sophisticated technology. Production and processing could represent a $1.5 billion market by 1993. Imports of this kind of equipment run high at 42 percent (the US has a small six percent of imports). The sector is engaged in heavy capital investment and with BSN, France has the food multinational par excellence. The Commerce Department points to openings in the processing industries for meat, poultry, eggs and dairy products, preserved fruit, vegetables, so-called specialty products, and beverages.

ELECTRONIC COMPONENTS

The national market could touch $6 billion a year by 1991–1992. Domestic production is improving after various swings, but imports dominate the sector with a 73 percent share. The US has been the traditional market leader, but is now besieged by the Asians. Imports are scheduled to rise by some nine percent annually.

AUTO PARTS/ACCESSORIES

Suppliers to the major French automobile manufacturers (State-owned Renault, now linked with Sweden's Volvo, and the publicly quoted PSA group of Peugeot and Citroen) are in a $10 billion a year market. Automobile production broke record after record in the 1980s. The 1990s are a bit slower, but there could be 27 million passenger cars on the road in 1992—hopefully, not all at the same time. Italian tycoon Carlo de Benedetti went in early and bought Valeo, the biggest local manufacturer. The market must expand. Mandatory technical requirements will mean vehicles being modernized and made cleaner. Motorists want greater comfort, safety, and a better ride. Domestic technology is not up to all this, so imports could take half the market.

ANALYTICAL/SCIENTIFIC INSTRUMENTATION

The market could reach $2.2 billion soon. Real growth per year is running at six percent. Imports currently account for 68 percent of domestic consumption and in 1991 imports were worth $1.5 billion. Some 46 percent of imports come from the US. This healthy state of affairs shows no sign of ending—French industry and the government realize the importance of greater R & D spending, and, therefore, of US equipment.

CLOTHING

The French import $3 billion worth of clothing a year within a market valued at $20 billion. Imports of men's ready-to-wear clothes amounted to $1.13 billion in 1989, slightly higher than the import figure for women's ready-to-wear. Children's clothing is a growing market which has been estimated at around the $4 billion mark. There's strong French interest in US sportswear, hosiery, and children's wear. The British and Italians are prominent. Cheaper Eastern European clothes are now expected to compete with Asian and Mauritian imports.

SPORTING GOODS

The booming tennis and golf markets (the President and his men are keen, even fanatical golfers) are behind the fast growth of this sector. It's a $4 billion-plus market in which imports are rising at 16 percent a year. Strong demand also exists for fitness equipment, such as isometric toning tables. The national Gymnase chain of fitness clubs has machines from all over the world, particularly the US. Sales of mountain bikes and boots are climbing. In Beneteau and Jeanneau, France possesses the two leading pleasure yacht makers in the world, yet there is enormous demand for high performance—and well appointed—boats from the US.

SECURITY/SAFETY

France is importing close to $300 million worth a year of security and safety equipment, of which the US share is 15 percent. The market is growing all the time. A major, biennial security equipment fair is held at Le Bourget airport. The demand is for high quality US products such as electronic alarm systems, property protection equipment, infra-red sensors, and telesurveillance equipment.

S P O T L I G H T

• *Investment Incentives* •

European competition for foreign investment stretches from Limerick to Andalusia, from Jutland to Peloponnisos, so France's renascent regions are offering both the maximum aid permitted under EC rules, and throwing in the "clincher" of cheap, prime-site factory land. Albert Suissa, who offers aid packages for inward investors to set up in any of 12 former mining regions, says: "Land is available at FRF5. 50 a square meter in the North and East, two areas that will prosper with the opening of the Channel Tunnel in 1993 and from German unification before then. Ten francs a square meter just three miles from a highway is something investors won't find in the expensive and crowded southeast of England." His company, Sofirem, part of Charbonnages de France, the French Coal Board, has attracted British, American, Japanese, and also Italian companies to Saint Etienne.

This former black country city in central France has been transformed into a center of modern industry. The last colliery pithead is today a museum. Fountains play and Saint Etienne has escaped the kind of inner-city desolation sometimes found in Britain and the United States. In all, Sofirem has helped create 1,000 companies and 70,000 jobs across the country. CGM, the shipbuilders, Elf Aquitaine, the oil and chemicals multinational, and St. Gobain (glass, pipes, and building) have also helped to transform once-depressed areas. All work with Datar, the government industrial investment agency (known overseas as the French Industrial Development Board) and other agencies to offer 8.5 percent loans, grants up to half plant building costs, and cash incentives that can run as high as $9,000 per new job. The key regional grant here is the so-called PAT (prime d'aménagement du territoire). Twelve of France's 21 administrative regions offer special tax deals. Ten-year tax holidays are available for those, like Coca-Cola, who invest in enterprise zones such as the one around Dunkirk port on the Channel coast, or around the former shipbuilding areas at La Seyne and La Ciotat on the Mediterranean. Anvar, a French government agency dedicated to new and transferred technology, finances research and development projects with foreign as well as French capital. These include high-risk technological research. The Ministry of Research and Technology makes no distinction against foreign-owned, small and medium-sized companies when it comes to aid and tax credits.

Ernst & Young tax expert Jack Anderson says: "Foreigners coming in now are eligible for lucrative investment incentives. These are likely to disappear once the single market is in place and French industry has reached the desired level of competition." Disappearing slowly are the bureaucracy and the hundreds of procedures involved in obtaining aid. They are now down to a handful in most cases. Overlapping national, regional, and city authorities often confuse the newcomer. However, investors should be in no doubt that the French want them if they can offer jobs and new technology.

INVESTOR CHECKLIST

DATAR (FIDB) offices exist in New York, Chicago, Houston, and Los Angeles, Tokyo and Osaka, Berne, Frankfurt, London, Madrid, Rome, and Stockholm. Contact via French Embassy or consulate.

Datar office, Paris:
1 Ave Charles Floquet
75007 Paris
Tel: 33-1-4065-1234
Fax: 33-1-4306-9901

Anvar
43 Rue Caumartin
75436 Paris Cedex 09
Tel: 33-1-4017-8300
Fax: 33-4266-0220

Sofirem
Tour Albert 1ᵉʳ
65 Ave de Colmar
92507 Rueil Malmaison Cedex
Tel: 33-1-4752-9344
Fax: 33-1-4749-6493

An investor can always go straight to a big city mayor. Competition is strong between the budding Eurocities in the provinces. American industrialist Bill Packard headed for Grenoble—and its skiing—when choosing the site for a big Hewlett Packard factory.

The main rules governing investment in France today are the following: Foreign investors establishing new operations in France are absolved from advance notice and approval. Purchases of existing operations above FRF10 million (roughly $1.8 million), or more than 20 percent of the capital, need Treasury permission. A new two-week rule for replies applies only to investors from other EC countries. However, a more relaxed attitude is shown to all investors. The "nationalistic" reflex and a "non" came when Americans tried to buy one of the crystal glassmakers or the Japanese a famous Burgundy wine dealer. Certain prestige products are off-limits in France, unlike in Britain where buyers can take over Jaguar and other famous brand names.

Foreign companies created or safeguarded some 14,900 jobs in 1990, a record figure. Two-thirds of these jobs came from new or "green field" investment. As recently as 1985, foreign investors

seemed more anxious to take over existing French firms facing difficulties, but this kind of investment, which represented 70 percent of
the total in 1985, was just a few percentage points in 1990, showing
dramatically that investors preferred to set up their own, tailor-made
operations to attack both the French and EC markets. The thinking
was further underlined by investors building at sites that they themselves had chosen and not necessarily where DATAR was offering the
best incentives, the PATs. Half of the inward investment was outside
areas qualifying for aid. In fact, the EC Commission in Brussels said
that French aid was often too generous and said eleven *départements*
could be removed from the list of the needy—Charente, Cher, Indre,
Landes, Mayenne, Orne, Bas and Haut-Rhin, Ille-et-Villaine, Indre-
et-Loire, and Vienne. Investors were keener to stand on their own feet
in order to be present within the enlarged market. Close to two-thirds
of new Japanese investment was in non-aided zones, while a third of
the Germans and Austrians seemed unconcerned about the necessity
of *primes*. It is worth noting that DATAR considers a firm to be foreign
if more than 30 percent is owned by non-French interests.

INTERNATIONAL TRADE

France is learning to live with a foreign trade deficit each year in the
region of eight to ten billion dollars. Trivial, it might seem, compared
to the chronic deficits of the US and Britain. It causes much soul-
searching and the kind of long discussion deemed necessary in France
before action is taken.

Some of the reasons for the deficit are obvious—poor marketing;
reliance on see-saw Middle Eastern or African countries; a tendency
to propose mega-projects, ignoring smaller, lucrative deals; depen-
dence on arms sales. At home there has been the shortfall in production capacity due to years of under-investment, the need to buy
foreign machinery, and the way much of the consumer boom has to be
satisfied by imports. The country that built the Concorde supersonic
jet, advanced nuclear power stations and the world's fastest train, the
TGV, is often absent from more humdrum market sectors. While
France has been building space rockets, the Japanese have crushed the
French typewriter and watch industries, to name but two victims.

Thomson, the State-controlled defense and consumer electronics company, is committed to world sales of television sets and to acquiring a dominant position in future high definition television. Here, the French are showing the national will that built the rockets and the autoroutes but the Japanese may be first in the marketplace. Money is poured into both Thomson and Bull, the State-owned computer manufacturer. In Bull's case, State subsidies will continue for five years, whatever the cost. The French still believe in the role of large national enterprises, but these groups often find it difficult to operate on the world stage. Renault, the most symbolic of State firms, has linked with Sweden's Volvo in an effort to consolidate a strong export position, except in the US.

Many French firms have gone west across the Atlantic and acquired or bought into ITT, RCA, Union Carbide, Honeywell, American National Can, Pennwalt, Uniroyal, and publishers Diamandis and Grolier. Media and ministers have hailed the new boldness of French industry. True, but a detailed look at the trade figures shows big gaps at home, where a fall in the sales of just one product, the European Airbus, assembled at Toulouse, can have a sharp negative effect on the balance of trade. Doubt surrounds the outlook for arms sales which have earned billions in foreign currency since the Mirage jet fighters performed so well in the 1967 Six Day War in Israel. Cheese and wine sales should prove resistant, while perfumes and luxury goods sell in bad times as well as good. For the moment, however, the industrial balance is not at all healthy with a $16 billion deficit. Manufactured items account for only 20 percent of gdp in France compared to 30 percent in Germany, which is France's biggest export market and where France has recently reduced its deficit. France runs deficits in computers, computer-assisted manufacturing, the whole range of video goods, robots, machine tools, trucks, sound equipment, household electronics, clothes, and shoes. It holds its own in telecommunications, aerospace, pharmaceuticals, automobiles and automobile parts and, of course, in both perfumes and food sales.

Best reading

England language review of French economic performance and trends published by:

Economic Research Department
Credit Lyonnais
5 Ave du Coq
75009 Paris
Tel: 33-1-4926-5648

French Company Handbook
published by:
International Herald Tribune
181 Ave Charles de Gaulle
Neuilly-sur-Seine
Tel: 33-1-4637-9396.

S P O T L I G H T

• *Business Etiquette* •

British authoress, Roberta Dahdi, writes of formality in French business, compliments to the ladies, and conversational wit when writing on business etiquette in a French Government investment brochure.

Formality: "The atmosphere in the old French establishment tends to be formal, with strict attention to hierarchy and careful use of titles, such as 'Monsieur le President' for the head of a firm. Many younger French people find stifling the outdated system of power restricted to the top, and a large number of modern offices now practice decentralized decision making and the informal use of first names. There tends to be a 'new toy' feeling about such organizations."

Greetings: "A kiss on the cheek (never on the lips) will not shock a good friend of the opposite sex. Many Frenchmen have been brought up to believe that not to be complimentary to a female is rude. Hence their romantic reputation. *Tu,* the informal you, is a bed of nails. Safer to use *vous,* except for children up to 12."

continued

Lunch: "Break often as early as noon (particularly true in the provinces). The conversation may well turn from business and you could be asked your opinion on politics... Much value is put on lively wit...the motto for France is 'show you are dynamic.' " (A safe, international subject? Violence on the metro.)

TRANSPORTATION AND COMMUNICATIONS

AIR

Prairie-like space, thousands upon thousands of acres stretching into the distance, is the blessing enjoyed by Charles de Gaulle airport, north of Paris. That the French government seeks to dethrone Heathrow, London, as the major transport "hub" in Europe is understandable, but the ambition is backed by political will, a lot of cash, and all that space—they're even building a golf course. More pertinently, there's room to add three terminals to the existing two that already handle 20 million passengers and, incredibly, three more runways to the pair now in operation. One billion dollars were allocated recently to upgrading Charles de Gaulle and its twin airport, Orly, south of Paris. Charles de Gaulle is to get a TGV (train à grande vitesse) station at the airport, new office parks (some built by the British), freight zones, and hotels. Longterm, Charles de Gaulle and Orly could handle 100 million passengers a year. In the much nearer future, de Gaulle will benefit from a unique air-high speed train-highway interconnection. France has other, smaller international airports at Bordeaux, Lyons, Nice, Marseilles, Strasbourg, and Toulouse. New terminal capacity and longer runways are being added at Nimes, Perpignan, and Montpellier as sunbelt industries move close to the Mediterranean. What remains is for the Brussels Commission to push ahead with deregulation so that competition reduces fares, notably the extravagant rates charged between Paris and Nice by Air France and Air Inter. Air Minerve is one challenger.

RAIL

The new generation TGV express train, a distinctive blue stripe on its sleek, silver sides pulls out of Montparnasse station in Paris at breakfast time, 8.20AM, glides through the suburbs at 19mph and, when the flatlands of western France are in sight, it takes note of the computer order *allez* (go). It hits 186mph—some 120 mph less than its maximum—and businesspeople are able to lunch with contacts in distant western cities. The new TGVs have radically changed the whole relationship of western seaboard cities, such as Nantes, with the rest of France—and Europe. Toulouse and Bordeaux are next. New lines will put Marseilles just three hours from the capital, Barcelona four and a half hours. London will be three hours away. A powerful political-railway lobby has ensured the availability of funds for these new lines, many of them costly due to environmental precautions such as rubber shock absorbers near stored wine in the Loire Valley. The 1990s will see these French networks linking with European networks, notably in Germany and Spain. Business travellers pay a 47 percent premium on some trains at peak hours—but, oh, the comfort. Small conference lounges, worldwide telephoning, good food. For freight, the State Railways have introduced 100mph *Fret Crono* trains for perishable goods and refrigerated containers. Another, Scan-Express, links France and Sweden. In addition, the two main ports, Marseilles and Le Havre, have expanded container facilities to approach Europe's two "super ports," Antwerp and Rotterdam.

ROADS

Roads, long regarded by the French as highly "strategic," have become clogged and this has meant a new masterplan for a 70 percent expansion of the autoroute system from 7,000 km to 11,800 km over ten years. Three-quarters will be toll roads. Some of these now start right at city gates. The plan has four major routes avoiding Paris: a link between Le Havre and the northeast autoroutes; Bordeaux-Clermont Ferrand-Lyons; Nantes-Tours-Orleans-Troyes, and Nantes-Lyons. There's an exciting north-southwest route planned between Calais, Bordeaux, and Spain, a Caen-Bordeaux route, and one from Geneva to Marseilles. A second ring around Paris nears completion. A futuristic scheme to drive road tunnels under the city awaits further study. Many plans have as their *raison d'être* the by-passing of Paris.

::::::MANAGEMENT AND WORKFORCE ::::::

When engineering staff, demanding a shorter week for the same pay, walked out at British Aerospace, workers at the Aerospatiale company in Toulouse shook their heads in disbelief. Both groups of skilled workers are building the European Airbus jet airliner. The French pleaded with the British to end the strike, calling it harmful to Europe's largest joint industrial effort. Above all, they did not understand the importance of the issue of hours. Aerospatiale fitters are not looking for a 37-hour week like their British colleagues on Airbus. They work an hour or so longer than required each week. Ignoring extra pay, they seek to accumulate days off during the year. Thus, the French worker, fairly low in the European pay league, prizes vacations and job security particularly now that employees have a stronger case for firing. Days lost to strikes have fallen 65 percent in the past decade. Despite the fact that legal vacation time has been raised to five weeks a year, French workers long ago shed their reputation for taking things easy during the working day. Productivity between countries is difficult to compare. Some studies put German productivity 20 to 30 percent higher than French, adding that salaries and social charges across the Rhine are 50 higher. The French are anxious to do better and many firms spend far more than the required 1.2 percent of their payroll on training courses for employees, which in some cases include English lessons. EC statistics point to a low level of pre-tax wages in France, placing the country in ninth position amongst the 12 member countries. However, there are wide differences in France between the pay of highly skilled workers and the less skilled, plus a complicated system of bonuses. The EC figures, referring to April, 1989, put six countries above the $10 an hour level with Denmark way in front with $15 an hour. Others were Germany, Luxembourg, Netherlands, Belgium, and Britain. Below the ten dollar line were Italy, Ireland, Spain, Greece, and Portugal, as well as France. Since the beginning of 1989, many French workers won six percent raises or more on the back of booming company profits. These declined in 1990. The major automobile firms, Peugeot and Renault, will probably offer less in the various bargaining rounds of 1991 and 1992. This would mean pay rising in line with inflation—or no more than 3 percent. The government has asked the state sector to limit raises to 2.5 percent.

Industry in France has problems finding sufficient engineers. The *grande écoles,* mainly in Paris, dominate training: Polytechnique, Central, Mines, Pont et Chausses, and Arts et Metiers. A few others are in Lille, Lyons, and Toulouse. Altogether, the French engineering schools turn out 14,000 graduates a year, compared to 20,000 in Britain and 29,000 in Germany. Thomson, the major electronics company, takes one in ten of these graduates, squeezing severely the number available for smaller companies—and foreign investors.

Worker participation? Yes, but not to the extent that it interferes with day-to-day management. Companies with more than 50 workers must have works councils, but these deal with conditions, not policy. Likewise, profit-sharing is mandatory in companies with more than 100 employees, but is far from crippling.

A sign of French Socialist pragmatism was the decision to allow mass layoffs for economic reasons without prior authorization from the labor authorities. A major change. The other is the declining power of the once highly troublesome Communist trade unions. Combine this with a low rate of unionization in general, plus the lack of strike funds, and one has the reasons for the rarity of general strikes.

S P O T L I G H T

• *Advertising* •

The French advertising industry has been doing well, despite 1990's problems. Until then, spending on advertising had shown 12 percent annual growth, which dropped to eight percent in 1990. Newspapers, radio and tv took in less than expected, but the poster sector and the cinema did better in the $13 billion market. These days, the industry is not only large but facing changes as agencies look towards the single market. Agencies are buying, merging, allying. The current drive for size reflects both a new Pan-European vision and an effort to diversify beyond pure advertising. But even so, the Euro-advertising agency finds it has yet to target the Euro-

continued

consumer. In 1989 seven French groups—Eurocom, Publicis, RSCG, BDDP, FCA, CFP, and TBWA—shared 85 percent of the market with ten Anglo-Saxons: Young & Rubicam, Interpublic, WPP, DDB, Saatchi & Saatchi, Leo Burnett, BBDO, Grey, DMB & B, and Ayer. While the Anglo-Saxons have been the undisputed leaders in the world advertising field, the 50 top French agencies together accounted for 4.2 billion francs out of a total of 6.0 billion francs ($1.1 billion) in revenues.

"Anglo-Saxon creation is better," says Isabelle Musnik, journalist at CB News, the leading trade journal. "But France is trying to catch up, little by little. We can't slack off." These efforts include a wave of acquisitions and joint ventures: WCRS buys into SGGMD, Eurocom increases its stake in WCRS, RSCG takes over KLP, etc. As the English and Americans seek a foothold on the Continent, the French are extending their networks in Europe and beyond.

"The French agencies all have a long-term strategy for both a European and an international expansion," notes Laurent Saillard of Publicis. And increasingly, clients are demanding a global rather than local approach. But once the international structure is in place, and the local marketing directors have been replaced by a single European marketing director, the problem becomes one of finding a "Euro-campaign" that will work across the board.

"It's a real nightmare," admits Bernard Petit of Grey. "A single campaign is extremely difficult to achieve. Such a commercial will always be a compromise, and that's an enormous danger. Compromise will never make a great campaign."

For new products there is less danger, because positioning is the same everywhere. Problems arise when the product is a leader in one country, lower down in the next." Petit notes that a two-tiered approach can often work, with a dual campaign tailored to reflect strong/weak markets or north/south regional differences.

"It's the eternal problem," Isabelle Musnik agrees. "It's

most difficult in food. Cognac, for example, is drunk very differently in France than it is in Germany. But a single campaign can work in some areas, jeans for example. Young people wear jeans in the same way all over Europe." Indeed, the youth market appears to be the most promising for Euro-advertising. "The Euro-consumer doesn't exist yet," says Musnik, "but we can try to create him, starting with young people. They're the ones to target." Petit concurs. "We're still a long way away from a single market. But we'll get there, product by product."

REAL ESTATE

France's boom years—four percent growth in 1988 and 1989, followed by 2.6 percent in 1990 and an estimated two percent in 1991—have led to demand for more and better offices by companies, local and foreign. Strong demand for all kinds of property has sustained the Paris property market for investors. Prime yields during the boom period were four to five percent. Owner-occupiers were paying over 100,000 francs the square meter for well-located downtown commercial property in the so-called "golden triangle" around the Champs-Elysees, as well as in the Opera district. Top rents reached 4,500 francs the square meter. The western suburbs were sought after because of lower prices. In one major deal, C. Itoh sold a building to a French insurance group. Business parks found takers, while the Swedes were active in Paris and cities such as Lille, Lyons, and Nice. The rental market was strong west of Paris in what property agents now call the "golden crescent," or inner-suburban ring. Suburbs such as Nanterre and Reuil attracted oil companies Shell, Esso, and Fina, and insurers Sedgwick, Guardian Royal and Norwich Union. Rents have ranged from 1,200 to 1,500 francs the square meter. The northwest suburbs have been opened up by the RER express metro lines. Top sites are Espace Clichy, Saint Ouen and Genevilliers. These areas were part of the postwar Communist "red" belt around Paris, but nowadays, are workplaces and home to briefcase brigades. Rents are cheaper than to the west and Federal Express has negotiated with Jones Lang Wootton for offices renting for as low as 650 francs and 850 francs the square meter. Another booming area is in and around Roissy/Charles de Gaulle airport, which the French government hopes will one day overtake London as *the* European hub, Aeroports de Paris, the national airport authority, has encouraged modern offices, warehouses, and hotels (the latest is a new Hyatt). The added attraction is the TGV express train station at the airport. The TGV line will loop around Paris to the East, taking in Eurodisneyland before heading south and southeast via a second interconnection station at Massy, site of more Jones Lang Wootton buildings, notably Atlantis (1992 rents are expected to be 1,500 francs the square meter). East Paris suburbs are not too far behind. Areas with fast public transport links to Paris are set to boom—Vincennes, Charenton, Bagnolet and Fontenay-sous-Bois.

• *Getting To Know the Capital* •

The Seine River snakes sinuously through Paris, dividing it into left and right banks. On the *Rive Gauche*—the Left Bank—are the Latin Quarter, the Sorbonne University, the National Assembly and Senate (parliament), government ministries, wide boulevards, and a maze of narrow, winding streets (Baron Haussmann didn't get his hands on much of the Left Bank). Dwarfing everything is the Eiffel Tower, the very icon of Paris. The view from the top is remarkable.

The *Rive Droite*—the Right Bank—is dominated by the Avenue des Champs-Elysées, a century old in 1989, with the Place de la Concorde at one end and the Arc de Triomphe at the other. Beyond the arc, going west, is the equally grandiose though lesser-known Avenue de la GrandArmée, Neuilly with its advertising agencies, and then the newish office development of *La Défense,* home to many multinational companies. La Défense has its own, contemporary Arc de Triomphe—and a diminished version it is of the original one—and a new exhibition center and World Trade Center. Other, increasingly popular business centers are Marne la Vallée, to the east next to Eurodisneyland, and in satellite towns: Saint-Quentin-en-Yvelines, Cergy Pontoise, and Evry.

Paris is divided into twenty *arrondissements*—administrative districts with their own *mairies* (town halls) that answer to the mayor and elected council of the city. The most fashionable and therefore expensive *arrondissements* are the eighth, which includes the Champs-Elysées; the seventh, particularly around the neighborhoods known as Invalides, close to the river, and the nearby Ecole Militaire; parts of the first and second; and virtually all of the sixteenth, west of the center. The sixteenth borders the large and famous Bois de Boulogne, a stretch of wooded parkland, within which are two racetracks, Longchamp and Auteuil; some excellent restaurants; a lake; and a bevy of excessively friendly (at a price) "ladies." The sixteenth's dignified and calm next-door neighbor is the suburb of Neuilly, a coveted address: close to the city center, to La Défense, and to the Bois de Boulogne.

Paris has one of the best rapid-transit systems in Europe, perhaps in the world. Taxpayers foot a high bill, in the form of massive subsidies from employers, central government, and the city of Paris. But—and it's a very important but—the result is a coordinated subway, bus, and railroad network that offers riders clean, fast transportation and notable value for money.

The subway system—the Métro—and the RER, which is run by the state-owned French railroad company, together offer the fastest transportation from Point A to Point B. Use the Métro for shorter distances, the RER for longer ones. At any Métro station you can buy *carnets* of ten tickets valid within the Paris area on subway and RER trains and on buses. Clear, detailed maps of the subway, RER, and bus routes are free. Note that though one ticket takes you all over Paris by Métro, you may have to use two tickets for a long bus journey; check the map at bus stops and in buses themselves. If you're staying in Paris for a few weeks, it's worth buying a Métro and bus pass entitling you to unlimited travel. Ask your hotel concierge for details.

Taxis are hard to find in rush hours, and too many drivers seem to be either off duty or determined to go in the direction opposite to yours. Most drivers will take only three passengers. Try to avoid unmetered limos lingering at airports and railroad stations; they are very expensive unless there are four or five people in your party and you bargain hard.

continued

Rental cars from major American and European firms are available, but expensive. We don't recommend driving in the city. Traffic is a headache, parking is scarce. There's really no reason to drive in a place that has such excellent public transportation.

EUROCITY LYONS

Lyons fought a long battle of statistics with Marseilles before recognition as the second city of France. Today, it displays its industrial strength, modern research centers, and growing financial marketplace—and a new youthfulness—to assert a Eurocity role, namely a metropolis combining both size and an influence extending well beyond the city walls. Geography is its other great asset, sitting as it does in the middle of the country, on the rivers Rhône and Saône. For the moment, north-south traffic both French and European is delayed by local traffic jams, but the city is linked to neighboring countries by excellent road and rail connections, but impatiently awaits an express rail service to Turin and Milan. More autoroutes are being built, some for the 1992 Winter Olympics in Albertville, others with a view to future Alpine tunnel links with Northern Italy. The record-breaking, French bullet train, the TGV, which has transformed Lyons' role in the contemporary French business world, is scheduled to go faster and faster, and will hook up with other high-speed railways across Europe. Lyons is not quite a fully fledged Eurocity like Barcelona or Frankfurt. The will, however, is very much there, despite age-old Parisian centralism of power. The city recently voted in a new political leadership under Mayor Michel Noir, a physical giant of a man with the ambition to match. Noir thinks his striking city with its southern air should rank with Turin or Birmingham, Stuttgart or Rotterdam. It is certainly a city on the move, with its eyes fixed firmly on the opportunities the Single Market brings to "hub" cities.

Lyons has been a crossroads for centuries. It was a leading banking and silk manufacturing center in the Middle Ages, with strong ties to Italy. Silk gave way to textiles and to chemicals. Plants were built for automobiles and commercial vehicles and these gave birth to today's broad range of precision engineering firms, with a network of sub-contractors similar to that in Italy.

The city also gained a reputation for composite materials, but per-haps its greatest claims to modern renown are the pharmaceutical and medical-vaccines industries, around giants such as Rhône Poulenc and Merieux, and the research labs they spawned. However, there was a period in the 1970s when Lyons slumped. The city was badly man-aged and there were fears that the sleek, orange-colored TGV trains, hurtling hourly on a special track between Lyons and Paris, would drain the city's talent towards the French capital. What happened in-stead was that the great train—speeding 22 times a day in both directions—opened up a vital, two-way "business corridor" between the two cities. A contemporary style business district rose around the Part-Dieu TGV station. Banks and venture capital funds set up there. The Lyonnais, long regarded as rather serious, introverted, slightly penny-pinching accumulators of wealth, seem now to have adopted a more jaunty lifestyle. One young Parisian doctor, typical of her gener-ation, who studied in both cities, opted without hesitation for Lyons. The city has an attractive new look, due to restoration of ancient buildings and careful, yet imaginative, city planning. A new congress hall and world trade center are being built along the river banks. Whole new business-cum-leisure centers are being constructed. The driving force is Mayor Noir, who, in his early forties, has undoubted, if unstated, Presidential ambitions, yet who says he first wants to make it as easy to enter France via his city as it is by "that other city" farther north. Lyons sits as the capital of the thriving Rhônes-Alpes area which stretches from the central French mountains across to Geneva in Switzerland, a spread of land with ten percent of France's popula-tion and national wealth, and a fifth of its exports. It is turned out-wards towards the rest of Europe. Hence Mayor Noir's forceful attempts to persuade the great Eurocities to work together in the New Europe. The have been planning better ways to create durable links in business, transport and culture. Lyons sees its partners in southern Germany, northern Italy, and Catalonia. And it has a good setting for the making of deals—the many fine restaurants in the city and sur-roundings. It is probably the greatest concentration of "gastronomic power" in the world. Master chef Pierre Orsi is in the markets at 5:00 a.m. selecting fish and vegetables before putting in a 16-hour day. "If you charge 400–500 francs for a meal, there's no room for error," he says. A sign of the times is that businesspeople can also lunch at Orsi's these days for half the price and in half the time.

Opportunities in the Regions

Geography plus opportunities offered by the Single Market point to six regions as high-flying investment and business areas. Limited on the strictly political front, the regions have taken their economic destinies increasingly into their own hands. Alsace delegations head for Japan, those from Rhône-Alpes for New York. These days an investor is often well-advised to deal directly with the mayor of a big city or the regional council rather than knock on the doors of the Treasury in Paris.

NORTH

Shrubs have been planted on the slag heaps, British investors and property buyers are swarming over the entire region, while in Lille, the capital, posters and banners proclaim: "The TGV, the tunnel: our destiny." The Channel Tunnel, when it surfaces near Calais in 1993, will be mainly for through traffic between London and Paris and, later, London and Brussels. However, there will be considerable spin-off for the North in warehousing and the relaying of goods. The North will be one of the main transport hubs of Europe and in anticipation of that day a huge freight zone, called Centre International de Transport, capable of handling 2,500 trucks a day, is being built outside Lille. Few areas of France are enjoying such a renaissance as this former black country of mines and mills. The popular ballads that are part of French daily life once referred to northerners being born "with a factory in their heads" (born to a life of hard work). It's called industrial culture now and it serves the new automobile and electronics plants and the region's growing service sector. Lille will be on the London-Brussels line and will be linked to Paris by TGV. The high-speed trains will put this urban conurbation of a million people within two hours of London, a mere half hour from the European capital in

Brussels, and just three hours from Cologne, Düsseldorf, and the Ruhr. A new main station, a European Business Center, a World Trade Center—Lille is adding all of these. Nearby, the once grim textile city of Roubaix has looked to the future, adding a teleport and extending its big mail order business across Europe.

EAST

"A smile, a wave, the perfume of childhood." Patricia Kaas, hailed as the new Edith Piaf, a one woman expression of the national mood, hails from the East, sings of her region in French and German and is an admirable ambassadress for her region. Strasbourg, the capital, has another with its female mayor. Like the North, the geographical position of the East gives it a high European profile. National leaders in Paris fear that the spine, or axis, of the new Europe will inevitably move East to a line running through the Ruhr and Rhine lands. Alsace and Lorraine, France's eastern approaches to Germany are next to the Rhine. Between them, the two regions touch Switzerland (Mulhouse-Basel airport straddles the frontier), Germany, Luxembourg, and Belgium. General Motors long ago saw the geographical advantage and built a plant. Some 100 German manufacturing companies have followed, as have a growing number of Japanese and British corporations. Transport connections, particularly train links, are not of the best, but long-range planners in Paris see a future high speed line to Moscow, passing through eastern France. A new Rhine bridge will be built in the more immediate future in Strasbourg, home of the European Parliament, the European Court of Human Rights, and the 22-nation Council of Europe. Alsace, lying in the Rhine River plain between the French Vosges Mountains and the German Black Forest, is an ideal distribution point for goods to the rich heartland of the EC. The area also has a concentration of research and development laboratories linked to Strasbourg's three universities and six engineering schools. In neighboring Lorraine the night sky is no longer red. Most of the steel furnaces have closed and massive reconversion is underway, backed by an efficient welcome service for foreign investors in the cities of Metz and Nancy. Science parks are opening, while France, Belgium, and Luxembourg are jointly promoting the European Development Area, offering startup packages of close to 40 percent of investment.

ILE DE FRANCE

The capital's suburbs are part of the Ile de France region of ten million people. The ban on new offices has been lifted and a new campaign started to persuade international companies that Paris is the *de facto* capital of the new Europe and, therefore, the obvious choice for a European headquarters. A poll of foreign CEOs was hardly encouraging, revealing as it did a preference for Brussels and London, and expressing a marked dislike for French social security charges, bureaucracy, poor command of English, and what was seen as protectionism against the US and Japan. The golf boom in Ile de France is softening the landing for the Japanese.

Paris and its surroundings, however, arguably form the most agreeable environment in Europe. There remains something of a "people problem" encountered daily, with rude and inefficient telephone operators. McDonald's and Disneyland, two US exports to France, run counter to French habits, but they and other foreign service industries have introduced a "have a nice day" approach. On a somewhat different level, the government sees the new symbols of the Fifth Republic—the cultural palaces, the glass pyramid in Paris, the triumphal arches and other great architectural works—as both flattering for the native-born and a form of enticement for well-heeled foreigners. Only London is seen as a challenger and the French point to their business city, La Défense, on the western edge of Paris as finished and functioning a decade ahead of London's Docklands. Most important, the Ile de France's transport structure is being upgraded in a manner unique in Europe, with new business parks, exhibition space, and an expanded Charles de Gaulle airport. Bordering Ile de France to the South is Region Centre, with its heavy concentration of US companies (John Deere, IBM, Tenneco), a tradition started with the US Army in the postwar years.

RHÔNE-ALPES

The energy and flair of Lyons' noted chef Paul Bocuse are shared by many of the businesspeople and bankers who eat at his tables. Long lunches in Lyons do not spoil the appetite for business. The two are inseparable and the citizens look as solid as the city's architecture. In this business city old fortunes co-exist with new money, earned from a panoply of industries. Lyons sees itself as a kind of French-style Milan, a counterweight to the capital. Prosperity began with the old silk industry which is now enjoying a revival. Prosperity expanded into oil refining by French and international groups, aluminum (Pechiney), glassmaking (BSN), chemicals and pharmaceuticals (Rhône-Poulenc), and trucks (Berliet-Renault). Other successful expansions have been in metallurgy and non-ferrous metals, machine tools, plastics, electronics, and vaccines—all supported by a range of institutes of higher technical education. Grenoble to the east is vibrant with an impressive student population, evidence of the relatively high French birth-rate. The city has a reputation as France's "Science City." National and international research centers are sited near major foreign operations, such as Hewlett Packard, French electrical giant Merlin Gerin, and European software leader Cap Gemini Sogeti. Lyons is near the "sun line" of France and so looks south to the Mediterranean coastal regions, and east and west to Italy and Spain. More than a half million visitors will arrive in 1992 for the Winter Olympics in the nearby Alps. Organizer is Jean-Claude Killy, triple Olympic champion turned businessman. The French are doubly proud of him.

SOUTH WEST

Ancient Toulouse is where Europeans are reaching for the visible sky—and deep space. Not far from here, French poet and soldier Cyrano de Bergerac flashed the steel of his sword. The dexterity of the modern aircraft, rocket, satellite fitter bears some similarity. Toulouse is the capital of the European aerospace effort. It provided an occasion 20 years ago for Europe's two leading aerospace nations to build jointly the revolutionary supersonic plane, the Concorde. This collaborative effort was extended to Germany, Italy, and Spain for the successful, wide-bodied European airliner, Airbus. Segments are flown in by freighter from around Europe and assembled in the vast halls of Aerospatiale. The plane has won orders worldwide, including many from the US. What is not generally known is that US sub-contractors supply many of the systems of the European plane. Honeywell has gone one better and established a flight systems department in Toulouse. The Franco-Italian regional jets of the ATR family are also built in Toulouse, as are Dassault fighter planes. Matra has its satellite manufacturing "clean room," while the French Space Agency (CNES) and Dassault are preparing the manned European space plane Hermes which will fly to the space station Columbus at the end of the century, if funds permit. Toulouse is a showplace of European cooperation. Motorola, Bendix, Rockwell Collins, and others generated a second boom in electronics and this has spilled over now to the Languedoc region on the Mediterranean, where high-tech plants are dotted among the vineyards.

CÔTE d' AZUR

High-tech has also breached the hedonistic paradise of the French Riviera. On the spectacular descent to Nice airport, the traveller sees the gorgeous villas of sheikhs, stars, and deposed dictators, and science parks. Who went to the Riviera in the old days? Somerset Maugham, Graham Greene, Pablo Picasso, Aristotle Onassis, the Aga (and Aly) Khan, Rita Hayworth, Saudi princes, Joan Collins, Sean Connery, and the Rolling Stones still go, but briefcase armies are marching through Nice Airport as the region seeks to establish itself as Europe's high-tech sunbelt. Technology parks have been built between glamorous hill villages, while office complexes rise next to the beaches. Today's revenues from high-tech and industrial sectors amount to a couple of billion dollars, the same sum spent by the region's eight million tourists. Sophia Antipolis technology park is probably Europe's most beautiful and successful, a choice location for Americans and Japanese. The late Pablo Picasso saw the trend, laid aside his brushes one day and turned the first earth at the park. Club Méditerranée has followed suit and opened a luxury center for businessmen seeking to recharge their batteries.

SUCCESS STORIES

3M

3M is a striking example of a multinational that prepared for the Single Market long before the fixing of the 1992 deadline. Ray Richelsen, president of 3M France, says the company came to treat Europe as a single entity as long as 15 years ago. European headquarters in Brussels oversees the manufacturing, research and sales of 17 subsidiaries in an area that accounts for $3 billion of total world sales of $12 billion. Europe is targeted as the main area of expansion, along with the Pacific Rim. 3M France is sole supplier to Europe of one of the company's most famous products, the Post-it adhesive note. Sales of Post-it, manufactured at a plant near Paris, are an example of how 3M does business, namely a mixture of mass orders sent by truck and small orders handled by a salesman's visit to the corner store in a village. The company has a well-structured organization across Europe with Brussels-based group directors and local managing directors, but with a lot depending on the sales teams and their day-to-day contact with the shopkeeper. Some 350 salesmen and women criss-cross France with their motto of *"Esprit d'Enthousiasme."* They are supported by a telephone advice service, ranked third nationally in 3M's sectors and 32nd among 1,000 tested companies. 3M engages in pan-European marketing in many cases, but has found that in France, as elsewhere in Europe, all customers want the same thing—fast delivery, accurate documents, and good follow-up. Aside from Post-it, 3M France makes visual systems, matchprints, and Scotch Magic Tape. Richelsen says the company long ago mastered the intricacies of Europe-wide transportation out of France, but that the Single Market will mean simplification of documents as borders come down. The Single Market also will drive prices down to the "lowest common denominator," as efficiency gains are passed on to customers. He thinks that those companies that have not rationalized their activities will be "in trouble."

3M has won some prestige fire barrier and anti-theft surveillance contracts for the famous glass pyramid at the Louvre Museum. Going European has meant only three Americans among the French workforce of 3,700. The company suffered a setback when the French government barred its purchase of local spongemaker, Spontex. The bid had come at a time when France was worried about foreign takeovers. The mood has changed as French companies invest and acquire in the US. 3M has shrugged off the "defeat," raised sales from its five plants to $800 million a year, notably in video cassettes, and won work on the European Airbus. Looking ahead from his office in the company's modern building in a Parisian satellite town, Richelsen adds, "The consumer is going to benefit from the Single Market. For us, it means better productivity and imagination—and, above all, quality and keeping close to the stores." On a broader front, 3M is one of the official sponsors of the 1992 Winter Olympics in ski-mad France.

SPIDER SYSTEMS

The pretty Chevreuse Valley, south-west of Paris, once known for its colony of famous British exiles—the Duke of Windsor, Group Captain Peter Townsend and Nancy Mitford—is today high-tech country with French, German, and Japanese firms—and a Scottish newcomer. Spider Systems, an Edinburgh maker of equipment for computer networking, has established a marketing center at the technology park in the valley at St. Aubin, near Versailles. The investment in France is "going very well indeed, exceeding our expectations for both turnover and profits," said Tony Bellhouse, group marketing manager for Spider, a company with worldwide sales of $40 million. The decision to be "close to the French marketplace and to operate like a French company" was dictated partly by a lack of strong distributors in France for the company's products, but mainly by the size and strength of the French economy. The French staff at St. Aubin, reporting to French-speaking staff in Edinburgh, is now selling directly to major concerns such as Renault, Unisys, Bull (the state computer company), and the Ministry of Justice. A sign of the times was Spider's ability to bypass the Ministry of Industry and the regional development agency, DATAR, hire its own consultants, and then pick its site. The ease of procedures shows how far France has gone in dismantling previous restrictions on investment. A decade ago there were delays, considerable red tape, and sectors considered "off limits," particularly to major American and Japanese investors. The former head of the glass multinational Saint-Gobain, Roger Fauroux, who became Minister of Industry, changed much of that kind of welcome. He approved continued backing for state firms such as Bull and Thomson electronics, and believed, like many other ministers, in a mixed state–private economy, but when it came to jobs he said things like, "Better Japanese than unemployed." Of the 200 to 300 foreign investment dossiers that do come the Ministry's way each year, perhaps 20 are examined closely and only one or two refused. The question mark is over the attitudes of the new French Premier, Madame Edith Cresson, who in the past has urged a joint US–European strategy against the Japanese. Premier

Cresson wants to protect France's automobile, high-definition TV, and computer sectors. Yet she is faced with high unemployment—now 2.6 million.

MARKS & SPENCER

Success in Britain limited further growth possibilities for retailer Marks & Spencer. The group turned to Europe and opened its first store on Paris's Boulevard Haussmann right across from the French capital's two top retailers, Galeries Lafayette and Au Printemps. Few British retailers of this size had ventured into France before, but the Marks & Spencer gamble has been successful. The British aimed deliberately at a segment of the market between France's huge and unique hypermarkets, which sell clothes as well as food (even yachts, in some cases), and the thousands of small, often expensive boutiques which provide much of the chic on the streets of Paris and provincial cities. Marks & Spencer seems to have found the right pricing, has offered more colorful clothes than it does in Britain, has heavily promoted its hassle-free refund policy—and has cleverly exploited the fact that the French spend twice as much on food as the British.

Clothes are mainly trucked from Britain and now the truck convoys continue south to Spain. Many foodstuffs also cross the Channel, for the French buy British food as much out of curiosity as for the taste. British biscuits, jams, pork pies, and puddings are to be seen in the best Parisian apartments. Some snobbery is involved—one up on the Duponts. The fact that Prince Charles and Princess Diana visited Marks & Spencer while on an official visit to Paris underlined the clout of the group, which also owns Brooks Brothers. It certainly impressed the average French shopper.

At the same time the Parisian store was established, the group also "tested" Lyons, France's second city, and Brussels. By 1991, there were nine stores across France, two in Belgium and one in Madrid. Marks & Spencer then made the $175 million decision to have 40 stores across Europe by the mid-1990s, 25 of them in France, but also eight in Spain where Marks & Spencer thinks retailing will continue its upward trend. All this represents huge investments but the $10 billion a year group prefers to be in top, downtown sites with secondary stores in the very best suburbs offering products that require space, such as home furnishings. In Paris, for example, Marks & Spencer is constantly expanding its flagship store which specializes in sweaters, tea and cakes, while offering different items in the out-of-town stores. French managers have been appointed at most stores, but the "look" remains very British. "We are seen as different—quiet, pleasant stores with goods presented differently," said a Marks & Spencer's executive. The two major French stores, opposite Marks & Spencer in Paris, certainly do things very differently. Both are packed with boutiques and stalls underlining the very strong presence of franchising in France. The British have discovered some marketing truths useful for the Single Market. French shoppers know what they want. If they have set out to buy all-wool or all-cotton garments they will settle for nothing less. They want colors. The women want fitting rooms (which they have at French stores of Marks & Spencer). They want "bargains," particularly in home furnishings where French prices are often astronomical. The choice in Marks & Spencer stores in France is now often broader than in Britain. Certainly, the marketing ideas flow back and forth and Marks is discovering that you can be one of the world's biggest retailers and still learn.

• *Eyewitness* •

French and Anglo-Saxon attitudes towards a deal differ greatly. Barry Stobbs explains why. He first set foot in France in 1948, runs a management consulting firm, and has watched both sides make mistakes. He advises: "The Anglo-Saxon deal is input-dominated: the objective is to give up as little as possible, to put as little as possible into the kitty before the other fellow signs. It follows that the happier *you* are with the deal, the more likely it is that the other fellow will become unhappy with it as time goes by, hence the legal emphasis on contractual escape clauses.

"The French deal, on the other hand, is output-dominated in the sense that it is based not on compromise, but on each side's continuing to pursue its own objectives while benefitting from the fact that many of these are shared by the partner. The French deal tends to be loose, optimistic. It very often does not envisage failure at all, and the only negative note may be the naming of a mutually acceptable referee to take care of disputes." Stobbs concludes that many potentially promising deals founder before they're signed because neither side is sufficiently aware of differences in culture and philosophy—even though they both agree on the value of the deal itself and are even enthusiastic about it. Stobbs' instructive reasoning is not necessarily applicable to the biggest Anglo-French deal of all—the Channel Tunnel. Here, the issue is more the cost calculation basis of major construction companies.

The Bois de Boulogne park in Paris contains exclusive clubs where discussion of serious money matters has replaced the century-old dallying of ladies looking like Michelle Morgan and gentlemen resembling Charles Boyer. That's the price of progress. These are not clubs in the London sense, but highly-fashionable, partly outdoor establishments with chic restaurants, tennis courts, and pools. Forget about membership, seek an invitation. The Polo de Paris says it's full for five years, the very snooty Cercle de Bois de Boulogne-Tir aux Pigeons is not taking newcomers for seven or eight years. The Polo is the place where the heads of Guinness talked merger with the Louis Vuitton Moët Hennessy group—a merger that forged the biggest drinks and luxury goods conglomerate in the world. Also in the Bois: the Racing Club. An invitation is necessary in every case. In town, favorite (and private) meeting places are the Travellers Club at 25 Ave des Champs Elysees and the Cercle Interallie at 33 Faubourg Saint Honoré, near the American and British embassies. Other haunts of businessmen: Maxim's Business Club, 3 Rue Royale, in the famous restaurant; the Automobile Club, very British in atmosphere, at 6 Place de la Concorde, just about the best address in the city, and the St. James's Club, Paris branch of the London club, at 5 Place Chancellier Adenauer, with a board ranging from Catherine Deneuve to the contemporary Marquis de Sade. The popular Cercle Japonais is at 97 Ave des Champs-Elysees.

:::::::::::::::::THE LEADERS:::::::::::::::::::

TOP 20 INDUSTRIAL COMPANIES (1989)

		Sales (1,000s FF)	*Profits*
(1)	Renault	174,477,000	9,289,000
(2)	PSA Peugeot	152,955,000	10,301,000
(3)	Elf-Aquitaine	149,802,000	7,218,000
(4)	CGE	143,897,000	4,937,000
(5)	Total-CFP	107,894,000	2,206,000
(6)	Usinor-Sacilor	97,042,000	6,763,000
(7)	Pechiney	88,472,000	3,542,000
(8)	Thomson	76,663,000	497,000
(9)	Rhône-Poulenc	73,068,000	4,092,000
(10)	Saint-Gobain	66,093,000	4,311,000
(11)	Michelin	55,255,000	2,449,000
(12)	BSN	48,669,000	2,698,000
(13)	Bouygues	47,005,000	573,000
(14)	Schneider	45,127,000	877,000
(15)	GEC-Alsthom	44,935,000	1,647,000
(16)	IBM-France	41,336,000	2,562,000
(17)	Shell-France	38,479,000	2,823,000
(18)	Beghin-Say	36,947,000	1,138,000
(19)	SGE	35,406,000	382,000
(20)	Aerospatiale	33,903,000	129,000

(Source: L'Expansion)

1990 Results

Falls

Renault F1.21b (−80 percent); Peugeot F9.26b (−10 percent); Rhone-Poulenc F2b (−50 percent); Michelin −F3.1b; Compagnie Financière de Suez F3.85b (−5 percent); Sanofi F853m (−8.9 percent); Bull −F6.8b (−90 percent); Thomson F2.16b (−18 percent); Saint-Gobain F3.35b (−22 percent); Au Printemps F317m (−41 percent); BNP F1.6b (−53 percent); Société Generale F2.68b (−25 percent); Gan F2.3b (−7 percent); Valeo F650m (−36 percent); CMB

Packaging F1.02b (− 13 percent); Cie Financière Paribas F2.54b (− 26 percent).

Gains

Cap Gemini Sogeti F623m (+ 19 percent); Elf Aquitaine F10.5b (+ 46 percent); Accor F900m (+ 8.6 percent); Club Med F395m (+ 5 percent); CCF F813m (+ 15 percent); LVMH F3.38b (+ 15 percent); BSN F3.1b (+ 14.6%); Credit Agricole F4.7b (+ 4 percent); Credit Lyonnais F3.7b (+ 18.5 percent); Lafarge Coppee F2.19b (+ 1 percent); Pernod Ricard F1.1b (+ 14 percent); Alcatel Alsthom F5.1b (+ 29 percent); Galeries Lafayette F140 million (+ 19.7 percent); Oreal F1.7b (+ 15 percent).

TOP 20 BANKS (1989)

		(1,000s FF)	
		Assets	*Profits*
(1)	Credit Agricole	1,400,647,100	4,520,400
(2)	BNP	1,339,707,822	3,413,765
(3)	Credit Lyonnais	1,219,685,000	3,130,000
(4)	Société Générale	1,017,455,000	3,561,000
(5)	Caisse d'Epargne	883,954,484	2,836,864
(6)	Paribas	802,608,000	3,449,000
(7)	Compagnie de Suez	724,444,000	4,062,000
(8)	CIC	432,509,000	1,026,000
(9)	Banques Populaires	374,492,000	1,275,000
(10)	Credit Mutuel	327,000,000	995,000
(11)	CCF	263,951,000	704,236
(12)	BFCE	258,116,475	1,321
(13)	Caisse Centrale BP	127,078,142	170,983
(14)	Fuji Bank	97,381,728	4,526
(15)	Sanwa Bank	94,537,503	2,449
(16)	BFCM	89,780,503	577,228
(17)	Worms	69,934,994	208,685
(18)	BP-Bred	67,447,264	110,768
(19)	Banque Arbitrage/Credit	53,470,081	87,088
(20)	Parisien Réescompte	52,535,568	300,514

(Source: L'Expansion magazine)

TOP 12 INSURANCE COMPANIES (1989)

		Premiums	Profits
		(1,000s FF)	
(1)	UAP	66,481,946	3,421,738
(2)	Groupe Victoire	50,734,929	1,743,797
(3)	Axa-Midi	44,679,400	2,321,000
(4)	AGF	38,221,506	2,570,377
(5)	GAN	27,450,000	2,467,500
(6)	Caisse Prevoyance	23,435,456	702,767
(7)	Groupama	22,261,000	1,747,000
(8)	Predica	21,625,463	360,341
(9)	Mutuelles du Mans	16,158,500	1,183,200
(10)	Athena	10,571,025	729,668
(11)	GPA Assurances	10,571,000	730,000
(12)	Générali France	9,500,000	250,000

(Source: L'Expansion magazine)

KEY CONTACTS

USEFUL PARIS TELEPHONE NUMBERS

Trade and Commercial Information

European Community Office: 33-1-4063-3800
Datar (Industrial Development Agency): 33-1-4065-1234

Ministries

Defense: 33-1-4065-3011
Economy: 33-1-4004-0404
European Affairs: 33-1-4755-8334
Foreign Affairs: 33-1-4753-5353
Industry: 33-1-4556-3636

Chambers of Commerce

Member Nations
Belgium/Luxembourg:
33-1-4562-4487
Britain: 33-1-4505-1308
Germany: 33-1-458-3535
Ireland: 33-1-4508-3500
Italy: 33-1-4225-4188
Netherlands: 33-1-4563-5430
Portugal: 33-1-4544-5339
Spain: 33-1-4752-4574

Others
Franco–American:
33-1-4256-0500
Franco–Arab: 33-1-4553-2012
France Canada: 33-1-4359-3238
France–Latin America:
33-1-4544-0340
Franco–Soviet: 33-1-4225-9710
Japan: 33-1-4563-0550
Norway: 33-1-4745-1490
Sweden: 33-1-4261-4232
United States: 33-1-4723-8026
International Chamber of
Commerce: 33-1-4953-2828

Embassies

Member Nations
Belgium: 33-1-4380-6100
Britain: 33-1-4266-9142
Denmark: 33-1-4723-5420
Germany: 33-1-4299-7800
Greece: 33-1-4227-7863
Ireland: 33-1-4500-2087
Italy: 33-1-4544-3890
Luxembourg: 33-1-4555-1337
Netherlands: 33-1-4306-6188
Portugal: 33-1-4727-3529
Spain: 33-1-4723-6183

Others
Canada: 33-1-4723-0101
Finland: 33-1-4705-3545
Iceland: 33-1-4522-8154
Japan: 33-1-4766-0222
New Zealand: 33-1-4500-2411
Norway: 33-1-4723-7278
Sweden: 33-1-4555-9215
United States: 33-1-4296-1202

KEY ADDRESSES IN THE REGIONS

North

Nord/Pas de Calais Développement
16 Residence Breteuil
Parc Saint-Maur
59800 Lille
Tel: 33-20.55.98.82
Fax: 33-2055-3915.

East

Strasbourg Regional Development Council
"Le Concorde"
4 Quai Kleber
67055 Strasbourg Cedex
Tel: 33-8832-5451
Fax: 33-8875-1590.

Apeilor Regional Development
1 Place du Pont à Seille
57004 Metz Cedex 1
Tel: 33-87.75.36.18
Fax: 33-8775-2199.

Ile de France

Agency for Corporate Development
Ile de France Regional Council
251 Rue de Vaugirard
75015 Paris
Tel: 33-1-4043-7370
Fax: 33-1-4043-7071.

Midi-Pyrénées

Bureau Regional d'Investissement et d'Accoull
Conseil Regional
14 Rue de Tivoli
31068 Toulouse Cedex
Tel: 33-6133-5084
Fax: 33-6125-6785.

Rhône-Alpes

Aderly (Lyons Development)
20 Rue de la Bourse
69002 Lyons
Tel: 33-7240-5858
Fax: 33-7240-5735.

Riviera

Cote d'Azur Développement
10 Rue de la Prefecture
BP 142
06003 Nice Cedex
Tel: 33-9392-4242
Fax: 33-9380-0576.

Facts on Germany

. . . .

Capital Berlin
Population (1989) 78.6m (West: 62m; East:
  16.6m)
Working Population West (1988) 26.9m; East
  (1985) 8m
Unemployment West: 7%; East: 15%
GNP Growth 1990: 4.5%; 1991 (est.) 3%
GNP Growth (East) 1990: −20%
Per Capita (1988): $19,581
Inflation 1990: 3%; 1991 (est.) 4%
Trade Total exports $420 billion
Trade Surplus 1989: DM134.5b; 1990:
  DM107.3b; 1991 (est.)—DM10–15b.
Current Account 1989 DM104b; 1990:
  DM72b; 1991 (est.)—DM10–15b.
German–US Trade
  US Exports (CIF) 1988: $16.6b
  German Exports (FOB) 1988: $26b

. . . .

GERMANY

"We can reach our objective, the economic, social and ecological unity of our country, in three to five years." Chancellor Helmut Kohl, Spring, 1991

"We will do everything to make sure that the upswing takes place in the whole of the economy, that there is no two-class society." Jorgen Möllemann, German Economics Minister

CHEERED BY RAPTUROUS EAST GERMAN CROWDS IN 1990, BOOED AND insulted by the same people in 1991, Chancellor Kohl is maintaining his optimism in public with messages like the above. The French have a word for such a posture—*pathétique,* meaning *moving* rather than *helpless.* The situation in the eastern part of the country has at times seemed helpless. Detlev Rohwedder, the strappingly tall business executive who was given the task of privatizing East Germany, was cut down by terrorists claiming they were acting for the jobless. Rohwedder had said: "The restructuring of East Germany will not fail for lack of money." That policy stands after his death. West Germany will reluctantly give up part of its wealth in order to lift East Germany out of the trough of collapse. Part of the problem is the sheer *Angst* (fear) of 17 million people removed from the cocoon of a centralized economy with its guarantees, even if these consisted of poorly paid jobs, cheap housing, and limited travel. Business initiative has been stifled, the market ignored. Some experts say it will take 15 years for the East's GNP to match that of the West. Now that the initial enthusiasm from the West German private sector has subsided, the government is liquidating East German firms with greater caution, subsidizing others and offering more to foreign, as well as German, investors.

The German mood has swung sharply from the euphoria of 1989 when the Berlin Wall came down and the joy of 1990 when elections were held and the country was officially reunited. No one still says that 1992 will be the year of another *Wirtshaftswunder,* or economic miracle, of the kind that the former West Germany experienced after the Second World War. The western part of the country saw a boom in 1989 and 1990, helped by initial demand in the East, and was set to continue its expansion in 1991. Meanwhile, the eastern economy went into a tailspin as the obsolete nature of its structures became only too evident. The former East Germany had lived on a cheap mark and exports, mainly to once secure Comecon markets that have evaporated. One for one monetary union, described as a disaster by former Bundesbank president Karl Otto Pohl, in one of the most celebrated comments of 1991, revalued the East German money by 300–400 percent, while wages rose sharply in the East. A Berkeley university team of economists concluded that at best one in ten East German companies could stay afloat in world markets. Unemployment and short-time working rose at a startling rate as companies went under and there were fears that the rate of the jobless could reach anything from 30 to 50 percent. This would have the effect of swelling anti-Kohl demonstrations from hundreds of thousands to millions.

Most outside observers counted on the Germans' organizational skills and disciplinary traits to overcome the crisis, but all agreed that radical measures could be necessary, particularly to overcome bureaucracy. One proposal, namely to subsidize most of East German wages in order to give eastern firms a better chance in world markets could run counter to German financial orthodoxy. Ironically, Germany's problems in balancing the economies of its western and eastern halves meant West Germans digging deeper into their pockets just as they longed for a life of comfort, security, and prosperity. A nationwide poll revealed this new German dream. The model for almost half the country, the pollsters learned, is Switzerland, admired for its wealth and independence. Sweden came a distant second with the major industrial nations, including the US, way back. The poll, conducted by the Infratest Institute for the *Süddeutsche Zeitung* newspaper in Munich, underlined Chancellor Kohl's problem in calling for generosity and national solidarity by citizens, industry, political parties, and unions. Before the all-German general elections at the end of 1990, the Chancellor had pledged no higher taxes. The government quickly changed course in 1991 announcing higher salary, income, and corporate taxes, as well as indirect taxes. Certainly, Germany had to pay a heavy contribution towards the Gulf War, in which it was very much a non-participant, but most of the $60 billion of extra taxpayers' money will flow east. More is needed to help the eastern länder with crash programs of housing, schools, hospitals and offices and for cleaning the environment—all on top of job creation, massive writing-off of company debts, and maintenance of some very shaky sectors in business. Until recently, the government agency, the Treuhandanstalt, has been closing many of the 9,000 eastern companies it was supposed to privatize. Billions will now be spent on trying to turn around "lame duck" companies prior to eventual sale. In the East, the services sector has been less buffeted by the slump, while the construction industry could pick up soon. The Bonn government may "twist the arm" of German companies to invest more east of the River Elbe, and so follow the big three banks, Deutsche, Dresdner, and Commerzbank, the car companies and the department store chains which were early to invest in the eastern half. Some foreign companies complain that the best East German companies have been "reserved" for West German concerns. The Germans are countering this impression—strengthened by Allianz buying the East German insurance industry—and both government and the Treuhandanstalt are seeking to persuade western merchant banks, as well as the big German banks, to take on mandates for groups of companies destined for privatization. One early example was Warburg bank, of London, which was charged with selling the East's Interhotel chain which covered the whole former East German state. The government has also changed the law to overcome the problem of one million land and property claims in the East by people claiming to be the former owners. Restitution is no longer the order of the day, whereas compensation is, enabling new investments to move ahead. In some cases, western concerns may be paid to move to the East to save companies, notably in chemicals. Inward investors will be helped to clear polluted land and water in many areas. Commerzbank and the Ifo Economic Research Institute in Munich have put chemicals, petroleum refining, rubber, and plastics at the top of the list of problem industries. These industries have only a "medium" competitive position *vis à vis* western Germany—a large technological gap and a "major" environmental problem. Metal production, non-metallic minerals, ceramics, and glass have the same environmental ranking, but do better with competitiveness and technology. Mechanical and electrical engineering, precision engineering, and steel are said to be competitive as are parts of office equipment and EDP production, consumer electronics, opto-electronics, and communications equipment. Some disagree with these upbeat rankings. For example, the office equipment, EDP, and related sectors have fallen behind in technology. Everywhere, there is a lack of marketing skills. Radical measures are no doubt needed in the East, but the new, hostile demonstrations have forced Bonn to adopt a strategy of massive grants blended with greater care for the human aspects of the drama. Planting an enterprise culture and a spirit of initiative in the East will take many seasons, for the area has not known freedom since the arrival of the Nazis way back in 1933.

:::::::::::MARKET OPPORTUNITIES :::::::::::

The German economic boom of 1989–90 was dented by increased income taxes, designed to help pay for unification, and high interest rates. Both consumer and company spending have been affected. In the new states in the East, the post-reunification spending spree has dwindled as collapsing industries and falling production have swollen unemployment and short-time working. The western part of the economy was set to grow at a lower three percent in 1991, while the East's "bottom" has been difficult to fathom. The upturn will come, but when is the big question—two years was the mid-1991 estimate of the German economic ministry. However, Germany is Europe's largest market and German industry, which worked at near full production in 1990, will still be buying in capital and intermediary goods, while the East's infrastructure needs will not go away, unrelated as they are to any fall-off in consumer spending. Increased imports led to a sharp decline in Germany's trade surplus in 1990 and purchases from abroad are expected to continue, albeit at a lower rate. It will take a decade to fulfill the Eastern region's need for telecoms, houses, offices, new plants, and road and rail links. The German market may no longer be lucrative, but it is still one that is full of opportunities. The West Germans continue to enjoy a very high standard of living. Quality and service remain the watchwords for the exporter to Germany. American goods are most highly regarded in the top end of the market where the latest technology is the factor—computer software and peripherals; electronic components; health care and medical devices; and synthetics.

American goods have been selling well in the past couple of years. For 1989, the latest full-year figures available, computer and peripheral sales amounted to $5.3 billion in a total market of $18.5 billion, while growth through 1992 is expected to be 10 to 15 percent a year. US companies sold $3.3 billion worth of software in a $10 billion market. A growth rate of 10 percent is expected in the U.S. import share. There is room too for considerable growth in personal computers. Michael Whittington, of the American company AST Deutschland, regards the German market as three to five years behind the U.S. "However, the PC user and decision maker is as informed as his or her US counterpart and the German market will continue to be the center of activity in Europe for the next three years." The CAD/CAM/CAE/CIM market is expected to reach close to $650 million in the western part of the country in 1991–92, with US companies supplying 70 percent. State-of-the-art technology is valued in Germany if it contributes to lower labor costs. Automation has enabled the Germans to remain competitive in automobiles and machinery. Other sectors of interest are laser and opto-electronics, electronic components, electronics industry production and test equipment, automotive parts and equipment, analytical and scientific equipment, chemicals, industrial process controls, telecommunications, and fiber optics. Opportunities are also to be found in the franchising, robotics, environmental, aerospace, sporting goods, and photographic fields. Trade fairs are the most cost-effective vehicles for introducing new or improved products to the German market. Hannover is a major fair city for aerospace and the CEBIT show. The latter attracts 4,500 exhibitors from four dozen countries involved in information technology. Frankfurt has its auto show and many others. Munich specializes in fairs for electronics and computer systems. Berlin has huge fair grounds. Stuttgart is increasing the number of its shows, while in Leipzig in the eastern half, the biggest, traditional, old-style communist fair, is being given a new look. The US Commerce Department supports exhibitors at the Ispo and IWA sporting goods fairs, the Heimtextil and Techtextile textile and apparel fairs, Automechanica for auto parts and accessories, Biotechnica for biotechnology, Analytica for analytical and scientific instrumentation, and the Cat CAD/CAM show. The size of the German market and the advent of the Single Market have seen a surge in takeovers of German companies by foreign investors. Most of the investment in the East has been by fellow German companies, although western multinationals are either expanding what had been a modest presence—the case of Dow Chemical, General Motors, Caterpillar, Eastman Kodak, General Foods,

IBM and others—or opening up, such as Philip Morris and Coca Cola. Old hands among the Americans number some one hundred, ranging from General Motors to small software companies. General Motors announced a joint venture between Opel, its West German subsidiary and the manufacturer of the former East German Wartburg car, Automobile Eisenbach, to assemble Opel Vectras. Newcomers include Salomon Brothers, Arthur D. Little, lawyers Baker & McKenzie, Arthur Anderson, Computerland, Manpower, McDonald's, Woodward-Clyde, Price Waterhouse, Avon, Marsh & McLennan, Kellog, and NCR. The American presence, however, remains a drop in the ocean among thousands of inter-German joint ventures, some real, some existing on paper. The clarification recently of ownership rights—former owners will receive government compensation rather than have property returned—will ease deals in the East. The key bodies are: Treuhandanstalt, the German government trust agency charged with selling 8,000 eastern firms, at Berlin Mitte, Tel: 49-30-3154-1037/1933; 49-30-3154-1982/1036 (fax); the American Chamber of Commerce, 12 Rossmarkt, Frankfurt/Main, Tel: 49-69-28341, and in Berlin at 31 Budapesterstrasse, 1000 Berlin 30, Tel: 49-30-2615586, Fax: 49-30-2622600. The Chamber now has a branch in Dresden. Above all, it has built up an excellent information series, *Investment in Eastern Germany.* This includes *Doing Business in Eastern Germany,* 40 pages of contacts and addresses plus information on the Treuhandanstalt with which the Chamber maintains close contacts; *Investment Incentive Programs; Opportunities and Obstacles* (in East Germany); and *Investment Opportunities in Saxony.* All are available at $25. The Chamber also offers East German company profiles and the Chamber membership directory is a good buy at $200. The role of the Berlin Economic Development Corporation (Wirtshaftsförderung Berlin) has grown with unification. It is at 1 Budapesterstrasse, Berlin, Tel: 49-30-264-880. Non-German hotel and real estate companies are active in the East, but retailing has been taken over mainly by the big West German department stores. Karstadt, the biggest, is now in Dresden, Halle, Leipzig, and Magdebourg. The latter is the site also of a future, high-tech business city by the British ITC project management group and the Irish contractors MF Kent. Another of the German Big Three retailers, Kauhoff, has stores—also of the ex GDR chain Centrum—in Berlin, Chemnitz, and Rostock, while the Hertie chain is expanding in Berlin. It is in Berlin that foreign retailers are the most visible—Benetton, and New Man. The Japanese are in and around Unter den Linden. Accor, the French hotel group, is expanding its three-star hotels in the eastern part of the country in collaboration with the former state-owned Interhotels, as is the German Kempinski chain. Radisson Hotels International has East Germany as part of its drive east, as does Britain's Forte. Berlin is the main attraction for hoteliers, but new western hotels are expected also in Leipzig and Dresden.

INTERNATIONAL TRADE

Germany remains an export-led economy, despite the dip in its trade surplus in 1990, a trend that continued in 1991. Imports rose because of the strong growth of the economy, while exports were affected by weakness in traditional export markets such as the US, Britain, France, and Italy. Sales of machine tools, textile, and construction machinery were down and even the chemical giants, Bayer and BASF, reported lower profits linked to the world slowdown. Other factors were a fall in orders from the former Comecon countries, notably the Soviet Union, and a strong deutschmark. The mark weakened at the outset of 1991 and there were hopes of avoiding the situation that BASF found in 1990 in Japan, where sales rose by ten percent in local currency, but fell by the same margin in Deutschmarks. Many companies have made heavy investments in the eastern part of Germany. It all amounted to a situation where profits fell by up to ten percent. Yet, as GATT, the General Agreement on Tariffs and Trade, stated in its annual report for 1990, united Germany is now the world's biggest exporter, ahead of the US. The dollar value of German exports of visible goods rose to $420 billion, some $26 billion above the US. However, the 1.5 percent rise in German exports was lower than the US increase of 8.5 percent and Japan's 4.5 percent (to $286 billion). A lower Deutschmark will improve Germany's market share, as will an economic improvement in the East—and some kind of resumption of orders from the Soviet Union. The German boom is far from over and recovery in the US and the EC could bring trade back to "normal."

S P O T L I G H T

• *AG or GmbH?* •

The German way of conducting business has its own acronyms. AG is for *Aktiengesellschaft*, a joint stock company with DM100,000 minimum capital and shares with a face value of at least DM50. An AG can be formed by at least five persons, individuals, or legal entities who need not reside in Germany. Shareholders are not personally liable for debts incurred. Shares of many AGs are quoted on one of Germany's eight exchanges. By law, AGs have a supervisory board *(Aufsichtsrat)* and a board of management *(Vorstand)*, but there is strict division of responsibilities, with the Vorstand carrying out day-to-day business.

The GmbH—*Gesellschaft mit beschränkter Haftung*—is a limited liability company in which shareholders' liability is limited to the amounts stipulated in the partnership agreement, a minimum of DM50,000. The GmbH is the most common form of organization for starting a new business.

There exist also general partnerships (OHG), where two or more persons trade jointly with responsibility for business debts being shared as well as borne by each individual partner; limited partnerships (KG) of two or more people, with a general partner being liable for business debts and containing at least one partner with limited liability; and the more recent, combined limited partnership and limited liability company (GmbH and KG). In this type of enterprise, the general partner is the GmbH, responsible for debts to the extent of its assets, with the limited partners responsible only to the extent of their shares. There is also the *Einzelunternehmen,* or sole proprietorship, where business and private property are put on the line.

Still, Germany was set to record a current account deficit—the first in a decade—and see the surplus of its purely trade balance dwindle from 10 billion DM to around 20 billion. More than half of Germany's trade is with other members of the EC. If the EFTA countries are included, the proportion rises to more than 60 percent. In the recent past, West Germany with 20 percent of the EC's population has been transacting a quarter of total internal trade and supplying a third of the imports of other members. Even more impressive was West Germany's 40 percent of the EC's internal imports in engineering and automotive products. It remains for Germany to "digest" the former East Germany and to find a "satisfactory" level for its currency.

German trade with the countries of eastern Europe represents only five percent of total German foreign trade, but German firms have long been in the market and are well-placed to benefit from an economic improvement in the other half of Europe. An examination of OECD figures shows that Germany has been responsible for 40 percent of OECD countries' exports to Hungary, 36 percent to Poland, and a quarter of those to Romania. Plus, of course, 22 percent of exports to the Soviet Union—until the political and economic crisis there in the winter of 1990–91.

TRANSPORTATION AND COMMUNICATIONS

Germany, the geographical and trading center not only of the EC but also of a future European Economic Area, embracing Eastern Europe, has excellent transportation and communications networks. Yet, it faces an enormous bill in the 1990s running into many, many billions of dollars. Certainly, the 5,000-plus miles of *Autobahn* started by Hitler form Europe's best road system and predate by many years Britain's motorways, France's *autoroutes* and Italy's *autostradas*. Yet they are taking a pounding from Europe's largest car and truck fleet and need to be extended and broadened in order to play their future East-West transit role. The Bundesbahn rail network is highly efficient for passengers and links major cities in just a few hours. The moving of growing quantities of freight is not perfect, but more money is being spent to improve the road-rail freight transfer system, Combi transport, which is better than most in Europe and which strives to emulate the US RoadRailer. Airports are modern, particularly Frankfurt, Europe's aerial freight hub. Munich has a brand new airport, while a super airport is planned for the capital, Berlin, to replace Tegel and Schönefeld. The German postal service is to join with five partners (France, Netherlands, Sweden, Canada and Australia's TNT company) to create an international courier service, GD Net BV, in Amsterdam; a major challenger to American courier services. Telephones, naturally, work well in the land of telecoms leader Siemens.

One German problem with transport is common to all EC states. It's rooted in history and has been amplified by the EC's failure so far to persuade nations to relinquish national control of their transport infrastructure development and hand it over to Brussels. The problem is that road and rail services in Germany—and elsewhere—look inwards and do not give priority to international links. The coming Channel Tunnel is the exception, as it will link London not only to Brussels and Paris, but also Cologne and other German cities.

Even Germany, to some extent, has neglected its railways. Germany's second, bigger transport problem is to link western and eastern networks. The Russians literally took away tracks after the war and train times rose above pre-war levels on often one-way lines. New west-east services have been opened, but the high-speed Hannover-Berlin line, on which work will start in 1992, will not be finished until 1996, the year that the former East Germany is expected to achieve more or less economic parity with the West. The immediate Bundesbahn projects concern traditional north-south links, such as the new, high-speed Hamburg–Munich line, a service that is similar to the French high-speed TGV trains. These two "rival" high-speed networks have yet to be linked, partly because of "buy national" policies of France with Alsthom and Germany with a Siemens-led consortium for the ICE express. The two countries collaborate on space rockets and armaments, but not yet on the more pressing matter of transport within the Single Market. One of the main "missing links" in high-speed European rail transport is that between Paris, Munich, and Central Europe.

Meanwhile, some estimates put Germany's bill for modernizing its eastern transportation and communications as high as $250 billion. A start has been made, but for the moment money is mainly going towards patching-up and planning for future, grander improvements needed for the future western and eastern markets of 430 million people in the European Economic Area—EC, EFTA, and the former East Bloc countries. Federal transport minister Günter Krause, a former East German, announced 1991 spending of DM9 billion for the eastern Reichsbahn as against DM11 billion for the Bundesbahn. However, the technological disparity is such that the two railways will be run under separate management for some years.

In the heady days of 1989, Frenchman Jacques Attali, then President Mitterrand's adviser, now head of the London-based European Bank for Reconstruction and Development (Berd), envisaged that the fall of the Berlin Wall would herald the day when high-speed trains, preferably French, would race between Paris and Moscow, via Germany and Poland. Unfortunately, that day is a very long way off and must wait until Germany unites its transport networks and everyone in Europe thinks more "horizontally." Minister Krause also announced outlays of DM2.5 billion on resurfacing and expanding decayed eastern roads, notably Berlin to the main Baltic port of Rostock, plus improvements on the Berlin to Hamburg road, scene of Europe's worst car and truck jams. The magnitude of the problem can be gauged from the fact that the former communist government built just 300 miles of new highways in 30 years. With roads, more than double is being spent in the West, but the Bonn ministry says the balance will change as the eastern modernization gets underway. Slowly, Europe's common approach is improving with harmonization of truck loads, containers and so-called "cabotage," or the right of outsiders to pick and deliver in other countries.

In the ports sector, eastern harbors have to be modernized to take advantage of their Baltic links and to avoid losing the bulk of their business to western ports. Eastern Rostock, however, will never regain its former importance. The respective shipping lines are coming together, while the Rhine–Main–Danube Canal is destined to play a major future role in German and European freight handling. As for air transport, the former East German airline, Interflug, has disappeared, leaving Lufthansa in a strengthened position as national carrier. Freight now accounts for a quarter of Lufthansa's revenues. The airline is also reinforcing contacts with Aeroflot without going as far as setting up a joint airline like British Airways with the new Air Russia. At home, it has linked with the Bundespost for a same-day letter and document air courier service.

Siemens is to the forefront in East German modernization and is present in practically all East European markets. For the moment, there are telecoms delays between the western and eastern halves of Germany. The federal government has opened up satellite links for voice and non-voice services to bidding by the private sector and claims that the current East-West telecoms problem will be resolved by the end of 1992 or the beginning of 1993. This may be an optimistic forecast, but there is certainly a new urgency across the whole board of infrastructure matters—rail, road, air, and telecoms. Good news for Germany and Europe as a whole, as anyone who has tried to call the East or drive there will confirm.

S   P   O   T   L   I   G   H   T

• *Euro-trains* •

High-speed trains in France, Germany, and Italy, already challenge airlines on journeys up to 500 miles. A step towards a truly European bullet train network will be taken when the Channel Tunnel opens in the summer of 1993. The British, admittedly have yet to build a high-speed line from London to the tunnel mouth, meaning trains from Waterloo station will chug along at 62 mph. They will accelerate to 100 mph in the tunnel and roar off at 186 mph to Paris on the French high-speed line. London–Paris by train will be cut to three hours, London–Brussels to a quarter of an hour less. When the British do build their $10 billion line then another half hour will come off.

The orange French TGV train showed the way on Paris–

Lyons with dozens of daily trains packed with businesspeople. More recently came the blue TGV Atlantique services to the southwest—20 mph faster at 186 mph. More lines are being built and France will have a 820-mile, high-speed network in 1994. Brussels–Paris will be cut to a unbeatable (by the airlines) one hour and twenty-five minutes, city center to city center. The Germans have put their 156–175 mph ICE high-speed train on Hamburg–Munich and are now building a Hannover–Berlin line. Other lines have been approved for the $12 billion ICE program. Spain is to spend $18 billion on modernizing its railways, notably with a Madrid–Seville high-speed train. The Italians have their swaying Pendolino train linking Turin–Rome at 150 mph, with a faster, 190 mph train coming soon. However, these high speed trains are not compatible and cannot cross borders because of different weights and widths. Signalling is different as are electrical systems, while Spain has broad gauge track.

The *Trans Manche* London–Paris train will be able to cross borders and will point the way forward for cooperation between the main train builders—the Anglo-French consortium GEC-Alsthom, Germany's Siemens, and the Swedish-Swiss group ABB. At stake is $50 billion worth of contracts for the trains and more than $100 billion for new track. The target date for a Europe-wide network is 2020, with the tunnel an important part. Businesspeople will pay the equivalent of business class air travel, but will have telephones, faxes, computer plugs, meals—and no airport delays.

MANAGEMENT AND WORKFORCE

Reunification has brought two-pronged tension to the German labor scene. Labor unions in the West have been holding out for ten percent pay rises, far higher than anything sought before, arguing that four percent inflation and the 7.5 percent "reunification" income tax increases threaten their standard of living, the highest among the EC labor forces. It is based on a 35-hour week, generous medical and pension schemes, long vacations, and high salaries—in the case of Volkswagen workers of $30,000 to $35,000 a year, three times higher than VW's Spanish workers in Pamplona working on the same models. In the end, the unions were settling for just over six percent.

Management had balked at paying the 3.8 million western metalworkers the ten percent, arguing that competitiveness *vis à vis* the Japanese would be adversely affected. BMW, at one point, talked of switching some production to the US, although the stronger dollar put paid to this policy—or ploy.

Whereas West German manufacturing firms will no doubt get by on traditional quality and productivity, the problems facing those in the East are much greater, although some of the names are the same, *i.e.* productivity and wage increases. First, production in the East fell 50 percent in 1990 following the collapse of the old Comecon markets, the collapse of consumer confidence among the 17 million East Germans who rushed to buy western goods, and the collapse of companies because of obsolescence or decision of the Treuhandanstalt, the government holding company which had life-or-death powers over eastern industry in 1990. The main reason, however, was the explosion of production costs. Prior to reunification, the ost mark was estimated to be worth, at best, some 23 western pfennigs. Monetary union in July 1990, on a largely one-for-one basis, sent East German production costs rocketing. It was sudden over-evaluation, the reverse of the sharp Polish devaluation at the beginning of 1990 which boosted Polish exports considerably. Additionally, eastern wages rose by a third and are set to rise again. The principle accepted is for the wages of East German metalworkers to match those of their western countrymen by 1994. The deal gave eastern workers 62.5 percent of western wages (58.5 percent for office workers) in 1991. The scale of increases will take the eastern metalworkers to 70 percent in 1992 and 80 percent in 1993. The deal has been extended to include workers in the electrotechnical branch of the metallurgical industry. Working time will be reduced from 40 to 38 hours a week by 1995. But, as one cynic commented, this will happen only provided the jobs are still there. The Treuhandanstalt has been told to "soft pedal" closures, a decision which has led some experts to calculate the cost of saving and reviving East German industry in the 1990s as $236 billion, four times the sum spent by the West on the East in 1990–91.

On the human side, Franz Steinkühler, head of the IG Metall union, admits that it will be difficult to change the mentality of eastern workers, marked by "docility and passivity." It will also be difficult to stop the flow of skilled workers to the West, which could be as high as 300,000 when the 1991 statistics are ready. Another half a million are expected to commute to work in the West by 1992. Unemployment at the end of 1991 was around 14 percent, with just as many working part time. Long-term, the answer to the chronic eastern labor scene can only come with increased investment. Siemens, BASF and Volkswagen have shown the way and are being followed by General Motors, Coca Cola, the British (GKN and Unilever were two 1991 examples), and the French (Alsthom, BSN, Air Liquide, and Lafarge Coppée). All observers agree that bureaucracy, the "beamte mentality" in both West and East should be reduced to ease the task of German and foreign managers.

Are Germany's noted managers up to a task that resembles the rebuilding of West Germany after the Second World War? Writer Ferdinand Protzman had this view: "They have created Europe's most powerful economy and become the world's leading exporters through the diligence, craftsmanship, and meticulous organization that are national hallmarks. . . . But management experts say those very achievements and attributes have also entrenched a corporate leadership structure that is often inflexible and mindless in its conformity and that discourages initiative and independent thinking. . . to meet the daunting challenges of rebuilding eastern Germany's ruined economy and to continue to lead Europe's economies will require more modern and innovative thinking."

On a more day-to-day level, consultant Michael Whittingdon, offered this advice: "American companies in Germany face cultural differences—vacation time, work hours, and business practices. Germans do work shorter hours than their US counterparts, but work just as hard and are easily motivated. One of the difficult things to manage in German companies is the amount of time Germans are away from work—six weeks' vacation is normal plus extra sick days. This usually means that some positions are not filled during these times. There are positive and negative aspects to six weeks' vacation. The positive aspect for the employee is that one can truly relax and regenerate one's energy. US companies' two weeks' vacation is just too short. . . . In general, do your homework before starting to sell products in Germany. You usually have only one chance."

S   P   O   T   L   I   G   H   T

• *Labor Unions* •

The former West Germany's 16 labor unions are strong, rich and disciplined. About 42 percent of nonagricultural workers are union members and union representatives sit on the supervisory board of all large companies (the companies' other board, management, deals with day-to-day matters.) Employers fought hard to defeat this legal requirement, the so-called *Mitbestimmung*, introduced by the Social Democratic Party government in the 1970s, but seem now to accept it as both permanent and even desirable. After all, labor union board members have learned some of the facts of economic life, one of them being that their country's prosperity rests largely on exports—and that means that it must remain competitive.

How do labor union leaders view *Mitbestimmung?* One of them described his tactics as "antagonistic cooperation" with the bosses. He contrasted this favorably with what he saw as the more hostile approach to union-management bargaining in Britain, France, and Italy. Whether that view is right or wrong, and whether the system is chiefly responsible, the facts are that half of all workers now enjoy working weeks of fewer than 40 hours, along with pay and fringe benefits that are the highest in the entire European Community.

Employers and unions alike are committed to the value of training future workers and retraining people. About 1.8 million apprentices attend special schools—ten times more than in France, for example. This means that employers can often recruit directly from the schools rather than placing help-wanted advertisements in the newspapers.

The high skills of German workers counterbalance their

high cost by world standards. When all barriers to intra-European trade are removed Germany will feel the full force of competition from such relatively low-wage countries as Spain and Portugal. Many German labor leaders are advocating the formation of transnational unions that would raise wage and employment standards elsewhere.

REAL ESTATE

Strong German and foreign investment activity in the commercial property market was evident in 1990 in key cities such as Frankfurt, Berlin, Düsseldorf, Hamburg, and Munich. The economy was still growing very strongly and the demand was there. Locals banks poured DM15 billion into the market via their property investment funds, the ubiquitous Swedes, active also in neighboring Belgium, laid out DM5 billion, while the Japanese, notably Nomura and Kajima, took a DM500 million stake in the towering Messeturm skyscraper in Frankfurt. Office rents rose to the highest national levels in Frankfurt to reach DM85–90 the square meter per month, double the level of five years ago. New banks and financial houses wanted to be in the traditional financial district, or in the neighboring Westend, and were prepared to pay for this. The city's property collapse of the mid-1970s, when some 500 buildings stood empty, is a distant memory, although many thought the rise in rents could not continue given 1991's slower growth, higher interest rates, and taxes.

Despite the difficulties being experienced by the government and private industry in bankrolling the eastern economy, property experts see Frankfurt continuing to benefit from unification, the Single Market factor, and its good location. Large new buildings include the Westend Carree, while rents are holding up at DM85 in the 15-year-old Büro City, one of the top business addresses. Shortage of space in the center of Frankfurt, plus the unlikelihood of more skyscrapers of the Messeturm kind, have led some companies like the Schweizerische Bankgesellshaft to move to Niederrad's highly-popular and normally full Büro city, which has attracted Bull, Nixdorf, Honeywell, Wang, and the West German Machine Builders Association. A new favorite is Eschborn, an out-of-town location, which has good transport links including an expressway, and which is much cheaper than downtown with its suburban rents closer to DM30. Others interested in winning part of the real estate action include Norwegians and Finns, as well as investors from Hong Kong and Taiwan. There has been a clear trend towards offices within a 20-mile radius of Frankfurt, making industrial and warehousing development less worthwhile from a developer's point of view, although Frankfurt remains a large distribution center.

Lack of space in the former West Berlin—and a serious undersupply in the eastern part of the city—have pushed office rents there to near Frankfurt levels with the limited space in the East going for a premium. The government's decision to cut subsidies for Berlin, including investment aids, might bring down prices, now DM70–80, once new accommodation becomes available and the outline of the master plan for the eastern part of the city is finalized. On the other hand, investors now have priority with disputed land and property as compensation rather than restitution to former owners is the order of the day until the end of 1992. The handicap of poor telephone, road, and rail links will take longer to overcome. The move to Berlin by the government will set the market ablaze.

Some British developers are looking seriously at the longer-term prospects of Dresden and Leipzig and it is expected that large companies, banks, and law firms will eventually set up there. Both cities are now well served by Lufthansa.

Back in the western side of the country, demand has been strong in the "gateway" port city of Hamburg and in the country's second financial center—and major trading center—Düsseldorf. Rents there have been rising to DM40. Downtown Munich has long been expensive at DM50 the square meter, but new office parks outside the city and near the new airport are proving popular and much cheaper—at around DM25—for companies such as Fujitsu, Prime Computer, and Sony.

• *Getting To Know the Capital* •

The physical barriers that divided the two halves of Berlin have disappeared with the Wall of which only small, symbolic sections remain. These have been left for the artists to depict their vision of the reinstated capital of Germany. Berliners, by and large, have made a good job of merging what were two distinct cities. City literature exaggerates a little when it proclaims "Berlin is now twice as good." The hyperbole is greater when it adds that today there exists "an undivided city with undivided fun." Fun remains scarce in many parts of former East Berlin with its rundown districts and rising unemployment. The administration of the Christian Democrat Mayor Eberhard Diepgen, however, is now back in the traditional city hall, the "eastern" Rotehaus, while Berliners wait for the government and parliament to return from Bonn—quickly or slowly. The Treuhandanstalt, the privatization agency handling the liquidation, preservation, or sale of the thousands of onetime state-owned companies, shops, hotels, and restaurants is working more efficiently. It survived early corruption and the assassination by terrorists of its head, Detlev Rohwedder, now replaced by Frau Breuel, formerly in charge of the Treuhandanstalt's regional offices.

Western Berlin is alive around the clock with trade, deals and construction followed by nighttime exuberance. Eastern Berlin now has its western-style stores and other investment in the form of office construction and the shingles of western companies and consultants. Yet, the stark reality of Europe's largest inner-city wasteland—the Zentrale Bereich, the old, historic center around the Potsdamerplatz and Leipzigerplatz—is a daily reminder of the need for a cohesive, even daring urban plan. Daimler–Benz, the giant corporation, took the lead with plans for a major complex, although this project ran into trouble over the conditions of sale of some of Europe's most valuable land. But things are on the move.

Greater Berlin is vast, as travelers can see from incoming planes. The central sector is now easily negotiable on a west-east line. The visitor can travel without hindrance from one side to

continued

the other, be it from the Tiergarten park area, scheduled one day to become a diplomatic quarter again, via the Brandenburg Gate to Unter der Linden. Or across the site of the vanished Checkpoint Charlie (and other former border points), across the bridges over the River Spree and the canals, or along once-divided streets in the colorful Kreuzberg sector. On a fine Sunday one can walk from the Funkturm (radio tower), at the large, western fairgrounds, to the "eastern" Alexanderplatz with its television tower. West to east, one can take in the restored Schloss Charlottenburg and the museums. Or go more directly along Bismarckstrasse, Kantstrasse, or the famous Kurfürstendamm with its elegant boutiques, cafes and hotels. There is no eastern equivalent, as yet, of the commercial and leisure complex that is the Europa Center, but work is underway to revive Friedrichstrasse in the eastern half and so provide a counterweight to the prosperity of the west. Beyond Friedrichstrasse, Unter den Linden begins to look like the grand avenue of old with the university, library, opera house, and palaces. Former Communist squalor was hidden behind this facade.

The magnitude of the task of restoring both eastern Berlin and eastern Germany is now fully understood by national and city government. Money will be thrown at problems that remain despite the free flow of automobiles, buses, trucks, and, therefore, trade. More foreign investment is being called for— and the opportunities are considerable for those willing to look to the medium-term. The euphoria that followed the collapse of the Wall is now a thing of the past, but there is little doubt that Berlin is destined to become a great and powerful metropolis again. As the situation improves, the easterners will cease looking west and hopefully stay put, making the capital really seamless.

S P O T L I G H T

• *Bonn vs Berlin* •

Bonn, once described as "a green and inoffensive" city on the Rhine, lost its title of federal capital to Berlin when German reunification came into force in October, 1990. It remained the seat of government, parliament, and embassies, while Berlin pressed its case to be capital in every respect, not just in name. Political and public opinion about moving the whole government swayed back and forth before a parliamentary vote, which went narrowly in Berlin's favor. The chancellor's office, the chief ministries, and the main house of the German parliament will now move, leaving the Bundesrat, or upper house, in Bonn with a much depleted population. All the embassies in and around Bonn will also move east to the city of 4.3 million.

The leading advocate for a total move to Berlin was always the Federal President Richard von Weizsäcker, a former mayor of West Berlin. He said repeatedly that Berlin, with its key East-West position, represented the future, no matter what the cost of moving. The pro-Bonn lobby put the cost at close to $40 billion, difficult to justify when other huge sums moved East to refloat the economy there. Berliners replied it would cost a mere $4 billion. A Bonn newspaper shot back with an emotional argument: "As the symbol of a centralized Germany, Berlin stands for too many dismal failures, false starts, and inglorious aberrations. In Berlin, one cannot escape the pull of the megalopolis beckoning even the most sensible politicians down questionable paths." Anyway, the politicians voted to move.

Berlin, jolted by the EC Commission's decision to look

continued

closely at the terms of Daimler-Benz's acquisition of a key site in the old no-man's land by the former Wall, a move that was supposed to mark Berlin's revival, planned to re-open the pre-war Tiergarten diplomatic quarter.

⠇⠇⠇⠇⠇⠇Eurocity Düsseldorf ⠇⠇⠇⠇⠇⠇

Düsseldorf, a handsome, even "swinging" city, is the financial capital of the Ruhr, the location of big international trading companies and a notable fashion center. A technology center is being set up for office and laboratory space for companies in branches such as information and communications, materials, surfaces, medicine, bioengineering, and the environment. People live well in the North-Rhine Westphalia capital, none more so than the Japanese. They came originally, as one Japanese executive said, to learn from big German companies which are often their competitors. Sportingly, the city welcomed the "invaders" and today there are more than 300 Japanese companies in and around the state capital (banks, trading houses, manufacturing concerns), plus a Deutsch-Japanisches Center downtown. Creature comforts for the 7,000 strong Japanese community among the 580,000 population include a department store, other shops, a hotel, restaurants, *karaoka* sing-along bars, distinct residential areas, and schools. Office rents in Düsseldorf can now run up to DM40 the square meter per month as advertising firms, PR consultancies, bankers, and accountants arrive to swell the now-dominant services sector. Space is scarce in the central area around the broad Königsallee with the result that Kennedydamm, between the city and the airport, has grown to accommodate top firms such as IBM, Mitsubishi, Nixdorf, and Veba, and some leading hotels. Other business centers have opened. Key contact:

Office for Economic Development
29 Muhlenstrasse,
Düsseldorf
Tel: 49-211-8995500
Fax: 49-211-8994776.

::::::::::: EUROCITY FRANKFURT :::::::::::

Fears that Berlin's resurgence would mean the Bundesbank (central bank) leaving Frankfurt have proved groundless and Frankfurt's leadership in finance and many related sectors is symbolized by the new Messeturm skyscraper office building, Europe's tallest, which has been completed in the famous fairgrounds. Citibank and the US developer Tishman Speyer got the skyscraper off the ground, so to speak, but the Japanese quickly saw its potential and today Nomura and its Japanese partner, Kajima, are the major shareholders in the 875 foot tall building, taller than London's new Canary Wharf. It dwarfs also the other symbols of a city known as Manhattan–am–Main, namely the twin towers of the Deutsche Bank and the tower of the Dresdner Bank with its top-floor pool. Both banks, along with Commerzbank, have invested billions in new networks in the eastern länder, but they have every intention of keeping their headquarters in Frankfurt. Also, the city is bidding to be the seat of the planned new EC central bank, the Eurofed. With its 370-plus banks, German and foreign, Frankfurt is one of the most "banked" city in Europe outside London, and is certainly on a par with Paris and Zurich. Bankers are to Frankfurt what lawyers are to Washington. Another sure sign of Frankfurt's innate financial strength is the expatriate financial community's growth by a third in the past two to three years. All this has not made Frankfurt cheap and top office rents now reach DM85 to DM90 per square meter per month, double those in Düsseldorf, Hamburg, and Munich and rivalled only by Berlin where the shortage of accommodation is even greater. Britons and Swedes, who can sniff a good real estate scene from way off, are active in Frankfurt. Possibly, rents will ease, but Frankfurt remains a "hot" city in European terms. New banks and financial houses are still arriving in the "Deutschmark's home town," seat of the powerful, independent central bank, the Bundesbank, whose influence is both national and Europe-wide. Reforms at the stock exchange in the past year have been designed to boost its importance. Trading hours have been extended and the Price Information Project Europe is seen as an initial step towards a European capital market. Frankfurt admits that it will never match London as a financial center, but it would like to be leader on the so-called Continental mainland and, likewise, have its airport as the continental mainland's number two, after Paris. The undoubted wealth that exists in the city is not flaunted and the architecture is often drab. But the city is destined to play a new key role—organizing the private financial side of bailing out the eastern part of the country.

Aside from banks, Frankfurt and its region have major industries in chemicals, electrical, and mechanical engineering. The Frankfurter Kreuz forms an expressway crossroads for traffic from Scandinavia, the Benelux countries, France, and neighboring countries to the south. The rail station is Europe's largest and the airport is mainland Europe's air cargo hub. Perhaps the best-known activity, outside of banking, is the exhibition business at the vast *Messe* (fairgrounds). It provides a motor show, plus fairs for industrial products, books, even furs. Many of these fairs are world-leaders. Key contact:

Messe Frankfurt GmbH
1 Ludwig Erhard Anlage
Tel: 49-69-75750.

EUROCITY HAMBURG

Hamburg, Germany's largest port, is a rival to Rotterdam, particularly for containers, but the city's new philosophy is to be a service industry center with a port, rather than the other way around. These service industries already account for three-quarters of the city's GDP of more than $60 billion. Competition, however, with both Rotterdam and Antwerp is tough, for all three port cities seek to become the dominant "Eurogate" for trade. Hamburg has a handicap in that its handling and internal waterway costs are somewhat higher, yet a look at a map of Europe shows that it is only 25 miles from the former East Germany and can therefore claim that much of East Europe is its natural hinterland.

This is Germany's second largest city after Berlin, a cosmopolitan city-state with close to two million people. The city has a lot of grace, sophistication, style, and wealth with the added environmental attraction of two inner-city lakes. The port has made Hamburg famous since the days of the Hanseatic League between the 13th and 17th centuries, but today there are big names in electronics and electrotechnology, AEG, IBM, DEC, Nixdorf, Philips and Siemens, plus branches of the aerospace, medical, pharmaceutical, biotechnological, and marine technology industries. Additionally, the city has become Germany's media center with many millions of copies of newspapers and magazines published regularly and a sizeable, accompanying advertising industry.

Hamburg practically came back from scratch after World War II, for massive Allied bombing destroyed most of the port and large sections of the city. Prewar, Hamburg handled a good proportion of the foreign trade of what later became East Germany. Reunification has seen the city begin to regain a similar role. The former communist regime in the East developed the port of Rostock to save on foreign exchange. However, Rostock's Baltic location, limited handling capacity, and poor rail connections probably will mean more and more trade passing through Hamburg, which prior to reunification was handling three times as much cargo and big container traffic. Taiwanese, Korean, Japanese and Chinese shipping lines prefer Hamburg. For China, Hamburg is the main European point of entry, while the Japanese have been extending their local manufacturing base. Hamburg's port, 70 miles up the River Elbe from the North Sea, also has strong maritime links with the US, while it is also a port with Baltic links via the Kiel Canal. Yet, Rotterdam and Antwerp are seeking to show that it is cheaper to move export goods by river, canal, road, and rail to their mega-ports. It is going to be a fascinating battle between the three ports as the Single Market comes onstream and as order and trade return to East Europe.

Hamburg will be spending many hundreds of millions of dollars on infrastructure during the 1990s. It can already claim to be a transit point for some Czechoslovak and Austrian trade, while hundreds of Scandinavian firms have set up to be within the EC.

Up to one billion dollars a year of foreign investment has been pouring into Hamburg with the electronics industry to the force. Some 400 more foreign firms have been attracted to the city-state in the past four years. Hamburg is one of Europe's wealthiest cities and among the landmarks are the opulent, Renaissance-style *Rathaus*, home of the city-state's senate and lower house, the Kunsthalle art museum and the famous Staatsoper (opera house), developed after the war by one of the great names of opera management, Rolf Liebermann. For businessmen, the best one-stop call is:

Hamburg Business Development Corporation
11 Hamburgerstrasse
Hamburg 76
Tel: 49-40-22701923
Fax: 49-40-22701913.

Office rents in Hamburg have risen to DM40 per square meter the month, but reunification and the Single Market have boosted building—the City Süd development with various schemes spread over a few years and the outer port area, notably the Kehrwieder-Spitze development in the free port zone. British investors have taken the lead and will build a commercial and services complex embracing 80,000 square meters of offices and a luxury hotel, an investment of DM300 million. In addition, the old, traditional commercial quarter, east of the city center, is being renovated.

EUROCITY STUTTGART (WITH BADEN–WÜRTTEMBERG)

Stuttgart, with its 620,000 inhabitants is a compact city with a Swabian no-nonsense, non-sophisticated approach to life. The main exception is the world-class ballet company, but otherwise Baden-Württemberg's capital is about business, symbolized by the Mercedes emblem atop a high-rise office tower. Daimler-Benz, (the brand new corporate headquarters of Germany's largest concern are just outside Stuttgart) SEL, and a host of big foreign firms are the high profile names, but the city on the River Neckar has a strong manufacturing "culture" stretching from IBM's major investment, including a second production line for four megabit chips, down to small engineering companies. Businesspark, with a total floor area of 50,000 square meters, is one of the largest private initiatives of its kind in Europe with 220 companies (Tel: 49-711-7287121, Fax: 49-711-7287151). A similar park is being built at Ludwigsburg, north of Stuttgart. The city has been gaining a reputation for trade fairs. Stuttgart Messe (Fair) has jumped from regional to international status and is collaborating with the former East Germany and with Czechoslovakia, Hungary and Poland for the staging of modern trade fairs. It is not yet in the same league as Frankfurt, Hannover or Munich, but has captured a food wine fair from the Bavarian capital. Fairs in 1992 include those for automation components, hotel and catering, heating techniques, telecoms, computer-aided technology, metal-working, cleaning, automobiles, and a consumers exhibition. Key contact:

Messe Stuttgart
Postfach 103252
D-7000 Stuttgart 10
Tel: 49-711-25890
Fax: 49-711-2589440.

:::::: OPPORTUNITIES IN THE REGIONS ::::::

SCHLESWIG–HOLSTEIN

The northernmost of the 16 states (länder) has long served as a bridge between Germany and Scandinavia for its neighbor is Denmark, while Kiel, also the state capital, and other ports open onto the Baltic. The region benefits too from modern road links with Berlin, but, above all, it curls around the city-state of Hamburg, an industrial, trade, and services metropolis, on its southern border. A division of labor, has developed between Hamburg and south Schleswig–Holstein. For many years, a joint state planning council has coordinated zoning, transport links in all directions, and population development. Companies setting up in Schleswig–Holstein have easy access to the local state market, but also to the extremely rich Hamburg market and the market of much of northern Germany just beyond, including Bremen, another city-state, and northern Lower Saxony. The four states are home to 12 million people and contributed one-fifth of the former West Germany's GNP. Forty years ago, Schleswig–Holstein was predominantly an agricultural area, but today this sector represents only 20 percent of exports now running over DM11 billion (north German region: DM82 billion). The state's exports have increased over 700 percent since the 1960s and demand now is for machines and vehicles, chemical and electrotechnical products, precision and optical instruments, as well as textiles. Ships are still built, even if far fewer than before. The chemical and petroleum refining industry has been attracted to Brunsbrüttel on the state's west coast. This North Sea port at the mouth of the River Elbe is linked by ship canal to Kiel, a journey taken by 60,000 ships each year and which lasts but eight hours. Kiel, Lübeck and the outer border ports of Flensburg and Puttgarden are integrated into the Bundesbahn Inter-City Express-Shipment Train System, which transports goods overnight to other German cities. Container and piggy-back terminals can be reached quickly. The move away from the land, where one in four worked in the 1950s, has led to a situation in which three out of ten work in manufacturing, two in commerce and transport, and four in private and public services. The most important industry currently is machine engineering with some 200 companies exporting 40 percent of production. Until now, two-thirds of Schleswig–Holstein had been classified as zonal border regions with special depreciation allowances and cheap loans. This will change. New industries include pharmaceuticals where one of the investors is Glaxo, the high-performing British company, and electronics. Other major investments have been made by Johnson & Johnson, Matsushita, Minolta, Volvo, and Alfa-Laval. Total foreign investment is well over DM1 billion, guided by the state's Economic Development Corporation. (43 Lorentzendamm, 2300 Kiel 1, Tel: 49-431-51446; Fax: 49-431-555178). Another contact is the state ministry for economics, technology and transportation (94–100 Dusternbrooker Weg, 2300 Kiel 1; Industrial promotion division—Tel: 49-431-5963930). The labor force is youngish, while the Christian-Albrechts University in Kiel, one of Germany's oldest, covers the scientific spectrum, focusing on oceanography, polar science, immunology, international relations and Scandinavian research. The GKSS research center in Geesthacht is involved in reactor security, as well as environmental and offshore technologies. This being Germany, there are strong technical colleges in Flensburg, Kiel, Lübeck, and other cities. The state's basic strength is geographical, aside from having Hamburg as a neighbor, it opens onto Scandinavia and the northern half of eastern Europe and the Soviet Union.

NORTH RHINE–WESTPHALIA

This is Germany's largest state with its 17 million people. It's also the country's economic powerhouse, producing a quarter of the former West Germany's GDP and a third of its exports. It includes the Ruhr–

Rhine industrial heartland of Germany where one major city merges into the next to form an urbanized area of eight million inhabitants, the most densely populated zone in Europe. NRW, as it is known, can trace its industry back some 150 years, but traditional coal and steel have given ground to chemicals, machine tools, textiles, paper, food, and consumer goods. Aside from the Japanese, other foreign investors, notably American, British, French, and Scandinavian, have opted for the state not because of investment grants, but more to be at the center of things and to tap local skills developed at technical schools and research institutes. Ericsson, for example, decided to spend DM100 million on a R & D center for mobile telephones at Aachen because of the chance to recruit the right people. Aachen, shaped in the past by iron and metal processing, has diversified into microelectronics and this and related industries draw upon huge research institutes with 17,000 employees of their own plus some 45,000 students. This is just one area of an increasingly high-tech state. Cologne also plays a major research role, as does, to a lesser extent, the region around the outgoing federal capital of Bonn, often thought of as a Rhine village which had a government dropped on it.

The Ruhr owed its industrialization to coal deposits estimated at 65 billion tons. After coal, came the steel industry, then machine tools. Chemicals followed and today close to 40 percent of the former West Germany's chemical industry is in NRW. The top dozen industrial companies include Bayer (chemicals), Veba (energy, oil, chemicals), Thyssen (steel, trading), RWE (energy), Ruhrkohle (mining), Mannesmann (pipes, machinery), Ford (automobiles), Krupp (steel, plants), Feldmühle Nobel (chemicals, paper, machinery), Henkel (chemicals), Klöckner-Werke (steel, machinery), and Hoesch (steel). Other major companies include Viag aluminium, Hochtief construction, Nixdorf/Siemens electronics and Oetker food. The area is crisscrossed with autobahns and railways, but the Rhine, Europe's main river and its most important inland waterway, continues to play a dominant role in life along its valley. Cologne, which rivals Düsseldorf in size, was a trading center in the Middle Ages. Later came the invention of the four-stroke engine and today engine and automobile production is a major industry there. Ford has been in Cologne since before the Second World War and is spending DM650 million on an engine plant at Cologne–Niehl. Toyota, Mazda and Renault are also in the region. More than 130 million tons of goods carried along the

Rhine (Duisburg inland port handles 50 million tons annually) have fed many industries, but the chemical industry now uses oil as its basic raw material and brings it by pipe from Rotterdam. There's a similar pipeline system for ethylene.

Although Düsseldorf, the Ruhr cities, and Cologne dominate activity, services, and the media industry the state has other expanding manufacturing areas where investors receive subsidies. In the past these have ranged from eight to eighteen percent in selected towns. Granting of subsidies is, however, coming under pressure as the federal government spends more and more in the former East Germany. The current investment aid map can be obtained from:

North Rhine–Westphalia Economic Development Corporation
8–10 Kavalleriestrasse
Düsseldorf
Tel: 49-211-59901.

The relatively small city of Mönchengladbach extended a helping hand with the result that one finds Toshiba making video cassette recorders and building up a European center for production, marketing, and distribution of a range of products. Cologne, which is also the center of the German retail trade as well as having a vast array of TV, radio, and media companies, has its economic development office at:

2–4 Richartzstrasse
Cologne
Tel: 49-221-2216123
Fax: 49-221-2216686.

BAVARIA

Bavaria has Alpine peaks and another variant—big business in the shape of Siemens, three BMW plants, the headquarters of Audi, a Volkswagen subsidiary, Allianz insurance, MBB aerospace, and US multinationals of the rank of Hewlett-Packard, Texas Instruments, and DEC. Japanese investment has grown, too, through companies such as Phoenix Electric and Toshiba. Over the years, the Bavarian state government in Munich has provided advice and money through the Bavarian Act for the Promotion of Medium and Small Business.

Some of these companies have been attracted by the presence of such giants as MBB and Siemens.

Bavaria is the largest of the German länder in size and second only to North Rhine–Westphalia in population. It has one of Germany's most pleasant lifestyles. The scenery is spectacular. However, its appeal for business has always been its proximity to central and southern Europe. It boasts a German equivalent of California's Silicon Valley and these days about a third of companies are working in the information and data processing branch.

Away from Munich are several industrial centers. Schweinfurt, in the northern part of the state, is the center of German—and European—ballbearing manufacture with FAG Kugelfischer and SKF. In all, the engineering industry employs close to 200,000 people and the sector's 850 firms export nearly half of their production. In Würzburg industry producing traditional printing machinery has gone over to computerization. Nuremburg, the state's second city after Munich, has both industrial and services sectors and works closely with neighboring Furth and Erlangen. Publishing—above all in Munich—pharmaceuticals, and the traditional porcelain industry complete the picture. Regensburg, chosen by Toshiba for an expanding plant making laptops and also the site of Siemens, BMW, and AG plants, has good road and rail connections with the rest of Germany, but also looks East to Prague and South to Vienna. Here, the port on the River Danube will benefit from the coming Rotterdam–Black Sea connection now being completed by canals. Munich's brand new, second airport, is nearby. This new hub is creating business opportunities in the surrounding area.

Munich itself, with its 1.5 million population, is also in the forefront in banking, fashion and textiles, and movie and television production. It has one business park near the first airport, Riem, and a second, the Euro Industrie Park in Munich–Freimann. It's an expensive place to live and to rent offices. For living, however, it is the place named by other Germans as the most desirable. For renting business accommodation, the rates are still below Frankfurt, but these days not far below. Helping to adapt the work ethic to contemporary needs are universities and technical colleges, several of which include information technology, data processing, biotechnology, experimental physics, materials study, engineering automation, and related subjects attracting highly qualified young people to the state.

Key contact:

Bavarian Ministry for Economic Affairs and Transport
28 Prinzregentenstrasse
Munich 22
Tel: 49-89-2162-2642
Fax: 49-89-2162-2760.

BADEN-WÜRTTEMBERG

In its short history since 1952, this youngest German state has developed into a presentable "model of German capabilities," a phrase of Theodor Heuss, the first federal president. The third largest of the states, it has experienced strong growth and considers its position to be ideal for exploiting the Single Market. It borders eastern France and northern Switzerland, an economic advantage which will be strengthened when France and Germany improve their interconnecting road and rail links, hopefully in the 1990s. It also borders Germany's other growth state, Bavaria. The capital, Stuttgart, is today a major industrial center, while Karlsruhe is expanding its so-called *Technologieregion* with the backing of Fridericiana University's computer sciences faculty and some one hundred other technological and scientific institutes. Karlruhe has a very high ratio of 32 scientists per 1,000 workers. Baden–Württemberg is home to such well-known companies as Bosch, Daimler-Benz, Porsche, and Zeiss. Standard Electrik Lorenz, now part of the French Alcatel telecommunication group, is also headquartered there, as are the German branches of IBM, Hewlett Packard, and Sony. Foreign-held investments total more than DM20 billion with US companies representing a third of this. Aside from Sony, the Japanese have plants for Minolta and Hoya Lense. The state contributes about a sixth of the exports of the former West Germany. The *Mittelstand,* or medium-sized firms, are also prominent in the local economy and as exporters. Roughly nine-tenths of Baden–Württemberg's economy is in the hands of the *Mittelstand.* These companies and inward investors do not receive start-up aid of any consequence, but once they are operating they benefit from a highly effective technological program, based upon Stuttgart's Steinbeis Foundation, which enables managers to call up and learn of German and world innovations, plus those developed locally. Key contact:

Ministry for Economic Affairs
Medium-Sized Firms and Techology
4 Theodor Heuss-strasse
Tel: 49-711-1232382
Fax: 49-711-1232126.

HESSE

The state includes Germany's counting house, Frankfurt, and is home to such major companies as Hoechst, Germany's largest chemical concern, and Opel (General Motors). There are also important manufacturing areas near the former East–West border which stand to benefit when the eastern länder begin to close the gap with the West. The state, the most centrally-placed in the former West Germany, has excellent rail, road, and air links, many of them running through Frankfurt. The city dominates the state, but the Hesse economic development office (HLT—Hessische Landesentwicklungs and Treuhandgesellschaft) is in Wiesbaden:

38 Abraham Lincolnstrasse
6200 Wiesbaden
Tel: 49-6121-7740
Fax: 49-6121-774265.

This organization is a good first call, for it sets up contacts in the state, advises on what aid is available, and suggests sites for investment. Its information and agency service is linked with external databases and has an EC service.

The up-state city of Kassel, near the old border, has developed as an industrial center and offers industrial sites and business parks with space available. As in Baden–Württemberg, local universities provide technology transfer as well as skilled labor for specialized suppliers working in the machinery and automobile sectors. Here, the north-south autobahn, Hannover–Kassel–Frankfurt, crosses the east–west autobahn, Dortmund–Kassel, for which a further link is planned to the east—Erfurt–Leipzig–Berlin. The opening of the border saw Kassel businesspeople among the first to examine the potential in the East. There's been no East–West boom, but Kassal says it has the know-how and contacts to profit from better times in the future.

EAST

Big names from the western side of the country—BASF, Daimler, Opel, Siemens, and Volkswagen—have been the main investors in the East since unification. The Treuhandanstalt, the agency in charge of disposing of 7,000 eastern companies and 25,000 shops and service outlets, has been actively seeking foreign investors. Foreigners to a large extent have been deterred by the poor state of most eastern companies—only 10 to 30 percent are considered competitive in western terms—the problems of ownership and a feeling that the East is a preserve of West German groups. The Treuhandanstalt is assuming most of the debts of companies to give them a greater chance of surviving. Compensation, rather than restitution, to former owners has been accepted in some cases where it is vital to save or create jobs. Aid—covering restructuring, assuming corporate debt, sums for redundancies and for new infrastructure such as telecommunications, roads and railways—could run as high as DM400 billion during the 1990s. Investors are advised to check with the finance ministry in Bonn (49-228-682-6241) for the latest on legislation on compensation versus restitution, as well as decisions on investment aids and possible tax breaks. The American Chamber of Commerce with its various offices in Frankfurt, Berlin, and Dresden is another important source. As is the Treuhandanstalt, Berlin Mitte (Tel: 49-30-3154-1037; Fax: 49-30-3154-1982/1036). Various tender information—for hotels, for example—can be obtained from Treuhand's GPH branch (Gesellschaft zur Privatisierung des Handels mbH, 70/72 Hans-Beimlerstrasse, 0-1020 Berlin). The Treuhand moved its main office to the former, wartime Air Ministry building in Berlin.

The regional bureaus of the Treuhand are as follows:

Berlin (1005)
26 Schneeglöckchenstrasse
Tel: 37-2434-2601

Cottbus (7500)
24 Gulbenerstrasse
Tel: 37-59-634800
Telex: 069-17-406

Dresden (8010)
5 Budapesterstrasse
Tel: 37-51-4852474
Telex: 2431

Erfurt (5010)
37 Bahnhofstrasse
Tel: 37-61-51751
Telex: 61 417

Frankfurt/Oder (1200)
Am Forum
Tel: 37-30-364-2450
Telex: 162 201

Gera (6500)
7 Puschkinplatz
Tel: 37-70-68274
Telex: 582 83Y

Halle (4010)
1–2 Alter Markt
Tel: 37-46-6270
Fax: 37-69-627288

Chemnitz (9006)
16–18 Henriettenstrasse
Tel: 37-71-38301

Leipzig (7010)
5 F. Engels-platz
Tel: 37-41-715-3040
Telex: 512 468

Magdeburg (3010)
27 O. Guerickestrasse
Tel: 37-91-38-3456
Telex: 08 446 spkm dd

Neubrandenbury (2000)
120 Leninstrasse
Tel: 37-90-580-2844
Telex: 33192

Potsdam (1581)
2 Am Bürohochhaus
Tel: 37-33-367-24
Telex: 15 461

Rostock (2500)
1 Freiligrathstrasse
Tel: 37-81-38-55-008
Telex: 31 436

Schwerin (2750)
18 Karl-Marx-strasse
Tel: 37-84-786-91
Telex: 32 216

Suhl (6016)
3 Strasse der DSF, PSF 220
Tel: 37-66-5336-11
Telex: 62 201

So far, there has been no large-scale US investment in the East, outside of Adam Opel, a division of General Motors. The French have been active—Alcatel's West German division, SEL, has won contracts for telephone exchanges and a cable plant. Also present are Lafarge Coppee, Air Liquide, BSN, CMB, and a private group, headed by Paris consultant Christian Tassin, that has acquired the Saxe porcelain works (Sachsisch Porzellan Manufaktur), near Dresden. GKN, the British components, industrial services and defense group, has bought a motor components maker. Finland's Nokia is supplying TV kits for local assembly by Kombinet Rundfunk und Fernsehen Stassurt. Japan's Sharp has shown interest in the Stern radio plant in Berlin. These investments are overshadowed by Siemens which is investing DM1 billion in 20 projects, notably in telecommunications, power generation, and automation. Siemens now employs 15,000 people in the East and is aiming for $2 billion of sales in 1991. The West German Company Act on stock companies, the law on private limited companies (GmbHG) and the commercial code (HGB) have been introduced in the East. Would-be investors are advised to check with western accounting firms, notably Coopers & Lybrand, which has an eastern network in place. Key contact:

Coopers & Lybrand (Frankfurt/Main)
Tel: 49-69-71100
Fax: 49-69-711466.

Saxony (capital Dresden), the largest of the five eastern länder with a population of close to five million, has a long industrial tradition, but many former key sectors—lignite mining, textiles, even brewing—have suffered closures or massive cutbacks since unification in 1990. Leipzig and Dresden, centers of the protest marches which led to the overthrow of the ancient regime, have seen the popular mood turn sour. The Buna and Leuna chemical plants have sharply reduced their workforces and will depend on substantial financial aid from the Treuhand, plus deals with Linde (industrial gases) and BP (refining) for survival. Unemployment has forced workers to move by the thousands to the West. Yet, Saxony has attracted inward investment, such as the purchase by Britain's GKN components group of Gelenwellenwerk Mosel, makers of constant velocity driveshafts, in the southern Saxon town of Mosel. The British investment is based on the hope that eastern production of automobiles will treble to 400,000 a year. The ugly Trabant and the bigger Wartburg have been scrapped, but Volkswagen will make Golf and Polo models at Mosel, which GM's Opel will be producing elsewhere in the East. Saxony, with its automobiles, machine tools, printing plants, and its Meissen china, was responsible for a third of the former East Germany's GNP. It was rivalled only by the neighboring land of Thuringia. BASF is committed to spending more than $300 million on the development of the Schwarzheide polyurethane foam plant, but sizeable reductions will be needed in the workforce before the new East German automobile industry swings into profitable production. The Saxonia metals group in Freiberg is looking to cooperation with Metallgesellschaft and Degussa, West German metals and chemical companies. In another move to stimulate new activity, Dresden is hoping to build a technology center-cum-science park. In Saxony, as in the other eastern länder, there is a need for more small- and medium-sized businesses of the kind which make up the backbone of the west German economy.

S P O T L I G H T

• *Leipzig Fair* •

It used to be the East's main commercial shop window. Western salesmen flocked to the Leipzig Fair to meet the managers of the centralized economies of East Germany and the other East European countries. But with the swing to market economies in the East, the managers of central purchasing agencies and foreign trade organizations have disappeared along with their once monolithic institutions. Attendance slumped at the two 1990 fairs—Spring and Autumn—and most exhibitors were West Germans. Only nine Soviet firms turned up, all from Lithuania or the Ukraine. Other eastern countries, now trading in hard currencies and therefore with little to spend, stayed away. Leipzig is the world's oldest trade fair, but now looks as sad as the overall facade of East German industry. Bonn's economic minister, Jörgen Möllemann has said he will subsidize future fairs, but the Leipzig organizers are demanding a hefty DM1 billion. The shop window is doomed to be reduced.

Thuringia was once known as the "green heart" of Germany, but it has not been spared postwar industrial pollution, notably the uranium mines of the former GDR–Soviet company, Sdag Wismuth, covering 40 square kilometers. This former, 29,000-strong "state within the state" is now the subject of a decontamination plan of the federal environment ministry. The huge conglomerate has been divided into various sections—services, construction, machinery and steel, consulting and engineering—under a plan drawn up by the West German consultants, Kienbaum. Elsewhere, the Treuhandanstalt has sought to bring together the two halves of the optics maker Carl Zeiss, forcibly separated for 40 years. It has already written off the debts of Jenoptik Carl Zeiss Jena in Erfurt and paid for the dismissal of workers to encourage a link with West Germany's Carl Zeiss Oberkochen. Reconversion is also necessary at VEB Mikroelectronik, the electronics group in Erfurt, which has dropped its hugely expensive one megabyte chip to concentrate on transistors, integrated circuits, and applications-specific chips. Experts say that possibly half of the former East Germany's electronics industry could survive in reduced form. Robotron, the computer and office equipment maker, which has worked with IBM in the past, has changed its name to Soemtrom and has made deals with NCR for cash registers and with Aquarius, the computer group in Taiwan for PC sales. The overall need to increase sales to the West has been made more urgent by the collapse of eastern markets, notably in the Soviet Union. Thuringia has been hit hard by unemployment and one of the most dramatic cases has been the closure in Eisenbach of the Wartburg automobile plant. Some encouragement has come from BMW's plans for machine tool production and by Bosch for consumer appliances.

SUCCESS STORIES

SEB

The French SEB group, maker of small household appliances, jumped to European size when it paid Chicago Pacific Corporation $170 million in 1988 for the Rowenta company in West Germany, maker of similar appliances. The decision was justified by the West German economic boom of recent years, while the market in the former East Germany, although affected by the grim economic situation there in 1991, is set to grow once the economy improves. SEB's confidence in the future is underscored by its DM130 million, three-year German investment program, designed to modernize Rowenta's manufacturing base, notably by moving from downtown Erbach, 50 miles south of Frankfurt, to a new plant outside of the town which will make Ultraglide steam irons. SEB/Rowenta products—scales, mixers, nonstick cookware, and coffee makers—are now familiar sights in both western department stores and small shops, while the eastern part of the country will see current sales increased by the arrival of big western chains such as Karstadt, Kaufhof and Hertie, which have taken over the supermarkets and department stores of the former GDR Centrum chain. SEB, in recent years, has become the top-ranking European group in small domestic equipment and a world leader with its cookware, pressure cookers, and electric fryers. The purchase of Rowenta, headquartered in Offenbach, near Frankfurt, made the group the world's second producer of irons and No. 3 in toasters and coffee makers. SEB sees Germany as the "locomotive" of its future European expansion following its domination of the French, British, and Benelux markets. Non-performing Rowenta lines have been dropped and sales concentrated on proven international successes, which include the Tefal cookware range, headquartered in Wiesbaden for the German market. Micro-wave ovens have been abandoned and a new emphasis placed on air conditioning. The German move has added 2,700 staff, bringing the world total to 10,000 for sales of $1.36 billion. The one cloud is future wage negotiations in Germany where the unions have been pressing for higher-than-customary increases following new taxes levied to pay for unification. Looking to the longer-term, SEB is taking part in the EC Eureka high-tech research program. In its case, this involves new, advanced treatment of enamel.

TRELLEBORG

Swedish miltinational Trelleborg took a number of steps to protect its market for rubber parts for German automobile makers, notably Volkswagen and BMW. It had rebuilt in the bombed ruins of Hamburg after World War II only to find later that the city had engulfed it in a way that hindered expansion. So the Swedes decided to move everything elsewhere. They went north to the state of Schleswig Holstein to a green field site that provided the space for an automated plant and higher productivity. They looked at some 30 sites before choosing Wasbeck, by the Hamburg–Flensburg autobahn, convenient for transport from headquarters in Sweden and geographically well-placed to send products by Autobahn to the automakers in the south of Germany. The Swedes now have two plants making $40 million dollars worth of shock absorbers, diaphragms, brake seals, and rubber axles for campers. They have adopted the German "qualität" way of doing things. Production is monitored by computers which track the entire process of manufacture. Trelleborg does not seem worried about gloomy predictions for the auto industry, believing the market for its carefully tested products will rise. Local manager Wolfgang Ehrhardt says: "Comfort will become increasingly important at the cost of speed. It's very likely that we will have speed limits on all the German autobahns. The development of components that make the ride more comfortable will be the way of the future. In eastern Europe, there is a vast amassed backlog for quality cars from the west."

THE LEADERS

TOP 20 INDUSTRIAL COMPANIES (1990)

		Sales	Profits
(1)	Daimler Benz	DM85.9b	DM1.7b
(2)	Volkswagen	DM65.35b (1989)	DM1b (est: 1990)
(3)	Siemens	DM63.2b	DM1.67b
(4)	Veba	$29,239m (1989)	$1,618m (1989)
(5)	BASF	$28,294m	DM2.7b
(6)	Hoechst	$27,273m	DM3.2b
(7)	Bayer	$25,728m	DM3.4b
(8)	RWE	$21,420m (1990: nine months)	$1,259m
(9)	Tengelmann	$22,104m	
(10)	Thyssen	$20,351m	DM1b (1989)
(11)	Bosch	$18,157m	
(12)	BMW	$15,755m	DM696m
(13)	Ruhrkohl	$13,831m	
(14)	Mannesmann	$13,269m	DM597m (1989)
(15)	Adam Opel	$12,363m	
(16)	Metallgesellschaft	$11,959m	DM201m (1989)
(17)	Ford	$11,768m	
(18)	Krupp	DM15.8b	DM350m
(19)	Man	$10,133m	
(20)	Preussag	$9,719m	

1990 Results

Falls

Deutsche Bank DM1.07 (−20 percent); BASF DM2.7b (−37 percent); Bayer DM3.4 (−18 percent); Hoechst DM3.2b (−22.5 percent); Deutsche Babcock −DM81m; Commerzbank DM557m (−0.01 percent); Krupp DM91m (19m 98.6/1989).

Gains

Bayerische Hypotheken DM1.075 (+2 percent); Schering DM258m (+15 percent); GEA energy DM88 (+25 percent); Volkswagen DM1b (same); Mannesmann DM505m (same); Klockner–Humboldt–Deutz DM3m (−DM170/1989); Commerzbank (10 months) DM 1.1b (+18 percent); Siemens Est DM1.7b (same); BMW DM696m (+24.7 percent); Dresdner Bank (plus Dresdner Berlin) DM 921m (+42 percent).

TOP 10 BANKS (1989)

		Balance Sheet (Millions DM)
(1)	Deutsche Bank	344,800
(2)	Dresdner	249,579
(3)	Commerzbank	191,554
(4)	DG Bank	186,925
(5)	Westdeutsche Landesbank	177,434
(6)	Bayerische Vereinsbank	173,611
(7)	Bayerische Hypothekenbank	153,021
(8)	Bayerische Landesbank	147,731
(9)	Kreditanstalt für Wiederaufbau	118,982
(10)	Norddeutsche Landesbank	116,603

TOP 10 INSURANCE COMPANIES (1989)

		Income (Millions DM)
(1)	Allianz Holding	31,833
(2)	Münchner Rückversicherung	12,459

(3)	Allianz Lebensversicherung	7,982
(4)	Allianz Versicherung	6,947
(5)	Hamburg-Mannheimer Versicherung	3,590
(6)	Deutsche Krankenversicherung	3,121
(7)	Volksfürsorge Lebensversicherung	2,827
(8)	Colonia	2,501
(9)	Vereinte	2,447
(10)	Bayerische Versicherungskammer	2,382

KEY CONTACTS

USEFUL BERLIN TELEPHONE NUMBERS

Trade and Commercial Information

American Chamber of Commerce: 30-261-5586
   30-262-2600 (Fax)
American Foreign Commercial Service: 30-819-7888
Berlin Chamber of Commerce: 30-315100
   US Desk: 30-3151-0326
   30-3151-0344 (Fax)
Berlin Economic Development Corp.: 30-264880
Berlin Law Letter: 30-310241
Berlin Marketing Council: 30-3151-0329
Berlin Press Conference/Media Center: 30-83-9100
BIG (Berlin Innovation/Business Venture Center): 30-693-7064
German Institute of Economic Research (DIW): 30-82911
International Congress Center (AMK): 30-30380
   30-38-2325 (Fax)
Trade Fairgrounds: 30-30380
Treuhandanstalt, Berlin Mitte: 30-3154-1037/1933
   30-3154-1982/1036 (Fax)

Other Useful Business Numbers

Business Center (western half): 30-251-8087
   30-251-1393 (Fax)

Business Center (Berlin Mitte): 30-229-3459
  30-209-23540 (Fax)
Office Rentals/Real Estate: 30-219-0040
  Jones Lang Wootton: 30-2190-0440 (Fax)
German Chamber of Commerce & Industry/New Länder
  Berlin office: 372-489-5857
  Länder Branches
  Chemnitz: 37-71-682-3801
    37-71-643018 (Fax)
  Cottbus: 37-592484143
  Dresden: 37-51-479547
    37-51-479970 (Fax)
  Erfurt: 37-61-3456-58
    37-61-62105 (Fax)
  Frankfurt/Oder: 37-30-311412
  Gera: 37-70-51513
    37-70-23301 (Fax)
  Halle: 37-46-37991
  Leipzig: 37-41-7153438
    37-41-51030 (Fax)
  Magdeburg: 37-91-33951
  Neubrandenburg: 37-90-41101
  Potsdam: 37-33-21591
  Rostock: 37-81-37501
  Schwerin: 37-84-78922
    37-84-83390
  Sudthuringen Suhl: 37-66-24112

USEFUL BONN TELEPHONE NUMBERS

Government Offices

Chancellery: 49-228-561
  Public Relations: 49-228-208-2030
Construction: 49-228-337-3050
Economic Cooperation: 49-228-535451
Economics: 49-228-6151
  Public Relations: 49-228-615-4295
Environment: 49-228-3050
Foreign Affairs: 49-228-170
  Public Relations: 49-228-172059

Finance: 49-228-6820
  Public Relations: 49-228-682-4241
Food/Agriculture: 49-228-591
  Public Relations: 49-228-529-3707
Labor: 49-228-5271
  Public Relations: 49-228-527-2224
PTT: 49-228141
Transport: 49-229-3000
  Public Relations: 49-228-300-2040
Research & Development: 49-228-591
  Public Relations: 49-228-593037
German Chamber of Commerce and Industry: 49-228-1040
  49-228-104158 (Fax)

Consulates (Western Part)

Japan: 49-30-8327026

Member Nations
Belgium: 49-30-324-4031
Britain: 49-30-305-9292
Denmark: 49-30-832-4001
France: 49-30-881-8028
Greece: 49-30-213-7033
Ireland: 49-30-3480-0822
Italy: 49-30-261-1591
Luxembourg: 49-30-310050
Netherlands: 49-30-883-5173
Portugal: 49-30-815-6027
Spain: 49-30-261-6081

Others
Brazil: 49-30-881-9756
Canada: 49-30-261-1161
Finland: 49-30-882-7727
India: 49-30-313-4091
Indonesia: 49-30-831-5076
Malaysia: 49-30-261-4271
Nigeria: 49-30-304-6309

Norway: 49-30-882-1224
Pakistan: 49-228-823-2601
Philippines: 49-228-261-9188
South Africa: 49-228-241-517
Soviet Union: 49-228-832-7004
Sweden: 49-228-891-7091
Switzerland: 49-228-394-4021
Thailand: 49-228-831-2715
Turkey: 49-228-892-5033
United States: 49-228-819-7454
US Embassy Office, Berlin Mitte:
0372-220-2741

Former Comecon Countries
Bulgaria: 49-228-823-4108
Czechoslovakia: 49-228-832-4083
Yugoslavia: 49-228-826-2091
Hungary: 49-228-803-6063
Poland: 49-228-825031
Rumania: 49-228-803-3019

USEFUL FRANKFURT TELEPHONE NUMBERS

Trade and Commercial Information

Bundesbank (Central Bank): 49-69-1581
German Chambers of Commerce:
  Industrie und Handelskammer: 49-69-21970
  Handwerkskammer Rhein-Main: 49-69-710-0010

Chambers of Commerce Economic Offices

Member Nations
France: 49-69-729353
Greece: 49-69-291-879
Italy *(Mezzogiono)*:
49-69-708024/294151
Spain: 49-69-638031

Others
Australia (Victoria):
49-69-666-6028
Austria: 49-69-702866
Finland: 49-69-728148
Ghana: 49-69-234313
Hong Kong: 49-69-740161
India: 49-69-252254
Israel: 49-69-722821

Japan (Jetro): 49-69-283215
Mauritius: 49-69-284348
Philippines: 49-69-748048
Puerto Rico: 49-69-721242
Singapore: 49-69-233838
Taiwan: 49-69-610742
Thailand: 49-69-281091
United States: 49-69-283402
  Connecticut: 49-69-282055
  Iowa: 49-69-233858
Old West (North and South
  Dakota, Montana, Nebraska,
  Wyoming): 49-69-20516
Louisiana State: 49-69-591808

Consulates

Member Nations
Belgium: 49-69-590578
Britain: 49-69-720406
Denmark: 49-69-770391
France: 49-69-740137
Greece: 49-69-595750
Italy: 49-69-75310
Luxembourg: 49-69-236611
Netherlands: 49-69-752021
Portugal: 49-69-702066
Spain: 49-69-638071

Others
Argentina: 49-69-233644

Austria: 49-69-707-2558
Bolivia: 49-69-728205
Brazil: 49-69-290708
Cameroon: 49-69-254-2311
Chile: 49-69-550194
Egypt: 49-69-590557
Finland: 49-69-728148
India: 49-69-271040
Iran: 49-69-714-0050
Japan: 49-69-770351
Kenya: 49-69-2825512
Korea (South): 49-69-563051
Mexico: 49-69-235709
Morocco: 49-69-231737

Norway: 49-69-411040
Philippines: 49-69-627538
Peru: 49-69-20301
South Africa: 49-69-723741
Sweden: 49-69-230479
Switzerland: 49-69-725941
Tanzania: 49-69-745989

Thailand: 49-69-20110
Turkey: 49-69-772048
United States: 49-69-753040
Uruguay: 49-69-518510
Venezuela: 49-69-287284
Yugoslavia: 49-69-439923

USEFUL DÜSSELDORF TELEPHONE NUMBERS

Trade and Commercial Information

North Rhine–Westphalia: 49-211-130000
Economic Development Corp.: 49-211-130-0054 (Fax)
City Economic Promotion: 49-211-899-5500
Economy/Technology Ministry: 49-211-83702
Igedo Fashion Fairs: 49-211-858-4823
Nowea (Trade Fair Headquarters): 49-211-858-4853
Venture Capital: 49-211-878974

Chambers of Commerce

Member Nations
Britain: 49-211-43740
   Northern Ireland:
   49-211-719011
Denmark: 49-211-392035
East Germany: 49-211-391031
France: 49-211-139920
Ireland: 49-211-353951
Italy: 49-211-387990
Netherlands: 49-211-498-7201
Spain: 49-211-480-621

Others
Düsseldorf Chamber:
49-211-35571
Austria: 49-211-324036
Canada
   British Columbia:
   49-211-353471
   Quebec: 49-211-320816
China: 49-211-8662905
France: 49-211-139920

India: 49-211-360598
Indonesia: 49-211-452908
Iran: 49-211-451018
Israel: 49-211-325272
Japan: 49-211-369001
   EIAJ (Electronics):
   49-211-369816
   Jetro: 49-211-136020
Korea: 49-211-362044
Norway: 49-211-45890
Singapore: 49-211-499269
Sri Lanka: 49-211-593053
Sweden: 49-211-452074
Switzerland: 49-211-434488
Taiwan: 49-211-84811
United States: 49-211-596798
   Missouri: 49-211-592025
   North Carolina: 49-211-320553
   US Embassy, Bonn:
   49-211-0228-3991

German Business Associations

Boilers, power plants: 49-211-485006
Chemical industry: 49-211-83890
Construction: 49-211-67031
German foundry: 49-211-68711
German steel: 49-211-370094
German welding: 49-211-154040
Glass industry: 49-211-168940
Iron, steel union: 49-211-8291
Iron, tin, metal: 49-211-454930
Ironworks engineers: 49-211-67070
Publishers: 49-211-363333
Retail trade: 49-211-498060

USEFUL MUNICH TELEPHONE NUMBERS

Trade and Commercial Information

Bavarian Chamber of Industry & Trade: 49-89-51160
Bavarian Foreign Trade Association: 49-89-557-7701
Munich City Information: 49-89-23911
Trade Fairs: 49-89-51070/500610
Bavarian Ministry for Economic Affairs Transport: 49-89-2162-2642
49-89-2162-2760 (Fax)

Consulates

Member Nations
Belgium: 49-89-397096
Britain: 49-89-394015
Denmark: 49-89-220441
France: 49-89-475016
Greece: 49-89-470-1061
Ireland: 49-89-985723
Italy: 49-89-418-0030
Netherlands: 49-89-594103
Portugal: 49-89-299932
Spain: 49-89-985027

Others
Argentina: 49-89-263787
Austria: 49-89-921090-0
Brazil: 49-89-227985

Canada: 49-89-558531
Finland: 49-89-221493
Indonesia: 49-89-294609
Japan: 49-89-471043-5
Jordan: 49-89-282953
Malaysia: 49-89-1232178
Mexico: 49-89-981617
Morocco: 49-89-476031
Netherlands: 49-89-594103
Norway: 49-89-224170
Philippines: 49-89-400482
Sweden: 49-89-264089
Switzerland: 49-89-347063
Thailand: 49-89-781997
Turkey: 49-89-176093

Facts on Greece

Capital Athens

Population 10,010,000

Unemployment 8.6%

GDP Growth 1988: 4%; 1989: 2.3%;
1990: 2%

GDP per Capita 1989: $5,399; 1990
(provisional): $5,611

Inflation (May to May) 1988: 12.5%; 1989:
13.1%; 1990: 22%; mid-1991: 18.1%

Industrial Production 1989: +1%; 1990
(est.): 1.5%

Trade ($ millions)
Trade Balance: −9,500
Invisible Receipts: 10,600
Current Account Deficit: −3,000
US Share: Foreign Investment 28.3%
US Share: Greek Imports 3.5%

GREECE

"Not even Latin America has such debts. We are on the verge of economic and moral ruin. We need hard work and sacrifice to avoid the last place in the EC." Constantine Mitsotakis, Greek Premier

THE LEADER OF THE NEW DEMOCRACY PARTY (CONSERVATIVE), which had scraped into power in the third general election within a year, was exaggerating—but only just—when he explained the need for sharp increases in the prices for light, gasoline, public transport, cigarettes, and alcohol, surtaxes on profits, and an end to the automatic indexation of State employees' wages. The drastic prices and incomes "medecine" is aimed at reducing demand and inflationary pressures. Its initial effect was to accelerate inflation by at least four points to the mid-twenties to triple the EC average before bringing it down to around 18 percent. The goal with inflation is to reduce the figure to 15 percent by the end of 1991 and to ten percent in 1992. If achieved, this latter figure will enable Greece to enter the exchange rate mechanism of the European Monetary System ahead of the Single Market. A second, accompanying aim is to reduce public sector borrowing which had rocketed to 27 percent of gross domestic product, and to cut the fiscal deficit by 50 percent in two years. Former economy Minister George Souflias blackened the picture—while blaming eight years of Socialist misspending—by stating dramatically: "We have reached a dead end." It seemed that the Greek economy had entered a fog in 1991 as thick as the notorious, suffocating, yellow *nefos* (pollution), which hangs over a capital burning cheap fuel and packed with aging automobiles. Then comes the breeze, and the Acropolis, and the Parthenon atop it, stand out with the Greek flag— first run up by resistance fighters to replace the wartime swastika— fluttering proudly. Mr. Mitsotakis wants to blow fresh air through the way the Greek economy is conducted, but some of his declarations ring hollow, given his tiny, one-seat majority in Parliament, the strength of the self-serving unions and lobbies, the incompetence and corruption of much of the civil service, the bad and slothful habits encouraged by previous forms of government based on give-aways and, last but not least, the rapidly-dwindling patience of Jacques Delors, head of the EC Commission in Brussels. The Commission has granted billions of dollars of regional and agricultural aid to Greece since it joined the EC in 1981, and wants, not unnaturally, to see some results. Eight, eleven or twenty billion dollars? No one will swear to the exact total of past, present or future EC aid. A lot went down some kind of Greek "black hole" during the years that the government was run by the profligate Socialist Andreas Panpandreou. Coming to power on the slogan "Out of the European Community," he decided to keep Greece as a member, after all, and took EC money for his decentralization program—and other less laudable spending which has since landed some ex-Ministers in the courts. These excesses gave way in 1989 to electoral stalemate and a form of left-right coalition government that amounted to no government at all. M. Delors was obliged to deliver an unprecedented warning to this all-party government over Greece's failure to honor the terms of the emergency EC grants of several billion dollars made in 1985. Similar sums are now being sought by Athens to tide the country over until the Mitsotakis government moves to the second, or medium-term stage of its "restructuring." Provided that it survives in Parliament, the New Democracy government will privatize or close some 40 heavily-indebted industries that have been under State control, a move not dissimilar to the recent privatization of State industry in Portugal. An early example of the change in policy was the decision to sell 49 percent of the heavily-indebted and loss-making Olympic Airways to other European carriers, and Olympic Catering to the private sector. The Olympic move was symbolic as the airline had been founded by the famous entrepreneur, the late Aristotle Onassis, before purchase by the state in 1975. The government will also grant tax breaks for foreign investment and re-investment in new technology, renewable energy, infrastructure, telecommunications, and tourism. Investment approvals will be faster (maximum delay: four months), while the stock market is to be opened up. Price controls have been abolished completely, and labor markets are being liberalized through the introduction of part-time employment and free collective bargaining.

Will it all work or will many proposals be watered down, as have been those designed to end the monstrous tax fraud of the 1980s which saw workers paying more than members of the professional classes? For one thing, membership of the EC condemns Greece to succeed. This time Brussels is going to keep a strict eye on internal Greek policy in exchange for guaranteeing market borrowings of $2 billion by Greece, matching finance for $9 billion to be borrowed by Athens for various major modernization projects up to 1993. Closer control will be the norm in future financial dealings between Brussels and Athens. Even Mr. Mitsotakis, a lawyer by training, was a couple of billion dollars "vague" in announcing some big figures of required EC aid. Yet his stand on public sector wage demands (and the many strikes) has been firm, always with a touch of dramatization belying his cold exterior. "Lack of money is the final law," he says over and over again to those at home, while seeking to persuade EC governments—and Washington—that the Greek house is being put in order finally. "The Socialist decade of the 1980s is over, the Liberal decade of the 1990s is in," he says. The would-be savior is no newcomer to Parliament, housed in the old royal palace on Syntagma square, the center of Athens life. At 71, Mitsotakis is a veteran of Greece's highly-charged political scene where cut-throat politics have long been a national vice, and 16 afternoon newspapers with sensational headlines vie for readers. The son of a prominent politician from the island of Crete whose brother was prime minister three times between 1910 and 1932, Mitsotakis became an MP at the age of 27. This was just after the end of the Second World War and at the time of the civil war, during which communist insurgents were defeated by rightwing nationalists, helped by Britain and the US. He served in many posts up to the "colonels coup" of 1967, which saw him arrested and exiled, as was Papandreou. Back from exile in Paris, Mitsotakis joined Constantine Karamanlis's New Democracy Party, becoming minister for economic coordination and then foreign minister. Later, as party leader, he lost three elections to Papandreou's Pan-Hellenic Socialist Movement (PASOK), before prevailing finally in the spring of 1990. The opposite of the charismatic, scandal-tainted America-baiter Papandreou, Mitsotakis set about mending bridges with Washington where then President Ronald Reagan and Vice President George Bush had removed Greek leaders from the invitation list. The new premier, announcing his free market policy in the US capital, remarked also that he was the first Greek leader to visit the US in 26 years. President Bush visited Athens in 1991. Settling the issue of the renewal of US bases in Greece and toughening the stance on international terrorism has also improved Greek-American relations significantly. Mitsotakis has traveled to give similar explanatory talks to leaders such as Chancellor Kohl, President Mitterand and, of course, to M. Delors.

Leading commentator George Pavlides had this to say: "The government has been trying hard to put across the message within Greece that the EC does not look upon the raising of taxes alone as the means to get the Greek economy back on the rails; rather it is the implementation of our development program which counts most with Brussels. Greece is virtually sitting for an exam before an EC board of examiners to prove its will and capability to streamline its economic system to one acceptable to the EC. If the Greek government bows to any kind of domestic pressure, be it from the Opposition or trade unions, then it will have lost the game for good. The EC underlines that the excessive surplus of workers in the public sector will have to be tackled as it is the principal cause of budget deficits and the inability to finance economic growth."

The first exam result seemed positive. First came an EC loan of $1.6 billion towards the cost of major infrastructure works—road construction, widening, and improvements, as well as better railways, marinas and harbors. Then the EC in 1991 granted Greece a $3 billion balance of payments loan, but there was a tart comment in the margin that the country had to try much harder, notably by reducing the inflation rate to the region of seven percent by the end of 1993. To achieve this, Greece is going to be forced to reduce government spending drastically—and with it State jobs. It was only this kind of effort, said Brussels, that would enable the drachma to enter Europe's exchange rate mechanism. The fierce Meltemi North wind whips the Cyclades islands before dropping to a whisper. The Greeks are hoping for the same calmer period in their politics.

MARKET OPPORTUNITIES

A new development law, designed to eliminate many bureaucratic obstacles, passed Parliament. It broadly revised earlier socialist legislation, known as Law 1262, which failed to attract any substantial foreign investment because projects of more than Dr2 billion ($13 million) required mandatory participation by the Greek State.

The new law abolishes the requirement and seeks to accelerate procedures for approval of investment proposals. It also seeks to direct investment towards particular areas, such luxury tourism and high technology. Other measures were included to reform the labor market, modernize the State banking system and bring Greece into line with its EC partners on real estate purchases.

In the past three years—the runup to the Single Market—most foreign investment has come in the form of takeovers and minority participation in private Greek companies in the food, insurance, and packaging sectors.

Greece is divided into four zones for investment-siting and incentives vary considerably. Zone A includes the major population centers of Athens and Salonika where investment and interest subsidies are not generally granted. Exceptions include investments which reduce pollution, conserve energy, introduce advanced technology, or involve relocation of existing industrial plants to less-developed areas.

The ratio of own capital is set at no less than 40 percent of total investment cost in subsidized Zone B, which includes most well-known tourist areas and smaller cities; at no less than 35 percent in Zone C, which includes provincial towns and the majority of the islands; at 25 percent in Zone D, which includes the outlying Dodecanese and the other border areas; and at only 15 percent in Thrace, which is the least-developed region of the European Community.

As Greece has lagged behind in high-tech investment, private investors will be allowed to bid for participation in the introduction of mobile telephones and other new communications. Standard incentives may be increased for investments that provide for swift introduction of information technology. The new law also permits the establishment of private clinics with a view to bringing in advanced medical technology.

To streamline procedures, investment applications can only be submitted in January and February, or in July and August each year. A uniform tax or fee will cover the various permits needed; the assessment period is to be shortened. The minimum investment covered by the new law is Dr30 million ($200,000) for farming projects and Dr60 million for industrial projects. The Dr2 billion ceiling on tax deductions has been lifted. Repatriation of capital and profits as well as royalties and service fees is permitted. Greece already conforms to EC rules on capital inflows and is due to come in line with its partners on capital outflows. This hopefully will result in considerable Greek capital held abroad.

The law sets the framework for the privatization of State-controlled companies, which has been proceeding extremely slowly. The first group consists of 29 industrial companies nationalized in the early 1980s, plus a second group of 80 concerns controlled by State-owned banks—several leading hotels, shipyards and mines. Incentives are being introduced for companies to join the Athens stock exchange which has fewer than 150 listings at the moment. Mergers, too, are included. The aim is to have more mergers and so make Greek industry, largely composed of units employing fewer than 100 people, more competitive in the new Europe. There are no restrictions on the percentage of foreign ownership in Greek companies.

Greece has long had in place legislation which gave advantages to foreign firms setting up branches to conduct business outside the country (Law 89/67). These firms are exempt from significant customs duties, taxes and other liabilities. The Greek incentives were introduced to attract firms fleeing Beirut. The US Embassy in Athens has a Regional Trade Development Office, which specifically helps regional marketing offices of US companies in Greece and Cyprus to promote trade in the Near East and North Africa. The British and other EC Embassies offer advice. The man who is regarded as the leading expert on the legislation is Gordon Ball, longtime British resident in Athens, president of consultancy firm Commissioners International, and chairman of the Eightynine Liaison Committee which represents Law 89 companies with the Greek government. (Key numbers: Tel: 672-4284/671-9890; Fax: 6479659). Ball states that Greece is the least-publicized base offering special privileges. Yet, hundreds of multinational corporations have taken advantage of the facilities. For two decades, companies have managed multi-country operations from Greece with staffs of from one to more than 200. Unlike many other business centers and offshore locations, this special Greek legislation does not require an enterprise to invest capital and to register a new legal entity, which may account for the relatively-low profile. Almost any legitimate foreign registered company can establish a branch office in Greece, from which to do business outside the country. None of the 'offshore' business activities are subject to Greek fiscal reporting requirements, nor is there any liability for Greek taxation of commercial business conducted outside Greece. Work permits are granted to foreign personnel, who have other privileges, too.

The early 1980s saw a downturn in these Law 89 companies. Then came an upsurge, with three hundred companies in the commercial sector, 800 in shipping. These provide a net gain annually in the region of some $300 million, which has been estimated as the equivalent of the spending of one million tourists "without the same strain on the nation's infrastructure." Mr. Ball continues, "It's a good time to make onshore investments in Greece for those with staying power over five to ten years. Law 89, too, is functioning better than ever. Don't forget, this country has a terrific location at the meeting of three continents." Others, however, say Greece is unfortunate that its immediate communist/ex-communist neighbors to the North are among the poorest of the old Warsaw Pact bloc with Yugoslavia falling apart. Yet, it is more than likely that Athens and Salonika, will eventually regain their traditional entrepôt roles, dating back to the Ottoman Empire.

A look at Law 89 companies gives an idea of who is putting money into Greece: advertising, banking, construction, communications, insurance, military hardware, and pharmaceuticals. The regions covered by these offices are not only the Middle East and Africa, but extend, in some cases, to Asia and Europe. Athens has had bad press—politics and pollution. The airport is improving, with a wider range of services. Though one time lax, security at the airport is now strict and is up to international standards. Apartment and house prices are rising but there are sufficient international schools. Personal security for executives is higher. Minor extremist groups make bangs in the night but could be on the way out in a climate tilted to pragmatic solutions of the nation's problems.

Greece's main problem remains the bureaucracy. The government is committed to reducing the size of the army of civil servants, but, then, most new-broom governments are. Still, a Law 89 company can be set up in three months with local advisers. Slightly different rules apply in the Marine sector of the 1989 legislation. How will the Single Market affect these offshore operations? The Greek Government is ready to sustain facilities by the introduction of modified regulations within the terms of EC membership. Adds Ball: "It could be said that the recent expansion of the Law 89 community in Athens is being stimulated by the evolving Single Market, as companies recognize the opportunity to use the south-east corner of the continent as a base to expand into other international markets."

S P O T L I G H T

• *The EC to the Rescue* •

The Greeks, warned by leftwing politicians at the start of the 1980s that they would be "enslaved" by the multinationals in the advent of the country's adhesion to the EC, have come to love the Community's generosity, which is based on a policy of raising the living standards of the poorer Southern, or Mediterranean, countries. As one rather cynical Athenian pointed out, how can you not love someone who has handed over $20 billion in less than a decade? This funding has saved whole regions from disaster, particularly the mountainous North, raised farmers' incomes, built roads, and propelled coastal zones and the Greek islands (or most of them) from an age of tending flocks to tending St. Tropez-style bars for tourists.

Not to put too fine a point on it, the EC is fed up with shelling out when obviously so much money has gone to waste. More money depends on the Greeks continuing to satisfy Jacques Delors and ECOFIN (European Finance Ministers as a group) that they are putting their house in order. Mitsotakis has promised "blood, sweat and tears," despite the waves of strikes that have greeted his austerity program. Anyway, says Brussels, the program is not tough enough. ECOFIN deregulations and the Eurocrats are calling for the restructuring of debt-ridden State-controlled insurance and pensions funds, and for much tougher measures on tax evasion, which has been described by Stelios Argyros, of the Federation of Greek Industries, as "theft on a national scale." Mitsotakis' ministers and senior officials are refining projects to make them more effective—and to make them more pleasing to Delors, whose new policy is that major infrastructure projects should have pan-European spinoff. Deputy Greek foreign minister, Esthinios Christodoulou, was named the government's new Mr. Europe and a coordination office was opened at the ministry (Tel: 361-0581). The office will match projects for all the regions, including Athens and surroundings, with the appropriate Euro fund, be it Feder, the European regional fund, or the Integrated Mediterranean Program, which has allocated some $4 billion to Greece. All this money will aid the small olive grower, but also help build the metro stations and, perhaps, a bridge across the Gulf of Patras. It will electrify railways, and bring in natural gas from Italy. Some say Athens is "condemned" to mend its ways as a member of the EC. Others point out that EC money could well go to Eastern Europe. The latter fear will hopefully provide the main impetus for reform. The table shows how Greece depends on trade with Europe, although its merchant fleet sails the world's seas:

TRADE WITH THE EC

	1980	1988
Exports to EC (as % of total)	47.6	65.1
of which: W. Germany	17.9	24.3
France	7.4	8.6
Italy	9.7	16.2
UK	4.1	8.2
Imports from EC (as % of total)	39.7	59.3
of which: W. Germany	13.9	22.2
France	6.2	7.8
Italy	8.2	12.3
UK	4.6	4.9

Source: OECD

continued

EC commissioners and senior officials meet regularly with the Greek government to discuss funding of infrastructure such as roads, railways, bridges, telecommunications and public works. The answer to the question asked by the Greeks as to how much they will receive depends greatly on Athens-Brussels entente, especially after previous rows over the way Greece has spent funds. The major planned projects under review are as follows.

THE ATHENS SUBWAY

Difficult in a city of such historical interest, but the system will skirt the famous ruins. A Siemens-led consortium, Olympic Metro, has been awarded the $1.5 billion contract for two lines with the main intersection under Syntagma Square. The Germans have gathered together 26 firms from different countries. There is a strong French presence, but more spin-off is expected, for the successful conclusion of the contract is vital for Athens' future.

RIO-ANTIRIO BRIDGE

This four or five year project is for a 1.8 kilometer suspension bridge to link the Peloponnese and the mainland at Patras. The plan is highly logical from a transport viewpoint, but Greece has been lacking in drive in asking for EC funds.

SPATA AIRPORT

This scheme is for a new international airport near Athens to relieve congestion. The current airport, except for those lucky enough to hold Olympic Airways business class seats, is primitive—long queues for undrinkable coffee in plastic cups. Phase one calls for one runway and several buildings for charter and cargo at the new airport. Olympic would like two new runways. Cost: Close to $300 million. Completion: A hopeful 1996.

RAILWAYS

There is a $2 billion project to modernize track, rolling stock, and equipment. The plan also calls for electrification and signalling equipment.

PORT HANDLING

A program calls for upgrading and expanding 15 international ports and smaller points. Piraeus and Sabnika are naturally in the first category.

HIGHWAYS

There are longstanding plans for a $1.8 billion modernization of the nation's highways. Again, thanks to EC money. (The EC office in Athens is next to Parliament:

2 Av Vass. Sofias
Tel: 7243-9824
Fax: 724-4620

Contact: Dr. Georges Tsouyopoulos, Director.

AIR TRAFFIC CONTROL

A $90 million modernization program to include a radar simulator, a datar processing and display system, a switching center, and a flight plan processing system. Delays are envisaged.

RADIO-TV

Greece legalized in late 1989 private and municipal TV and local radio. There are now 20 government and 300 private municipal radio stations, and three government and nine private TV stations. Major opportunities exist here

continued

for foreign firms that can provide equipment, consulting, and broadcasting services, and, of course, for programming.

TELECOMMUNICATIONS—VALUE ADDED SERVICES

Greece is opening up to services that could provide contracts worth $400 million to foreign firms. The Hellenic Telecommunications Organization (OTE) has, in the past, put local needs at: videotex, teletex, electronic mail, electronic funds transfer: 26 million drs; cellular phones: 19.5 million drs; international infrastructure networks: 15 million drs; and telex: 6 billion drs.

DIGITALIZATION

OTE also began a $4–5 billion program in 1990. Much of the work went to a German-Swedish-Greek consortium (Siemens, Ericsson, Intracom), but there remain subcontracting opportunities.

SATELLITES

OTE has a budget for turnkey earth stations and additional systems.

ACHELOOS RIVER

A $1.8 billion irrigation and hydroelectric project up to the year 2000 (five dams, five hydroelectric power stations and tunnels). Bechtel is involved.

FOOD PROCESSING/PACKAGING

The Ministry of Agriculture, the Agricultural Bank of Greece (AE), and the government-controlled agro-industrial cooperatives want new, modernized food processing and packaging units. The AE has a program of $500 million for some 300 projects.

HOSPITAL MODERNIZATION

The Health Ministry wants six, 300-bed, regional hospitals. Cost: $37 million each. Another plan is for a 700-bed University Hospital in Larissa, Central Greece.

ALUMINA

A 600,000 ton-per-year alumina plant is not expected before 1994. The Russians were coming, but now Kaiser Engineering is there.

NATURAL GAS

Another Greco-Soviet project, this time for one to two billion cubic feet of natural gas per year. A 437 kilometer pipeline.

LIQUEFIED NATURAL GAS

Algeria will provide 12 billion cubic meters of LNG over 12 years if all goes well. The US firm, Kellogg, is involved.

TRANSPORTATION AND COMMUNICATIONS

SHIPPING

The Greek shipping industry, in the minds of many people, is the huge fleet of ocean-going merchant vessels which carry cargoes all over the world, very few of them from or to the home country. Certainly, it was this section of the industry which created the image of the Greek shipping magnate, with his private island and plane, his homes in world capitals and his jet-setting lifestyle. Yet, there is another section of the industry more important to the Greeks themselves, namely domestic shipping comprising coastal passenger ships and ferries, coasters, and cruiseships flying the Greek flag. These three "trades" are protected under Greek law by cabotage regulations, preventing foreign vessels from entering the market.

An ongoing dispute within the EC has brought the subject to the fore. While most other member states favor lifting the restrictions, Greece has strongly opposed such a move for many years. With the Single Market virtually a fact, the Greek government has realized that it is impossible to hold out against change, but it is working hard to secure the best possible terms for its ships.

Some 26,000 seafarers work on ships enjoying cabotage protection in Greece. Greek legislation on employment and social welfare conditions differs from that of other countries. For example, hotel staff on cruiseships are considered under Greek law to be seafarers, a status that does not exist elsewhere. There is concern about jobs should the market be opened to permit foreign vessels to cruise in Greek waters using Greek ports as points of embarcation and debarcation.

Greece has a coastline of 1,600 kilometers and hundreds of populated islands. There is further concern that the social need to link the islands with the mainland through a boat service may be disrupted if foreign companies operate vessels only at peak tourist periods. Until now, the Greek government has subsidized the island lines.

The Greeks also say that cabotage is linked to national security. Greece and neighboring Turkey are both members of NATO, but have been in a state of animosity for decades over divided Cyprus. Clashes frequently occur between Athens and Ankara over territorial waters, airspace rights, and other aspects of control of the East Aegean. Many Greek islands are infinitely closer to Turkey than they are to the Greek mainland.

Greece wants the EC to implement a 1990 decision to make a full study of the effects of change. It also wants the eventual freeing of cabotage to be part of the framework of a common shipping policy. The opening up of domestic shipping is unlikely to take place in 1993, as planned by Brussels.

AIR

Greece's state-owned Olympic Airways has been plagued with debts and lack of profits for years and the government has decided to sell a minority stake which may be as high as 49 percent. Talks were opened with KLM, SAS and Swissair, while shares may be offered to the public. The Gulf War was the coup de grâce to an already ailing company which had lost 10 billion drachmas in 1990 and which started 1991 on a similarly depressing note. The airline was forced to trim domestic and international flights, including New York, Amsterdam, Stuttgart, Vienna Zurich, and other European destinations, by almost one third. Work on new buildings, renovations and modifications to installations were suspended. Efforts were also made to privatize Olympic Catering, which supplies inflight meals. A Lebanese firm registered in Greece made a bid. Also for sale is Olympic Aviation, a fleet of small turboprop planes serving the Greek islands. Meanwhile, it is not known when construction of the new airport for Athens at Spata, 12 miles from the capital, will begin.

MANAGEMENT AND WORKFORCE

In the 1980s, the public and semi-public sectors in Greece came to absorb an incredible 80 percent of national resources, compared with a more normal 30 percent in the previous decade. Heavily-subsidized public companies competed unfairly with private ones, sometimes forcing them into bankruptcy, into foreign hands or into the orbits of State banks, thus swelling the public sector even further. Small wonder that the new government and its leader started talking about closing ailing industries "immediately" when it won a vote of confidence following the closely fought election. Mitsotakis, in fact, talked of acting "next week. . . we have no time to lose" in his dash for modernization. Some notorious, Socialist-created barter trading companies were closed virtually on the spot, but the pace has been much more measured because of problems in finding takers. There's also the social problem of laying off thousands upon thousands of workers. Still, there's even agreement on the Left that the so called "problematic companies," swept up into the State sector in the later 1970s and the early 1980s have no place there. Mitsotakis has pledged to cut and cut again in order to reduce the public sector drastically and make room for a competitive private sector. The privatization program will involve 100 firms of all sizes, including the country's largest cement, textile, and mining concerns, most shipbuilding and ship-repairing units, and the entire paper industry. Nearly one third of these, the "problematic firms," came under the auspices of Papandreou's Organization for the Economic Restructuring of Industry. Professor George Yannopoulos, who came in to head the organization with the singular aim of closing it down, said the State's attempt to run these 30 firms was a "dismal failure." In six years it wrote off close to $2 billion, while the companies accumulated losses of another one billion dollars. Yannapoulos planned to shut down all non-viable companies, particularly those which are also corrupt and which have been engaged in coffee and wood trading, as well as Yugoslav grain trading for which special EC payments were illegally obtained. Attempts have been made to find buyers for others—shipping, textiles, canning, and more. Public offerings are being considered in a few cases only, for the government wants to stop the flow of funds into ailing companies and to pocket as much as possible as quickly as possible by sales. But the government will have to await the final rulings of the European Court of Justice and an Athens court, which have indicated that EC company law had been broken by government aid in the mid-1980s. Many of the ailing companies had come to belong to the State banks: the National Bank of Greece (Tel: 321-0411, Telex: 214-931/8); the Commercial Bank of Greece (Tel: 321-0911, Telex: 216-545); and the Hellenic Industrial Development Bank (Telex: 215-203, Fax: 362-1023). Meanwhile, Michalis Vranopoulos, head of the Commerce Bank, Greece's second largest after the National Bank, says the process in Greece should really be called "reprivatization," as many industries had been driven by rising labor costs and the strict price controls of 1982–85 into the arms of the official restructuring organization (OAE). The process of closing or selling 100 companies will be a long one. There have been auctions in some cases; in others OAE has had to make even lengthier inventories in order to attract private interests. Greek and Foreign banks—such as ETEBA and Citicorp—have made assessments. Among the bigger deals was that involving Ciments Francais' purchase of 85 percent of Halips Cement, one of the several "ailing" companies in the portfolio of the National Bank. The French assumed liabilities of $50 million and then set about looking for other companies to add to concrete firms and quarries it already owns in Greece. In general, new owners will be absolved from paying old debts.

S P O T L I G H T

• *Tourism* •

"Greece's search for rich tourists continues," said the mid-1990 headline. Then came the Gulf War, which put an 18 percent dent in tourism in the first half of the 1991 season. Greece, just like Spain and Portugal, wants to upgrade its tourism via more free-spending visitors as opposed to backpackers hopping the islands by boat. Even now, visitors spend $2.7 billion a year. The Mediterranean region attracts some 170 million tourists and business travelers a year. Greece's share, namely nine million, is but five percent, although it sometimes seems higher in the overflowing Plaka district of Athens or on fashionable islands such as Mykonos. Wooing better-off tourists means not only trying to persuade Greek-Americans "to go back to the land of the ancestors," or telling Jewish-Americans that the climate has changed with the new government's full recognition of Israel; it means improving hotels built in the 1970s, airports, railway stations, roads, water, communications, and the cleanliness of the beaches. And lowering the capital's smog level. Greece has so much to offer visitors, with its incomparable heritage and thousands of islands, but a lot of new investment is needed in services, buildings, and training in what is the largest, foreign currency earning sector of the economy,

continued

representing six percent of the GDP. The mid-1990 national development law, the major attempt by the center-right government to break with the past, offered tax breaks for those, Greek and foreigners, willing to spend on new hotels, conference facilities, yacht marinas, and the like. Big question marks may remain over the date for a new Athens airport, and the city's long-planned metro, but Olympic Airways is renewing its fleet and installing a new *esprit de corps* to return to the standards established by tycoon Aristotle Onassis when he created the airline in the 1950s. It served caviar in those days. Pilot Loukas Grammatikos, who quit as the airline's boss when Mr. Andreas Papandreou's Socialists came to power in 1981, returned to the top job, and wants to see the airline privatized as soon as possible and then made profitable. Many new routes are being opened—to Tokyo, for example—and from Salonika to other Eurocities. The laws protecting many of the islands from foreign investors are being scrapped. The Rothschild family took the Greek government to the European Court over their right to have property on Corfu island and won. The way is now open for property investment, not only in Corfu, but in other former "border zones," such as Crete and Santorini. Take the island of Paros. Prices are rising as new investors enter the market. A major new hotel with golf links is to be built at Naoussa, the artists' town. German restaurateurs have opened fancy new eating places with English kitchen staff. The Greeks are taking the plunge. General Athanassios Papanikolaou (retired), who saw Korean War service, and his daughter, Lila, have built the magnificent Philoxenia Hotel at New Golden Beach, and have captured much of the lucrative market of gourmets-cum-windsurfers. Naxos is getting a new airport. Buy now and double your money? No longer quite true in the Cyclades Islands, but there are fine investment chances—and the ubiquitous Swedes and other Scandinavians are stepping ashore from ferry boats clutching check books. Greece, however, knows it has to offer more if it wants to win back the jet set. There are signs that this is happening. Much of Greece's beauty is eternal, the drachma is cheaper, and competition from other Mediterranean holiday and leisure investment zones is forcing the tourist industry to make a new effort. The government is insisting that each island should retain its distinctive colors when it comes to new building. It also plans to sell off state-owned hotels. One big boost came when President Bush was pictured, smiling, at the Acropolis.

REAL ESTATE

High-class office accommodation is cruelly lacking in Athens. A new mayor intends to change radically the way the city goes about its daily business and maybe he will turn his attention to the problem of business offices. The current shortage has led to a situation in the main business area around Syntagma Square in which monthly rents have risen to 6,000 drachmas the square meter. In one case, the owner asked for six years rent in advance. Rents are slightly cheaper in the commercial area around Omonoia Square. Otherwise, the best bet is the suburbs, but then there's Athens traffic to contend with—and that's daunting. In fact, business in Greece is daunting.

• *Getting To Know the Capital* •

The hub of Athens life is wedged between the Acropolis to the southwest and the little conical mountain to the northeast, Lycabettus. Roughly equidistant between them is Syntagma (Constitution) Square, with its sidewalk cafés facing the old royal palace, now the Parliament Building. Near Syntagma and the other main square, Omonoia (Concord), is the Plaka, a cluster of winding, cobblestoned streets that comprise the heart of the old market district. The smaller Monastiraki

Square is near the Plaka, which is nestled beneath the Acropolis. Whereas Syntagma is modern and emphatically touristy, Omonoia has more local flavor and is teeming with Greeks haggling and debating on the sidewalks. Clearly, they don't pay the first price asked.

On a first or even second visit to Athens, you will do better to take taxis than risk the hazards of overcrowded buses bearing destination boards in the Greek alphabet. All taxis have meters so make sure the one in yours is switched on before the journey starts. Most drivers speak English of a kind, or at least understand it, but some become surprisingly tongue-tied if you try to negotiate a fare instead of relying on the metered price.

EUROCITY SALONIKA

The city, known to Greeks as Thessaloniki, is capital of Macedonia and northern Greece, the natural port of the Balkans. The opening of East European markets is expected to have a considerable impact on the Greek economy, although this may take time. It is in Salonika—not Athens—that the changes are viewed as the beginning of a new era and commerce and industry are preparing. Until a few years ago, more than half of Greek industry was concentrated in Attica, around Athens. Today the balance is tilting towards the north.

Central Macedonia is responsible for a large volume of exports, particularly to other EC member countries. Exports from northern Greece, as a whole, now account for half the country's total. This export activity has meant Salonika taking over from Piraeus as the leading port.

The growing importance of northern Greece was reflected in recent EC assistance for infrastructure works. Out of the 776 million ECU for Greece, Central Macedonia will receive 213 million and Thessalia, which belongs to the greater area of Salonika, 123 million. Macedonia and Thrace, additionally, have been allocated 863 million ECU for the EC's special program, known as the Integrated Mediterranean Program for 1986–92.

Aside from its archaeological attractions—the city dates back to

316BC—Salonika is known outside Greece for its annual international fair. The 1989 fair, for example, attracted 3,400 Greek and foreign companies. The fair will increasingly become a Balkan "shop window." Air links to European cities, West and East, are being improved, notably by the national carrier, Olympic. Salonika seems set to challenge the leadership of Athens and become the major financial and industrial center.

┊┊┊┊┊┊SUCCESS STORY—DOW HELLAS ┊┊┊┊┊┊

Dow Hellas has increased production capacity eight times in the 30 years it has operated as a wholly-owned subsidiary of Dow Chemical. There are no strikes and the technologically-advanced plant produces 15 types of polystyrene around the clock, with a fifth of output going for export. Happy days? Not quite. Dow in Greece hopes the new government will move fast to answer longstanding complaints by it and other multinationals over frustrating legislation, restrictions, and bureaucracy in the important fields of profits and taxes. Dow and the others want Greece to relax regulations on the repatriation of profits and to stop hitting them out of the blue with various retroactive taxes. (Other companies complain of the past tendency to disallow the books on technicalities.) Only when these reforms are firmly in place, says Dow's regional general manager and managing director Efstathios (Steve) Asvestis, will the top management at Dow and elsewhere agree to invest heavily in Greece, as opposed to elsewhere in Eastern and Western Europe. Managers in Greece who propose excellent projects to headquarters receive answers like: "All right, so you make profits, even increase them, but the stock owner sees only 12 percent of this." Asvestis adds: "As a Greek, the situation to date has not made sense to me, given the drive to attract investment and technology. I don't think there would be a drain of more than $50 million if total profit repatriation was allowed for Dow and two or three other companies. Against that, I could bring in twice as much in two years. We could expand exports tomorrow by 50,000 tons for we have the markets..."

Dow's modern plant at Lavrion employs a small staff of 80, given that production is highly computerized. Another 80 people work in the offices at Nea Smyrni, Athens. Asvestis, a Dow veteran, puts the total lack of work stoppages down to the fact that Dow Hellas treats its workers as "partners," and thus has avoided the indiscipline rife in many other sectors. He's also proud of what he says is "zero pollution" at Lavrion. The water is cleaned after use within the plant and is then sprayed on the 5,000 trees planted in the once-barren surroundings.

Dow, says Asvestis, will be investing some $300 million dollars a year in Western and Eastern Europe, including the Soviet Union, in the next few years. Half will go on modernization, half on new units. He has to compete for funds with other Dow companies across Europe, notably in Italy and Spain, and now with future units to the East. He spoke of another aspect which influences headquarters back in Midland, Michigan, namely those retroactive taxes. "Dow has never made use of investment grants (now being phased out) as it seeks stability not subsidies. A recent, retroactive tax of five percent was the third in 15 years and this kind of thing ruins my economic evaluations in the eyes of management. In my view, a multinational in the full sense is not going to be induced by any amount of money. If you offer me 50 percent free money or a freeze of the tax situation for 15 years, then I'll take the freeze." This philosophy has gained rapid ground with the new government, with its new investment incentives. Until the 1990 elections, US executives were more than hinting to the authorities that there was no great secret to the success of Ireland, Portugal, and Spain. Conditions there were more stable. Now the warning concerns Eastern Europe where many workers are disciplined, hard-working—and relatively "cheap."

• *Eyewitness* •

Jean Bourne

Greece has a triple personality—European, Balkan and Mediterranean. The new government has provided Greeks with a sharp reminder of the importance of their European "face."

For the moment, Greek lifestyle remains as casual as ever, and the staple nightlife gatherings at tavernas with tables full of friends, food, and wine continues. The carefree and spontaneous way of life for which the Greeks are known could soon be a thing of the past, as double-digit inflation combined with austerity measures limit their spending power.

Greece is virgin territory for almost every kind of project, ripe for everything from new technology to new trends. Yet, the country's lack of infrastructure makes both living and working somewhat difficult. There are strikes—banks, transport, electricity. The maze of bureaucracy on bad days seems personally vengeful. The lack of easily obtainable information can also be maddening. Everything from getting a residence or work permit to finding a telephone number usually requires personal contacts.

Apart from this bureaucratic disorganization, Greece's atmosphere, even in Athens, remains friendly. It is perhaps one of the few European countries where people aren't afraid to walk the streets after dark. Despite rising rents and inflation, Greece remains one of the least expensive countries in the EC. Greece's informal attitude, a quaint part of its problem—businesspeople, for example, are often expected to turn up late for appointments as a matter of practice—will probably be lost in the move to the "real" Europe.

THE LEADERS

TOP 10 INDUSTRIAL COMPANIES (1989)

		(1000dr)	
		Sales	*Pre-tax profits*
(1)	Aluminum Greece	52,216,620	11,444,982
(2)	Titan Cement	33,348,265	4,730,167
(3)	Hellenic Bottling	40,666,960	4,567,470
(4)	Thassaloniki Refineries	46,631,691	3,599,144
(5)	Herakles Cement	39,146,993	3,464,724
(6)	Papastratos Cigarettes	20,300,469	2,801,929
(7)	Sidenor Iron	18,135,787	2,643,099
(8)	Intracom telecoms	12,250,094	2,458,933
(9)	Hellenic Steel	11,334,798	2,430,620
(10)	Thessaly Steel	14,425,895	2,254,992

TOP 10 COMMERCIAL COMPANIES

			(1000dr)
		Sales	*Pre-tax profits*
(1)	Dutyfree Stores	12,883,472	4,296,647
(2)	Theocharakis Autos	32,146,235	1,891,013
(3)	Toyota Hellas	34,548,318	1,851,033
(4)	Zamba Machinery	3,501,384	1,166,737
(5)	Philips Hellas	13,922,391	1,063,094
(6)	Siemens	11,666,711	972,683
(7)	Procter & Gamble	12,758,603	881,838
(8)	Texaco Hellas	36,079,975	807,142
(9)	Jason	7,551,325	789,570
(10)	3M Hellas	2,631,549	689,567

(Source: ICAP Hella SA)

KEY CONTACTS

USEFUL ATHENS TELEPHONE NUMBERS

Trade and Commercial Information

European Community: 30-1-724-3982
European Parliament: 30-1-723-3422
United Nations: 30-1-322-9624
UN Environment Program: 30-1-723-6586
Association of Commercial Agents: 30-1-323-2622
Exports Promotion Organization: 30-1-322-6871
   Fine Arts: 30-1-323-1230
   Handicrafts: 30-1-363-0253
   Hotels: 30-1-323-6641
   Shipping: 30-1-411-8811

Government Offices

Prime Minister's Office: 30-1-364-2640
Agriculture: 30-1-529-1111

Commerce: 30-1-361-6241
Defense: 30-1-644-2918
(Switchboard: 30-1-646-5201
Economy: 30-1-324-7742
(Switchboard: 30-1-323-0931
Finance: 30-1-322-4071
Foreign Affairs (plus Euro Office): 30-1-361-0581
Education: 30-1-323-5730
(Switchboard: 30-1-323-0461
Environment, Town Planning, Public Works: 30-1-643-1461
Health, Social Security, Industry, Energy: 30-1-523-2820
Technology: 30-1-770-8615
Labor: 30-1-523-0385
(Switchboard: 30-1-523-3110
Merchant Marine: 30-1-411-3340
(Switchboard: 30-1-412-1211
Presidency: 30-1-724-8721
Public Order: 30-1-692-8510
Transport, Communications: 30-1-325-1211

(Switchboard numbers given can sometimes reply quicker than "direct" lines)

Chambers of Commerce

Athens: 30-1-360-4815
American Hellenic: 30-1-363-6407
British Hellenic: 30-1-721-0361
International: 30-1-361-0879

Embassies

Member Nations
Belgium: 30-1-361-7886
Britain: 30-1-723-6211
Denmark: 30-1-724-9315
France: 30-1-361-1663
Germany: 30-1-685-1164
Ireland: 30-1-723-2771
Italy: 30-1-361-1723
Luxembourg: 30-1-417-9515
Netherlands: 30-1-723-9701

Portugal: 30-1-729-0096
Spain: 30-1-721-4885

Other
Canada: 30-1-723-9511
Japan: 30-1-775-8101
United States: 30-1-721-2951

Facts on Ireland

. . . .

Capital Dublin
Population 3.5m
Working Population 1.3m
Unemployment 18.5%
GDP Growth 1989: 5%; 1990: 5.5%; 1991
   (est.): 2%
GDP per Capita 1989: $8,684; 1990: $10,298
Inflation 1988: 2.7%; 1989: 4.7%; 1990:
   3.4%; 1991 (est.) 2.7%
Trade Balance $3.5b
Irish–US Trade (1989) Exports: $2.8b
   (+ $1.16b)

. . . .

IRELAND

"Someone who is not strong has to be clever." An Irish banker addressing a European investment symposium in Seville

IRELAND, AT THE WESTERN EXTREMITY OF THE EC, HAS LONG TRIED harder than any other Community country to attract foreign investment. The going has been rough sometimes as other nations improved their incentives to match those of the Irish. However, the Irish have always offered the lowest tax levels on corporate profits and have created an export-oriented society in a couple of decades with a ratio of exports to GNP of 65 percent, as high as Belgium the EC's frontrunner. All in all, some 1,000 foreign companies have set up in Ireland, often on green field sites. They have been British, German, and Japanese, but, above all, American. For example, Michael Smith, former Minister for industry and commerce in the Charles Haughey government, proudly stated that of the top 15 US pharmaceutical concerns, some 14 were present in Ireland. Electronics, too, is a major industry and exporter. The growth of exports slowed slightly in 1990, rising only 11 percent, but Americans sold 40 percent of the total and were therefore largely responsible for maintaining Ireland's trade surplus. A US trade official in Dublin put it another way: "American companies in Ireland are still smiling."

Most companies have stayed and expanded not only because of the "famous" 10 percent Irish corporate tax, but also because of a young and skilled workforce. All political parties, the government Fianna Fail, and others, agree that these youngsters are Ireland's best hope for the future. In addition, Ireland's scenic attractions have helped pull in the businessmen as well as the golfers and fishing folk.

Some analysts were claiming not so long ago that Ireland's future in the Single Market was far from guaranteed, given that 18 years membership of the EC had failed to promote the country from the bottom group, or trio, of member states—Greece, Portugal and Ireland—and that gross domestic product by head remained some 60 percent of the EC average. There is fear that future foreign investment could go elsewhere, given the geographical factor, a population of only 3.5 million (half the size of London or Paris), a labor force of 1.2 million, accompanied by unemployment that remains stubbornly at around 18 percent. Certainly, the local economy is miniscule in European terms, representing a tiny one percent of the total of the EC. Government policies in the not-so-distant past were reckless, based on borrowing and spending a way out of the worldwide slump of the 1970s. Not surprisingly, the national debt soared with the inevitable result for the Irish of high personal income taxes.

Yet, the Irish persevered, attracted more companies, achieved higher growth and trade surpluses, and proved themselves excellent Europeans—something which has and will stand them in good stead when the EC makes regional grants. A program of national recovery was worked out in 1987 and was signed by government unions, employers, and farmers. Things began to look up after the bleak period of the early 1980s. There was real gross national product growth of 4.25 percent in 1989, compared with about one percent in 1988. It was 5.5 percent in 1990 and the continuing surge in exports meant Ireland was exporting more per head than Japan. The Irish government has also been successful in trimming the budget deficit and stabilizing national debt although the latter remains a drain on resources with debt servicing costing I£35 a week for every worker. Unemployment, always a serious problem in Ireland, fell after 1987 due to significant emigration and moderate success in job creation. It rose again when some emigrants returned, but overall Ireland's efforts to join the advanced EC countries by the year 2000 are bearing fruit.

As the American Embassy in Dublin states in its latest review of the Irish economy: "The past two years represented a watershed...after more than a decade of poor economic performance, rapidly-rising government debt, high inflation, and unemployment, the economy showed promising signs." The chances also are good for a prolonging of the "program of national recovery," with its private sector wage increases of four percent, which has made a significant—some would claim dramatic—difference to the government's fiscal position, as well as to business and consumer confidence. The importance of cash grants ranging from 45 to 60 percent cannot be underestimated.

Among the foreign manufacturers, Ireland has attracted IBM, General Electric, NEC, Kodak, and Nixdorf, to name but five. More recently, Nissan Diesel, part of Japan's second largest car maker, said it would assemble medium duty trucks near Dublin, its first assembly operation in Western Europe. Software leaders, such as Ashton Tate, Lotus, and Microsoft, have been drawn to Ireland. Among the industrial zones in what was once a farming society is that around Shannon Airport. Now, the government's aim is to attract major names from the world's financial community to the ambitious, offshore International Financial Services Center, rising in Dublin's Custom House Docks area.

The US pharmaceutical presence with its heavy R & D spending is of particular importance to the Irish Development Authority when selling the merits of the country. Michael Smith, the development minister says that these companies during high-profit years need to be researching the next generation of winning products and that Ireland's low tax system makes this possible.

In two decades, the Irish electronics industry has gone from nothing to one employing 26,000 people and providing a third of exports. Smith offers these thoughts about the place of smaller countries in the New Europe. "The theory is that in 1993 all member states of the EC will be equal, that all will be the same throughout the Community. It's more likely that there will remain strong regional differences. Labor skills and conditions, for example, will be very different between Germany and Portugal. Both countries are good industrial locations, but for very different reasons. Ireland might not be an attractive location if a company has to be in the center of the market. If, however, the company needs people or low tax or both, then Ireland is very attractive ...Other, less-developed regions should concentrate on these factors if they are to offset the attractions of the central, developed regions. In the spirit of the commitment to economic and social cohesion enshrined in the Single European Act, the European Community must ensure that the less-developed regions are helped in building on these strengths."

The Irish authorities believe there will be even greater export opportunities in the Single Market despite the government's political problems of 1991. The National Economic and Social Council in Dublin published in late 1989 an exhaustive, academic account of Ireland within the EC. It concluded: "Ireland's strategic approach to the European Community should be based on creating a genuine European economic and monetary union," by which it meant not just the Single Market, but also common social policy, R & D development, and protection of the environment. That said, the Irish are not altogether happy with the way the Commission is undertaking the task.

Be that as it may, the European Commission is happier with Ireland. The EC in 1990 granted some £800 million to improve road, rail, and air links, both within the Republic and between Ireland and the rest of Europe. The grant was one of the largest ever made to a single country and the hope is that this massive handout will make a decisive difference to the development of trade and tourism. The EC said the money would be used to tackle two of the fundamental problems of Ireland's economy: high access costs resulting from the country's peripheral position, and the poor transport infrastructure. These are EC Objective One funding projects, for across-the-board infrastructure improvements and the main aim is to help reduce transport costs for Irish exporters to Europe by a quarter in the mid-1990s. The aid will be spent on improving main national roads, airport development, and upgrading the leading ports. Among the improvements are the main roads between Rosslare and Northern Ireland, work at Dublin airport on both runways and the terminal, and better roll-on, roll-off ferry services between Dublin, Waterford, and Rosslare to the rest of Europe. The Dublin-Belfast (Northern Ireland) rail link will be modernized. These improvements will be of immense help to groups such as Kerry, the one billion dollar a year dairy concern in the extreme southwest, whose managing director Denis Brosnan has long complained about Brussels not doing enough for those "on the edge."

MARKET OPPORTUNITIES

When it comes to the electronics and engineering sector, the fanfare of the Irish Industrial Development Authority is justified. Fifteen years ago, this sector consisted of just a few companies with less than 5,000 employees, generating a mere six percent of the country's industrial exports. Currently, there are more than 400 electronic companies, employing 26,000 people and accounting for 29 percent of Ireland's total exports, with a value of IR£3 billion, or more than 16 percent of GNP. Some big names invested in Ireland in the 1989–90 period. Intel (US), the semi-conductor manufacturer, announced an IR£300 million investment which will create some 2,600 jobs. SCI Systems set up in Cork. Pratt & Whitney established a joint venture with Airmotive to re-manufacture engine casings. Motorola will produce radio communications products and systems in Dublin, while Cork will become a European center for cellular phones. General Motors, via its information technology subsidiary, Electronic Data Systems, of Dallas, is establishing a systems engineering development center in Dublin to support 15 centers in Europe. Fujitsu Isotec, a leader in printer technology, has just established a computer printer component operation in Dublin, while Brother, the Japanese electronics company, is expanding its capacity for components for dot matrix printers, microwave ovens, and electronic typewriters. These companies join prominent names in electronics already established in Ireland. Among them are Digital, with three plants and rapidly-expanding Apple. AT&T has chosen its Irish plant as the center for rural telecommunications products. Ireland has attracted much of this investment as a result of relatively high numbers of computer and engineering graduates. Research projects at Dublin City University, for example, include robot guidance with artificial vision, computer-aided control system design, and semi-conductor research. Dublin's Trinity College, in a joint venture with Hitachi, has established a lab for research into networks and high-level language involving super computers. In addition, Limerick University is linked with Sumitomo in an optoelectronics research and development center.

Investment has been varied. Kromberg & Schubert opened in Waterford in 1973 as a satellite production unit supplying cable harnass to its sister company in Germany. The next stage involved the manufacture of insulated wire and cable assemblies and the setting up of sales and technical engineering units. Today, the Germans employ 950 at the Waterford plant. Underway is a wire drawing facility to produce multicore cable for the computer industry. Kromberg says its operation in Ireland has been "highly profitable." Customers include Daimler Benz, BMW, Ford Opel, and Vauxhall for cable harnass, while cable assemblies are sent to IBM Scotland, England, France, and Sweden. In all, Kromberg now employs some 3,200 people.

In 1971 Digital Equipment Corporation (DEC) opened its first high-volume manufacturing plant outside the US at Ballybrit, Galway. Since then, the Irish company has progressed from a US-managed final assembly and test site into three separate Irish-managed manufacturing facilities, each of which is now heavily involved in R&D. Now, DEC Ireland makes complex DEC products. Hardware R&D has been created at Clonmel and Galway, while there has been software buildup at Galway.

Again, it was the pool of computer sciences graduates that persuaded Andy De Mari and his partners in Santa Monica-based Retix to set up in Ireland. De Mari had been a frequent visitor to Ireland over 20 years and knew many software engineers. Retix started up a unit for the design and development of communications software and began employing several dozen of Ireland's top graduates. Retix says its market is expanding at the rate of 40 percent a year, notably with IBM and Boeing, while it reckons the total information systems market worldwide will be $142 billion in 1992. In fact, some 55 percent of total European GNP is covered, touched upon or connected with information technology, making it by far the largest industry sector. In a related area, General Electrics Informations Services established a software center in Blackrock, Co. Dublin, where the company, Geisco Software Development, creates software for the international banking community, as well as for the new Dublin financial services center.

Ireland's Industrial Development Authority (IDA) is probably the most efficient inward investment organization around, relying in part on the famous "Murphia" oldboy network. The IDA takes care of everything—or so it seems. But of all these "advantages," the greatest is perhaps the well-trained graduate in a Europe with a distinct "graying" problem. One-third of school-leavers in Ireland go on to university or college education. Major companies—Philips, Siemens and ICI, to name but three—have taken advantage of this.

The US stake in Ireland is by far the biggest among foreign investors. Of the 950 odd foreign firms in the Republic, some 350 are American, employing close to 40,000 people. The US is the largest source of inward investment, accounting for 48 percent of all overseas manufacturing jobs and more than 18 percent of total manufacturing employment. US Department of Commerce figures show that the average return on US manufacturing investment in Ireland has been 22 percent—four times the EC average in the 1980s.

HOUSEHOLD PRODUCTS

This market, estimated to be worth $584 million in 1989, is growing at a rate of five percent a year. Imports in 1989 were $182 million, with domestic electrical appliances the principal items. In recent years, metallic cookware, brooms and brushes, wooden products, lawnmowers, and hand tools have all experienced growth. Real average annual growth in imports between 1989 and 1991 is forecast at six to eight percent. US imports account for five percent of all imports. There has been a shift in sales away from traditional outlets (hardware and grocery stores) towards supermarkets and do-it-yourself superstores, though not on the same scale as in other EC countries because of the lack of large population centers. US exports to Ireland in general increased by 14 percent in 1989 to $2.5 billion (computers and peripherals, drugs and pharmaceuticals, electronics) but opportunities exist in a wide variety of areas, including domestic electrical appliances, hand tools, wooden products, lawnmowers, glassware, metallic cookware, cutlery, plastic housewares, and ceramics.

INTERNATIONAL FINANCIAL SERVICES

The new Dublin International Financial Services Center had 130 committed projects last spring, with another 25 in the pipeline. A quarter were from the US and Canada. The center offers US companies the chance to establish an EC financial base—maximum tax of ten percent until the year 2000 for all non-Irish pound financial transactions. The five principal activities are asset financing, captive insurance, fund and investment management, corporate treasury management and insurance/re-insurance. Companies in the following sectors are likely to be attracted to the center: banking, legal, securities, accounting, insurance, stockbroking, leasing, computer software, factoring, information technology, credit/charge card, and treasury operations of multi-nationals.

FRANCHISING

This is a growth industry expanding at an annual rate of 25 percent. It is limited in terms of the size of the population, but the country can be considered as an entry point into the EC market of 320 million by US franchisers. The principal markets served by franchising systems in Ireland are fast food, home improvement and fitting, home cleaning and repair, health and beauty, clothes and accessories, convenience retailing, transport, printing, and leisure.

FOOD PROCESSING

This is Ireland's largest indigenous industry and has been targeted by the Industrial Development Authority (IDA) for development. The IDA estimates that $1.1 billion will be invested in buildings and plants by 1992. Between 1983 and 1987, the IDA invested $500 million in the industry and has earmarked $950 million by 1992. Rapid growth is foreseen as many of the larger co-ops and food commodity firms reorient themselves in producing processed, value-added food products. Food processing companies are expected to invest at least $90 million per annum in Ireland in the next five years. Machinery imports, with 95 percent of the market, are dominant. Export opportunities exist particularly in meat processing with the $750 million spent in the beef industry in recent years and up to 1992. Dairy food processing is another sector of heavy investment, as is the fish processing market.

MEDICAL EQUIPMENT

The medical instruments, equipment and supplies market, estimated at just over $100 million, is set to grow by five percent a year, reflecting higher government health expenditure. Consumables are up, but capital equipment has declined. Imports are higher than demand, as Ireland is used as a distribution point for EC countries. The US dominates the import market and exporters work through four or five major distributors.

PROCESS CONTROL

Process control equipment is important in manufacturing plants, particularly the dairy, pharmaceutical, and brewing sectors. Irish manufacturing industry has been a strong growth sector in recent years, creating 35,000 new jobs between 1987 and 1989. Foreign investment has played a large part in this growth with over 80,000 people employed in the 900 foreign companies. Fourteen of the top 15 international pharmaceutical companies are located in Ireland. There's also a substantial number of breweries, distilleries and creameries which need process control equipment.

HEAVY CONSTRUCTION

Activity grew by nine percent in 1989 after a period of decline. A vital element in this revival has been money from the EC. Between 1989 and 1993, the Irish government will spend about $2 billion on strengthening Ireland's transport infrastructure alone, with the EC providing some $866 million. Heavy-duty construction equipment imports were more than $100 million in 1989, particularly excavating machinery, and special purpose vehicles.

BUILDING MATERIALS

The building materials sector has also picked up along with expanded construction. It is relatively open compared with other EC countries. Imports of construction materials remained static throughout the 1980s, at about $600 million, but the forecast growth in construction is expected to lead to higher imports, especially of wooden, mineral, and metal products.

SAFETY AND SECURITY

The Irish safety and security equipment market is close to $80 million a year. Over half is security equipment. Imports rose 16 percent in 1989 to $61 million. Safety doors and windows and burglar alarm systems are high export areas. Protective footwear sales are rising, while opportunities exist in the security equipment segment for access control systems, closed circuit television, and fire protection equipment.

S P O T L I G H T

• *The Key Incentives* •

What exactly are the much-vaunted Irish investment incentives that have persuaded 900 foreign firms to build in the emerald isle? IDA lists them. First, corporation tax at ten percent, Western Europe's lowest. This covers manufacturing, finance, and some service activities and is guaranteed until the year 2000.

Second, depreciation allowances which enable both buildings and machinery to be written off against tax liability so that tax is, in effect, less than 10 percent in the initial years.

Third, a repatriation system which allows profits to be sent home "without hindrance." Capital and employment grants, say the Irish, are "competitive," while grants are non-taxable. Fixed asset costs eligible for grants include sites, buildings and equipment. International service activities are eligible for employment grants. Training grants are available via IDA. The State Investment body says that these grants towards the cost of initial training programs are "generous." R & D grants are available for product research and development. Advance factories (ready-to-occupy factories) in many parts of Ireland can be found, as well as "up-market" offices. Another aid to investment: venture capital funds available through the business expansion scheme. Individuals can invest up to IR£25,000 in one year, which is allowable against personal income tax. (IDA key number: 353-1-686633.)

TRANSPORTATION AND COMMUNICATION

The Emerald Isle—with its tax concessions—has proved an attraction over the years for millionaires, writers, and others. Then came the problem of inadequate telephones—and many of these hunting and fishing and literary tax exiles quit. More recently, the Irish have been seeking to improve their telecoms and raise them to high EC standards. Hence, a $1.5 billion program of new lines and all-round modernization. Telecom Eireann appointed a leading businessman, Michael Smurfitt, as part-time chairman—and more lines became available. In addition to some 100,000 new lines, the telecoms body launched a crash cabling program in Dublin, which, of course, was needed with the advent of the International Financial Services Center. Telecom Eirann is spending IR£10 million on a new network claiming that their new packet-switching system is the cheapest in Europe. By the end of the 1980s, most customers had fully automated service. More satellite links came into being. With hindsight, Ireland's decision to "go digital" a few years ago has proved an advantage. One telecoms man commented: "Our late start with a modern network has proved a blessing. It enabled us to take a leap over the stages between an old technology and the digital 'age'."

Improvements are being made at Dublin Airport where the Dublin/London route, served by six carriers, is the second busiest in Europe after London/Paris. Aer Rianta, the airports authority, has already opened a IR£35 million runway system, first part of a IR£100 million capital development program running up to 1993. Traffic is scheduled to rise, but the Irish say they have no air traffic control problem. It's almost unheard of for planes to be 'stacked over' Dublin. Another advantage for the incoming businessperson is the mere 20-minute ride into the city center.

MANAGEMENT AND WORKFORCE

Ireland has placed the emphasis on technological education for the past two decades and has achieved a sharp increase in business graduates. More than 55 percent of higher education students now pursue business, engineering, or science disciplines. The result has been a 23 percent increase in the number of these graduates between 1988 and 1991, with computer sciences leading the way. Irish universities and other higher education institutions have been encouraged to link with industry, for example, through contract research work, academics setting up in business, 'incubation' centers and business and technology parks. Three programs of advanced technologies, known as PATs, aimed at harnassing the knowledge and expertise of universities in key areas for the benefit of industry, are working successfully. They are focused on advanced manufacturing technology, biotechnology, and opto-electronics. There are now three microelectronics institutes: the National Microelectronics Research Center (NMRC) in Cork; the Microelectronics Application Center in Limerick; and, thirdly, a cross-border initiative involving the Institute of Advanced Microelectronics at Queen's University, Belfast, the NMRC in Cork and University College Dublin.

Dr. Eoin O'Neill, director of Innovation Services at Trinity College, Dublin, has this to say about a younger, more educated workforce: "In the key areas which underpin modern technological manufacturing and international services, there is going to be a ready availability of trained personnel ranging from technicians to post-doctoral researchers with skills in optical electronics, software, hardware design, VLSI design, CAD, CIM, AMT, biotechnology, and genetic engineering, while laser specialists, plant breeders, synthetic organic chemists, polymer technologists, toolmakers, civil engineers, and architects will seek to apply their skills."

REAL ESTATE

The building of new offices in Dublin is proceeding at a rapid pace prior to the Single Market. Leading agents, such as Jones Lang Wootton, report the appearance of two distinct markets. One is for well-located, high-specification modern buildings renting for around IR£16 the square foot to companies looking for accommodation between 10,000 and 50,000 square feet. The other is at the new International Financial Services Center, one of the most ambitious projects in the EC. Rents for this "high-tech" space are between IR£22 and IR£30 the square foot. These much higher rents are being asked for much-higher quality accommodation than in the first letting market. When completed, the center will have some 750,000 square feet in seven buildings. Allied Irish Banks has bought the completed West building containing 100,000 square feet. Two other buildings of similar size have been taken by the Bank of Ireland, the country's No. 2 bank, and National City Stockbrokers. A fourth building has been let to accountants Arthur Andersen, and a fifth to lawyers McCann Fitzgerald. Two more buildings are due to be built and will constitute phase two of the project. Elsewhere in the city, secondary accommodation is proving difficult to let despite low rents. Companies already in Dublin or which are moving there are looking for quality. In all, office rents rose 15 percent in 1990 with industrial premises increasing 11 percent.

S P O T L I G H T

• *Finance* •

Dublin's new financial city, rising on the banks of the River Liffey, will consist of blocks of modern buildings housing the international financial services center, plus apartments, stores, a hotel, restaurants, and fountains. The Allied Irish Bank group moved into one building in 1990, while two other buildings are due for occupancy from mid-1991. The whole IR£450 million project will be finished in 1993, some five years after launch. It is a hugely ambitious idea, dictated both by the need to provide jobs for Ireland's graduates—and stop

continued

them emigrating to Britain, the US and elsewhere—and to create an industry not handicapped by questions of distance.

There were many skeptics both within and outside Ireland, when the plan was launched. The key to success was to offer a package of attractive tax rates, low rents, and inexpensive telecoms to international financial institutions and so provide them in the Irish capital with a secondary international support unit to London, New York, and Tokyo. "It was never the intention to attempt to rival these well-established centers, merely to provide an inexpensive, alternative back-up," said the IDA. In addition, the Channel Islands, Zurich, Luxembourg, and Hong Kong were proving increasingly expensive. Dublin had the advantage of being in the same time zone as London, having an English-speaking population and offering tax sweeteners—10 percent corporate profits tax even while in temporary accommodation waiting to move in. Some 130 institutions had signed up by the end of 1990.

The IDA has targeted five financial sectors: asset financing; trading and dealing; fund management; insurance; and corporate treasury. The targeted markets are Germany, Japan, North America, Benelux, and the UK. Asset financing will probably be most popular, particularly as Guinness Peat Aviation ($2 billion a year sales) is moving partly to the center, followed by Japan's Orix, Belgium's Banque Brussels Lambert, Holland's ABN, the US's Citibank and the UK's Nat West. The major Irish bank, Allied Irish, and its fellow Bank of Ireland will be present in trading and dealing, accompanied by Chase Manhattan, Nat West, James Capel, and other names in the sector. Dozens of insurance and "captive" insurance companies have also signed. They include Sedgwick, Willis Faber, American International, Sinser, Alexander and Alexander, and special operations such as BMW and Sweden's Ericsson. Thus, the new Dublin center will be challenging the leader in financial services, Luxembourg, but the pickings could be big given that in the Single Market most underwriting risks for Europe will have to be underwritten in Europe.

Other big names set to move include: Deutsche Bank Capital Corporation, New York; Dresdner International; Belgium's Kredietbank; Mitsubishi; and at least one of the builders of the center, McInerney Properties, the Irish contractor, well-known in the Middle East, Portugal and elsewhere. British Land and Ireland's Harwicke are the other members of the building consortium.

"Intelligent" offices with 4.6 meter high ceilings and room for cabling will rent for IR£27.50 the square foot, with more standard offices renting for just under IR£20 the square foot. Tax write-offs will make these rents more attractive, says IDA. The center is also proud of its sophisticated air conditioning.

Certainly, if all goes to plan, the 27 acre site, known locally as Customs House Dock, will be one of the most attractive in Europe. It has had top priority with a committee, chaired by the office of the Taoiseach (prime minister), and made up of bankers, brokers, accountants and insurance executives. To complete the center on time, the IDA has slashed through red tape.

European Community approval of the 10 percent tax rate cleared the way for the center to be promoted worldwide. Brussels recognized the Irish need to stem the flow of well-educated people abroad. Other developments have been the zero rating for tax purposes of unit trusts. Ireland has implemented the EC directive relating to "undertakings for collective investments in transferable securities" (UCITS), enabling fund managers to market their products throughout the EC.

Some of the IDA's most effective arguments with the 130 firms that have signed concern costs. They point to London rents being five times higher, while the Irish bank teller's average salary, $19,600 a year, is 40 percent that of his Zurich counterpart.

The IDA handles the formalities for setting up. Potential investors have to present a detailed business plan at the outset of any new project.

• *Getting To Know the Capital* •

The River Liffey flows gently through the city center on its way to the sea. On both banks are quays that are less commercially important than they were half a century ago, but still are crowded with the country's exports and imports. Joining the northern and southern sections of the city are several bridges, the most notable being O'Connell's. This leads from the university and administrative districts to the busy commercial heart of Dublin, concentrated around broad O'Connell Street and to the east and west.

Most of business Dublin can be walked within an hour, but not all of it. Some companies have moved to the suburbs, so check addresses very carefully.

Ireland's national bus and rail transport company is the Coras Iompair Eireann (CIE). Dublin also has an efficient city bus and rail system, called the Dublin Area Rapid Transit (DART), which connects north Dublin from Howth with the south of the city, Killiney. If you're going to be traveling a lot, it's worth buying a weekly commuter ticket at *Bus Atha Cliath,* 69 O'Connell Street; this is valid on both buses and trains. Taxis are usually plentiful.

Dublin has its first street guide. Before, no one seemed to have need of one. Everyone knew everyone else. The city has become 'international,' hence the decision to publish an A to Z street listing, complete with "what's on" information. The promoter is entrepreneur Simon Williams and the Independent Newspaper group. Some half a million copies have been published, listing not only streets, but also theaters, cinemas, buses and more. It is called *The Independent Directory.*

EUROCITY CORK

Ireland's second city and capital of Munster has long played an important role in the moving of goods to Ireland's export markets. The deepwater harbor handles close to six million tons of cargo a year, a quarter of national seaborne trade. Traditionally, Cork was a port of call for transatlantic passenger liners—but today's traffic spans liquid bulk and dry bulk cargoes, containers, roll-on, roll-off car ferries, and freight, too. Cork is also the offshore exploration capital feeding the natural gas national grid from Marathon's Kinsale field.

Ashore, the greater Cork area, with its quarter of a million people, has 130 foreign concerns among the 770 manufacturing companies. The IDA, Cork Corporation, and Cork County Council have helped inward investors. Some leading electronics companies have come to Cork—Apple, Boeing Computer Software, Motorola, and Western Digital from the US, and Alps from Japan. Among the pharmaceutical companies are Pfizer, Penn, Henkel, FMC, and Sandoz. Cork business and technology park has been developed by both the city and the IDA, while Ireland's first, 800-acre, port-based freeport is being built at Ringaskiddy. New roads, bridges, and airport improvements are underway, aided massively by the EC.

Time and again, the Irish stress their computer-literate young workforce and the 150-year-old University College Cork has courses straddling science, medicine, law, engineering, food, and the humanities. The food processing center of Ireland is located in North Cork, where the country's dairy industry is concentrated.

Key Contacts

Cork Corporation
City Hall
Cork
Tel: 353-21-966222
Fax: 353-21-314238.

Cork Enterprise Board
Rotunda Unit
Enterprise Center
North Mall
Cork
Tel: 323-21-397711
Fax: 323-21-395393.

Cork County Council
County Hall
Cork
Tel: 253-21-276891
Fax: 253-21-276321.

:::::OPPORTUNITIES IN THE REGIONS :::::

SHANNON

Mix high-tech industry and golf galore and there's a certain appeal for American and Japanese industrialists. Shannon, an area in southwest Ireland of some 3,000 relatively unspoiled square miles has had success in attracting US, Japanese and other foreign investment because of its "package"—tax breaks, airport, environment and young workforce. Shannon's industrial and high-tech side took off after the decline of the international airport, once the obligatory, fuelling stopover of all trans-Atlantic flights, now less so. IDA and Shannon Development, another government agency, built upon Shannon's evocative past as one of the world's oldest international airports and set up a duty-free industrial zone, an international aviation leasing and maintenance center, and a Japanese parts center. The area has survived ups and downs in its development.

Shannon rents are half those asked in the new financial district of Dublin. In 1990, these rents were not much more than Irish £12 per square foot. The greatest proportion of overseas companies originate in the US, which accounts for about 60 percent of overseas investment, Germany 20 percent, UK 10 percent. Shannon has one-third of the country's computing and electronics employment. It is also strong in engineering and services, with software and international financial services showing impressive growth. The region is home to Irish-grown world players, such as the GPA aircraft leasing group, which has North American, Japanese, and other European shareholders, as well as Irish. A recent deal has brought togehter GPA and Switzerland's Sulzer for the re-manufacturing of jet engines, notably blades and vanes.

:::::::::::::::SUCCESS STORIES :::::::::::::::

SHANNON AEROSPACE

This Irish–German–Swiss company was established to service planes of the Lufthansa and Swissair lines, and others. The Irish partner, GPA, is charged with building the IR£80 million, 300,000 square foot facility, initially for Boeing 737s and MD-80s. Other aircraft will be handled by the mid-1990s. The company is owned 30 percent by GPA and 35 percent each by Lufthansa and Swissair. GPA itself is a group of privately-held financial service companies, with headquarters in Shannon. Planes are both leased and sold. GPA has also moved into investment banking and financial engineering. The company's portfolio is some 225 aircraft worth more than $3 billion, on lease to 69 airlines in 37 countries. GPA is big these days, having ordered or taken options on 800 new planes in the next decade. Principal shareholders are Mitsubishi Trust Bank, Aer Lingus, Air Canada, Prudential Insurance, Long Term Credit Bank of Japan, and Irish Life Assurance.

ANALOG DEVICES

This wholly-owned subsidiary of the Massachusetts company is the world business center for the production of complementary metal oxide semi-conductors devices (CMOS) and has full responsibility for product development, manufacturing and marketing. It now has a workforce of 750 in Shannon, with one in six engaged in R & D projects. Products developed to date represent over 90 percent of annual sales. A world leader in the manufacture of microchips, Analog has close links with Limerick University where it has endowed a fellowship. Analog likes the environment as it battles to stay ahead of competition. A spokesman said: "The key reason for coming to Ireland, rather than Scotland or Northeast England was the engineering talent coming out of the universities of Limerick, Galway, and Dublin." At the outset, IDA supplied Analog with buildings, but the company now has its own custom-built plant on a Limerick industrial estate. In all, it has poured $100 million into the investment which puts it well inside the EC.

SUMICEM

Sumicem Opto Electronics, part of Japan's Sumitomo Cement, set up only two years ago in the spectacular Plassey Technological Park, "to meet the challenge of advanced technology in both Japan and Ireland." It's another springboard into Europe for the Japanese, but they have "played the game" by establishing both manufacturing and a new R & D center, Lightwave Technology Research. In all, it is estimated that the export of goods and services from Plassey is worth more than IR£500 million a year. The Park has an international board of directors from Europe, North America and Japan. The new research center is run by a professor from Limerick University but its research capabilities are open to all companies.

THE LEADERS

TOP 10 BANKS (1990)

		IR£
(1)	Allied Irish Bank	1.13 b
(2)	Jefferson Smurfitt	1.06
(3)	CRH	606.3 m
(4)	Bank of Ireland	574.4 m
(5)	FII	260.5 m
(6)	Woodchester Investments	218.5 m
(7)	James Crean	186.0 m
(8)	Waterford Wedgwood	177.2 m
(9)	Elan	171.6 m
(10)	Aran Energy	166.9 m

TOP 10 COMPANIES (1989)

		IR£m Pretax profits
(1)	Smurfitt	245.5
(2)	CRH	80.6
(3)	Fyffes	25.0
(4)	James Crean	21.5
(5)	Kerry Group	17.1
(6)	Independent Newspapers	15.5
(7)	Avonmore	13.1
(8)	Fitzwilton	12.1
(9)	Waterford Foods	11.3
(10)	Power Corporation	10.3

KEY CONTACTS

USEFUL DUBLIN TELEPHONE NUMBERS

Trade and Commercial Information

European Community: 353-1-712244
Industrial Development Agency (IDA): 353-1-686633
Industry, Commerce: 353-1-614444
Information Service: 353-1-607555
Labor: 353-1-765861

Transport

Airports
Cork: 353-21-865388
Dublin: 353-1-370011
Shannon: 353-61-61666

Ferries
B&I: 353-1-788077
Irish Ferries: 353-1-610511
Sealink: 353-1-807777

CHAMBERS COMMERCE

Member Nations
Germany: 353-1-789344
Italy: 353-1-767829
Portugal: 353-1-618222

Others
Dublin: 353-1-764291
Dun Laoghaire: 353-1-793733

Ireland: 353-1-612888
Canada: 353-1-970692
Japan/Jetro: 353-1-714003
Joint Arab/Irish: 353-1-605276
Taiwan—Confederation House: 353-1-779801
United States: 353-1-793733

Embassies

Member Nations
Belgium: 353-1-692082
Denmark: 353-1-756404
Britain: 353-1-695211
France: 353-1-694777
Germany: 353-1-693011
Greece: 353-1-767254
Italy: 353-1-601744

Netherlands: 353-1-693444
Portugal: 353-1-884416
Spain: 353-1-691640

Others
Canada: 353-1-781988
Japan: 353-1-694244
United States: 353-1-688777

Facts on Italy

. . . .

Capital Rome
Population 57m
Working Population 24m
Unemployment 11.9%
GDP Growth 1989: 3.2%; 1990: 2.7%; 1991:
    1.7%
GDP per capita 1989: $15.051
Inflation 1990: 6.2%; 1991 (est.): 6.6%
Trade 1990: − $14b; 1991 (est.): − $19b
Budget Deficit − $119b

. . . .

ITALY

"It's Andreotti versus the deficit." Newspaper headline upon the nomination as prime minister for the sixth time of veteran politician Giulio Andreotti

ITALY'S ILLS HAVE BEEN SO WELL-PUBLICIZED, SO THOROUGHLY documented, so widely discussed at home and abroad that some out-siders wonder about the country's chances in the bright, new, and highly-competitive world of the Single Market. What chance a land that has public spending and bureaucratic inefficiency on such a scale? Where one half of business activity is directly controlled by the State through the mega-holding companies, such as IRI (industry in a very broad sense), ENI (oil exploration, refining and petro-chemicals), and EFIM (aluminum, aircraft and glass)? In this trio alone, the five parties of the government coalition "control" 15,000 managerial jobs, through the patronage system known as "la lottisa-zione." Price Waterhouse, in Milan, gives this view: "Italy has enor-mous tasks ahead in order to bring its postal, telephone, and power generation, railway and social security systems up to more acceptable levels of efficiency. The functioning of the judicial and taxation sys-tems is a brake on business operations, while the general inability of the political class to take difficult decisions, notably on the public defi-cit, raises the levels of uncertainty and risk for businessmen."

Then, there's the shaky government—the 50th since the Second World War—of veteran Christian Democrat politician Giulio An-dreotti. Yet, the government benefited from Italy's 1990 presidency of the European Community—and from Andreotti's long experience on the Italian and European stages. He is the only statesman who was there when the 1957 Treaty of Rome was signed and the Common Market, as it was then known, came into being. Then, there has been the flair of Gianni De Michelis, the controversial, hardworking, hardliving foreign minister with his ideas for newstyle groupings in Central Europe, which would position, for example, Italy, Austria, Hungary, and eventually Yugoslavia as something of a counterweight to the united Germany. Again, on the positive side, Italy has sought new European "credentials," after some decades of seeking exceptions to Euro rules. Italy has freed capital movements ahead of time, allow-ing Italians to send money overseas. A daring move, given that the government has always tapped savings to finance its budget deficits. Italians are now allowed to open bank accounts abroad and to hold unlimited amounts of foreign currency in domestic accounts. There have already been steps towards liberalizing foreign securities transac-tions. The government has decided, however, that the war on tax evad-ers and organized crime must be stepped up before 1992 and restrictions are aimed at preventing overseas money laundering. In-vestors sending abroad more than ten million lire, just over $8,000, must declare this while foreign transactions exceeding 20 million must be done through Italian banks. The timing is right, given a strong lira and the feeling that, despite problems of competitiveness, Italy has sufficient entrepreneurial ability—or call it salesmanship—to take on the Single Market.

Gianni Agnelli, the head of Fiat, once told the author of this book that the strength of Italy lay in its small and medium-sized machinery firms. He pointed to an elderly Italian leaving his office—a prominent sub-contractor for Fiat—saying: "That man is richer than I am." Hardly true. Mr. Agnelli sits atop an industrial, family pyramid that is the most impressive since the Fords in America. Bid-proof Fiat is pumping enormous sums into industrial investment and moderniza-tion. Agnelli is the most prominent member of the modern *condottieri* (renaissance mercenaries-turned-modern entrepreneurs), who exer-cise almost as much power as the State. The Italian multinational is dominated by family, not only at Fiat, but also at Ferruzzi, Olivetti, Pirelli, Berlusconi, Benetton, and elsewhere. These companies have a strong domestic market and, until now with automobiles, protection against the Japanese who have had only a tiny percentage of the mar-ket. The tax system favors small cars. The domestic market is domi-nated by Italian brand names, while public purchasing has been "Buy Italian." This has to change with the Single Market and the new EC arrangements with Tokyo. Alliances are being forged by the bigger companies—Olivetti's Benedetti in auto components, Berlusconi in the audiovisual and publishing fields, and Benetton and Stefanel in textiles.

Lower stratas of Italian business are also family-controlled. There is the famous Italian entrepreneur, the Verona shoe salesman capable of selling his goods in war zones, such as Lebanon. The family sectors range from machine tools to textiles and clothing; from agricultural produce to construction equipment; specialty chemicals and pharmaceuticals; food, paper, plastics, and furniture. Many of these companies are used to trading abroad and so offer good partnership possibilities for foreign investors. A recent European Community document, the so-called *Cecchini Report,* stated that small and medium Italian firms would benefit from the Single Market. The report said that Italian–EC trade, pre-1992, was more costly because of formalities and local charges than that between any other country and the rest of the EC. So, it concluded, the potential gains for the Italians were "greater," given their flair for exporting. One management consultant put it this way: "Smaller companies are concerned about larger organizations in the Single Market but this is not new and certainly does not undermine basic self-confidence."

"Small business Italy" is in the center of the country—textiles in Prato, tiles in Sesto and Montelupo, clothes in Empoli and Signa, leather in Santa Croce, shoes in Monsummano and Fucecchio, furniture in Cascina. Next door to Tuscany is Emilia, with knitwear in Carpi, tiles in Sassuolo, machinery in Bologna, Modena and Reggio nell' Emilia.

Enthusiasm for the Single Market runs high in Italy because these entrepreneurs see the abolition of frontiers as a chance to broaden the area in which they can exercise their flair for selling. Italians also view with optimism a future European Economic Area, the provisional title for an even bigger free-trade zone embracing non-EC states in Western Europe and the emergent democracies of East Europe. Aside from new links within the EC, the Italians have continued to push into Budapest, Warsaw, and Moscow with Fiat leading the way followed by Ferruzi, Beneton, and others. At home, the situation *looks* bad. One main problem is the staggering budget deficit and the seeming inability to reduce it to the levels of other major nations, although a new Andreotti government made a new effort with the 1991 budget. The Italian state employs a record 17 percent of the non-agricultural workforce and these armies of public servants perform badly on the railways, in the PTT and other vital services. Privatization has been resisted by government and the unions. The former argues that the existing big private groups would benefit most, but Treasury Minister Guido Carli is pushing for share sales to Italy's large cooperative movement. Unions fear more job losses of the kind that have already affected Fiat and Olivetti, squeezed by the relative downturn in growth. Companies have also made an expensive settlement with the engineering workers and are complaining that their competitivity has been hit. Time will tell. There are no signs of greater efficiency within industry to meet the latest challenge. There are no guarantees yet that the "Italian way" of ducking and bobbing will not find the solution before the next general elections in 1992.

MARKET OPPORTUNITIES

A closer look at trade patterns shows, for example, that the US now sells more office machinery parts than coal to Italy. The market is becoming more sophisticated. Another factor is modernization. Both the public and state sectors are updating and improving and so are actively seeking reliable foreign suppliers, notably of computer systems and services. A third factor is that Italians, Europe's largest savers, have been enjoying new wealth. One US diplomat stated: "American lifestyles have become part of Italian everyday culture. High added value, high quality products—those which are less vulnerable to exchange swings—are the best bet in this market." The liberalization of exchange controls in mid-1990 made payment terms for Italian importers much easier. The best sectors are computer hardware, peripherals and software; energy-saving devices; electronic components; avionics; aircraft parts and accessories, and ground support equipment; while services, such as insurance, personal financial advice, and franchising are open fields.

COMPUTER HARDWARE AND SOFTWARE

Italy trails other European countries in spending on electronic data processing (EDP), but looks like catching up. Imports of EDP hardware are expected to grow 14 percent through 1991. Mini and super computers with vector features sold much better and industry experts say the outlook here is for continued growth. The US has a dominant position in the EDP market, although Italian software is becoming more competitive.

MEDICAL EQUIPMENT

This is an expanding market, particularly in the high-tech fields of imaging, NMR scanners, and other neurological equipment, digital radiology, and cardiology equipment. It should reach $700 million. Italy, most likely, will continue to rely on foreign suppliers offering state-of-the-art apparatus. American products are relatively cheaper since the dollar's decline.

POLLUTION CONTROL EQUIPMENT

The authorities are under increasing pressure to place more controls on polluting industries. The pressure comes from local Greens and from Brussels. Stricter enforcement of existing regulations—combined with new legislation to control air, water and soil contamination—will induce private and public industries to install more anti-pollution devices. Sales went above one billion dollars in 1988 and should grow by 15 percent a year through 1991.

APPAREL

The country has long been a leading manufacturer and exporter. Demand within Italy has been traditionally high—$7.6 billion in 1988 with an average of six percent growth forecast through 1991. Imports have grown faster, rising 13 percent to $1.3 billion. Most incoming clothes are from low-cost countries, but there is demand for quality US leisure wear—and for smart British clothes, even tweeds, among the Milanese business community, the most powerful in the country.

AGRICULTURAL PRODUCTS

Bulk and intermediate commodities—forest products, oilseeds and products, cotton, tobacco, hides and skins, wheat and seeds—

dominate Italian purchases from the US which have risen above one billion dollars. In the consumer area, the best prospects are for dried fruits and nuts, corn oil, fruit juices, health foods, fish and crustaceans, wild rice, snack foods, blueberries, and breakfast foods, as well as regional and ethnic foods such as Cajun and Mexican specialties. "High-tech" items such as bovine semen and cattle embryos are sought by the Italians. For these and other sales opportunities, exports should study at the Milan Fair dates (see Spotlight). The US and Foreign Commercial Service (US & FCS) is particularly active in Italy promoting trade and supplying market research. The US Chamber of Commerce in Milan is a rich storehouse of contacts and a guide to the thousands of American companies in Italy.

INTERNATIONAL TRADE

It can be no surprise that the biggest surplus earner for Italy's merchandise trade account is the broad sector comprising textiles, clothing, and leather goods. Italian style is a worldwide winner. Shoes, clothes, and accessories from top stylists like Ferragamo, Gianfranco Ferre, Valentino, Armani, and Laura Biagiotti are joined by the products of many other makers in conquering foreign markets.

Flair in design and flexibility in manufacturing have given Italian firms a sharp edge for carving out substantial shares abroad. However, low labor cost countries have been blunting the impact of Italy's fashion exporters, whose sales abroad have been growing less rapidly than those of engineering firms. Indeed, it seems likely that the surplus from engineering goods will overtake those of textiles, clothing, and leather goods.

Italy is a transformation economy, exporting manufactured goods and importing the raw materials needed for their production. This explains the heavy deficit in ferrous and non-ferrous metals. Elsewhere, a lack of indigenous materials is strongly evident in energy, with the country needing to import more than three quarters of its needs. Soft oil prices and a weak dollar were great advantages to the balance of payments, but this has been changing.

As the country known for the Mediterranean diet, Italy spends surprisingly heavily on importing agricultural and food products, particularly from northern Europe, and its trade in these sectors is significantly in deficit. Notwithstanding a strong agricultural tradition and a large workforce, Italy exports relatively little and imports a lot.

Chemicals are another sector where imports significantly exceed exports, and, again, northern Europe is a major supplier. The former West Germany is one of the contributors, with its chemicals industry one of the factors in the country's top ranking as Italy's number one supplier country. More than one fifth of all Italian imports come from West Germany. But trade also flows in the other direction, with West Germany as Italy's principal foreign market, taking nearly one fifth of total exports.

France ranks second both as customer and supplier, with about one seventh of exports and imports. The US is Italy's third largest trading partner. But, clearly, the European Community is the focus of Italian trade.

TRANSPORTATION AND COMMUNICATIONS

Roads are the arteries for channelling the flows of goods and people in Italy. In the past two decades roads' share of long distance freight traffic increased from 44 to 63 percent, the volume of goods carried increasing by 150 percent and the number of trucks doubling to about two million.

With more than 6000 kilometers of 'autostrade' highways (generally toll charging), most of the country's essential trunk network is in place. Two principal links join north with south; one follows the Adriatic coast from Bologna to Bari and the other goes from Milan to Bologna, Florence, Rome, Naples, and the Calabrian toe. A third north-south axis, down the west coast from Genoa, is partially complete, the 240 kilometer section from Civitavecchia to Leghorn still unbuilt. Two major transverse 'autostrade' are the basis for west-east traffic in the north, and other trans-peninsular links exist in the center and south.

Good international 'autostrade' connections assist traffic to France at the Riviera frontier, at the Swiss frontier point of Chivasso north of Milan and into Austria through the Brenner Pass and Tarvisio. Top priority is being given to completing the vital Aosta-Mont Blanc link with France.

When not hit by strikes affecting any permutation from the large number of different air transport staff categories, or disrupted by autumn-to-spring Po Valley fog at the key Milan airport, Italy's internal air services are generally good.

The principal hub is Rome's Leonardo da Vinci Fiumicino airport, handling over 16 million passengers annually, more than one third of total Italian air passenger traffic. Milan's Linate handles about one quarter. Milan's second airport Malpensa, Turin, Venice, Bologna, Naples, Palermo, Catania, and Cagliari all handle more than one million passengers annually. With regular scheduled services to a further 15 airports, Italy can boast a well-developed air network.

Plans are in-hand for important strategic development projects at Rome's airport, where terminal area will treble and aircraft handling capacity will be boosted by one third over the next 15 years, and at Milan's Malpensa to ease pressure on city-center Linate. The Rome project is very big indeed and plans have been established jointly by Aeroporti di Roma and Reynolds, Smith and Hill, the US engineers. In many respects, Italy's state airline, Alitalia, is vulnerable, particularly in its services from northern Italy, where it suffers customer leakage from travellers crossing borders to take flights from France and Switzerland.

A second point of vulnerability are services joining the north to Rome, frequently subject to delays from fog, air traffic congestion and labor disputes. But in spite of new extra-fast *Pendolino* services giving center-to-center service between Rome and Milan in under four hours, state railways, Ferrovie dello Stato, have not exploited their opportunities.

A center of controversy and scandal, the railways suffer from several adverse factors: a low level of electrified track and advanced control systems; a high level of elderly locomotives, freight cars, and carriages; stagnant freight traffic; high over-manning; high losses and enormous subsidies. Massive injections of new finance are needed to bring about a turnaround at the railways. Strategic plans underline the need for funding, but Italy's high public sector borrowing requirement seems to present an insurmountable constraint.

While travellers are loquacious in their criticism of air and rail services, their complaints are probably outvoiced by the widespread discontent from family and business about the post and

---

S P O T L I G H T

AT&T has learned that in Italy one cannot walk in and tell the proud Italians how to run things—even if you are offering what amounts to a lifeline to a troubled sector. AT&T's "global" alliance of 1983 with Olivetti, the office automation group, has been scaled back. Now, the US giant has a new global alliance with Italtel, the state-owned telecommunications equipment maker, for manufacturing and technology transfer. Switchmaker Italtel (part of the Iri-Stet group) is much smaller than AT&T, but has a guaranteed 50 percent of local switching equipment orders. AT&T has pumped $135 million into the venture and given Italtel access to Bell technology. There are advantages all round: AT&T wins access to an Italian telecom market valued at $21 billion in 1994 (compared to $15 billion in 1989) plus another foot into Europe. Italtel wins the know-how to improve Italy's notorious telephones. Many sectors of Italian industry could dramatically improve their results—if the telephones worked. AT&T and Italtel have secured the first major third-world order for digital exchanges in Nigeria.

telecommunications services. Few believe the claim that average letter delivery time was cut from 8.5 to 4.5 days in the closing three years of the 1980s. Where possible, users try to avoid entrusting mail to a public system in which additional charges for express delivery are no guarantee of delivery within a week.

Crossed lines, dropped lines, and appallingly bad lines seem to characterize Italy's telephone system. But even getting a connection is a gamble. National telephone company SIP claims that the overall figure for answer-service ratio is just over 50 percent. On long-distance calls the figure is probably lower than 30 percent. Division of responsibilities, deep-rooted bureaucratic mentality and high politicization of the public sector are reasons for the poor telecommunications service that leaves Italians and foreigners in despair.

Handicapped by the low level of public infrastructure, business is increasingly impatient. The gap between Italy and its European neighbors is a matter of serious concern because it adversely affects overall business competitivity.

MANAGEMENT AND WORKFORCE

An unacceptably high rate of unemployment is the biggest blot on the Italian economic landscape, for not only is the national average rate of 12 percent high by OECD standards, but it conceals disparities between the two halves of the country. There's more or less full employment in the north, while in the south over 21 percent of the workforce is without a job, and youth unemployment is pushing towards 50 percent.

OECD says correcting these staggering regional differences is one of the major challenges for policy-makers. It's no new challenge. Trillions of lire have been "thrown" at the south. Regional disparities in both income per head and unemployment rates are larger in Italy than in the other major European countries—and certainly an anomaly in the world's fifth largest economy.

The country, in effect, is split in two between the advanced and prosperous north and the poor, under-industralized south, the *Mezzo-*

giorno. Here, productivity is weaker and almost on any measure of economic performance the results compare unfavorably with those in the north. The unemployment rate is three times higher, while those who are working have had an output per head, just half that of their northern cousins. Purchasing power in the north is higher than the average in the more affluent European countries, while in the south it's on a level with Spain and is not much higher than Greece or Portugal.

The postwar *Cassa per il Mezzogiorno* first financed infrastructure, then changed policy and subsidized industrialization projects, few of which paid off. The funding of the Cassa was raised, public enterprises were obliged to invest in the south and, additionally, social security costs were reduced for newly-hired workers. Then came administrative decentralization in Italy. Regional authorities acquired more powers and the role of the Cassa was substantially curtailed. Its expenditure fell by 45 percent in the decade up to the end of the 1980s. This new policy led to the creation of a Ministry of the Mezzogiorno in 1986, which was given the task of promoting "strategic projects." Its new role was one of coordination and supervision, not funding. The public sector enterprises made matters worse by not meeting their investment targets in the south.

In farming, proportionally more cash went to the north from the EC's Common Agricultural Policy. Then, the Italian government abolished regional differentials in wages—irrespective of differences in productivity. This meant that labor cost differences narrowed to the point that, because of the productivity gap, unit wage costs became higher in the south! A crazy world.

Still, economic conditions in the south have improved dramatically, says the OECD. Its 1990 review of the south said: "The north-south gap in total available resources narrowed to 29 percent by the late 1980s from 39 percent in 1951 while, most significantly, GDP per employed person rose from 54 percent of the northern figure in 1951 to 75 percent in 1987."

Many of the problems remain daunting. The plants in the south have not produced spin-offs for small firms as they tend to import raw materials from abroad and hire specialist services from the north. The OECD concludes, tactfully, that regional wage parity is "inappropriate" and that the Mezzogiorno needs to regain its competitive edge in costs and so attract investment. A new wage gap could create a new wave of southerners heading for the north. The government will no doubt have to juggle its subsidies, despite the poor state of public finances. The three national labor confederations, which claim a combined membership of ten million, are anxious to protect their position and "rights" in the run-up to the Single Market. The calm of the mid-1980s, which coincided with a boom period, gave way to a wave of strikes at the end of the decade—and to higher wage settlements. Manufacturers claim that high wages and a strong lira have hit exports. Overall labor costs have been rising at ten percent per annum. Government pension, health and assistance funds prove much more expensive in Italy than almost anywhere else. The Nomisma research firm estimates that non-pay contributions add 43.5 points to the Italian wage bill as against 44.8 points in France and 18.1 points in Britain. Unit labor costs in the United States ranked 79.4 against Italy's 117.3. Italian unions are strongly in favor of the EC Social Charter and would like a Europe-wide union structure. But they have not rejected the Single Market, for they say that Italy's large productive capacity is not being fully utilized. Problems, such as the *scala mobile* link between wages and inflation, high social security payments and massive tax avoidance were at last being discussed in some depth in 1991 in tripartite talks between the three main union groupings, the employers, and the government.

REAL ESTATE

Shortage of top quality offices in prime central sites has driven rents as high as 800,000 lire the square meter per year in Milan, Italy's leading business city. Some other offices just below this range can be had for between 650,000 and 750,000 lire. London and Edinburgh Trust, the British developers, are refurbishing space and are also associated with the planned international business park, near Linate airport, which will provide 28,000 square meters when the bureacrats finally supply all the necessary approvals. Also in the planning stage is a large office development in the Garibaldi area. Other very large, if more isolated, projects are planned in the Pirelli–Bicocca area (400,000 square meters of offices and apartments) and Montecity (700,000 square meters of offices, hotels, shops, and apartments). Snam, the State energy group, is planning a business complex at San Donato, southeast Milan, but this is longer term. If and when these schemes are brought to fruition, Milan will close the office gap currently existing between it and other leading European business cities.

S P O T L I G H T

• *Bari Science Park* •

One of Italy's most successful science parks has been created in the deep south by marrying the mathematical and data skills of the old university at Bari, labs set up by some of Italy's and Europe's leading high-tech firms—and plenty of government aid. The origins of the science park were in a small data calculating center in 1984. Word got around, State money became available and Fiat, Olivetti and IRI (the holding company), IBM, and the French software leader Cap Gemini built labs. It was all a link between fundamental research and pragmatic manufacturing. Bari researchers have acquired special knowledge in chips as well as software for space and telecom units. The teams are hoping to work on Hermes, the future European space plane, now mooted as a supply and rescue vessel for the Freedom space station. More down-to-earth work is on robots for Fiat, a vital area if Italy's and Europe's leading automobile manufacturer is to head off the Japanese. High barriers against Japanese autos will begin to crumble in the 1990s. Bari science park also works on new semiconductor materials, as well as agricultural research into the development of an advanced form of cereal grain. Not bad in less than a decade. It will soon double its 800-acre site. The driving force is former construction king Gianfranco Dioguardi, who is proud that his researchers are at their desks straight after lunch, despite the torrid heat. His motto: Power through imagination, but also by virtue of organization.

• *Getting To Know the Capital* •

The roads leading to Rome are as straight as they were in the days of the chariots, but the city itself can be confusing at first because of the north-to-south meandering of the Tiber River. The Vatican and Saint Peter's, as well as the ancient and romantic quarter of *Trastevere* ("across the Tiber"), are on the west bank. Political and business Rome, the commercial and shopping areas, and the major hotels are on the east bank. However, one twist in the Tiber means that part of historic Rome on the east bank, the area around the Piazza Navona, juts like a peninsula toward the Vatican.

The best way to fix the city's topography in your mind is to divide the main, eastern part of the city into east and west of the Via del Corso, the main artery that runs from the Piazza del Popolo in the north down to the Piazza Venezia. Here stands the massive and ugly Vittorio Emanuele monument that marks the unification of Italy. Nearby are the Capitoline Hill, the Colosseum, and the ruins of the Forum. This is where Rome began.

Another way to understand the city's topography is to view it from the Janiculum ridge above Trastevere. From this vantage, you can take in the honey-brown mass of Roman roofs and pick out the monuments and church domes. There are other great views, notably from the gardens of the Villa Medici, up behind the Spanish Steps. Close by is the celebrated Via Veneto; like New York's Fifth Avenue and the Champs-Elysées in Paris, its name is a synonym for luxury and elegance. See for yourself.

Rome traffic is fierce and very often gridlocked. There are four rush hours, because most shops and offices close for lunch and many people go home to eat. Being on time for an appointment means that you are up to half an hour late. One solution for the business visitor who wants to get around fast is to hire a guide. If the guide has a car, he or she will know the short cuts and the complicated parking rules. Ask the hotel concierge to recommend a guide, and be sure to negotiate a price in advance. Don't rent a car unless you know the city well.

In theory, much of the center is closed to nonresidents' cars—but still the jams persist. However, the heart of Rome is small enough for any point to be reached on foot within 15 minutes.

There are only two subway lines, useful because they connect the main railroad station with downtown Piazza di Spagna and Piazza del Popolo and serve the Vatican neighborhood as well as the satellite city of EUR *(Esposizione Universale Roma)*, seat of several ministries and state companies, notably Alitalia and ENI.

Rome has about 5,000 buses, but half the fleet is usually being repaired. One ticket takes you anywhere in the city—but a ticket may be hard to find. You have to buy one before boarding the bus, and newsstands and *tabacchi* (cigarette stores) often have none. The big cafés at the Termini station are usually a better bet. However, hardly anyone uses the ticket canceling machines on the buses, so if you don't have a ticket, well...

The 5500 taxis are not nearly enough for a city of Rome's size and are scarce at peak periods and at shift changeover times (7:30 a.m. and 2:30 and 10:00 p.m.). The Romans don't wait in line for anything, so stand up for your rights if you're first at a taxi stand.

EUROCITY MILAN

Smoggy, but dynamic, Milan will take care of the practicalities of adapting Italy to the Single Market, while Rome looks after the politics. There's a long rivalry. Unfortunately, Rome is more daring on the European political front than in cutting the historical, but restricting ties between Italian political parties and the business world. Milan gets things done.

Milan, with a population of close to four million if the suburbs are included, is more than just the capital of Lombardy. It is the commercial and financial powerhouse of Italy. Tycoons, such as Fiat's Gianni

Agnelli and Olivetti's Carlo de Benedetti, may have their plants else-where, respectively Turin and Ivrea, but their counting house is Mi-lan. The city was an early innovator in banking—Lombard Street in London is now a generic term for the British money market. Today, the leaders are the ubiquitous merchant bank Mediobanca with the fabled octogenerian Enrico Cuccia at its head, and the Banca Com-merciale Italiana, the most international of Italy's 1,200 largely State-controlled banks. New laws enabling banks to sell 49 percent of their shares to the public, and to extend their branch networks, have been welcomed in Milan. The city is conscious that banking is an area—along with the small Milan stock market with its old boy networks—that needs overhauling and strengthening if Italy is to compete effectively with British, French, and German banks for corporate cli-ents. Only 217 companies are listed in Milan, a tenth of the number traded in London, and Italy has trailed in setting standards of trans-parency and efficiency in market transactions.

Nor has Milan's reputation gained from the unseemly power strug-gles between the clique of tycoons, named after renaissance merce-naries, the *condottiori*. Media baron Silvio Berlusconi fought de Benedetti for control of Mondadori, the country's largest publishing house, and Raul Gardini, the agribusiness king from Ravenna, slugged it out for control of the public-private chemicals company Enimont, a battle involving his Milan-based Montedison group and the State holding company ENJ. Gardini has been sidelined, but de Benedetti, and Agnelli have considerably strengthened their pan-European alliances—Fiat's telecoms deal with France's Alcatel was the most notable. De Benedetti warns that Italy—therefore Milan—must develop even bigger industrial "players" as the country has only seven private-sector companies with sales of more than $1.5 billion, com-pared with Britain's 71 and France's 38.

Yet, Milan is booming in many areas. In fashion, a one-billion-dollar-a-year business, Milan is challenging Paris and is winning in sectors such as ready-to-wear women's clothes for the Japanese mar-ket. The city is also a household name in design, notably furniture de-sign. Its advertising agencies dominate Italy's $3.3 billion publicity market. Mr. Berlusconi, from his villa outside the city, controls through his Fininvest company three national TV networks, Publita-lia, an advertising agency with a third of the market, much of Monda-dori; the country's largest publisher, and a chain of retail outlets and cinemas.

Milan also is industrial—automobiles, steel and Italtel, the state's telecoms equipment maker. Italy's efficient, family-owned, medium-sized companies are there, too, plus a new breed of yuppie-style managers and entrepreneurs, or rampanti.

Milan's strengths are its outward-looking attitude and its hellbent pursuit of money, which makes it more German than Italian in many ways. These factors have inflated city center office prices, now higher than Rome's. In fact, at $776 the square meter for central, air-conditioned offices, Milan ranks third in Europe after London and Paris. As a result, the city edges are being developed at Pirelli-Bicocca, Montecity, and the Garibaldi and Portello sections.

Visitors will find that most Italian companies have headquarters or sizeable offices in Milan. Major American concerns, too, like IBM, 3M and many of the other 7,400 U.S. companies in the Italian market have offices here. The key directory is that of the American Chamber of Commerce in Italy:

Via Cantu 1
20123 Milan
Tel: 39-2-869-0661
Fax: 39-2-805-7737.

FAIRS

Milan boasts 80 trade fairs a year, or 33 percent of total exhibition space sold in Italy. In all, there are some 170 international trade fairs throughout the country. The northern "capital" stages no fewer than 22 in the month of November. Milan, in fact, is second in Europe only to Paris for the number of fairs, and second to Hannover for actual space. After the summer, in October, MIFED brings together makers, buyers, and sellers of movies and television programs. Industry leaders debate such hot issues as video piracy, protection of authors' and producers' rights, and international coproductions. MIFED is held at the original fairgrounds on the edge of the city. Contact:

Fiero Milano
Largo Domodossola 1
20145 Milan
Tel: 39-2-49971
Fax: 39-2-499-7375.

South of Milan is *Il Girasole* (The Sunflower) fairground, hub of the new commercial center at Lacciarella, or City of Fashion. That's where buyers from many countries look at the latest ready-to-wear clothes and accessories. Among other important shows are: home furnishings; gardening equipment; leather goods; food, drink and catering; franchising; textile technology; do-it-yourself gadgetry; chemical and medical equipment; motorcycles and scooters. The BIT travel show is second only to Berlin's. April is the month of the *Great Milan Fair,* "mother" of all the others, attracting 3000 exhibitors and a million visitors. *What's on in Milan,* is a good English language guide. Elsewhere, up-and-coming Bologna has more than a tenth of national business. There's also the Bari fair as the gateway to the Mezzogiomo.

:::::: OPPORTUNITIES IN THE REGIONS ::::::

APULIA

Italy's Apulian heel with its lengthy coastline extending from the southern Adriatic round the instep of the Ionian Sea is Italy's seventh largest region in terms of both area and population. Apulia (Puglia in Italian) is divided into seven provinces, Foggia the most northern, to Lecce deep in the Salento peninsula that points towards Greece and the Levant.

Notwithstanding the resources allocated to encourage industrial development, the region retains a heavy rural bias. This is partly because Apulia has the highest proportion of flat land in Italy, more than one half of its surface area. The hot climate helps the cultivation of grapes, olives, tomatoes, and vegetables, even though the region suffers from inadequate indigenous water supplies. About one sixth of Apulia's working population finds employment in agriculture.

In contrast to the northern part of the Adriatic, long stretches of the Apulian coast are unspoilt, and the sea is generally unpolluted. Tourism on the scale of Rimini is absent and the development of the holiday industry unsophisticated. Increasing environmental awareness has caused delays in the construction of a mega power station at Cerano on the border of Lecce Province, south of Brindisi, and has led to demands that it should be gas- as well as coal-fired.

Most of the region's industry is concentrated in and around the main city Bari, and at Taranto in the instep. While Bari's industry is broadly based, Taranto's is centered on Italy's largest steelworks, oil refining, and cement production. Though there has been talk of an industrial take-off in Apulia, generally, and Bari, in particular, such claims are often exaggerated. (See spotlight.) Apulia, has done better than other *mezzogiorno* regions but is still heavily dependent on regional aid and incentives.

Good communications are a positive factor for a region which is nevertheless handicapped by being far from markets for its products. Apulia is distant both geographically and culturally from northern Italy and the rest of Europe. Productivity is significantly lower and there have recently been signs that organized crime, a feature of Sicily, Calabria, and Campania, is starting to appear.

LATIUM

With the national capital Rome, Latium (Lazio in present-day Italian) ranks as a leading region. It is ninth largest of Italy's 20 regions in terms of surface area, and third largest when measured by population. Rome, which has province status, is the country's biggest metropolis with three million inhabitants.

Rome's problems are well-known; traffic is chaotic, exacerbated by rapid urban expansion that has not been matched by growth in infrastructure and services. Yet the presence of ministries, state holding corporations, official organizations, and major banks and associations means that the city's role will continue growing.

Against the drawbacks, Rome enjoys the benefits of having Italy's leading international airport at Fiumicino and a climate that is considerably kinder than that in the large northern cities. These factors and the magnet of the ministries has led to the establishment of a sizeable foreign business community.

Rome's closeness to the area benefitting from southern regional development funds has been another factor attracting foreign firms. The line for regional incentives was at Pomezia, about 20 miles south of the capital, though, an EC ruling means this is being redrawn further south. Large numbers took advantage of the grants, tax breaks, and holidays from social security contributions while funds were available.

Pomezia was chosen by several multinationals siting production facilities in Italy, including Litton, Johnson & Johnson, IBM, and Wellcome. Non-Italian firms are also numerous in neighboring Latina Province, center of the Pontine marshes further south down the coast in the direction of Naples, with pharmaceuticals strongly present.

The good road and rail connections that join the Latina Province to Rome are also enjoyed by Frosinone Province, mid-way down the Rome-Naples autostrada. Multinationals are well-represented in Frosinone's various industrial parks, though Italy's own Fiat is the biggest, with its auto plant at Cassino.

Two Latium provinces are located north of Rome, agricultural Viterbo that has not enjoyed regional development aid and Rieti that has. With Fiat's telecommunications subsidiary Telettra and Texas Instruments, Rieti is an important electronics center. So also is Rome, where the presence of Selenia, Elettronica, and Ericsson subsidiary Fatme on the Via Tiburtina once led the district to be called Rome's Silicon Valley.

VENETO

Six provinces comprise the Veneto, probably the region that has produced the biggest surprises in terms of economic development over recent years. After many years ranked among the poorest regions, and suffering largescale emigration, the Veneto's resurgence has been based on small and medium sized manufacturing firms.

Many foreigners know the region, having visited cities like Venice, Verona, and Padua on vacation. The Veneto enjoys a wealth of history from the Venetian Republic to the period of Austrian occupation and the battles of the Great War earlier this century. The region's artistic and cultural heritage is enormous, with minor cities like Vicenza offering jewels of Palladian architecture.

However, the Veneto's tourism is not restricted to culture. Lake Garda, the largest of the Italian lakes, is a playground for foreign visitors, particularly from Austria and Germany. The region's Dolomite Mountains offer excellent skiing at resorts like Cortina d'Ampezzo in Belluno Province.

In addition to its strong tourism and a continuing firm agricultural base that includes fruit and quality wines around Verona, the city that hosts the country's largest agricultural fair, the Veneto has benefitted from a buoyant manufacturing base. Textiles and clothing are among the leaders, with world famous Benetton in Treviso Province and Marzotto in Vicenza Province.

Vicenza is also one of Italy's gold and jewelry centers. A major employer, generally in small workshops, the industry is an important earner of export revenues, though the downturn of Middle East markets caused by the soft oil prices and weak dollar of the late 1980s has had a negative impact.

A feature of the Veneto region, where light engineering and chemicals industries at Marghera near Venice are also major manufacturing sectors, is the absence of significant urbanization. Medium and small cities and towns are the norm. The region has exploited its strategic position close to the Brenner Pass and the goods flow to and from Germany, Italy's top trading partner. It is well-placed to benefit from developments in Central and Eastern Europe.

PIEDMONT

The name is the giveaway. Piedmont, in Italy's northwest corner, lies at the southern foot of the Alps. Nearly as large as Sicily, about 40 percent of the region's surface area is mountainous. Its boundaries follow a broad arc from where the Alps touch the Mediterranean on the Riviera to Switzerland. North of Turin the autonomous Aosta Region separates Piedmont from France.

Turin is the principal city of a region that has a wide mix of industry and agriculture, notwithstanding the heavy presence of auto giant Fiat, with its headquarters and several large plants. Distance markers on the Turin-Milan autostrada serve as Fiat billboards.

Travellers heading towards France and Switzerland on the Turin-Aosta highway get their distances by courtesy of office automation equipment maker Olivetti whose headquarters and main plants are at Ivrea, 50 kilometers from Turin.

Turin can also boast Italy's biggest clothing maker, Gruppo Finanziario Tessile (GFT) which produces for several of the top stylists.

There is a clear link to high-quality textiles manufactured in the Biella area of adjacent Vercelli Province. By opting for the upper market segments, Piedmont's textiles and clothing industries have avoided a head-on competitive clash with low labor cost Third World producers.

Piedmont has six provinces, three in the north and three in the south. Turin and Vercelli are joined in the north by Novara, at the eastern edge. Thriving food processing, chemicals, textiles, and engineering industries combine with proximity to Milan to make Novara one of Italy's wealthiest provinces.

Overall, Piedmont's southern provinces, Alessandria, Asti, and Cuneo, are poorer than their northern sisters, though Cuneo has the smallest gap. Agriculture and food processing are significant in all three, with wine an important product. The Langhe area of Cuneo Province produces Italy's most highly-regarded red wines, Barolo and Dolcetto. Asti is well-known for its sparkling wines. And it should not be forgotten that Turin has the headquarters of Martini & Rossi and Cinzano vermouths.

Piedmont felt the economic crisis of the late 1970s and early 1980s, and was a center for Red Brigade political violence. Always known for hard work and conscientiousness, after a period of industrial restructuring and enjoying a calmer social climate, Piedmont ranks high in Italy's industrial table.

LOMBARDY

Many say that Milan is Italy's true capital. The Lombardy capital has a hustling, bustling liveliness and aggressiveness that set it apart from Italy's other large cities. The city's stock market is responsible for ten times the total business on Italy's nine other exchanges. Its retail banks include four of the country's largest, while Milan's merchant banks lead the way in their field.

Undisputed financial capital, Milan and its surrounding province also head the industrial rankings. Automobile maker Alfa Romeo, tire and cables maker Pirelli, steelmaker Falck, and chemicals leader Enimont (the Eni-Montedison joint venture) are Milan corporations. Light industry from engineering to consumer goods firms is strong, and Milan holds top position as Italy's design and fashion capital.

However, Lombardy is certainly not just Milan, though the metropolis tends to be the focus. With nearly nine million inhabitants, Lombardy is almost twice as large in terms of population as the second largest region. And in terms of surface area it nearly matches Sicily, Italy's biggest geographic region.

Brescia Province in Lombardy's northeast is known for its steel-making and arms factories, Beretta being the leader. North of Milan, Como Province's silk industry enjoys a world reputation. Varese's shoes and clothing continue to thrive, though the smuggling of lira banknotes into neighboring Switzerland has been disrupted by a calm political domestic scene and the removal of exchange controls.

While best known for its industry, Lombardy's agriculture is a leader in size and efficiency. Farming is large-scale, in contrast to the smaller plot subsistence farming that characterizes the *mezzogiorno*. Leading agricultural provinces with related food processing industries are Pavia, Piacenza, Mantua, and Cremona. The latter is probably better known for the tradition of violin making started by Stradivarius, Amati, and Guarneri.

SUCCESS STORIES

TEXAS INSTRUMENTS

Since 1987 purchasers of Texas Instruments' calculators, even in the US, have been buying Italian-made products. All consumer items in Texas Instruments wide range of hand, pocket, and desk calculators are produced at the corporation's Rieti factory, about 50 miles northeast of Rome, putting Texas Instruments in the position of being the largest company making such products in Europe.

The Rieti plant, which started production in 1973, was Texas Instruments' second Italian production facility. The first, established at Aversa just north of Naples in 1958 and now employing about 700 workers, makes electro-mechanical and electronic components for the white goods industry.

Manufacturing in central Italy has clearly been a positive experience for Texas Instruments. In September 1990, its third Italian plant came onstream at Avezzano in the Abruzzo Region, about 60 miles east of the capital. The 400 employees at Avezzano make four megabyte chips to supply the requirements of the Rieti plant, where the corporation has centered its European production of computer memories.

That Texas Instruments has chosen Italy for the production of computer memories says much for the cost and quality competitiveness of Rieti, where the corporation has a payroll of about 1200. Considerably more than half of annual sales of L400bn are achieved in export markets. Successfully challenging producers with factories in low labor cost countries in the Far East is a significant achievement. Texas Instruments' positive experience coupled to financial incentives for investment in the Abruzzo Region underlay the decision to locate in Avezzano.

One of the factors determining the choice of Avezzano was Texas Instruments' corporate policy of keeping plants below a defined size threshold. Adding Avezzano's staff requirements would have taken Rieti above the threshold. Recruiting a further 400 employees would also have created tension in Rieti's labor market.

Though Avezzano lies in Italy's mountainous center, Texas Instruments encountered no problems in staffing its new factory. For each of the 100 graduate jobs advertised, the corporation received seven replies. This good response was probably due partly to the presence of other electronics companies at Avezzano and nearby L'Aquila. Relative closeness to Rome and the autostrada toll highway connection may also have been a factor.

Logistically Avezzano is better placed than Rieti whose connection with the capital is along the Via Salaria Roman consular road. However, Texas Instruments in Avezzano looks as much towards Rieti as to Rome. For the 50 miles cross-country journey there are promises of major road improvements.

Texas Instruments has reason to expect that the road linking its two main Italian electronics plants will be improved rapidly. Records were broken in obtaining approval for the L1500bn investment at Avezzano, a project that seemed to disprove the notion that Italian bureaucracy is a brake. But the fact that the minister responsible for southern development happened to be from the Abruzzo Region might have played a part.

WELLCOME ITALIA

Pharmaceuticals maker Wellcome Italia is the largest British-owned manufacturing company in central/southern Italy. Wellcome, based at Pomezia about 20 miles south of Rome, has a payroll of nearly 600 and sales of L120bn in financial year 1988/89.

The company set up in Milan as Burroughs Wellcome in 1905, but left after nine years at the outbreak of World War I. Following a lengthy absence, Wellcome's products returned to the Italian market in 1949 through a local distributor. Six years later the company established its own importing and packaging operation in Rome. A decision to manufacture led to the move to Pomezia in 1962.

The 1980s was a period of rapid growth. From turnover of L17bn in the opening year of the decade, revenues moved to L50bn in 1985. Growth is expected to continue during the present decade, and next year the company is budgeting for sales approaching L200bn. The success of Wellcome's anti-viral preparations has been a major factor in the growth of the Italian company.

Anti-herpes drug Zovirax and AIDS treatment Retrovir are important revenue producers. So also is Lanoxin, a heart treatment drug which ranks as the second most-prescribed drug in Italy. Wellcome produces a broad range of pharmaceuticals at Pomezia, including over-the-counter preparations like Actifed, the anti-cold medicine that enjoys a footnote in history by being taken on a US mission to the moon.

Wellcome's decision to develop its over-the-counter business in Italy is partly due to the particular characteristics of the country's pharmaceuticals sector, which complicates the marketing of prescription drugs. Only products on the State's register can enjoy prescription subsidies. Moreover, their prices are government controlled and revision of these prices is irregular.

The notorious Italian bureaucracy combines with the State sector's financing problems to create serious difficulties in getting paid promptly. Wellcome Italia reports that payments by hospitals are delayed for as much as ten months, though by law the supplier should be paid within three months.

Dealing with the suffocating red tape of Italian bureaucracy, whether for obtaining registration and payment for its products or for getting building permits and regional incentives for development of its production facilities at Pomezia, has called for considerable effort by Wellcome.

The choice of Pomezia as Wellcome's Italian location owes much to its closeness to the decision-making ministries in Rome. However, Pomezia itself offers little to be recommended. Rambling, seemingly uncontrolled development has created an ugly town with little for its residents and nothing for visitors. Set on the Pontina highway that links Rome to coastal resorts Circeo and Sperlonga, road communications with the capital are reasonable. Though the highway has the unfortunate reputation of being one of Italy's most dangerous, many of Wellcome's staff commute from Rome.

Wellcome is completing a L23bn expansion program to extend research and development facilities, enlarge production and warehousing, and improve ancillary services. The project, which will bring the Pomezia site to saturation, is benefitting from regional incentives, though these are now being phased out for the Pomezia area. Whether the benefits of financial assistance have outweighed the disadvantages of being in Pomezia is open to question.

HONDA ITALIA INDUSTRIALE

Atessa, about 20 kilometers inland from the Adriatic in the Sangro Valley, is the location of a major production center for Japan's Honda. The 11,000 square meter motorcycle plant on a 60,000 square meter site, representing about L12bn investment, started production in 1977. For four years previously it had served for storage and distribution.

Atessa was chosen for a combination of reasons. First, its central position about 60 kilometers south of Pescara on the central Adriatic coast allows rapid links with both north and south. Second, the Sangro Valley was scheduled for significant industrial development with promises of both suitably skilled labor and the possibility of local subcontracting. Third, being in the Abruzzo Region, factories in Atessa qualified for southern development incentives.

In mid-1990 Honda Italia Industriale employed nearly 300 at its Atessa plant. Over 24,000 of its four 125cc motorcycle models left the Atessa production line in 1989, about 40 percent destined for export markets including Honda's home territory Japan. Eager to avoid accusations of economic and industrial "imperialism," the corporation emphasizes that its presence has helped create a strong local engineering sector and has boosted the Abruzzo economy. Italian components account for 85 percent of the motorcycles leaving the Atessa plant. Underlining the Italian nature of its operations in Italy, Honda had just six Japanese employees with its subsidiary in 1990. The corporation has tried to avoid any form of culture clash. Strategy has been to take the best of Japanese manufacturing technology and marry this with Italian technical know-how and flair. Relations with the regional authorities are excellent and the company has encountered no particular difficulties that Italian business does not itself face when dealing with the obstacles and delays of bureaucracy.

Japanese motorcycle makers have won a reputation for quality and Honda Italia Industriale is convinced that the products leaving Atessa in no way fall short of corporate standards. Moreover, productivity in terms of output per worker, aided by the high technology of the production system at the plant, allows Honda's Italian manufacturing subsidiary to hold its head up against factories in Japan and elsewhere in the world.

Atessa, nestling in an attractive and fertile valley sided by smallholdings and orchards, is hardly the place where a visitor would expect to find a major motorcycle plant. Honda's zippy 125 models are themselves somewhat out of tune with the pastoral, arcadian scene. Yet the Japanese corporation has integrated well into the local scene and is looking aggressively to the future. With the Single Market due to become a reality, Honda expects to exploit still further its Abruzzo plant. It aims to boost annual production to 40,000 units and to produce engines for its other European factories. Honda Italia Industriale's turnover of L200bn looks set to rise substantially.

THE LEADERS

TOP 20 INDUSTRIAL COMPANIES (1989)

		Sales	*(Millions lire)* *Net income*
(1)	Fiat	22,288,377	614,928
(2)	ENEL Electricity	17,010,792	155,904
(3)	SIP Telephones	14,572,874	471,022
(4)	Agip Oil	12,234,656	28,492
(5)	ILVA Steel	9,486,579	160,395
(6)	Snam Gas	7,746,078	494,729
(7)	IBM Italia	7,379,165	587,653
(8)	Iveco Fiat	5,205,563	74,320
(9)	IP Italiana Petroli	4,619,736	12,700
(10)	Esso Italiana	4,600,696	− 2,585
(11)	Enichem Chemicals	4,053,794	230,946
(12)	Alitalia	4,022,776	− 151,126
(13)	Olivetti	3,909,400	233,500
(14)	Tamoil	3,370,088	5,025
(15)	Autogerma	3,249,039	72,617
(16)	Rinascente Retail	2,942,113	77,043
(17)	Rai TV	2,801,542	528
(18)	Standa Retail	2,535,099	5,013
(19)	Publitalia	2,183,616	2,012
(20)	Fincantieri Ships	2,175,926	− 254,312

(Source: La Classifiche Del Mondo)

1990 Results

Falls
Banca Nazionale del Lavoro L72b (− 35 percent); IRI Holding L800 (− 50 percent); Pirelli Tyre Holding − $5m (+ $115/1989).

Gains
Benetton L133b (+ 15.5 percent); Italtel L121b (+ 10 percent); Banci di Roma L159b (+ 55 percent); Banco Ambrosiano Veneto L170b (+ 19 percent); Stefanel clothing L54b (+ 40 percent); Olivetti L60.4b (L203b 1989); ENI L2,072b (L1,613b 1989).

TOP 20 BANKS (1989)

			($m)	
			Assets	*Pre-tax profits*
(1)	Cariplo (4,513)		82,103	961
(2)	Banca Nazionale del Lavoro (4,153)		100,967	106
(3)	Istituto Bancario San Paolo di Torino (3,697)	107,403		986
(4)	Monte dei Paschi di Siena (3,625)		66,560	543
(5)	Banca Commerciale Italiana (3,415)		88,594	559
(6)	Istituto Mobiliare Italiano (3,199)		27,004	533
(7)	Credito Italiano (2,491)		75,233	316
(8)	Banco di Roma (2,075)		64,472	162
(9)	Crediop (1,656)		24,636	254
(10)	Banco Popolare di Novara (1,436)		28,514	345
(11)	Banco Ambrosiano Veneto (1,221)		22,081	265
(12)	Mediobanca (1,110)		10,953	195
(13)	Casa di Risparmio di Torino (1,094)		20,361	272
(14)	Banca Popolare di Milano (1,050)		24,122	262
(15)	Banco di Napoli (973)		67,004	111
(16)	Banco di Santo Spirito (968)		20,603	65
(17)	Cassa di Risparmio di Roma (902)		25,417	199
(18)	Credito Romagnolo (895)		14,101	179
(19)	Cassa di Risparmio di Verona & Belluno (866)		13,470	259
(20)	Banca Popolare di Verona (839)		7,111	136

(*Source: The Banker*)

KEY CONTACTS

USEFUL ROME TELEPHONE NUMBERS

Government Offices

Finance Ministry: 39-6-59971
Foreign Affairs: 39-6-36911
Foreign trade: 39-6-59931
Telecommunications: 39-6-54601
Rome Chamber of Commerce: 39-6-570071

Federations

Aerospace (AIA): 39-6-460247
Building: 39-6-84881
Chemicals: 39-6-679-4954
Construction materials: 39-6-864314
Electrical energy: 39-6-864602
Food: 39-6-59031
Leather: 39-6-581-0854
Pharmaceuticals: 39-6-311073
Quarrying: 39-6-860959
Rubber: 39-6-679-2598
Textiles: 39-6-474-4457

Embassies

Member Nations
Belgium: 39-6-322-4441
Britain: 39-6-482-5441
Denmark: 39-6-320-0441
France: 39-6-654-4241
Germany: 39-6-805338
Greece: 39-6-854-9630
Ireland: 39-6-678-2541
Luxembourg: 39-6-578-0456

Netherlands: 39-6-322-1141
Portugal: 39-6-873801
Spain: 39-6-687-8172

Others
Canada: 39-6-855-3421
Japan: 39-6-475-7151
United States: 39-6-46741

USEFUL MILAN TELPHONE NUMBERS

Trade and Commercial Information

EC Office: 39-2-801505
Lombardy Trade Board: 39-2-88231
Milan Trade Fairs: 39-2-49971

Federations

Building: 39-2-657-1861
Chemicals: 39-2-63621
FAI (Federazione Associazioni Industriali): 39-2-324846
Leather, skins: 39-2-7750
Machinery: 39-2-8242101
Office machinery/electronics: 39-2-878941/32641
Pharmaceuticals: 39-2-879087
Rubber: 39-2-498-8168
Textiles, clothing: 39-2-805-3536

Chambers of Commerce

Member Nations
Belgium: 39-2-498-7647
Britain: 39-2-670-2870
Denmark: 39-2-498-5251
France: 39-2-805-3890
Germany: 39-2-652651
Greece: 39-2-670-2779
Ireland: 39-2-709068
Netherlands: 39-2-498-0581
Portugal: 39-2-470659
Spain: 39-2-861137

Others
Canada: 39-2-657-0451
Italian Chambers of Commerce
    Abroad: 39-6-321-5660
Japan: 39-2-865546
Milan Chamber of Commerce:
39-2-851-51
Rome Chamber of Commerce:
39-6-570071
United States: 39-2-869-0661

Facts on Luxembourg

Capital Luxembourg City
Population 377,000
Unemployment 1.6%
GDP (1990): $8b
GDP Growth 1988: 5%; 1989: 4%; 1990: 3.5%
GDP per Capita (1990): $19,800
Inflation 1988: 1.4%; 1989: 3%
Trade Balance 1989: − $760b
Services Balance + $1.9b
Luxembourg-US Trade Sales to US (1988):
$246m; Imports from US (1988): $129m

LUXEMBOURG

"A one issue country. . .they're digging in their heels."
Western diplomat on Luxembourg bank secrecy

BANKING SECRECY IS AS DEAR TO THE HEARTS OF LUXEMBOURGERS AS tea is to the British and the Marseillaise is to the French. But Luxembourg's system of financial policing came under attack following the debacle of the Bank of Credit & Commerce International (BCCI), which was shut down in mid-1991 in a coordinated international move following charges of fraud described by one New York prosecutor as "the largest this century" and by the governor of the Bank of England, Robin Leigh-Pemberton, as "massive and widespread."

BCCI was run by Pakistan and technically owned by Abu Dhabi, but had its headquarters in the Grand Duchy of Luxembourg. Alarm bells rang when two BCCI subsidiaries pleaded guilty at a court hearing in Florida to drug money laundering. The bigger financial scandal that came to light in 1991 wiped out many depositors around the world.

Luxembourg's reputation as a reputable financial center was tarnished, a serious matter in a "one issue country." *The Washington Post* editorialist said: "It is pretty safe to say that no other bank will be allowed to put its nominal headquarters in a small country like Luxembourg, with weak financial policing, while it carries on its main business elsewhere." Luxembourg replied that it was not planning to tighten banking regulations or increase protection for creditors, but admitted that a "legal loophole" that allowed BCCI to operate across the world while keeping a nominal base in Luxembourg "should be closed." In recent times, there has been renewed pressure on Luxembourg from its EC partners to open up its bank accounts to investigative forces from other countries. The banking community in Luxembourg, which has burgeoned from 37 banks in 1970 to 170 in 1990, is resisting this pressure. It puts forward vigorous economic arguments for preserving some of the strictest banking secrecy laws in the world, not least because this secrecy has helped to attract a lot of its private banking clients. They fear any cracks in this armor will send the funds flying to rival centers outside the EC, like Switzerland and Austria.

Private banking played a vital role in the expansion of Luxembourg's financial sector during the 1980s. It has attracted investors from mainly continental Europe who like to be able to pop in and see their account manager, and who appreciate the multilingual capabilities of most of the staff.

In 1984, 21.57 percent of all deposits at Luxembourg banks came from private banking, but now this has doubled.

Private banking effectively evolved in Luxembourg after 1981, when the banking secrecy law was first promulgated. This law was given extra teeth in March 1989, for bank accounts in Luxembourg were rendered virtually impenetrable to any investigating tax authority.

On the other hand, accusations that Luxembourg was laundering drug money prompted the government to introduce very strict criteria for all banks to apply to new clients.

This second law is one of the strictest in the world and has forced the private banks to vet potential clients very thoroughly, and some have turned down applications which did not meet the rigorous new criteria.

They keep a watch for obvious signs of dubious activity, like large cash deposits, suitcases of used $20 bills, and people who bring in large sums of money and then take them out again quickly. (One Italian financier carried an enormous sum in suitcases and was judged to be honorable.)

Bank secrecy applies to Luxembourg's own tax authorities, not just to those from other countries. It is considered to be something which protects the individual. Bankers argue that nobody wants his neighbor to know his wealth and, therefore, they consider it as a case of human rights which needs protecting. But they stress that this does not mean they apply this ruling to money from criminal operations.

It is not always easy to distinguish between what is legal and what is not, but the secrecy law is the strictest in Europe. Luxembourg has cooperated with the US authorities in several cases and the US Attorney General Richard Thornburgh, had expressed his satisfaction with the cooperation over the affairs of drug barons and General Noriega, the former Panamanian dictator, in 1990.

Prime Minister Jacques Santer says that Luxembourg banks will always cooperate with police if the investigating authorities can provide clear evidence that funds have derived from criminal sources.

S P O T L I G H T

• *Local Economy* •

A large middle class—its numbers swollen by several thousand Eurocrats, or functionaries at the various EC bodies in the Grand Duchy—enjoys a high standard of living. Senior Eurocrats are on duty when the EC Council of Ministers meets in Luxembourg. Others work at the Court of Justice, the secretariat of the European Parliament or at the European Investment Bank. The squares beneath the Grand Duke's castle are alive with well-fed merrymakers on summer evenings. Television and film people are adding an extra zest to life which was, in the past, rather dull, if comfortable. Luxembourg shares a common currency and customs facilities with Belgium, and is partner with its neighbor in the Belgium-Luxembourg Economic Union (BLEU), which is already adapting to the Single Europe by dropping its two tier franc system. There's also close integration with the Netherlands. The industrial sector, until recently dominated entirely by steel and the giant Arbed company, is increasingly diversified. Steel, which has benefitted from the world upturn, still contributes a good chunk of GDP, but banking and the services sector are now the largest contributors to government revenues. Agriculture is based on small, highly productive, family-owned farms.

This cooperation on judicial matters was ratified in November 1989 when the Prime Minister met President Mitterrand, then president of the European Council of Ministers, to discuss whether Luxembourg should relax the bank secrecy laws. An agreement was reached which allowed Luxembourg to keep the accounts of its banking clients under wraps unless criminal links could be established.

The Luxembourg banking community does not regard as its role the policing of the tax affairs of non-residents who use their banks, arguing this should be left to the investor's home country. Luxembourg, in addition, successfully collects nearly all the taxes it is entitled to from its taxpayers and argues that every country should do the same with its own taxpayers—and stop hassling the Grand Duchy.

Luxembourg attracts banking clients from what is known as the "middle rich." This means customers who can lay their hands on assets of between $500,000 and $5m, net of borrowings and freehold ownership of a permanent residence. This may seem a lot, but it is small beer when compared to the amounts rival private banking centers like Switzerland demand. Clients get all the usual benefits of private banking, including comprehensive financial advice on their assets and deployment. But one of the most significant carrots Luxembourg bankers can offer customers aside from secrecy is the absence of any withholding tax, a tax at source on investment income. This has helped to give Luxembourg banks an edge over many of their rivals within the EC. So Luxembourg was understandably relieved when the proposal of the European Council of Ministers to introduce a uniform withholding tax throughout Europe fizzled out in 1989.

And yet . . . the EC directive on the freedom of capital movements, which took effect from July 1990, removed the major financial barrier within the community and could renew pressure on Luxembourg and its EC partners to reach some agreement about a uniform withholding tax. Madame Christiane Scrivener, the European Commission member in charge of taxation and customs union in the EC, is pressing for fiscal "approximation," which is an EC term for similar levels of taxation.

At the moment, decisions on European fiscal policy require unanimous approval from all 12 EC members, but Madame Scrivener argues that decisions should be made on the principle of a qualified majority vote in lieu of unanimity. At present, even the smallest member state can scupper fiscal proposals with a veto. Madame Scrivener began discussions on the measures necessary to achieve fiscal approximation at the inter-governmental conference.

Luxembourg clearly has a vested interest in maintaining the status quo. Prime Minister Santer argues that when West Germany introduced a withholding tax for the first time in 1989, money flooded into Luxembourg. He concludes that if fiscal harmonization existed throughout the EC, capital would flow out of the community. Madame Scrivener disagrees with this argument countering that when Austria introduced a withholding tax at the beginning of 1989 no money left the country. Luxembourg bankers maintain that fiscal harmonization is not a prerequisite of a free market in financial services. They cite the example of the United States where there are standard federal taxes, but state taxes vary considerably. They note there are states which offer a person from another state some advantages in the same way that Luxembourg offers advantages to people from France, Belgium, and Germany. Purists say that harmonization is what the Single Market is all about—or at least what it should be about. Others—less pure—regard the harmonization of tax in Europe as faintly amusing. It was on the agenda when the EC was first put together and one only has to drive from Luxembourg to Belgium to realize how far away Europe is from common taxation. Just before leaving Luxembourg to enter Belgium on the expressway there is a whole line of every kind and brand of gas station. That is because gas, cigarettes, and alcohol are much cheaper in Luxembourg than in Belgium. The two countries have differential rates of tax on these items, although they use the same currency and have no border controls. They have had 20 years to sort out the anomaly and their failure makes the goal of tax harmonization look distant.

A continuation of Luxembourg's attractive fiscal regime will help maintain the boom in the number of managed funds which have set up in Luxembourg during the 1980s, both from inside the EC and from far-away places like Japan.

Luxembourg initially enacted a law for the operation of investment funds in 1983 and since then the number of funds based in Luxembourg has risen exponentially. Numbers have gone from 114 in 1984 to 687 in March 1990. The most popular type of fund is known as a SICAV, which is a French invention and is an investment company which works as a variable capital investment fund and operates rather like a unit trust.

Before the change of law in 1983 all funds were under an obligation to pay one percent of their share capital in a sort of stamp duty. So if someone formed a fund worth $450m then $4.5m was paid straight to the exchequer. That was eliminated immediately and funds were asked to pay a single payment of LuxFr60,000 which was less than $2000. Naturally this made a phenomenal difference.

Funds were drawn to Luxembourg because of its fiscal regime and the fact that it was in both the EC and the OECD, an advantage it has over some other rivals.

Luxembourg was given an additional boost when the EC directive on Ucits funds was implemented in March 1988. Ucits is an ugly acronym for Undertakings for Collective Investments in Transferable Securities. The directive allows a Ucits fund to be marketed throughout the EC once it has been approved in one of the EC countries. Luxembourg was the first country to react to this legislation and consequently attracted a lot of Ucits funds, scoring a significant coup in 1989 when it secured the first Ucits fund to be launched by a European subsidiary of Nomura, the giant Japanese securities house.

By March 1990, the assets of all the funds reached LuxFr2,770b. Despite knocks to investor confidence in the wake of stock market fluctuations, Luxembourg has been able to sustain a steady growth in the amount of funds coming into the country. According to banking experts in the Grand Duchy, this success has been helped by the concurrent expansion in the private banking sector which has invested significantly in Luxembourg-based funds.

As Luxembourg is such a small country with the financial sector accounting for 15 percent of its GDP, it has learnt that it must exploit any chances to expand its financial sector following changes in EC legislation.

Luxembourg has no domestic fund industry; it can therefore posture its law to cater for the needs of an international environment, and has much more flexibility than the UK, for example, which has a significant domestic fund industry. The UK cannot introduce laws which are favorable to German investors if this compromises its own industry.

The most recent success story in the expansion of the financial community is the growth in insurance services. So far, Luxembourg has concentrated on reinsurance business, but in December 1989, the EC agreed on a directive which will allow life assurance to be sold throughout the EC. The legislation will not be in place until late 1992 or early 1993, but Luxembourg is already paving the way so that it will be in a strong position to expand in this new sector.

Luxembourg knows only too well from its recent economic history that over-reliance on one sector of the economy can be disastrous. During the 1970s, the steel industry collapsed, leaving a huge hole in the Luxembourg economy. Steel still accounts for nine percent of GDP but competition from the heavy industries in Eastern Europe could place the steel industry in Luxembourg under renewed pressure.

The government is trying to encourage diversification and has begun to develop satellite TV and chemical production. Nevertheless, if Luxembourg wants to continue to enjoy its phenomenally high standard of living it will have to sustain and expand its financial sector in the face of European pressures for fiscal harmonization, which could strip the country of its comparative advantages.

S P O T L I G H T

• *The Man at the Helm* •

Luxembourg's prime minister Jacques Santer has such a low profile around the world that few will recognize his name despite his being one of Europe's longest serving premiers.

"Every Luxembourger is a famous Luxembourger because he is known by all the other Luxembourgers. Some, however, are more famous than others." This observation made by George Erasmus in his commentary on Luxembourg, "How to remain what you are," neatly sums up the size of Luxembourg society—small.

Within the Grand Duchy, Prime Minister Santer is a giant. He has been prime minister since 1984 and following the general elections in July 1989, he was returned to power with increased personal responsibilities which include the Ministries of State, Treasury, and Cultural Affairs.

continued

Despite this position in national politics his equivalent of 10 Downing Street is easily found near the main shopping area in the city of Luxembourg, and shoppers stroll by his prime ministerial office as they take a short cut to a car park. This relaxed relationship between elected and elector says volumes for the consensus politics of Luxembourg where everyone, including the opposition parties, clubs together to come up with policies which will ensure the continuing prosperity of the smallest member (but the richest member per head) of the Community.

Government in Luxembourg is typically conducted under a coalition. Mr. Santer's Christian Social party is currently in dual control with the Socialist party. However, the ideological differences between the parties are marginal. The main election issue in 1989 was confined to whether private pensions should be upgraded in line with the five-sixths of final salary received by the state's civil servants.

Without the chin-to-chin debates between conservative and socialist parties elsewhere in Europe, politics in Luxembourg is regarded by outsiders as the European equivalent of Japan, where individual politicians try to keep a low profile, unless of course they get embroiled with geishas.

But, unlike Japan, which has the economic power to dominate its sphere of influence in South-East Asia, Luxembourg relies heavily on its EC neighbors for its labor force and economic survival. Consequently, any Luxembourg prime minister must box clever on European issues as well as dealing with national affairs. Mr. Santer has played this double role for seven years and has learnt that he must be very imaginative in his negotiations behind the scenes in Brussels in order to protect the interests of the Luxembourg economy. This often requires diplomacy rather than publicity and is another reason why Mr. Santer remains an unknown quantity to many inside and outside the EC. Sometimes Luxembourg acts as a mediator between the larger members of the class of 12. The best example of this was the negotiation of the Single European Act under the Luxembourg presidency of the European Council of Ministers. The Grand Duchy's politicians again showed themselves to be past masters of "Euro diplomacy."

As the Single Market approaches, the moves afoot to standardize policies on financial services have pushed Mr. Santer into a corner. He is keen to retain the fiscal advantages which have helped to make Luxembourg so attractive to foreign investors during the 1980s. He does not think that fiscal harmonization which establishes a uniform withholding tax on dividend or interest payments for non-residents and common banking secrecy laws should be conditions for the liberalization of capital movements within the EC. And he has argued that if a withholding tax is introduced in the EC, then the capital would fly out of the EC to rival centers in Switzerland and Austria, or even Singapore and Hong Kong.

Mr. Santer stresses (mostly privately with fellow EC leaders) the need for strong financial centers within the Community; centers which are competitive with one another but complementary.

However, he takes a strong line following widespread accusations that Luxembourg banks have been laundering the ill-gotten gains of drugs smugglers and dictators, and he has given his word that no money from criminal origins is housed in Luxembourg banks. At the time of the BCCI crash, he maintained that local banking regulations were "in line with those existing in the most reputable finance centers," that the BCCI affair was unique. He ensured the passage of the severest law in the EC, which obliges bankers to reveal the identity of the owner of the money if it originates from drug trafficking or other illegal sources.

But he is adamant that Luxembourg banks should not co-operate with the tax authorities of other countries who suspect an account-holder of tax evasion, which is not a

continued

criminal offense in Luxembourg. No day-to-day, run of the mill, mutual assistance of tax authorities. This is a good example of when the national interests of Luxembourg coincide with what Mr. Santer perceives to be in the best interests of the EC. Under these circumstances, he is willing to take a stand and oppose any measures to change these rules which may come from Brussels. For under article 100 of the Single European Act, there must be unanimity on this issue from all member countries and Mr. Santer will vote against it if he has to. The "mouse" can do more than just roar.

Mr. Santer makes it very clear indeed that, although the Luxembourger is the quintessential European, he will stand up and fight for the national interests of Luxembourg. Perhaps it won't be long before everyone inside and outside the EC knows exactly who Jacques Santer is.

MARKET OPPORTUNITIES

Government incentives, the country's central location in the EC, multilingual staff, good communications—and a minimum of red tape—have helped lure US investment to Luxembourg in the past 35 years. There are some big names for a small country. Dupont de Nemours has polyester film and photographic film plants; Commercial Shearing makes steel-building systems and also hydraulic pumps; Goodyear produces tires and has a technical center with a test track; General Motors makes machine tools for other GM plants in Europe; General Electric is linked with Japan's Fanuc for automation products; while Guardian has a float glass factory supplying the walls of Frankfurt's skyscrapers, among others. More investment is being made—Dupont has just spent $280 million, Guardian another $100 million, while Goodyear, which employs 4,000 workers—the largest workforce outside of Arbed, the national steel company—is adding a $15 million facility. Luxembourg does not publish figures on foreign investment, but estimates put foreign investment—of which 60 percent is from the US—at around 35 percent of total industrial investment. US manufacturing investment in Luxembourg is probably around one billion dollars, one of the highest concentrations anywhere. There's always been a pro-American attitude since Perle Mesta served as a postwar envoy and had her diplomatic and social life portrayed in the musical "Call Me Madam." More important, perhaps, is the welcome mat of the Ministry of Economy and the State Investment Bank (SNCI). The SNCI, a government body, finances corporate investments and exports through ten-year equipment loans (at 4.5 percent), plus medium-and long-term loans at favorable rates, exports credits, equity loans or temporary equity participation. No restrictions whatsoever exist on the transfer of capital and profits. Top corporate tax has been reduced to 36 percent, while there is low value added tax with rates ranging from 3 to 12 percent. Investments in fixed assets are eligible for up to 25 percent government assistance in the form of cash grants or interest rebates on bank loans. Cost-sharing is also there for R&D and personnel training. Taxes paid by new companies are reduced by such measures as a 25 percent exemption for eight years for those supplying new products or services in the Luxembourg market; investment tax credits; depreciations for production equipment and R&D. Quick, high returns are the objective, say the authorities.

Luxembourg has linked with its neighbors, Belgium and France, to create the EC's first cross-border, development area which has the attractions of geography, low land costs, subsidies up to 37.5 percent of capital investment, and the pooled resources of three nations. It's called the European Development Area, or EDA, and has now "taken off" after a slow start in 1985. EC Commission president Jacques Delors has called the 1300-acre EDA "a living example of the great European economic space."

Then there is the Schengen Agreement, named after a Luxembourg town, whereby five EC nations (the afore-mentioned trio plus Germany and the Netherlands) agreed to scrap border controls in the region ahead of the Single Market. Firms within the EDA zone have created 2,800 jobs, of which 1,600 are in the French part. One of EDA's raisons d'être was the need to find new jobs for redundant steel workers in France and Luxembourg. The Grand Duchy offers new-comers to the tripartite zone its low taxation, cheap gasoline, efficient banks, American schools, and the expanding Findel Airport in Luxembourg city, 30 kilometers away. Belgium "contributes" a backup network of dynamic, small-sized companies. France puts into the "pot" a skilled labor force and most of the startup subsidy (25 percent) from its regional development grant. The EC pays the rest from its European Regional Development Fund and has given a commitment to helping EDA until 1995. One of the firms that has moved to EDA is Britain's Cape Building Products, makers of safety panels, which paid a low $128,000 for a 15,000 square site for its new factory. It was attracted by the incentives and EDA's "hub" position between Paris, Amsterdam, Frankfurt, and Geneva. The three nations have signed also to build a joint European technology college and the hope is that another 5,000 jobs can be created over the next five years.

Key Contact

Apeilor Development Agency
1 Place du Pont-a-Seille
57045 Metz Cedex
France
Tel: 33-8775-3618
Fax: 33-8775-2199.

S P O T L I G H T

• *Television* •

Luxembourg's audiovisual law takes up just one page and contains two clauses. A remarkable conciseness in the face of rapidly-expanding satellite and multi-channel TV. The Grand Duchy's "no frills" attitude towards radio and TV "sans frontières" is symbolized by Radio Luxembourg, now in its 60th year and part of one Europe's biggest audiovisual and publishing groups, and the Société Européenne des Satellites, with its successful Astra TV satellite, Rupert Murdoch's Sky TV and others. There is also a new tax incentive plan to allow American and other film and television production companies to recoup a significant proportion of investment in Luxembourg. The expansion of Compagnie Luxembourgeoise de Telediffusion (CLT), the parent company of Radio Luxembourg and RTL television, the launch of a second Astra pan-European satellite, and the efforts to boost local production are all moves in advance of the Single Market—and the growing demand for more TV programs in Europe. Until, now, around half of all programming in Europe has been imported.

CLT operates extensive TV programming to and out of Luxembourg and Eastern France (RTL-TV), Belgium (RTL-TVI); Germany (RTL+), France (M6), Bavaria (Tele 5), and the Netherlands (RTV). The company also operates radio programming, notably in France, Germany, and Britain, and owns book interests that include Robert Laffont, the Paris-based publisher. It has ambitions to expand, notably via the RTL International channel on Astra. Britain is a main target for programming and accompanying advertising, while Spain is also in CLT's sights. The company's plan for new programs, baptized CLT-2000, will link its own production offshoots, such as Hamster, with production companies in Canada, Britain, and France. This batch of joint programs will help CLT's penetration of new worldwide markets, give it access to various subsidies for programming, as well as help meet national and European quotas. More co-production deals are envisaged with major players such as the ZDF public channel in Germany, but even CLT with its experience and resources is finding it

continued

arduous to produce significant numbers of hours of quality European shows. Still, it sees the huge market ahead. This is mouth-watering, with a united Europe of 135 million homes, the largest TV market in the world. Currently, Europe's top five markets, France, Britain, Germany, Italy, and Spain, have 95 million homes receiving 125,000 hours of programming. CLT, chaired by former Luxembourg premier and European statesman Gaston Thorn, associated with Frenchman Jacques Rigaud, has essentially Luxembourg, Belgian, and French shareholders (Audiofina & Fratel, a Luxembourg holding company for the Belgian financial group, Bruxelles-Lambert and the French advertising group, Havas, have 56.7 percent of the shares, with Banque Paribas of France holding 22.4 percent).

Pierre Werner, former Luxembourg Premier, launched plans in 1982 for a medium-power, private satellite system for European TV. Werner is now chairman of the board of Société Europeénne des Satellites (the Grand Duchy holds 20 percent with the rest in private hands). SES has a 22-year franchise. Astra 1 was launched at the end of 1988. Signals are transmitted from European TV studios to the Luxembourg uplink site in the Grand Duke's former hunting lodge, and are transmitted 36,000 kilometers up to Astra. The satellite in turn re-broadcasts these signals down across Europe, where, two years after the launch, some 14 million homes equipped with a cable connection or direct-to-home dish receive all or some of Astra's 16 programs. These include a range of Sky TV movies, news, and sport; the Children's Channel; the MTV rock channel; Scandinavian programs and the Swedish Filmnet with subtitles; RTL Veronique Dutch programs and, most recently, eight German channels. Astra 2 will add 16 more channels. The State Banque et Caisse d'Epargne de l'Etat and the SNCI hold 10 percent each. The remaining 80 percent (a different class of shares) is divided between Aachener und Münchener Beteiligungs Aktiengesellschaft; Banque Générale du Luxembourg; Benson S.A.H; Bil Participations (Banque Internationale à Luxembourg); Deutsche Bank Luxembourg; Dresdner Bank Luxembourg; Stuvik A.B (Kinnevik); Kirkbi A.S.; Natinvest S.A.H.; RITA S.A.H.; Société Nationale d'Investissement de Belgique; Societe Generale de Belgique; Thames Television; TSW Television South West Holdings, and Ulster Television.

Under the tax incentive plan for locally-based media companies (or holding companies), some 36% of expenditure can be recouped. The Grand Duchy is not yet a European Hollywood (a rival is Portugal with its more varied scenery and sunshine), but one joint venture company brought together the government, local banks, the Paribas bank and the US production company, Harmony Gold. The plan is to finance some $300 million worth of filming in Luxembourg with even the bar bills of the producers earning the 30 percent-plus rebate. The new company, Harmony Gold Finance of Luxembourg, will produce children's programs, Sherlock Holmes, and more.

Key Contacts

CLT-RTL
Villa Louvigny
L-2850
Luxembourg
Tel: 352-4766-2114
Fax: 352-4766-2730.

Astra/Société Européenne des Satellites
Chateau de Betzdorf
L-6832
Betzdorf
Luxembourg
Tel: 352-717251
Fax: 352-71725 227.

• *Getting To Know the Capital* •

With a population of 80,000, Luxembourg city is a metropolis only in Grand Duchy terms. Some people find it charming, others dull.

A deep ravine divides the city. On one side is the old town, dominated by the Grand Duke's castle. This section has become newly fashionable, is being restored, and houses some fine restaurants. On the other side is commercial Luxembourg.

The Luxembourg royal family is a branch of the House of Nassau. During World War II, the Grand Duchess Charlotte personified national identity. She ruled in all for 45 years. Her son, Grand Duke John, now reigns. His wife is Princess Josephine-Charlotte, sister of King Baudouin of the Belgians. Traditionally Luxembourg's ruling family has been discreet, even secretive. Crown Prince Henri is changing that tradition: he likes to get out and about and smiles for photographers. His wife, the Grand Duchess Hereditary, Maria Teresa, is a bombshell by Luxembourg standards: beautiful, outspoken, of Cuban origin, with polish and self-assurance.

There's more to see and do in this apparently dour city than first acquaintance might suggest. The old town is worth a wander. The castle itself is open to the public from the middle of July until early September, during the Grand Ducal vacation.

The *Place d'Armes* and *Place Guillaume* are two central squares that bring together the twin influences of France and Germany. Also in this downtown area, on Avenue de la Porte Neuve, is the *stock exchange,* the only one in Europe that's over a row of boutiques and next to a supermarket.

The Jean-Pierre Pescatore Museum (Villa Vauban), Avenue Emile Reuter, houses a collection of paintings bequeathed to the city by two nineteenth-century bankers. Painters represented include Flemish and Dutch masters, and Canaletto, Courbet, and Delacroix.

One of the fathers of the European Community was Luxembourg-born Robert Schumann, so a visit to the Kirchberg Plateau is appropriate. *European City* is almost that—certainly a town almost in its own right. A visitors' bureau arranges guided tours.

::::::::::::::::SUCCESS STORY::::::::::::::::
GUARDIAN EUROPE SA

The presence in Luxembourg of the world's most advanced float glass factory is the result of a vision by a local businessman anxious to expand outside his country, the commitment of American money and know-how, and German-inspired last-minute trucking of fragile glass.

Glass retailer Ferd Kohn, in the late 1970s, wanted to grow much bigger, and even have his own float glass operation in the Grand Duchy. The big European glassmakers were not interested, so Kohn set off for Guardian, a major US manufacturer based in the Detroit suburb of Northville. It took him some time to persuade William Davidson, owner of the company, to make the investment. Davidson had a team study the Grand Duchy from every angle—geography, transport out of the country to the rest of Europe, government aid, and labor availability. All made sense, including converting redundant steel industry managers and workers. The Luxguard I plant was built in 18 months and broke even a year later. Luxguard II has just followed, bringing the investment to some $270 million. Today, Guardian Europe SA is headquartered in Dudelange, Luxembourg, and Kohn is Davidson's partner. The American has made use of the Luxembourgers wide range of contacts and has brought in the German truckers who have clocked up 40 million kilometers, transporting over a million tons of glass.

Americans and Luxembourgers seem to know how to supply glass. They have major market shares in Europe (60 percent in the Netherlands; 30 percent in Britain, bastion of the world's No 1, Pilkington; 30 percent in Germany; and 20 percent in France).

Guardian has received unspecified aid from the Luxembourg government. In return, it promised to create 150 jobs and has in fact found employment for 750, including those in a research and development company. "We've proved you don't have to be in Paris, Brussels, or Amsterdam with your headquarters in order to succeed." Europe is now making a major contribution to Guardian, a company with close to a billion dollars a year in sales, and one that is up there with the Big Four of glass: Pilkington, PPG, St Gobain, and Asahi. The difference with Luxguard is that it imports everything for the production of glass and then exports the entire output.

⋮⋮⋮⋮⋮⋮⋮⋮⋮⋮THE LEADERS⋮⋮⋮⋮⋮⋮⋮⋮⋮⋮

TOP 10 COMPANIES (1989)

			Workforce
(1)	Arbed	Steel	10,830
(2)	Goodyear	Tires	4,090
(3)	CFL	Railways	3,660
(4)	Banque Internationale	Finance	2,150
(5)	Group Cactus	Food	2,070
(6)	Banque Générale	Finance	1,750
(7)	Du Pont de Nemours	Plastics	1,450
(8)	State Savings Bank	Finance	1,430
(9)	Villeroy and Boch	Tableware	1,240
(10)	Monopol Scholer	Supermarkets	1,050

1990 Results

Falls
Banque Internationale à Luxembourg (BIL) Lfr1.03b (− 31 percent);
Minorco/Anglo American (six months) $96.3m ($98.9m)

Gains
Banque Generale LFr1.26b (+ 12 percent).

GROWTH OF MANAGED FUNDS IN LUXEMBOURG

Year	Number of funds
1970	102
1980	76
1983	99
1984	132
1985	177
1986	261
1987	405
1988	525
1989	629
1990 (March)	687

KEY CONTACTS

USEFUL LUXEMBOURG TELEPHONE NUMBERS

Trade and Commercial Information

Bankers Association: 352-29501
Luxembourg Chamber of Commerce: 352-435853
Monetary Institute: 352-478888

European Bodies

Commission: 352-43011
Council: 352-43021
Court of Auditors: 352-47731
Court of Justice: 352-43031
European Parliament: 352-43001
Conference Center: 352-478560
Investment Bank: 352-43791

Government Offices

Foreign Affairs: 352-4781
International Economic Relations: 352-478611
Economics: 352-479-4224
Government Information: 352-478224

Embassies

Member Nations
Belgium: 352-26957
Britain: 352-29864
Denmark: 352-20964
France: 352-471091
Germany: 352-453444
Greece: 352-445193
Ireland: 352-450610
Italy: 352-443644
Netherlands: 352-27570

Portugal: 352-473955
Spain: 352-460255

Others
Canada (via Brussels):
322-735-6040
Japan: 352-464151
United States: 352-460123

Facts on the Netherlands

. . . .

Capital Amsterdam
Seat of Government The Hague
Population 14.7m
Unemployment 8.3%
GDP 1990: $277b
GDP per Capita 1989: $15,063
Inflation 1987: −0.6%; 1988: 1.2%; 1989:
    1.25%; 1990 (est.) 2%; 1991–94 (est. annual
    rate): 1.75%
GNP Growth 1988: 2%; 1989: 4.25%; 1990
    (est.): 2.75%; 1991–94 (est.): 2.5%
Foreign Trade + $5b
Dutch–US Trade + $6b (for US)

. . . .

THE NETHERLANDS

"The Netherlands has consistently supported a dual process of European integration—by underlining internal liberalization within the European Community on the one hand, while at the same time advocating a Community with open doors to non-members." Premier Rudd Lubbers

THE LARGE DUTCH MULTINATIONAL COMPANIES—SHELL, UNILEVER, and Akzo—built their empires on global trading flair, but there were other ingredients such as hard slog, an attention to the fine print of contracts (both to earn an extra guilder as well as satisfy the customer), and a kind of overall business competence, even dedication. By contrast, the politicians were an irksome lot, certainly in the 1970s. Dutch government, previously a succession of painfully patched-up pacts, these days has a more efficient look with its center-left label. (The center-right government fell over financing a national plan to clean up the soil and air, a mistake the center-left government is unlikely to make, given the strong feeling on the issue. It has wisely promised and planned to reduce pollution by 70 percent in 20 years). One man has been responsible for most of the change. He's affable, unpretentious, slightly rumpled and loves nothing more than examining the smallest points of social and industrial policies. Ruud Lubbers, head of the Christian Democrats, a center party embracing both Catholics and Protestants, has been premier since 1982. He began a third term after the "environmental elections" of late 1989 and set off into the 1990s in alliance with the Socialists, led by the erudite, former trade union leader Wim Kok, now finance minister. Lubbers, still only 51, is breaking records for longevity at the top and will be remembered no doubt as the man who reformed the ultra-expensive Dutch Welfare State, which had ballooned out of control and infected the country with what became known as the "Dutch Disease." The situation has improved considerably under Lubbers—high growth, rising exports, a consistent trade surplus, greater productivity, and one of the EC's lowest inflation rates. A pity, therefore, that the Netherlands still trails the reputation, particularly in some US business circles, of being a country with abnormally high wages and social costs, and a troublesome workforce. The statistics and graphs point the other way, but it will take time, even the Dutch admit, before reality is generally accepted. One sign of the times is the pragmatic label now attached to Mr. Kok, as well as to the Premier. The finance minister, who is willing to talk with foreign companies about hiring and firing (provided there is compensation), has said that the fiscally favorable status for foreign companies, designated as NV, will continue after 1993 and has agreed with bankers and brokers that the tax on stock exchange transactions was driving business abroad and therefore should be scrapped. What surprised the nation at the end of 1989 was the speed with which the Christian Democrats and the Socialists agreed on joint policies—a brisk three weeks instead of the previous paralyzing seven months. Lubbers is both easing austerity and trimming the spending ambitions of his new Socialists partners. Wage demands will resurface and make Mr. Lubbers' life difficult, but there's no doubt as to his popularity. A look at the past is highly instructive. Up to the oil crisis of 1973, Dutch annual growth was six percent and investment in industry a percentage point higher. Unemployment was a mere two percent. Growth fell to one percent in the next decade, investment plummeted, and the unemployment level soared to a startling 17 percent. The Lubbers government won agreement on wage restraint and reduced the tax burden on industry. Private consumption picked up after 1985 as a result of higher national income, lower social security contributions, lower interest rates, and virtually zero inflation. Government expenditure was reduced, as was the government's financial deficit. Competitiveness, not unnaturally, improved and helped the export of goods and services which account for 65 percent of GNP. There's been some "fixing" of the unemployment figure which stood at 11.3 percent at the end of 1988, only to fall to 8 percent when statistics began excluding those not registered as unemployed. Structural problems exist with half the "official" unemployed out of work for more than a year. In addition, the Dutch population has an unusually low participation rate in the workforce—75 percent of the male population of working age (15–64), well below the EC average, the United States (85 percent) and Japan (88 percent). Why? Well, social benefits are about the same as the minimum wage, while taxes paid by the average worker are 40 percent above the EC average. Still, if the Lubbers-Kok team cannot solve this problem of incentives, then it is unlikely that anyone can. Meanwhile, taxes are being eased and the social security system streamlined.

S P O T L I G H T

• *Dutch Investment* •

Direct Dutch investment in the United States in 1990 stood at $60.5 billion, putting the Netherlands in third position behind Britain ($122.8 billion) and Japan ($66.1 billion). Most Dutch investments are in manufacturing. On the other hand, the US has its largest bilateral trade surplus in the world with the Netherlands, over $6 billion. The Netherlands, in fact, is America's ninth largest export market.

Dutch investment in the US has traditionally been led by the big multi-nationals—Philips, Shell, Unilever, and Akzo. More recently, the Nationale Nederland and Aegon insurance companies have taken up the running, as has the Ahold supermarket chain.

While the government seeks to cut costs with a new four-year program, the Single Market has seen even the very large Dutch firms girding themselves for increased competition and opportunities. The two largest banks, ABN and Amro, merged to become a major player in European and world financial markets. Insurance giant Nationale Nederland linked with NMB Postbank, itself the result of a merger of the fourth and fifth largest banks, while concentration continued among the food companies with Unilever buying into Mora/Saltos. In another area, Nedlloyd, the transport and energy group, held talks with Norwegian suitors. The Netherlands, as a leading exporting country, depends for its prosperity largely on the state of other major economies, and the Dutch have been beneficiaries of extra demand in neighboring, united Germany—West Germany was taking almost 30 percent of Dutch exports before reunification. Thousands of Dutch firms, which trade with Germany, stand poised to benefit from Germany's increased needs for goods and services.

MARKET OPPORTUNITIES

The domestic market is small when compared to some others within the European Community, but its attraction lies in its sophistication coupled with strong, recent growth. Growth was a healthy 4.2 percent in 1989 and 3–4 percent in 1990 and even if these levels fall to 2.5 percent in the period to 1994 then some $42 billion will be added to the national income. OECD has noted very buoyant private consumption and investment in plant and equipment. The country ranks tenth amongst the world's leading economies, and average earnings are close to a country like France. Government housing support is being cut back which will dent fixed investment, but firms are positioning themselves to take advantage of the Single Market. American firms, for example, are alert to these new opportunities. The US Embassy in The Hague notes: "The pace of new investments and the establishment of new business arrangements by US firms in the Netherlands clearly is on the rise . . . there has been a marked increase in the number of US products imported into the Netherlands." The "gateway" philosophy of the Dutch has meant a respectable surplus in their foreign trade, although one deficit is with the US. But then again, the Dutch make massive property investments across the Atlantic. An examination of sales openings shows the following.

POLLUTION CONTROL EQUIPMENT

This is more than just fashionable. Environmental awareness plays a major role in the daily lives of the Dutch. The Dutch now spend 1.344 percent of their GNP on environmental protection, twice as much per capita as in the US. The Ministry of Environmental Affairs, in its ambitious and expensive plan extending to 1994, calls on Dutch industry to double its spending on environmental protection. So by 1994, industry will be obliged to spend an extra $1 billion a year to meet the stricter norms on pollution. Imports of this kind of equipment are expected to rise well above the previous level of around $210 million.

AEROSPACE

Heavy investment is coming both on the ground and in the air. Schiphol Airport is spending to raise annual passenger capacity to 35 million by the end of the decade, and freight to two million tons. The fortunes of Fokker, the long-troubled aircraft manufacturers, are on the mend, as mid-1990 orders for the Fokker 100 medium-haul passenger jet airliner rose to 219 with options for another 163. Orders grow also for the smaller Fokker 50. The company is expanding in the Netherlands now that its plans for US assembly at Lockheed have been abandoned. KLM, the national carrier, Martinair, Transavia, and Air Holland will be investing four billion dollars in new aircraft in the next three to four years. The US will win the lion's share of these orders, but the European Airbus will also benefit, as will Saab of Sweden—the commuter line NLM is acquiring eleven Saab 340Bs, and a 30 passenger jet. Some 34 firms are grouped within NAG, or Netherlands Aerospace Group, working on parts of the European space lab, Columbus, a turn-of-the-century project administered by the Paris-based European Space Agency, which has a large satellite testing unit on the coast at Noordwijk; the Ariane V rocket, and the European space plane, Hermes. The US sells a steady $700 million a year in this market.

AUTOMOTIVE

The total market for equipment, tools, parts, and accessories (imports and production minus exports) is expanding to $4.5 billion. A quarter of all automotive expenditure in the Netherlands is for car purchase and the remaining three-quarters for maintenance and repairs. Equipment sales have grown with the increase in compulsory safety checks, while a do-it-yourself trend is boosting sales of maintenance items. Nearly all products, or some four-fifths, are imported.

TELECOMMUNICATIONS

A growth market following the end of the PTT's monopoly which was replaced at the beginning of 1989 by a government-granted concession. The PTT keeps its responsibility for providing the telecommunications infrastructure, but the new set-up relaxes the monopoly for peripheral equipment and services. The PTT plans to replace all electro-mechanical public switching exchanges with digital exchanges by 1996. Digitalization of the network is well underway and the introduction of Integrated Digital Network Services (ISDN) is envisioned by the year 2000. Imports of telecom items have been running at $700 million a year. The liberalization measures, particularly for customer premises equipment, will mean imports growing between 15 and 20 percent a year. The overall telecom equipment market is growing at seven percent.

SECURITY EQUIPMENT

Competition is strong between US, Japanese, German, and British firms in this $250 million market, driven by a doubling of both home and automobile burglaries in the past decade. Private companies purchase most of the imports which, in turn, dominate the market. Prime Minister Ruud Lubbers himself chased and caught a thief in a celebrated incident. His fellow citizens are turning to gadgetry, rather than a sprint in the street, to protect their paintings and silver.

COMPUTER SOFTWARE/SERVICES

The market is bursting. Imports and production, which stood at around $2.65 billion in 1988, leapt to $3.29 billion a year on the back of substantial contracts placed by government departments. The forecasts are ever upwards over three years—15 percent a year for application packages, 10 percent for custom software and consultancy. The Dutch buy personal computers in a big way—in one recent year they were the biggest buyers in the whole of Europe.

BUSINESS AND OFFICE EQUIPMENT

Exhibitions held annually in Amsterdam, under the title "Efficiency," offer an excellent showcase for those seeking to enter what is now a $2 billion dollar a year market. The sector expands by 15 percent a year. The fine new skyscraper offices in Rotterdam for Unilever, Robeco, and major insurance groups all need to be fitted out, as do the spreading business and industrial parks close to Amsterdam and the sprouting science parks.

SCIENTIFIC INSTRUMENTS

The market expands regularly and now stands at the $500 million mark. Growth, says the US Embassy, could be at six percent annually into the mid-1990s. Imports account for more than four-fifths of Dutch purchases, with US firms supplying a quarter of these incoming goods. In the related measuring and test equipment sector—now around $700 million a year—the US again supplies one in four. Growth is measured at ten percent.

SPORTING GOODS

Strong national growth, high national income, and generous vacations combine to produce an attractive market for US and other exporters of sporting goods and recreational equipment. Sales are pushing the $450 million mark and grow at a steady five percent. When they go abroad, notably to their vacation homes in France, the Dutch take everything with them so all these leisure goods are bought in the local stores.

S P O T L I G H T

• *Investment Incentives* •

The Netherlands, as well as Belgium and Denmark, has received a note from the EC Commission calling for a cut in subsidies outside of depressed regions. The Hague's reply: It will be business as usual, aside from a few book-keeping changes, when it comes to aiding investors. So Dutch grants continue. The Dutch also have a special corporate status, the famous "NV," adopted by some giants of world trade such as Alcatel, Nissan, Renault-Volvo; declining profits tax to match lower rates elsewhere in Europe; an in-depth, yet friendly dialogue with the taxman to avoid any "surprises" after opening for business; expansion of the venture capital market—all are measures by the Dutch to ease the financ-

continued

ing of investments. The regional incentive is known as the IPR capital grant, usually 25 percent, sometimes 35 percent. This covers the first $10 million of investment, with optional aid for a further $10 million. Examples: the new province of Flevoland grants a 25% subsidy up to around 20,000 guilders per employee, provided the investment is at least half a million dollars and creates ten jobs. Gelderland, already a center for high-tech and service industries, offers 35 percent. North Brabant helps with venture financing. The welcome mat is usually somewhat broader for companies in distribution, biotechnology, information technology, new materials, and medical technology. The Netherlands has an almost complete network of tax treaties to avoid double taxation, exempts from taxes the transferred profits of subsidiaries—hence the popularity of the NVs, has reduced the tax on company profits over 250,000 guilders to 35 percent, a necessary alignment with Europe, granted a 35 percent tax reduction to foreign managers, and instituted a system under which the foreign company and the inland revenue department sit down and reach a binding agreement on future rates. In addition, the new Amsterdam Financial Centre (Herrengracht 136, Amsterdam Tel: (31) 20-208769, Fax: (31) 20-208861) has worked on a 23 point plan to expand the city's financial clout, based mainly on the massive reserves of the Dutch pension funds and insurance companies. Amsterdam wants to stay as close as possible to Frankfurt and Paris and be at least the equal of other second-tier markets such as Brussels, Luxembourg, Madrid, and Zurich. The growing number of venture capital funds also look to the institutions as they expand within the Netherlands and across the borders prior to the Single Market. The Netherlands ranks third after Britain and France for venture capital. The MIP fund invests in larger, high-tech projects. Now, the Financial Centre is helping to create small company funds. The Dutch reputation for driving a hard bargain is one thing; more interesting is the fact that there is so much liquidity in the country and too few projects.

TRANSPORTATION AND COMMUNICATION

Heavy trucks, formed into seemingly endless convoys, trundle day and night along the highways of the Randstad, the "coastal city" area that embraces the important population and transport centers in the Netherlands. There are perhaps 8,000 Dutch road haulage firms and a good quarter—those with fleets of more than twenty vehicles—are engaged in the long haul from the ports and airports to the edges of Europe. The Dutch traditionally have been intermediaries in international trade and have invested heavily in dockside facilities and airport cargo centers, as well as the actual highways and waterways. The Dutch see mainly advantages from the Single Market, particularly with the extension of cabotage, or the freedom of truckers to collect and deliver loads outside their home country. An empty Dutch truck heading back from Southern Italy or Greece would use contacts, reputation, and computerized European data to pick up all kinds of loads. Dutch single-mindedness when it comes to road transport impresses, as well as frightens, other European truckers. The Dutch have a one-stop shopping center for customers in the Holland International Distribution Center in The Hague which groups truckers as well as bankers and insurance agents. Its policy is to make Dutch warehouses more centralized and computerized so that the country keeps its 36 percent grip on European road freight. The other advantage is a bonded warehouse system that in many ways transforms the entire country into a free zone. This customs system is called Femac, and a company can operate a *de facto* bonded warehouse in its own facilities—even the boss's home—and under its own administrative control. Nowhere is the Dutch sense of business more apparent.

Successful European ports in the era of the Single Market will be those that have not only invested in the latest forms of container-handling, but also in the rapid moving of goods from the ship into Europe. Rotterdam has rushed to build a new rail service center for all kinds of freight with the aim of further reducing travel time to destinations such as Italy. Huge sums have been earmarked by both the central government and the cities of the Randstad to improve highways and tunnels over the next two decades. One Minister spoke of $1.5 billion, another of five times that amount for a new storm-tide barrier between Rotterdam and the North Sea and for similar works. From

Rotterdam and Amsterdam, some 6,000 inland freighters, the world's largest fleet, take cargo to Belgium, Germany, France, and Switzerland, and the Dutch want to keep this two-third share of Europe's inland shipping.

However, along with this mega-spending, exists the fear that the industrial importance of the German Ruhr could decline with the rise of newer production and distribution centers in the south or south-east (the Mediterranean zone, for example, or Munich with its growing importance in electronics). And, of course, in Eastern Europe. For the foreseeable future, Germany's raw materials and energy "pipeline" remains the Netherlands. Another unknown factor is the Channel Tunnel and the new road and rail transport network surrounding it. Could Antwerp in Belgium, Rotterdam's rival in the super-port league, benefit because it will be nearer the Chunnel? While the Belgians argue over the route for new highspeed trains (TGV), the Dutch have started building their rail stations.

S   P   O   T   L   I   G   H   T

• *Ailing Giant* •

Business at the very top can be volatile even for Europe's mega-companies. Philips, a household name, suffered because it over-reached itself. The company made its first millions in lightbulbs and then repeated the success with consumer electronics. Later, it diversified into computers, PCs and silicon chips like the S-Rams (static random-access memory chips) for laptops and mobile telephones, but has suffered in the face of intense Japanese and US competition. At Eindhoven, the company town, Jan Timmer, who had turned around the consumer electronics division, replaced Cornelius van der Klugt as chairman when profits collapsed for the first time in decades and the company posted a 1990 loss of $2.4 billion. Profits rebounded in 1991.

The extent of the crisis at a company known worldwide for its shavers, hairdryers, radios, video recorders, and compact disks led to massive provisions and write-offs plus 40,000 job losses, bringing the total world workforce down to 260,000. The cuts affected not only the Netherlands, but also some of Philips' worldwide collaboration deals. In mid-1991, Philips pulled out of the appliances industry when it sold 47 percent of its joint venture to its partner, Whirlpool Corporation. Shortly afterwards, it unloaded most of its information systems division to Digital, saying it would focus in the future on the personal computer sector. The crisis also halted its membership of AT&T Network Systems International, created to seek domination of the European telecommunications market along with Italy's Stet and Spain's Telefonica. Philips needs to overhaul management and improve stock control prior to the Single Market. In the past, it operated on decentralized management—a British company in Britain, a German company in Germany. One view is that the Japanese have shown that this system is not necessarily the best in the global market, let alone the EC.

MANAGEMENT AND WORKFORCE

The presence in government of Socialist Wim Kok, longtime head of the Dutch labor movement, is one guarantee of stable management–workforce relations. Another is the fact that Kok, as deputy prime minister and finance minister, has been hailed as a realist and fiscal moderator since he took on the job of working out the details, under Prime Minister Lubbers' leadership, of a much-needed reform of state finances, particularly the Dutch social security system. For two decades, critics of the system have coined the phrase "Dutch disease" to describe abuses which have resulted in a situation in which 3.4 million people received an income without working while the total of employed was not much higher at 4.5 million. The 3.4 million total, of course, includes pensioners and genuine job-seekers, but there is also a hard core of 900,000 people who receive "disability" benefits of up to 70 percent of a salary until "retirement" at 65 without being unfit for work in a normal sense. This hard core represents a sixth of the workforce and a third of them have long claimed to be psychologically unfit for work because of "stress." It's a unique situation within the EC and one which gives the Dutch workforce a somewhat unjustified bad name, given that the majority of those in the private sector are highly-skilled and educated. The coalition partners are agreed that disability payments should be cut off after five or six years, taxes fine-tuned in an upward direction and, above all, that motivation be restored among the work-shy. Several billion dollars are being expended on various employment schemes so that, as Kok tactfully put it, "The relatively low percentage of active workers be increased and the numbers of unfit people reduced." He meant an "end to the comedy," although there is no Dutch phrase expressing that sentiment.

The positive side of the labor scene is that unit labor costs have decreased, while the country as a whole has one of the lowest strike rates—only 22 days lost per 1,000 employees. A new realism has taken hold within organized labor and an established mechanism is in place which permits smooth labor–management negotiations in liaison with the government. The three Dutch labor organizations, the Federation of Christian National Workers' Unions, the Federation of Netherlands Trade Unions, and the Council for Middle and Higher Grade Employees, represent one-third of workers. They deal with the two central employers' bodies, the Federation of Netherlands Industries and the Federation of Dutch Christian Employers which embrace some of the major Dutch multinationals. In turn, the government in its policy-making is required by law to consult with the joint employer-employee social and economic council. In addition, works councils at firms with more than 35 employees recommend candidates for company supervisory boards.

The labor situation has also suffered from lower profits—or losses in the case of Philips—among the once highly-prosperous multinationals. The Philips workforce dropped by more than 40,000 in 1991. Conservative, old-line families are still prominent in many boardrooms across the country, although the multinationals have prepared for the Single Market by establishing "1992 departments" to supplement their already considerable cross-border trading experience. Shell, with its joint headquarters in The Hague and London, has put together a special presentation on the Single Market for senior and middle management in its main areas, notably chemicals, gas, and downstream oil in the Netherlands, and manufacture and materials coordination, personnel, and group finance in London. The "briefing" has been extended to affiliates throughout the EC and EFTA.

Kok, long regarded as one of the smartest labor leaders within the EC, now has a large hand in revitalizing the Dutch economy.

REAL ESTATE

Office rents in central Amsterdam and at prime sites in the high-flying suburb of Amsterdam South have risen sharply to reach 500 guilders the square meter per year, a level that is still below most European capitals. The Amsterdam market is the largest in the country and only ten percent of the total office space of 4.4 million square meters was vacant at the beginning of 1991. In its environment bill, the national government estimated that total Amsterdam office space could increase by almost three million square meters during the next 20 years. High prices and lack of sites in the center will mean that most of this expansion will come in the suburbs. Aside from Amsterdam South, favored areas are suburban Buitenveldert (275 to 350 guilders the square meter per month) and Amsterdam South East (225 to 300 guilders the square meter per month), as well as the new teleport city of Sloterdijk to the west. Demand from the service sector is high. Agents Jones Lang Wootton estimate that this sector, notably lawyers and notaries, accountants, architects and engineering consultants, occupies half of existing offices. The local drive for more Japanese, Taiwanese and Korean banks will push up inner city, canalside rents. In Amsterdam South East, the Korean government and investors are planning a Euro-Asian Business Center of 30,000 square meters of offices, hotel, and exhibition hall. The area around Schiphol Airport is popular, but rents are the highest in the country. Amsterdam city authorities are seeking to balance environmental concerns with the need to build up Amsterdam as a financial center. On the one hand, land prices for office sites have been increased by 30 percent, but the long leasehold system of the municipality has been made more flexible, as have the rules governing inner city parking sites. City Hall knows that top foreign financial companies will insist upon a central location. The completion of the city's ring road and light rail transit system will improve facilities for those renting outside the center. Various other rail projects are to be undertaken. They will link both city and airport with neighboring towns as well as suburbs. Rents have risen with demand in The Hague—300–400 guilders the square meter per month—but Rotterdam rents are closer to 250 guilders. Major office areas being developed around the port city are Brainparks 1 and 2.

• *Getting To Know the Capital* •

Amsterdam's street plan is dictated by the canals. Many of these are lined by buildings several hundred years old: tall, narrow-fronted, elegant. With their brick façades, some of them bulging with age, the buildings of old Amsterdam offer little grandeur. What they do offer is the comfortable proximity of venerable neighbors, and the white lace curtains in the windows are a homey touch. There are no grand avenues, no spectacular perspectives, in the style of Paris. Amsterdam is a bourgeois city rather than a noble one.

Until a few years ago, much of it was shabby. Then the municipal council and real estate developers started to clean up the Central Station area and the streets leading from the Dam square. Amsterdam today has recovered some of its charm without trying to find its salvation in skyscrapers (which would probably sink, anyway).

Huge streetcars—jointed in the middle, air-conditioned, and equipped with loudspeakers—trundle along the streets and around sharp corners. They are among the best ways of traveling. There are buses, too, many of them able to bend around curves, and except when it's raining (rather often) there are plenty of taxis. Most drivers of streetcars, buses, and taxis speak English, or at least understand it. You can buy books of discount rate mass-transit tickets at the central tourist office (marked with the initials VVV) near the Central Station and the Dam.

EUROCITY ROTTERDAM

The Dutch call it "the city with its sleeves rolled up." In their very physical way, the Rotterdamers have been expanding the size and strengthening the efficiency of their great port, which handles some 292 million tons of freight a year, way ahead of Kobe, in Japan, the nearest challenger. With 30,000 vessels, some of them 350,000-tonners, calling each year, there seems little danger of the port losing its number one ranking in the world, a position held now for two decades. (The Port of New York, when it was the largest, sent a festive "You've won" cable of congratulations.) Yet the Dutch want to make sure, hence the burst of activity and building along the River Meuse from Rotterdam's city center with its office towers to the new container terminals on reclaimed land, way out by the North Sea, 30 miles away. Along Europort's waterfront is stored enough oil to supply Europe for a year. Chemicals, grain, and coal are unloaded, stored, and moved. Million of containers come and go on fleets of inland craft or on thousands of trucks headed for all points in Europe. With the approach of the Single Market, many countries, or their ports and airports, claim to be the Gateway to Europe. The Dutch have been using the slogan for a long time—Rotterdam for a century. Rotterdam's doubts stem from the future of the German Ruhr, linked to Rotterdam by the Rhine. Perhaps it was the suggestion that its arch-rival, Antwerp in Belgium, as well as Hamburg, would somehow benefit from changed trade routes that galvanized Rotterdam into launching a multi-billion dollar investment plan for new waterways, airport extension and a project for putting the main railway under the Meuse. The plans are not free from trouble. Powerful environmental groups are holding up some works, while the government says it does not have the kind of money needed for improving railways and thus easing the congestion caused by 30,000 trucks currently moving freight. Rotterdam also wants to add more housing and cultural centers and so beautify itself as well as consolidating its position as the European hub for heavy goods. Prewar, the city was extremely lively, even raunchy, with the fine canal houses of the merchants backing on to dance halls and disorderly bars. The Luftwaffe bombed and fire-bombed all of that into oblivion in May 1940. Just before the end, the Germans spent ten whole days blowing up the docks—and quite a few houses. Rotterdam did an incredible job of reconstruction after 1945, but the city was dreary and polluted until the 1970s. The 1970s oil crises halted expansion, and many companies and people left the city. Premier Lubbers, is a Rotterdamer—gutsy, rumpled, a stickler for details, yet a man of action. There are a lot like him in the city of half a million. As in Amsterdam, the place runs on an American-style public-private partnership. A new storm tide barrier is underway in the New Waterway between the city and the North Sea for everything depends on sea defenses. An extra container terminal is being built and Sealand, the US company that dominates the container world, has chosen Rotterdam. "Distriparks" are being built around the city to improve dispatching, aided by a teleport where port documents are handled electronically. Waterside cafes, restaurants and fine public buildings have added style downtown among the office towers of the Dutch multinationals, banks, and insurance companies.

OPPORTUNITIES IN THE REGIONS

The country's 12 provinces have directly-elected provincial councils, which appoint provincial executives for day-to-day administration. Presiding over both are the Queen's Commissioners. The four regions are generally known as West, South, North, and East and each one is made up of three provinces.

WEST

Much of the provinces of North Holland, South Holland, and Utrecht, including Schiphol airport, are below sea level but are protected by dykes and dunes. The area, also known as Randstad, is the country's core, for here are Amsterdam, The Hague, Rotterdam, and Utrecht. Amsterdam, the commercial capital is in North Holland province (the provincial capital is Haarlem to the West). Amsterdam has 80 odd European headquarters and is now seeking to strengthen its rank as an international financial center, notably by attracting more major Japanese banks and brokers. The city is undergoing a new wave of development that will ultimately push the historic skyline somewhat higher. A commercial zone is being developed around the main railway station—400,000 square meters of smart offices, shops, a science center, a theater, and a massive new hotel, the latest contribution to the city's hotel boom. Other developments include the renovation of a key downtown area known as Spui; a major teleport to the west of the city; new offices, ateliers and apartments along the IJ (or Y) River; luxury apartments for foreign executives and bankers; continued expansion of the business areas to the southeast and to the southwest at Amstelveen and Hoofddorp, plus a special EC passenger terminal at Schiphol, the country's most famous "gateway." The burgomaster has proved himself an effective and energetic businessman in promoting a US-style PPP system of doing things—private-public partnership. Office rents are the cheapest among the main West European capitals, while water and electricity rates are low. Haarlem is a printing, pharmaceuticals, and electronics center, while to the east is Hilversum, with the national radio and TV studios—and the Philips/AT&T joint venture in telecommunications. Densely-populated South Holland province, which includes the seat of government in The Hague and Rotterdam, has attracted 550 foreign companies, four out of ten of them American. Historic cities like Delft, Dordrecht, Gouda, and Leyden have added high-tech activities, yet agriculture remains prominent—the world's largest agricultural greenhouse, all 33 million squares meters of it, is south of The Hague. The third province, Utrecht, is where the Netherlands has its roots. It forms the expressway and transport hub of the country and as such is not a dispenser of the IPR, or regional capital grant, which is lavished on investors going to the Northern tip of the country or to other less-developed regions. All parts of the Netherlands are within three hours drive of Utrecht, the fastest growing of all the provinces. In fact, the arrival of a number of foreign and Dutch computer companies has earned Utrecht the sobriquet, Software City.

SOUTH

Limburg, the southernmost province bordering both Belgium and Germany, has the country's second-ranking airport at Maastricht, which handles 40 percent of Dutch freight transport to the rest of Europe, and is home to several multinational and parcel companies. New city buildings include a high-tech exhibition and congress center. The province offers various aid packages which the Limburg investment bank calculates as amounting to half of start-up costs. A trade park is underway at Venlo, next to Germany, in anticipation of a "tilt" eastwards of European distribution centers in the wake of German reunification. Even before the drastic changes in Germany, Limburg had attracted half a billion dollars worth of investment in just one year, including Electrolux and GPA Expressair. Medtronic, the American pacemaker manufacturer, was drawn by the university and university hospital in Maastricht. British Steel uses a subsidiary there as its spearhead into Germany. Big industrial names, such as Fuji Film, Johnson & Johnson, and Allied Lyons are among the 300 foreign companies in North Brabant province where BOM, the local, public-private investment company contributes cash grants up to 25 percent, venture capital, and training facilities. American and British companies are thick upon the ground. Eindhoven, dominated by Philips to the extent that it is the Dutch equivalent of a US company town, just grows and grows. Philips and newcomers to the Eindhoven science park are backed by the many thousands of students at the city's technological university. The third province, Zeeland, has been reclaimed from the sea. Nearly 2,000 people died when the area was flooded on Feburary 1, 1953, a disaster which led to the closing of the estuaries as part of the Delta Project completed in 1986 when the Queen inaugurated the storm-surge barrier in the Eastern Scheldt. The deep harbors can take vessels in the 100,000 to 150,000 ton range and have attracted Dow Chemical and other petro-chemical companies. Terneuzen is Dow's biggest site outside the US and the Americans are sinking another half billion in a third cracker.

NORTH

The once largely agricultural northern part of the Netherlands began changing fast with the discovery in the 1960s of huge natural gas deposits near Groningen, capital of the province of the same name. The find worked wonders for the national balance of payments and brought the ancient city of Groningen back into focus. Groningen is also a beet sugar center. The Northern Investment Company (NOM) works with British sugar brokers and the Dutch Suiker Unie in running the sugar trans-shipment center at Eemshaven port. Alongside the sizeable, local cardboard industry is a chemicals sector noted for a recent link between DSM of the Netherlands, and Idumitsu of Japan for production of polycarbonates. NOM hands out the 25 percent IPR regional grant, but the real excitement is over the arrival of computer centers and high-tech industries, many from Scandinavia, which is not far away and will be even more accessible when the Groningen road network is linked to the German autobahns in 1992. And, said one local, "the mentality of the people from northern Netherlands is similar to that of the Scandinavians." Local pride also centers on the Zernike Science Park, one of the most promising in the Netherlands, integrated with Groningen's university and specializing in biotechnology and pharmaceuticals. Friesland province, next door, known globally for its cattle, is now earning a name as an area of continuous working—one American businessman said his company, John Controls, had not lost an hour since the plant went up 30 years ago. This kind of reputation could help the Dutch who have discovered that studies by American consultancy firms have a negative side, namely the view held by some American companies that problematic Dutch labor outweighs the proven ability of the Dutch to move goods right across Europe. The remaining northern province of Drenthe sells itself as a place of space, a young workforce, plus beautiful surroundings for industrial plants.

EAST

Gelderland, largest of the nation's provinces, backs onto the German Ruhr and in Arnhem, the capital, situated at the junction of the Rhine and Ijssel rivers, it is said that businessmen look in two directions—to the Dutch and German markets. Close to 300 foreign companies are in Gelderland and many of those in manufacturing have chosen Midden, or middle, Gelderland around Arnhem and Nijmegen and benefitted from 35 percent grants, the highest in the country, or tapped the local venture capital fund. German firms are predominant among foreign investors, but American companies are the largest employers, while the British have long appreciated the grants, the road network and the skills of the Gelderland workforce. So has Philips, which has constructed Europe's largest chip factory. Digital is there and Du Pont is arriving. Neighboring Overijssel province has special grants to attract industry and so overcome the unemployment problem caused by the rapid decline of the textile industry.

Twente University is a technology transfer point to the business community, while Enschede business and science park in the province's largest city is probably the most successful park of its kind in the Netherlands. Flevoland province is brand new—well, since 1986—and consists largely of reclaimed land. The province has a clean environment conducive to farming—and, of course, bulbs. It offers high grants for newcomers.

SUCCESS STORIES

INTERGRAPH

Service is the key in his business, says Jim Meadlock, CEO of Intergraph, the $900 million-a-year computer graphics company based in Huntsville, Alabama. Meadlock sited his European headquarters in the Amsterdam area and his assembly plant 70 miles to the East in the high-tech industrial park at Nijmegen. Components and semi-finished products are loaded onto 747 "combi" freighters at Atlanta and flown to Schiphol. Once made up locally, they can be dispatched by truck to most European clients in a day or so. It's the same with spares. Clients include national water companies who are able to see the complex layout of their pipes on Intergraph screens, postal authorities with their cables, offshore companies with their ocean drilling, land mappers, and builders of chemical complexes.

Intergraph offices in the small town of Hoofddorp are a few minutes drive from Schiphol. A new combined headquarters-sales building is planned in the area, where growing numbers of large, glass-fronted corporate offices are rising along the canals. Jeffrey Heath, Intergraph's vice-president for business operations and financial questions in Europe, says fast Dutch reaction to the company's request to build at Nijmegen enabled the plant to open just one year after the announcement. Intergraph obtained a "substantial" high-tech grant to go to Nijmegen. Land was cheap. Digital was there—and Philips—which was reassuring. It's an open secret also that a company such as Intergraph, which claims to be the world's largest in "complete systems" in computer-aided manufacturing, design and engineering (cad/cam/cae) receives special treatment. Nijmegen extends a special welcome, with grants and tax concessions. The company says it chose the Netherlands over France, Luxembourg, Scotland, and Wales because of the skills of the labor force and their command of English. Another factor was the banking sector in Amsterdam, with its strong international flavor. And, Intergraph pays no withholding taxes on dividends transferred from subsidiaries in Europe and Africa.

Since the first computer graphics system was sent out from the Dutch city in 1986, air suspended, climate-controlled trucks have been delivering the goods around Europe, from Finland to Yugoslavia. Many journeys are just one day. Some 350 of Intergraph's total European complement of 1,600 staff work in the Netherlands. Many of the American executives wear jeans, a relaxed style that suits younger Dutch personnel. Microcad on PCs is what Intergraph hopes will be the big post-1992 expansion. In all, some 1,400 American companies are now in business in the Netherlands, and a good quarter of them are engaged in manufacturing.

CANON

Japanese industry, in general, and the larger consumer goods groups, in particular, like the geography of the Netherlands. The big port, the slick airport, the bonded warehouses, "understanding" customs and tax authorities, plus the thousands of trucks ready to head off in all directions—all these excite the Japanese executive, anxious to inundate dozens of countries with thousands of products. The Japanese also like that important intangible factor, the business climate. They sense that the way government and industry pull together, a kind of Netherlands Inc. mentality, is similar to the way things are done back home. Take Canon's statement: "The Dutch government has supported the company in its European business activities." Canon went first to Geneva in 1962 but moved to the Netherlands when bulkier products such as copiers made ship transport necessary. The company has spent $60 million on a new European headquarters in the Amsterdam suburb of Amstelveen, just across from Schiphol. Canon Europa NV looks after Canon's $3.1 billion market in Europe, including the Canon plants in France and Germany and the research operations in Britain. The new headquarters building contains not just offices; the groundfloor is devoted to a showroom, training center, clean rooms for testing mask aligners with automated storage space next door. Here, Canon plans its European marketing, organizes its spares network, trains personnel, and generally looks after business in some 40 countries. The Netherlands now has 150 Japanese companies and 45 manufacturing plants, the second largest Japanese presence in the EC after Britain. The Japanese Finance Ministry estimates that its countrymen now account for more than two percent of the Netherlands' national product. Like Intergraph, Canon says it values distribution and financial services available in the Amsterdam area.

SANDVIK

Sandvik, which is Swedish metal in a big way, moves many thousands of metalworking products, lengths of special steels, tools and saws, as well as process systems into the EC from Sweden and other points, sends thousands more around Europe from plants scattered all over and, additionally, trucks, flies or ships even more goods to far-away countries. Capital, directors, and managers at Sandvik are Swedish, so the company is not a multi-national in the accepted sense, but it is heavily involved in Europe and ready for the Single Market. Admittedly, it has kept its administrative base in Lucerne, Switzerland, for the company has done business in the Swiss Confederation for some 145 years and, in the postwar years, it found that only its fellow neutral offered good banking, telecommunications, and language skills. Changing times have moved the company's focal point to the Netherlands. Lucerne handles the one and three quarter million orders a year, but Santrade, Sandvik's distribution arm, receives, stores, and expedites the goods from its warehouse complex at Schiedam in the Rotterdam port area. Sandvik's products and steels arrive around the clock and some 20,000 different products are stored in the Netherlands and then dispatched to the main European markets within 24 hours. Metalworking products predominate and most of these go by truck. Santrade says it had to prove that Schiedam was as efficient, preferably more so, than Swedish warehouses. That has been the case and distribution operations are to be extended, probably via a second site within the Netherlands. Michael Mott, Sandvik executive, said: "We have agreements with a panoply of land, sea, and air forwarders, chosen for performance, dependability and price—in that order.

We're happy with the Dutch. I think they will be well-suited to take advantage of 1993's opening of the land freight market when loads can be picked up anywhere." This is also of considerable interest to Santrade customers, not only in metalworking but also in chemicals, oil, construction, and the wine-growing industry.

················THE LEADERS················

TOP 20 COMPANIES (1989)

		(NLG millions)	
		Sales	*Profits*
(1)	Shell	181,537	12,447
(2)	Unilever	66,285	3,249
(3)	Philips	57,224	1,374
(4)	Akzo	18,736	873
(5)	Ahold	17,075	162
(6)	SHV Holdings	13,437	245
(7)	PTT Nederlands	12,741	1,460
(8)	BP Nederland	12,630	211
(9)	DSM	10,772	1,320
(10)	Vendex International	10,243	96
(11)	Hoogovens	9,011	751
(12)	Heineken	6,668	325
(13)	KLM	6,460	340
(14)	Exxon Nederland	6,092	153
(15)	Nedlloyd Group	6,009	252
(16)	Dow Benelux	5,875	826
(17)	Sara Lee/DE	5,413	300
(18)	DAF	5,266	172
(19)	Buhrmann-Tetterode	5,151	219
(20)	Cargill Nederland	4,722	74

(Source: Het Financieele Dagblad)

1990 Results

Falls

Philips − $2.4b; NMB Postbank Group Fl 635m (− 3.5 percent); ABN-Amro Fl 1.33b (− 6.8 percent); DSM Fl 811m (− 22 percent); Hoogovens Fl 292m (− 28 percent); DAF − Fl 227m (+ Fl 171m/ 1989); VNU Publishing Fl 146m (− 7 percent).

Gains

Fokker Fl 83.4m (+ 100 percent); Rabobank Fl 971m (+ 8.1 percent); Heineken Fl 366m (+ 12.4 percent); Alcatel NV Ecu 688m/ $826m (+ 25 percent); Aegon Insurance Fl 645m (+ 14 percent).

TOP 20 BANKS (1989)

		(NLG millions) Balance Sheet
(1)	Amro Bank	179,720
(2)	ABN	173,182
(3)	Rabobank	172,429
(4)	NMB Postbank	161,274
(5)	BNG	79,163
(6)	Credit Lyonnais Nederland	31,839
(7)	Mees & Hope	24,492
(8)	VSB Group	14,912
(9)	Pierson, Heldring & Pierson	9,490
(10)	Dai-Inchi Kangyo Nederland	9,072
(11)	Nat. Investeringsbank	7,678
(12)	F.van Lanschot Bankiers	7,616
(13)	Yamaichi Int. (Ned)	6,056
(14)	Banque Nationale de Paris	5,812
(15)	Roparco	5,356
(16)	Albert de Bary	4,407
(17)	De Lage Landen Group	3,833
(18)	Bank of Tokyo (Holland)	3,830
(19)	Friesland Bank	3,475
(20)	Daiwa Europe	3,458

(Source: Het Financieele Dagblad)

INSURANCE COMPANIES

Name		General	Life
		(Premium income, millions of guilders)	
(1)	Nationale-Nederlanden	6,318	7,707
(2)	Aegon	2,830	3,589
(3)	Amev	3,702	2,613
(4)	Delta Lloyd	906	1,106
(5)	Interpolis	936	613
(6)	Stad Rotterdam	631	873
(7)	Central Beheer	515	831
(8)	Zilveren Kruis Verz	1,064	15
(9)	NRG	732	306
(10)	Zwitzerleven	—	860
(11)	UAP Nederland	378	264
(12)	Nieuw Rotterdam	567	50
(13)	Avero	277	337
(14)	Ohra	473	84
(15)	Zurich Vita	231	257
(16)	Royal Nederland	469	—
(17)	Zwolsche Algemeene	334	118
(18)	VGZ	353	—
(19)	Goudse	280	59
(20)	Equity & Law	—	336

(Source: Het Financieele Dagblad)

KEY CONTACTS

USEFUL AMSTERDAM TELEPHONE NUMBERS

Note All former six-digit numbers are now preceded by 6.

Trade and Commercial Information

City Hall Investment Office: 31-20-552-3328
City Promotion: 31-20-575-3026
Financial Center: 31-20-620-8769

Rotterdam Port
  External/Commercial
  Affairs/Public Relations
  PO Box 6622
  3002 AP Rotterdam
  Tel: 31-10-489-4177/489-4199
  Fax: 31-10-477-8240.

City of Amsterdam
City Hall
Amstel 1
1011 PN Amsterdam

American Embassy
  Lange Voorhout 102
  2514 EJ The Hague
  Tel: 31-70-362-4911
  Fax: 31-70-363-2985.

Tel: 31-20-552-9111
Fax: 31-20-5523426.

Offices/Rental Information

Jones Lang Wootton
Tel: 31-20-664-1611.

Science Parks

Zernike Groningen
Zerniker Park 2
9747 AN Groningen
Tel: 31-50-745745
Fax: 31-50-634556.

Enschede
c/o City Hall
PO Box 20
7500 AA Enschede
Tel: 31-53-818181
Fax: 31-53-317445.

Leiden
City Hall
PO Box 9100
2300 PC Leiden
Tel: 31-71-254276
(Economic Affairs)
Fax: 31-71-254225.

Amsterdam
City Hall
PO Box 202
1000 AE Amsterdam
Tel: 31-20-5523179/5529111.

Delft
c/o City Hall
Oude Delft 137
2611 BE Delft
Tel: 31-15-602960.

Maastricht
University of Limburg
PO Box 616
6200 MD Maastricht
Tel: 31-43-888888

Eindhoven
Stichting Technopool
Stadhuisplein 6
5611 EM Eindhoven
Tel: 31-40-444010
Fax: 31-40-444065.

Science Park Builder

Wilma Vastgoed BV
Weferstede 53
(Postbox 632, 3430 AP Nieuwegein)
3431 JS Nieuwegein
3700 Al Zeist
Tel: 31-3402-96411
Fax: 31-3402-50874

KEY ADDRESSES IN THE REGIONS

Netherlands Foreign
Investment Agency
PO Box 20101
Bezuidenhoutseweg 2
2500 EC The Hague
The Netherlands
Tel: 31-70-798818
Fax: 31-70-796322.

West
Bureau for Regional
Development
PO Box 3007
2001 DA, Haarlem
Tel: 31-23-319199
Fax: 31-23-326053

South
Provincie Zuid-Holland
Economic Affairs Dept.
PO Box 90602
2509 LP The Hague
Tel: 31-70-117057.

Limburg Investment Bank
PO Box 800
6200 AV Maastricht
Tel: 31-43-280280
Fax: 31-43-280200.

Stock Exchange: 31-20-623-9711
Teleport: 31-20-660-6500
Trade Information Center:
31-20-575-3140
World Trade Center:
31-20-575-9111

Chambers of Commerce

Member Nations
Britain: 31-20-627-7359
France: 31-20-626-9691
Italy: 31-20-644-2351

Other
Amsterdam: 31-20-523-6600
Japanese: 31-20-678-7111

USEFUL HAGUE TELEPHONE NUMBERS

Note All former six-digit numbers are now preceded by 3.

Embassies

Member Nations
Belgium: 31-70-364-4910
Britain: 31-70-364-5800
Denmark: 31-70-365-5830
France: 31-70-356-0606
Germany: 31-70-342-0600
Greece: 31-70-363-8700
Ireland: 31-70-363-0993
Italy: 31-70-346-9249
Luxembourg: 31-70-360-7516
Portugal: 31-70-363-0217
Spain: 31-70-364-3814

Trade and Commercial Information

European Community:
 31-70-346-9326
Netherlands Foreign Investment
 Office: 31-70-379-8818

Chambers of Commerce

Britain: 31-70-978881
United States: 31-70-3659808

Others
Argentine: 31-70-365-4836
Australia: 31-70-364-7908
Austria: 31-70-324-5470
Brazil: 31-70-346-9229
Canada: 31-70-361-4111
China: 31-70-355-1515
Egypt: 31-70-354-2000
India: 31-70-346-9771
Indonesia: 31-70-346-9796
Israel: 31-70-364-7850
Japan: 31-70-346-9544
Korea: 31-70-352-0621
Malaysia: 31-70-350-1703
New Zealand: 31-70-346-9324
Nigeria: 31-70-350-1703
Norway: 31-70-345-1900
Pakistan: 31-70-364-8948
Philippines: 31-70-360-4820
Poland: 31-70-350-2806
South Africa: 31-70-392-4501
Sweden: 31-70-324-5424
Soviet Union: 31-70-345-1300
Thailand: 31-70-345-2088
United States: 31-70-362-4911

USEFUL ADDRESSES

Trade and Commercial Information

Netherlands Foreign Investment
 Agency
 PO Box 20101
 Bezuidenhoutseweg 2
 2500 RC The Hague
Tel: 31-70-379-8819
Fax: 31-70-379-6322.

New York Office
 One Rockefeller Plaza
 New York, NY 10020
Tel: 212-246-1434
Fax: 212-246-9769.

World Trade Center
  Strawinskylaan 1
  1077 XW Amsterdam
  Tel: 31-20-575-9111
  Fax: 31-20-662-7255.

World Trade Center
  PO Box 30099
  3001 DB Rotterdam
  Tel: 31-10-4054444
  Fax: 31-10-4054400.

City of The Hague
  City Hall
  Burg de Monchyplein 14
  2585 BD The Hague
  Tel: 31-70-353-2000 (General)
  Fax: 31-70-365-4904 (External
    affairs).

City of Rotterdam
  City Hall
  Corolsingel 40
  3011 AD Rotterdam
  Tel: 31-10-417-3447
  Fax: 31-10-417-2154.

Holland International
  Distribution Council
  Bezuidenhoutseoeg 27, PW
  2594 AC The Hague
  Tel: 31-70-383-6905
  Fax: 31-70-383-8341.

Amsterdam Financial Center
  Herengracht
  1015 BV Amsterdam
  1016 BE
  Tel: 31-20-208769
  Fax: 31-20-208861.

North Brabant Development
  PO Box 3089
  5203 DB's-Hertogenbosch
  Tel: 31-73-408240
  Fax: 31-73-423557.

North

Drenthe Economic Institute
Stationsstraat 20,
PO Box 142
9400 AC Assen
Tel: (31) 5920-12547
Fax: (31) 5920-10157.
(Also via Eurosite database)

Northern Development Authority
(NOM)
PO Box 424
9700 AK Groningen
Tel: (31) 50-267826
Fax: (31) 50-261475.

East

Gelderland Development
  Authority
PO Box 206
6800 LT Arnhem
Tel: (31) 85-511334
Fax: (31) 85-516361.

Facts on Portugal

. . . .

Capital Lisbon
Population 9.78m
Unemployment 4.5%
GDP Growth 1989: 5.5%; 1990: 4%; 1991
  (est.): 3%
GDP per Capita $6,048
Inflation 1989: 12.6%; 1990: 13.4%; 1991
  (est.) 12%
Trade
  Imports 1989: Esc2,973b
  Exports 1989: Esc1,994b
Foreign Investment 1990: $5b
US Share (1980–89) 12.6%
EC Share 64.5%
($1 = 148 Esc)

. . . .

PORTUGAL

"They have the cars. Now I have to provide the roads." Anibal Cavaco Silva, Prime Minister of Portugal

THIS NATION OF TEN MILLION PEOPLE ON THE ATLANTIC FRINGES OF the European Community has acquired some three-quarters of a million extra vehicles within the past five years, more than over the previous decade and a half, and for these trappings of prosperity the Portuguese have their membership of the EC to thank. Since accession in 1986, the Community's different treasuries, or *fonds,* in Brussels have committed several billions of dollars to Lisbon for infrastructure, public works, industry, tourism, job training, technical education, agriculture, the modernization of small businesses, and more. All this has been done largely on the basis that Portugal, the poorest EC member, is a "special case" following the twin traumas of the 1970s: the colonial wars in Africa and the final retreat from empire, and the disastrous lurch to the extreme left that followed. This largesse from EC headquarters—partly the result also of tenacious bargaining on the part of Portuguese politicians—is now being matched by billions more from foreign investors, European and American, with the Japanese about to increase their stake in the economy. This second wave of money involving big names such as Ford, General Motors, Volkswagen, and Valmet has not only been attracted by the first wave (for example, the large sums available for improving the skills of workers), but also by the newfound political stability in the country. The popular Socialist President and the center-right government of technocrats were elected in 1987 with a rare, overall majority. This particular government scored a remarkable success in 1991, proving that democracy, with its demand for change, can also mean stability. Most qualified observers believe that a new course has been set. Both Right and Left (and the vast majority of the population) are wholeheartedly pro-European and the political debate generally turns on the speed of adaptation to the Single Market. The near-catastrophic economic consequences of the 1974–75 Revolution have been erased by the post-1986 rate of growth which has been just about the highest in Europe.

371

A "counter-revolutionary" program has been instituted for the progressive privatization of practically all the banks, insurance companies, and manufacturing concerns swept up by the State in those heady, ruinous days of 16 years ago. April 25 remains a national holiday in honor of the marxist-military seizure of power (later rejected at the ballot box). However, the crowds in the 1990s, led by trade union stalwarts, grow thinner each spring as they march, red carnations in hand, from the statue of the Marques de Pombal, rebuilder of Lisbon after the 18th century earthquake, and down the broad, tree-lined Avenida da Liberdade, centerpiece of one of Europe's most beautiful cities. These days, bigger crowds head for the Atlantic beaches in their automobiles. The first generation of Portuguese motorists drove like snails, so afraid were they of damaging their hardwon means of transport, paid for often by work as emigrants across Europe. Today, prosperity is accompanied by bravado. The country with the highest economic growth rate in Europe (along with its neighbor, Spain) has the highest growth also in fatal accidents on its inadequate roads. The state of their highways should serve to remind the Portuguese of another bigger risk, namely that the country will not be ready for the Single Market, even allowing for extensions of one or two years in some areas. The positive changes in Lisbon—the new pragmatism, the new attitudes, the new business class—are strikingly obvious, yet many problems remain. For one, the inflation rate has to pulled down from double digits so that Portugal can enter the European Monetary System (EMS). Then, the privatization program needs to be accelerated and firm guidelines fixed for those foreigners interested in investing in the couple of hundred companies that are being sold. Thirdly, Brussels has to be convinced that its generosity has been well-rewarded and that Portugal deserves more money for roads, natural gas pipelines, scientific research, agricultural development, and other essentials.

And the notorious bureaucracy has to be streamlined in time for the Single Market. This thicket of regulations, inhabited for decades by petty officials, has been the bane of Portugal since the long years of the dictatorship of Antonio de Oliveira Salazar (1928–68) who not only kept the country isolated, but imposed a paternalistic style under which the State official was always right and the citizen wrong. This dictatorship, the 1974–75 upheaval, and the ensuing chaos all meant that Portugal entered the EC in a relatively poor condition. In all, it has taken some 14 years before mentalities changed and new laws were passed enabling the all-important privatization process to begin. Portugal needs to use the proceeds usefully and not to meet debts. Despite the problems, membership of the EC is probably the most momentous event since the voyages of discovery of the great Portuguese navigators of earlier centuries. The writer and leading Portugal-watcher, Diana Smith, estimates that when Portugal joined the Community "the development gap between it and EC 'averages,' measured in years, was about a quarter of a century. Per capita income was less than half that of Spain and less than a quarter of the former West Germany." Inflation was staggering, as was illiteracy. Few had cars, telephones or other consumer necessities. This is changing rapidly. Also, as Ms. Smith points out, the Portuguese brought to the Community a "growing pride and the will, given time and help, to rise to EC standards of living, productivity, and competitiveness." Or, as a Japanese executive in Lisbon put it: "In Portugal people work harder than elsewhere in Europe because they still want to be rich. This work ethic is not the current mood in the richer countries, where leisure and consumerism are the fashion."

Certainly, the changes since 1986 have been dramatic. There has been annual growth of around four percent, while in 1989 the figure touched 5.5 percent. Investment in that year was close to ten percent of gross domestic product, foreign investment doubled, exports rose by a quarter, unemployment fell to below five percent. People were earning more (although some textile workers in the north were making under $3 an hour) and so credit had to be restricted to cool consumer demand. Portugal, however, remained the European country with the highest rate of personal savings, further proof of the seriousness governing so much of Portuguese life. The country will have to face many more challenges in the future. Wages and production costs are rising, and there will be a lag before new skills and services become established features.

:::::::::::MARKET OPPORTUNITIES :::::::::::

The US Commerce Department advises "aggressive selling" by Americans in view of the competition from Europeans, notably the British and the French. The internal market is small, but the country is a stepping stone both into the EC and those areas of Africa, even South America, where Portuguese influence remains strong. The Portuguese consumer has greater spending power, and greater aspirations for better houses, cars, and all kinds of goods. The country, in a manner reminiscent of Spain, is modernizing its basic infrastructure—telecommunications, roads, railways, and airports, and many contracts will go to foreign companies. First priority says the Commerce Department, is "a commitment to the Portuguese buyer (wholesaler) through business support networks for training, service delivery, and information. Firms should remember that doing business effectively in Portugal requires personal contact. This means visiting clients, while after-sales service is critical. Both persistence and patience are required; deals are not made in a day—orders may not be large but the business is there. US know-how and technology can be an important element in Portuguese modernization efforts." Where exactly? Relatively low US prices are helping sales not only of specialty chemicals and other intermediate goods, but also of industrial machinery and sophisticated equipment. Demand for security equipment, automobile parts, and medical equipment is strong, as is that for construction and mining machinery. Meanwhile, unglamorous coal remains the biggest American export to Portugal, almost all for use by the national electricity company's (EDP) coal-fired power station at Sines. Construction of a 1200-megawatt unit is underway at Abrantes, and a third plant is expected to be completed in northern Portugal by 2000. In the telecommunications sector, the government's air navigation authority, ANA, the telephone utility, CTT-TLP, and the armed forces are modernizing or introducing a variety of communications systems, including air traffic control, and telephone switching and transmission. Private TV channels and cable television are on the way. Major investment opportunities will arise, too, in the natural gas sector, with the EC backing trans-European pipelines bringing the gas to Portugal via Spain, and a liquefied gas terminal at the port of Setubal, just south of Lisbon. Natural gas networks, as well as new cross-border highways, will offer tremendous opportunities for Portuguese-Spanish cooperation (the Portuguese gas pipeline will most likely extend to Galicia, Asturias, even Andalusia). Elsewhere, the reorganization and expansion of the Portuguese retail system, with European groups linking with Portuguese companies to build hypermarkets and supermarkets, offer markets for food and other daily consumer items.

In London, the Department of Trade and Industry has been advising British firms of the "attractive market over the next four years for industrial machinery, office machines, and ADP equipment." Traditional Portuguese industrial sectors, such as textiles, clothing and footwear manufacturers, as well as mining, are re-equipping and introducing automated and computer-controlled production lines. This revolution of Portuguese commercial activity extends to the updating of cargo handling facilities, particularly roll-on, roll-off terminals. Another priority is health care, while in the more remote regions there is need to improve water supply and distribution, as well as the treatment of sewage and effluents.

Tax holidays, probably the most appreciated of investment incentives among multinationals because they help optimize global tax positions, are now on offer in Portugal. Added incentives are payment of the bill for training of new workers in new skills, and other EC and locally-funded startup grants. In all, the packages for inward investors are probably the most generous in Europe and have enabled Portugal to "outscore" Ireland, Greece, and Spain for some important manufacturing investments. Banking, finance, real estate and tourism still attract the bulk of investment, but car components, vehicle assembly, electronics, and fine chemicals are attracting new money at a faster rate. Additionally, Portuguese workers cost relatively little, yet are both productive and adaptable. Along with the political stability of recent years, the country's manufacturing sector has enjoyed a virtually strike-free record. Many, if not all, of the incentives were available to General Motors when it extended its investment in Portugal with a new, $55 million Delco Remy plant for electronic ignition systems on a green field site at Setubal, near Lisbon, an area which had suffered from the decline of traditional industries such as shipbuilding. Some foreign companies admit openly what they receive in the way of aid. Ford, for example, said it had obtained 52 percent of the $120 million cost of another major investment in Setubal for car audio equipment. Ford and Volkswagen announced a $3 billion investment to manufacture a new, multi-purpose passenger vehicle near Lisbon—and negotiated a $620 million incentive package. Burly Robert Langelier, head of GM in Portugal, chuckles when he recalls that some members of the Portuguese government expressed, or at least feigned, surprise upon hearing the incentives he had obtained. These various deals, offering 50 to 60 percent in grants, have had the dramatic effect of boosting foreign investment from $410 million in 1987 to $5 billion in 1990.

General Motors, a longtime investor in Portugal, stepped up its stake in the assembly of vans and commercial vehicles, and of components. A large percentage of production is for export to GM markets and plants around the world. General Motors' Delco Remy branch looked at Austria, Ireland, and Spain before opting for Portugal where GM has six autonomous subsidiaries, including a Kadett van plant, near Lisbon; an Inlan division plant, 100 miles east of the capital, making steering wheels, horn caps, brake hose assemblies and other parts for customers as far afield as South Korea and Australia; and a Cablesa division plant, in former Renault premises in the northeast of the country, where the 3,300-strong workforce includes 2,500 nimble-fingered women making wire harnasses for GM in West Germany and Spain. Langelier said that heavily-subsidized training was a major factor in GM's investment decision, adding that not one hour had been lost from labor disputes in his eight years in the country. In fact, GM reckons that the quality of the Portuguese automobile worker "is on a par with anything in Europe." The new plant in Setubal benefitted from a special grant for the depressed area and will begin production in 1991, exporting $120 million worth of systems. General Motors' exports from Portugal in 1990 topped $300 million, making its expansion doubly attractive for the government. The company says it pays "over the going rate" for its skilled workers. How much? Around $650 a month.

Ford, via Ford Electronica Portuguesa, looked at Ireland, Great Britain, and Spain before choosing Setubal, where more workers from heavy industry, such as steel, will be retrained—courtesy of Brussels. The new investment comes on top of Ford production of Transit commercial vehicles and pickups. It's likely that Ford will put more money into Portugal. Among other major investors are Neste Oy, of Finland, which has moved into chemicals, and by Sweden's Stora in paper. Renault has considerable investments in Portugal, although its former one-third share of the local market has been dented by the opening of frontiers. The Japanese involvement, limited until now to the assembly of mini-buses and commercial vehicles, is set to grow, for the Japanese have been looking at Portugal in depth. Finland's Valmet Corporation has acted and set up a joint venture for tractors and tractor parts with IPE, a Portuguese state-owned holding company with stakes in 100 different companies and which has the brief to help modernize the national economy. Valmet secured subsidies of 36 percent for its $28 million plant, also at Setubal, which will be producing

5,000 tractors a year by 1994 for Portugal, Spain, North Africa, and Portuguese-speaking Africa. Valmet said everyone would be trained "from zero" but that the existing skills of the future workforce of 400 made the whole deal "highly promising."

S   P   O   T   L   I   G   H   T

• *EC Aid* •

"By now," said the EC official, "Portugal knows its way around the European Community. It's one of the biggest, net beneficiaries of our aid. It remains for Portugal to show that it deserves every penny." Money has flowed from Brussels to Lisbon to the tune of ten billion dollars. Added the official: "The Portuguese government fought hard for specificity, the recognition that Portugal was a special case, and this tenacity paid off with the large grants of money." In addition, Portugal has added to its weight within the councils of the European Community by aligning itself in the voting process with other, "deserving"—and southern—states such as Spain and Greece. Ireland lends its vote, as does Italy, from time to time. The southern states have their lobby. Much EC money flows through the Portuguese Ministry of Planning and Territorial Administration on its way to regional authorities and town halls, to be spent on highways, dams and railways. Just what are these EC funds with their strange acronyms? Well, FEDER, or European Regional Fund, is making annual grants of $600–$700 million in the 1989–1993 period for infrastructure, public works, and local industrial and tourist projects. In fact, some 14.5 percent of all FEDER funds goes to Portugal on the basis of the country's special needs. FSE, or the European Social Fund,

continued

grants $400–$500 million a year for job training, technical information, apprenticeships, special employment assistance, and aid for young workers—packages that are tempting to big employers such as General Motors. From FEDGA, the EC Agricultural General Orientation Fund, has come $300 million for a scheme known as PEDAP, an acronym for Special Program Supporting Modernization of Portuguese Agriculture, with the Community paying for up to 75 percent of approved projects. But staff at the EC office in Lisbon (on Jean Monnet Square, just behind the Tivoli Hotel) say the most important is PEDIP, the 1989–92 Special Program for Portuguese Industry, namely individual project financing for the modernization of small businesses, and the development of new products and new technology. For these projects, some one billion dollars will come from the coffers of FEDER and FSE, plus another $600 million in the form of a special fund for Portugal. EC figures and those of Columbia University's Camoes Center also note one billion dollars from the European Investment Bank and NIC, yet another EC acronym, this time for New Community Financing Instrument. Again, this EC financing can run up to 75 percent of the cost of a project to improve Portuguese industry's competitiveness.

To understand the special terms obtained by Portugal in its negotiations with the Brussels Commission one needs to know that by 1996, ten years after entry into the EC club, Portuguese agriculture must be ready for full integration into the Common Agricultural Policy, with the same prices as in the other eleven countries. In the case of the EC's Common Fishing Policy, Portugal must allow EC boats free access to its waters—again after a ten year period with some limitation. The customs union must be complete by 1993, with the removal of all internal tariff barriers. The Portuguese point out that these have been lowered by ten percent a year since 1986. In the last two years, they are being lowered at a faster rate of 15 percent. By 1993, external trade with third countries will adjust to EC tariffs, and the establishment of EC banks and other companies. At the

moment, there's automatic authorization for EC companies spending up to 2.7 million escudos ($3.3 million). Big-
ger projects officially can take up to two months to approve,
but the competition from countries such as Spain and Ireland can mean faster decisions. Portuguese workers also
will be able to move across Europe, with the exception of
Luxembourg where 11 percent of the workforce is Portuguese and where the free flow of labor will be delayed until
1996.

PRIVATIZATIONS

A magazine article, describing the biggest economic change in Portugal in the early 1990s, had the headline, "Capitalism's big comeback...counter-revolution going ahead full steam." Full steam? Not
quite, for the massive close-out sale of the banks, insurance concerns,
and manufacturing companies that were nationalized in 1975 by the
military and civilian marxists has been proceeding somewhat more
slowly than planned. It's not that the center-right Cavaco Silva government has had second thoughts about the wisdom of drastically
pruning the sprawling- and heavily loss-making-State sector, although
the Prime Minister has been accused of being a technocrat with built-
in reservations about relinquishing control of a third of the economy.
He knows that entry into the European Community has presented
Portugal with two great opportunities: the chance to overhaul its infrastructure, and to change direction towards a market economy. The
problem has been political for, as in Spain, there have been criticisms
that the country risked being sold off to foreigners. Certainly, the leading groups in the rest of Europe have the financial means to buy out-
right many of the 70 odd companies on the privatization list. The
companies being privatized come, in the main, from the six conglom-
erates nationalized in the mid-1970s and which formed the economic
backbone of the "old" Portugal—Espirito Santo, banking, real estate,
insurance; Champallimaud, cement, banking, manufacturing;
Quimical, formerly Companhia Uniao Fabril (CUF), banking, chemicals, agri-industry; Quinas, banking and agri-industry; Brito, finance; Bulhosa, banking and oil.

Despite good intergovernmental relations between Madrid and Lisbon, there would be an outcry—and loss of votes for the government—if Spanish banks and firms were seen to be acquiring the best jewels in the Portuguese economy. Still, the debate on the size of the foreign stakes has convinced the majority of people that foreign partners are desirable. This is a view shared, for example, by leading local businessman Americo Amorim who wishes to expand his empire of cork, paper, and real estate through partnerships with the likes of Carlo de Benedetti, the Italian financier, and Robert Maxwell, the British tycoon. So the limit fixed initially for foreign stakes has been lifted from five percent to between ten and twenty. Additionally, there's been the problem of the former majority shareholders, the old families who ruled the roost before 1975 and who received little after having their companies confiscated. Some were also jailed, while others fled the country. They will not receive anything like full compensation, for one of the government's aims is to use most of the proceeds from the sales to help pay off the $34 billion public debt. Yet, the old guard is back. The best-known, Manuel Ricardo Espirito Santo, rebuilt his financial empire "from scratch" during exile in Luxembourg and, after the 1989–1990 change of laws on privatization, bought 34 percent of Tranquilidade Seguros, the insurance company that once belonged to the billion dollar Espirito Santo empire. First, the government offered 49 percent of the big insurance company, ruling that no single investor could purchase more than 10 percent of the privatized capital, but Espirito Santo signed hundreds of purchase contracts with workers and other small savers, who had been cut in, as well as with larger shareholders, so the family was back in the driving seat. Their comeback accelerated when they bought 23 percent of the Banco Espîrito Santo e Commercial de Lisboa. Partial privatization was also arranged for the brewers Unicer, the bank Banco Totta e Acores, and another insurance company. Then came the sale of majority holdings in the Transinsular shipping firm, and another brewery, and part of the Banco Portugues do Atlantico, and so on. The remaining shares of the two insurance companies were sold, prior to more sales in this particular sector. The British, traditional partners of the Portuguese in finance, saw the French, in the form of the UAP insurance giant, step in and take 30 percent of one local insurance company, and then declare that they wanted both to dominate the Portuguese insurance market and other, under-developed insurance markets in the southern layer of the EC.

There are risks for the government of a nationalist backlash at the polls but the Prime Minister said, with some confidence, that "people will think twice about going back to State planning." Certainly, these State industries have run up around six billion dollars in losses since nationalization, but in published tables and charts showing the companies to be privatized over the coming years there is often a blank or the words *a fixar* (to be worked out later) in the column for foreign shares. The finance minister has stated that stable cores of Portuguese shareholders would be a priority in a process that could take ten years. Still, there are many opportunities here for astute foreign investors.

S P O T L I G H T

• *Free Trade* •

The charming Atlantic island of Madeira, an autonomous region of Portugal with EC status, has set up a free-trade zone and an offshore center. It now has other attractions than the famous Reids Hotel, so loved by the wealthy British. Francisco Costa, chairman of the Madeira Development Corporation, said he wants to attract four different kinds of activities: manufacturing and warehousing of goods; offshore financial activities; offshore international services, and an international shipping registry. The island's position, 625 miles from Lisbon, has not proved an insurmountable handicap. The tax holiday until 2011 has helped. The manufacturing and warehousing zone has been established on a 300-acre site five miles from Funchal airport and has attracted half a dozen companies in textiles, electrical goods, marble, and foodstuffs. They come from Portugal, Brazil, and Lebanon. Some Portuguese banks now have licenses to operate offshore activities. French and British banks are interested.

TRANSPORTATION AND COMMUNICATIONS

Long isolation from the rest of Europe in terms of land transport is being overcome slowly through heavy investment in new, narrow gauge track on the main rail lines leading to Paris and Madrid, in the lengthening of the few existing highways, and in improving the road network in the interior. EC grants are being used to finance all these projects, but more Euro-money will be needed before Portugal can be integrated into future, Europe-wide transportation networks. The century-old railway system is currently mainly broad gauge, whereas the rest of Europe has moved to narrow gauge, while most of the lines are single track. Modernization will require considerable financing from Brussels—in all, the track improvements, plus new trains and signalling, will cost $2 billion by the time of the creation of the Single Market. The main Lisbon-Hendaye-Paris line through the mountains is being upgraded, while work on the Lisbon-Madrid line has cut travelling time from twelve to eight hours. Alfa first-class trains now take three hours from Lisbon to Oporto along the main business artery, and will come closer to two hours when a new bridge is completed over the River Douro in Oporto by mid-decade. Speeds are increasing, too, on the main line south between the capital and Faro. It's the same story with roads, with work underway to complete the Lisbon-Oporto highway, which has a poor central section limiting driving time to four hours at the best. A fast road already links Lisbon to Setubal, the expanding industrial area, which can now be reached in half an hour. More EC money is being spent on the interior roads, or rather dirt roads.

TAP, the national airline, has a modern fleet, but its takeoff ability in European terms has been restricted by debt. State money will lighten this load, while partial privatization, hopefully, will attract more business. Iberian integration within the EC has led TAP and the LAR regional airline to provide connections between Portuguese intercontinental services and a range of Spanish cities.

Partial denationalization is also seen as a remedy in the telecoms sector—plus investment running as high as $700 million in 1990 and thereafter. At the moment, transition to a digital system is proving difficult for business. For example, there is often a waiting period in making a call from Lisbon to Oporto. Businesses have joined the queue in

S P O T L I G H T

• *Tourism* •

Tourism, which earned $2.3 billion in a year, is a leading sector for both local and foreign investors. But is Portugal "killing the goose that laid the golden egg," in the words of the tourism minister himself? Sharp growth has been accompanied by ugly buildings, and criticism grows that the poor quality is ruining the Atlantic coastline. The alert has reached the minister who has castigated the policy which "has brought ten-storey high apartment blocks to cities, towns and villages which had attracted tourists exactly because they had no ten-storey blocks." This has been true in the southern region of the Algarve, site of both quality development by British groups and by France's Club Méditerranée, as well as ugly time-sharing apartment buildings. Some tourist areas, said the minister, would bear the scars of the recent building boom for a long time to come. Danish and Dutch development in the Alentejo area, south of Lisbon, has also been attacked as unaesthetic. Portugal now has a National Tourism Plan to guide development. Laws were passed to empower central government to oversee the licensing of construction previously decided by local government alone. The minister added: "We want Portugal to go on being Portugal, not to be transformed into a coastline of cement towers. There are already too many examples in Europe where regions have been spoiled by predatory tourism. Portugal has about four areas where this has happened, but from now on, we intend to control this and even to recover these four spots as much as possible. This is very difficult because the buildings are already there, but public opinion is now in our favor."

S P O T L I G H T

• *Textiles* •

Portugal's large textile industry, based in the north of the country, realizes that it needs to increase the quality of its wide range of products—and maintain price competitiveness in the face of the South-East Asian challenge. Wage competitiveness is striking when compared with other European countries, but, then, Portugal to some extent relies on women working at home—and child labor. Textile wages in Europe range from $14 an hour in Denmark and the Netherlands; $13 in Belgium, Germany and Italy; $10 in France; $8 in Britain; $7 in Ireland; $5.60 in Spain; $4.30 in Greece, and $2, or just over, in Portugal. Add to this the tradition of hard work and flexibility and one understands why Luis Anton, a leading industry figure, says Portugal has the machinery, the workforce and the skills to produce ever higher quality textiles. He sees the danger zones as governmental red tape and the unprofessional attitude of some of the new managers entering the industry. He criticizes new generation managers who have the academic qualifications, but who are ill-equipped for the realities of the shopfloor. He reckons they will have to work harder to meet the challenge from Turkey, Bangladesh, Pakistan, India, Mauritius, and China. A little bit more boldness is needed, too, in signing joint ventures. "Let's stop fearing that these will entail loss of money or control." Provided these changes are made, the prospects look good for Portuguese textiles, a top money-spinner along with shoes, leather goods, ceramics, cork and wood products, and less-known sectors such as mould-making and foundries. In textiles, none of the main competitors is a member of the EC. "The advent of the single market should act as a spur for dramatic changes," says Anton.

Lisbon for new lines—the country's largest bank had to wait to obtain lines to hook up its street cash machines.

MANAGEMENT AND WORKFORCE

Portugal's lack of skilled managers could hamper the country's development. Expanding foreign companies and their needs have introduced a new element of competition for top talent, and this, in turn, is driving up salaries. Wage costs in the financial sector have risen about a quarter in the past year. Managers with five to ten years' experience are finding that their "value" has almost doubled. Although managerial salaries are still half those in richer EC countries, including Spain, senior managers in Portugal obtained 18 percent more year-on-year, according to a study by Hay Management Consultants, London. Hay's spring 1990 figure for senior managers in Portugal was $43,731 (Spain: $96,667), with top managers (director level of a medium-sized corporation with an annual turnover, or sales, of $50 million) earning $63,420 (Spain: $141,828). Lower-down, middle managers in Portugal were making $27,980 (Spain: $58,511). Santos Silva, of the Confederation of Managers, reckons that it will be necessary to double the present total of 200,000 trained managers if Portugal is to be on a par with other EC states. At the moment, he lamented, a meager 1,000 per year were being trained. Mr. Silva blamed "obstacles" of all kinds in the way of young people who wanted to pursue higher or further education. Lack of places was the greatest obstacle of all.

REAL ESTATE

When it came to property, Portugal used to be seen in terms of holiday villas on the Algarve. Today, the buyer or renter of property in the country is as likely to be dressed in a business suit, albeit a lightweight one—and be looking for a functional, hundred to two hundred square meters rather than a view of the sea. Current demand for offices in

Lisbon is pushing rents 50 percent higher each year. In 1990, downtown prices in the capital had reached Esc 5,500 a square meter a month, or an annual cost of $440 a square meter, putting Lisbon ahead of Brussels and not too far behind Frankfurt. Lisbon's skyline is changing as new blocks are built to house the new traders. The city now has one of the most remarkable shopping-office complexes in Europe, the Amoreiras Centre, an avant-garde, award-winning British bank on the main avenue, and a string of new office buildings on the peripheral ring roads towards the airport or the famous Benfica soccer stadium, home of Portugal's finest team. The government, too, built in preparation for the six month period in 1992 when it assumes the presidency of the European Community. So, from being an underdeveloped, unsophisticated, and, in international terms, an uninteresting market just a few years ago, Portugal, and, in particular, Lisbon has become a focus of attention for builders. And not just those from the EC—the British, French, Germans and, of course, the neighboring Spaniards. The Swedes have picked Portugal as they have Belgium as an EC bridgehead. Skandia, Aranas, Convector, and Byggfast are among the Swedish flagbearers and, in the case of Skandia, they have taken over German property interests.

This booming property scene is recent. High interest rates that reached nearly 30 percent, plus the economic uncertainties prior to the 1987 election of the center-right Cavaco Silva government, meant that the market was quite unprepared for a reversal from years of stagnation to a period of high demand. As a result, there has been enormous growth in all sectors. The new financial district, the local Wall Street, is growing up around the Praça de Espanha and the Avenida de Bernia, north of the traditional commercial sector off the Avenida da Liberdade and separate from the business district along Avenida 5 de Outubro. The Bank of Portugal is constructing a landmark building, while a very big development indeed, some 425,000 square meters, will rise opposite the Benfica stadium, a semi-suburban area already chosen by General Motors for its new headquarters. Portuguese groups, such as Sonae and Amorim, have gone big into real estate in addition to more traditional activities. These and other Portuguese groups are associated with the French in building supermarkets. Eric van Leuven, Dutch-born managing director of George Knight, the leading Lisbon real estate agency, says, however, that bureaucratic delays, although shorter, still remain and road infrastructure and telephones have to be improved at a faster rate. The influx of foreign bankers and executives has meant the introduction of computer-designed buildings on the outskirts of Lisbon, with the emphasis on security rather than the view. View and luxury (and golf) remain the priorities in the Algarve, the southern coastline, which has become a major European tourist destination in the past two decades. Speculative, unesthetic construction has brought many complaints, but the other kind of development—complexes with expensive villas and upmarket time-sharing—continues just west of Faro, on estates such as Quinto do Lago. This and others nearby are the largest, new tourist complexes in Europe and some have four golf courses. The Irish building firm, McInerney, has been prominent down south, as have British firms, such as Bovis and Trafalgar House. It's not cheap to set up in this Portuguese Florida. A decent-sized plot and a pleasant villa cost one million dollars and up.

• *Getting To Know the Capital* •

Lisbon is built on hills facing the estuary of the River Tagus. Virtually destroyed by an earthquake in 1755, Lisbon today is an architectural mixture of the few medieval buildings that survived, the visionary urban planning of the Marquès de Pombal after the quake, and, alas, the miserably narrow vision of today's commercial developers. Teotonia Pereira of the Association of Portuguese Architects said recently that "the people of Lisbon need to become aware of the fact that the architectural heritage of Lisbon is a public calamity. Today...everything is for sale. Advertising, for example, has taken over every public space."

That having been said, Lisbon is still an attractive city, if one closes one's eyes to the pervasive billboards and flashing neon signs. It has character, even if such critics as Senhor Pereira think that character is bad. It's also very obviously a poor city, with peddlers and beggars infesting the main streets. And on the outskirts are the shanty towns of the chronically impoverished, many of them immigrants from the countryside, gypsies, or Cape Verde islanders who moved to Portugal to work in the construction industry.

How, then, does one account for the traffic jams, the smart shops, the excellent restaurants, the well-dressed people who

continued

stroll the wide *avenidas,* the vivid contrasts of poverty and wealth? The answer is that incomes are distributed very unevenly.

Business Lisbon is compact, though more and more companies are locating their headquarters on the outskirts, thanks to skyrocking real estate prices in the central neighborhoods. Some of the best hotels are also in the city center, along with most of the outstanding restaurants. The easiest way to visualize the city is to imagine one is landing from the Tagus at the Estação Fluvial Sul e Sueste.

To the right, rising steeply to a peak, is what remains of medieval Lisbon, the picturesque and crowded Alfama neighborhood topped by churches and monasteries. This was the old Moorish quarter.

Straight ahead, again looking from the sea, is the "new" city built by Pombal. The huge Praça do Coméricio (Commercial Square), open to the sea at the front, is flanked by impressive, pinkish buildings at left and right, and leads through arches to another vast square, the Praça Don Pedro IV, known popularly as the Rossio. The area between these squares is known as the *Baixa* and is the central commercial and shopping district. The dominant

building in the Rossio is the National Theater, with its classical-style colonnaded facade. That square leads into Praça dos Restauradores and then the Avenida da Liberdade, which ends at the Praça Marquès de Pombal. Immediately beyond is the greenery of the Parque Eduardo VII.

Back to the waterfront. Left, looking inland, are more hills and a maze of streets, some wide, some narrow, some of them extremely steep. This is the *Bairro Alto,* home of *fado* houses and some of Lisbon's best restaurants. If one looks sharply left, the coast stretches along the Tagus to Estoril and Cascais, two fashionable resorts, the first with an elegant casino. Although not administratively part of Lisbon, these two resort towns and others in between are integral parts of the metropolitan area, which has an estimated population of more than a million.

Now turn your back on the city of Lisbon and look across the river's broad mouth. There are some of the most important industrial suburbs, with shipbuilding, shiprepairing and other maritime services. There also are some good, crowded, and noisy popular restaurants specializing in fish and seafood.

To reach this part of the Lisbon metropolis, either take one of the cheap and frequent ferries or drive across the *Ponte 25 de Abril* (25th of April Bridge), one of the longest suspension bridges in Europe, with a span of 1,013 meters (3,300 feet).

Lisbon has a subway system called the *Metropolitano*, as well as buses (some of them British double-deckers) and streetcars. Most are crowded; all are cheap.

Taxis are plentiful, except when you need them, and inexpensive by Western European standards. Many drivers speak English, or at least understand it.

I do not recommend taking a taxi—or driving yourself—along the coastal highway, the *Marginal,* to Estoril and Cascais. Recent studies have shown it to be one of the most dangerous highways in Europe. Instead, try the fast and frequent commuter trains, which start from a station near the ferryport on the river. The Estoril stop, for example, is only five minutes' walk from the casino, which you approach through well-tended gardens. There and back, the train will give you a magnificent view of the sea and the busy shipping.

EUROCITY OPORTO

A deep-rooted feeling exists both in and around Oporto, Portugal's second largest city, that northern people work harder, while those in the south, i.e. Lisbon, spend far too much time on politics and other frivolous pursuits. The popular saying is: "Oporto works, Coimbra sings, and Lisbon enjoys itself."

This is somewhat unfair on modern Lisbon. Maybe it was once true, but the traditional rivalry and differences between the two cities are diminishing. The Single Market is transforming Portugal's two main business centers and bringing them closer together. The fast, air-conditioned Alfa express train is a symbol. Business travellers can now make it between the two centers in little more than three hours. A new bridge over the River Douro in Oporto, plus other track improvements, will cut this by almost an hour. (This is part of the railway revolution in the Iberian peninsula).

Oporto is the financial, commercial, and industrial heart of the north, but it is more in the sense that it is the home of the "old money," sprinkled by lots of new money. The city has been the base of some of Portugal's most important banks, such as the Banco Portugues do Atlantico, of traditional industries, and of many old family businesses (*see:* British-Portuguese Chamber of Commerce, Oporto office: Tel: 2000825, Fax: 601513). Today, the city is also the business and power springboard of new aggressive entrepreneurs heading groups like Corticeira Amorin and Sonae, and private banks like the Banco Portugues do Investimento.

Since Portugal joined the EC, the north and Oporto have been quick to grasp the opportunities and funds available to help modernize Portugal's economy. The effects are visible: new roads, new factories, and new buildings have risen everywhere in, at times, near-chaotic fashion. All this activity is transforming a city and a region with important implications for the country. The north, with a population of 4.9 million—about half Portugal's total population and more than half its workforce—accounts for roughly half the national domestic product, half of manufacturing investment, and 60 percent of exports.

Private enterprise has flourished around Oporto more than elsewhere in Portugal, and as many local companies are small- and medium-size they can adapt more easily to changing circumstances than larger, State-owned concerns in the south. But their relatively small size is also a handicap in the face of tougher European competition.

The source of the north's strength is also a potential source of weakness. Most of manufacturing activity is concentrated in traditional industries—textiles, footwear, wood and furniture, pulp, cork, and wine—and many of these face painful restructuring. Most of the textiles industry is located in the north and a third of the 170,000 workforce may have to be fired.

The north is also home to some of the most powerful and highly-diversified private groups. The activities of Sonae, led by Mr. Belmiro de Azevedo, range from manufacturing (wood and associated products), to distribution (supermarkets and fast-food outlets), real estate, agribusiness, trading, finance, and the media. For example, Sonae launched *Publico,* a slick national daily with simultaneous Lisbon and

Oporto editions. Private TV is also in its sights. Elsewhere, Corticeira Amorin, a group headed by Mr. Americo Amorin, has equally diversified interests and ties with the de Benedetti group, of Italy. Also in the north, the pulp and paper industry is booming and is now a top foreign currency earner. Perhaps better than elsewhere, the north and Oporto have the dynamism to meet the challenge of the Single Market.

S P O T L I G H T

• *Setubal* •

Setubal, a onetime rundown industrial area with struggling shipyards and fish canning factories south of Lisbon, has become a boom town. The EC rated it a depressed region and poured in aid money. Ford, for example, which will open a car radio plant in Setubal by 1994 will receive EC-funded incentives worth half the investment. EC money and foreign investment has saved Setubal. A total of $520 million was invested in the town and its surroundings in 1989 alone and half of this came from big foreign concerns such as General Motors and the Finnish tractor firm, Valmet. The Portuguese government also gives substantial tax breaks for investors in the region. Setubal has now set its sights even higher— $700 million dollars to be spent before the turn of the century, on projects that include a 1,000 acre industrial park. An airport, rail terminus and port are planned and the aim is to attract 200 local and foreign companies. Certainly, Portugal's EC membership has transformed the lives of Setubal's 120,000 inhabitants.

:::::::::::SUCCESS STORY—LEICA :::::::::::

Two decades ago, pressure of Japanese competition faced Leica, the German manufacturer of prestige cameras and optical instruments, with the option of cutting costs or closing down. The company chose to reduce its labor bill by moving part of its manufacturing to Portugal. The Leica plant opened in 1973 near the northern town of Vila Nova de Familicao has since increased its workforce twentyfold and now accounts for almost all the group's output of consumer goods. "We would simply not be in business today were it not for our lower labor costs here," said Wolfgang Koch, Leica's general manager for Portugal. He said Portuguese employees match their German colleagues for quality and are only marginally behind in productivity.

On the cost side, the differences between the Portuguese plant and Leica's two factories near Frankfurt is some 65 percent. Overall, Portuguese workers earn on average $3.81 an hour, compared with $23.35 in Germany. Portuguese wages are a third of those in Spain and a quarter of levels in France, Italy and the US.

Leica Aparelhos Optica de Precisao produces precision binoculars and microscopes and accounts for a substantial part of Leica camera bodies, among the most prestigious and expensive in the world. The 500-strong labor force includes 12 German technicians, but the head of the quality department is Portuguese. Sixty percent of employees are women who have demonstrated prowess at close precision work. The Germans cite this willingness to learn new skills as one of the key factors in the success of Leica, a company that is now controlled by Cambridge Investments (UK) and Switzerland's Wild group. Today, the plant exports $21 million a year—a good return on a total investment of $10 million. Foreign companies invested around $5 billion in Portugal in 1990, but those already established in Portugal, such as Leica, accounted for 56 percent of the total through capital increases and expansion projects. Ford and Volkswagen made the headlines with mega projects, but most investment was by small- and medium-sized foreign firms. Only a handful of some 3,500 foreign investments projects went above $70 million. A fifth of EC grants of $1 billion in the two years up to April 1991 went to foreign investors.

Firms such as Leica are vital for northern Portugal. The high-tech plant is situated in the Vale do Ave, the most depressed industrial region in the country where 45,000 jobs could be lost by the year 2000 as textile, clothing and footwear companies—Portugal's traditional sources of export revenue—face increased competition.

:::::::::::::::::::THE LEADERS:::::::::::::::::::

TOP 10 COMPANIES (1989)

			ESC b
		Sales	Net Profit
(1)	Petroleos de Portugal	379.4	4.7
(2)	Electricidade de Portugal	274	0.2
(3)	Renault-Portuguesa (consolidated)	147	6.9
(4)	CTT Telecoms	113.5	0.2
(5)	Shell Portuguesa	90.9	3.5
(6)	TLP Telefones	80.6	1.0
(7)	Portucel	78.1	6.0
(8)	Mobile Oil Portuguesa	72.4	0.9
(9)	EPAC	60.5	0.6
(10)	Quimigal	54.7	2.7

TOP 10 BANKS (1989)

		($ million)		
		Capital	Assets	Pretax profits
(1)	Caixa Geral de Depositos	1,060	17,718	207
(2)	Banco Comercial Portugues	419	3,447	76
(3)	Banco Espirito Santo	290	7,743	43
(4)	Banco Totta e Acores	242	3,243	21
(5)	Banco National Ultramarino	237	4,489	5
(6)	Banco Portugues do Atlantico	144	9,271	35
(7)	Banco de Fomento Exterior	116	2,645	20
(8)	Banco Pinto e Sotto Mayor	106	5,771	9
(9)	Uniao de Bancos Portugues	106	3,465	12

:::::::::::::::::: KEY CONTACTS ::::::::::::::::::

USEFUL LISBON TELEPHONE NUMBERS

Trade and Commercial Information

Bank of Portugal: 351-1-541074
European Community: 351-1-541144
Lisbon Trade Fairs: 351-1-645341

Government Offices

Prime Minister's Office: 351-1-678808

Ministries
Finance: 351-1-878685
  351-1-879106
Industry/Energy: 351-1-346-3091
ICEP (Foreign Investment): 351-1-524983

Chambers of Commerce

Member Nations
Belgium: 351-1-572502
Britain: 351-1-661586
France: 351-1-549748
Italy: 351-1-778663
Netherlands: 351-1-365629
Portugal: 351-1-364133
Spain: 351-1-536758

Others
Arabia: 351-1-547312
Argentinia: 351-1-774207

Australia: 351-1-574104
Brazil: 351-1-367729
Canada: 351-1-577562
China: 351-1-771317
India: 351-1-574104
International (ICC): 351-1-363304
Japan: 351-1-689632
Morocco: 351-1-692277
South Africa: 351-1-553208
United States: 351-1-572561
Venezuela: 351-1-557180

Embassies

Member Nations
Belgium: 351-1-549263
Britain: 351-1-661191
Denmark: 351-1-545099
France: 351-1-526206
Germany: 351-1-563961
Greece: 351-1-616991

Italy: 351-1-546144
Ireland: 351-1-661569
Luxembourg: 351-1-881177
Spain: 351-1-549605

Others
Angola: 351-1-767041

Algeria: 351-1-616356
Austria: 351-1-547609
Brazil: 351-1-535639
Canada: 351-1-563821
Chile: 351-1-528054
Colombia: 351-1-557096
India: 351-1-683203
Israel: 351-1-570251
Japan: 351-1-562177
Mexico: 351-1-570683

Mozambique: 351-1-771994
Panama: 351-1-825830
South Africa: 351-1-535041
Soviet Union: 351-1-562424
Sweden: 351-1-606097
Switzerland: 351-1-673121
Turkey: 351-1-614275
United States: 351-1-726660
Uruguay: 351-1-689265

USEFUL OPORTO TELEPHONE NUMBERS

Trade and Commercial Information

Oporto Fairs: 351-2-995-7887
Oporto Investment Office: 351-2-384794
Portuguese Industrial Association: 351-2-644161
Shippers Association: 351-2-225191
Textile Association: 351-2-317961

Facts on Spain

. . . .

Capital Madrid
Population 39m

Unemployment 16%
GDP Growth 1989: 5.2%; 1990: 3.6%; 1991
   (est.): 3%; 1992 (est.): 3.5%
GDP per Capita $12,472
Inflation 1989: 6.8%; 1990: 6.5%; 1991 (est):
   5%
Trade 1990: −$32b
Current Account −$16b
Tourism 1990: $18.6b
Spanish–US Trade 1990:
Exports to US $3.3b
Imports $5.2b

. . . .

SPAIN

"Spain, for sure, is not yet Germany, but then neither is it Taiwan any more." Carlos Solchaga, Spanish Minister for the Economy

NEW, GLASS-WALLED BANK BUILDINGS OCCUPY MADRID'S STRAEGIC intersections. Modern office towers—the tallest shamelessly named after Pablo Picasso—rise against the skyline. City streets in the capital and in the main regional capitals are choked in rush hour with cars, made in Spain by global manufacturers, or imports of the more expensive kind. Department stores, despite the late 1990 slowdown, still attract shoppers on buying sprees. Many have been the highly visible signs of Spain's new-found prosperity, just five years after the country's entry into the European Community in 1986. "We joined late, so we had to speed up things," said Cesar Rodriguez, partner in the Madrid office of Price Waterhouse. Minister Solchaga has delivered an optomistic forecast for 1992 and beyond. Foreign tourists may be deserting Spain, but foreign investors are not.

Today, with the barriers lowered, the EC dominates trade. Much of it is in desirable, imported consumer goods with their novelty value for Spaniards. Even more is in machinery and technology for the modernization of Spanish industry, particularly the export sector. "For the moment," said the Minister for the Economy, "we are very dependent on the multinationals for our technology." German, French, British, and Dutch firms have been leading the invasion of foreign investment in the economy—$19 billion was invested in Spain by foreigners in 1989 alone, following three years of similar spending. A high level was maintained in 1991 with France's Credit Lyonnais buying banking networks, Buinness purchasing the largest brewery, and Germans moving into the detergent market. Can it last, and can the many inward-looking, small- and medium-sized firms that abound find the stamina to endure in the Single Market given the government's tight monetary policy designed to slow inflation and demand? An extra challenge, certainly as far as infrastructure is concerned, is that the Single Market coincides with two mega events in Spain that will attract worldwide attention—the 1992 summer Olympic Games in Barcelona, capital of Catalonia, and the Universal Exhibition, in Seville, capital of Andalusia. Both are linked to the 500th anniversary of Christopher Columbus landing in America. The celebrations will give a tremendous impetus to upgrading road and rail travel, particularly between Madrid and the beautiful, but underdeveloped Andalusian south—potentially Europe's California—and to improving the whole range of telecommunications. Transport and telephones are currently Spain's glaring weaknesses as it folds itself into Europe after decades of isolation during the Franco years. Yet another question is whether Spain can continue to find favor among European, but also American and Japanese investors, in an era when East Europe beckons as an even cheaper source of labor and as an even larger market, and when many Spanish companies have an inflated view of their value. The answer to these questions has been positive. Spain has already undergone dramatic changes in the past decade and survived them in a stronger and leaner shape. Industrial reconversion, started as Spain prepared for EC membership, cost some 85,000 jobs in shipbuilding, steel, textiles, and electrical engineering, mainly in the formerly protected nationalized sector. The country was then thrown open to foreign investors with the result that the late 1980s, unlike the first half of the decade, were boom years, with the fastest growth in the EC. In the nineties, this dramatic expansion has slowed. The pragmatic, market-oriented Socialist government of long-serving Prime Minister Felipe Gonzalez has been dampening the consumer's ardor, or *el gran festin* (the big feast), with interest rates that are the highest in Europe, while seeking to turn attention towards improving exports. The feast has created a yawning trade gap. Closing this gap is a major challenge for Gonzales before he takes his political bow at the end of his third term. One of his major aims is to control inflation—and with it wages—bringing it down from close to seven percent in 1990 to some four percent or less in 1993. Otherwise, Spain will price itself out of the market. Spain has until the end of 1992 to free capital movements.

Of late, competitiveness has been dented, although rates of pay remain the lowest in the EC, with the exception of Greece and Portugal. Companies complain both of high interest rates and the government's continuing commitment to a strong peseta. It has become urgent for industry to improve technology at home and its marketing and distribution abroad. In 1990, both Spain's trade and current account deficits ballooned, respectively to $30 billion and $16 billion. The answer to both ills was to put a brake on Spaniards' spending which has been rising more than production. Solchaga's fiscal and monetary measures showed signs in 1990 and 1991 that they were biting. Car sales, for example, which had doubled in the years after 1982, dropped 20 percent. Imports of consumer goods declined, while industrial production, if not the creation of new jobs, held up, providing a breathing space for a government with a tiny majority following the 1989 elections.

A decline in growth would undermine efforts to reduce Spain's high rate of unemployment, which stood at a record 22 percent of the active population in 1985, but which has since been reduced to a "mere" 16 percent, an achievement in Spanish terms, but almost double that to be found elsewhere in Western Europe. The forecast is for growth to settle down to around 3 percent and to permit what economists call a soft landing for the Spanish economy. The government made plain its commitment to an anti-inflationary strategy when it integrated the peseta into the European Monetary System at the end of the six-month period in 1989, when Spain, for the first time, assumed the rotating presidency of the EC.

The Gonzalez administration seeks to lift Spain's living standards into the higher European bracket, just as much as it seeks to push inflation down to the EC average. Hence, the costly modernization of Spain's backward public services, the teaching of new professional skills to workers, particularly the young, and the setting aside of more resources for technological development. The latter, however probably needs to be doubled. But, after all, this is a Socialist government and so pensions have to be increased and benefits raised for the jobless and sick. The priority for the Economy Ministry planners is to somehow balance the budget, not as a result of any painful cut in public spending, but through more efficient tax collection, even a war against rampant tax evasion, and more indirect taxes on drinking, smoking, and the like. The keys to Spain's success in 1993 are labor costs and therefore competitiveness. Gonzalez would like to see wage increases limited to 5.8 percent in 1991 through a "competitivity pact," or *pacto de competitividad,* but the pressure from workers for a better deal is strong. In 1990, employers agreed to pay 8.5 percent more to two million workers. Another one million staged stoppages in support of claims for similar increases. Gonzalez's achievements have been impressive since he helped anchor democracy in Spain, following the turbulent years following Franco's death in 1975 and the attempted coup of 1981. He needs a new consensus with the trade unions and other forces on the Spanish Left to check any move remain in favor of the man who has been one of the most charismatic leaders in the New Europe, but who is nevertheless preparing for the day when he will step down after a decade in power. The dauphin is the new vice premier, Narcis Serra, now 48, who comes from a middle-class background in Barcelona and who once worked at the Chamber of Commerce there. His intellectual air belies his force of character for it was he who, as Minister for Defense, persuaded the army to remain in its barracks when putschists sought to overthrow Spain's new democracy at the beginning of the 1980s. He is known as a pragmatic politician who stays above party squabbling.

MARKET OPPORTUNITIES

How is the money spent in a country where average earnings, or gross domestic product per capita, have reached $9,700 (a quarter below the richer European countries) and where many industrialists saw profits double in 1987 and 1988, before rising at a slower rate up to 1991? There's a love affair with the automobile. General Motors is making its small Corsicas in Saragossa in the north east, and components in the deep south in Cadiz, Ford produces its economy car, the Fiesta, in Valencia on the Mediterranean coast, Volkswagen its Polos in Pamplona, while the French, Fasa Renault and Citroen Hispania, have plants respectively in the Castille-Leon region, northwest of Madrid, and at Vigo in the north-west tip of Spain. Sales of household goods have risen considerably and Germany's Bosch Siemens Hausgerate has joined Sweden's Electrolux in the white goods market. The French, too, are big in supermarkets, the British in department stores and hotels. Building societies, such as Britain's Abbey National, are set to tap the growing house-buying market. Most Spaniards are eager to try foreign goods. In terms of contributions to gross national product, the services sector, which in Spain is mainly tourism and financial banking services, is easily the most important, with a 61 percent contribution, followed by industry (26.5 percent), construction (6.5 percent), and the once all-important agricultural sector, representing just 6 percent. Total capital investment (Spanish and foreign, public and private) grew by 14 percent in 1989–1990, and by almost 60 percent in the four years to the end of that period.

The countries pumping the most money into the stock market and throughout the land are European, with the Dutch showing particular interest in the farming lands of Andalusia. The US has not figured prominently in this recent investment, but its total investment is one of the largest. Spanish imports from the US jumped in both 1988 and 1989 and lifted the American share of the total import market to ten percent. These American exports benefitted from clarification of how the local import licensing system, including quotas, is applied to American-origin products. The Spanish government confirmed that, for most categories, the licensing system does not restrict imports from the US. Significant demand exists for a broad range of American agricultural and manufactured products, as well as for services. Trade analysts have pinpointed computers and peripherals, telecommunications equipment and services, medical and scientific equipment, food processing and packaging equipment, coal, security and safety devices, electronics, sporting goods, and sportswear.

With Spaniards still slow to take the initiative in the private sector, foreigners have been establishing positions in manufacturing sectors tipped to do well in the Single Market. Foreigners, for example, control more than half of the sales in the food, paper, pharmaceutical, and chemical industries. And they have complete control in technologically-advanced industries, such as computers. Although much of the machinery in plants is less than five years old, there's no end in sight for the inflow of capital goods. The Gulf War affected the pace of take-overs, but stringent application of European company law directives, particularly for audits and the filing of accounts, could well bring more family-owned businesses on to the market.

Spain needs to sell a lot more goods, and greater value-added ones—cars, machine tools and construction equipment, as well as wines and shoes—if it is to pay for its unfinished process of industrial modernization. The export drive, particularly to the other EC countries, has assumed greater urgency now that the flow of tourists—millions of visitors spending billions of dollars—has slowed. Until two or three years ago, a Spanish finance minister could sleep soundly in the knowledge that tourist pounds, deutschmarks, francs, lire, and guilders would always enable him to balance the books. The overcrowded *costas* are out of favor now, as the old form of travel package deal gives way to "higher class" vacation elsewhere. The threat to Spain's largest industry is well known but will take time to rectify. Meanwhile, the trade gap is around $30 billion annually and the current account with services a staggering, minus $16 billion. Fortunately, there are sizeable foreign currency reserves, but for how long, one may ask? Exports have been rising—10 percent in 1990—but not fast enough, and imports still outscore exports two to one. Spanish style "champagne," *cava,* may outsell the real stuff in the US, but this marketing success story is overshadowed by the foreign goods and drinks in Spanish stores. Spanish household "white goods" are challenged on home soil by imports and are sold under different names in other countries. Sophisticated machinery is pouring into Spain from the rest of Europe. Spain is today a major European automobile manufacturer, producing more vehicles than Britain, but they are all made by foreign firms now that Seat, the onetime national car maker, was bought by Volkswagen. The cars also are at the cheaper end of the market. Icex, the government agency with the task of promoting Spanish exports, is spending money on trade shows, and on training local businessmen to attack other markets, rather than sell out to foreign bidders. In general, Spain needs to polish its image as a manufacturing nation, beyond one that makes aerospace equipment and sophisticated food processing systems, as well as bottling excellent Riojas wines. A broad spectrum of trade fairs in Madrid and Barcelona is beginning to push Spanish goods more actively. The Barcelona Games and the Seville World Fair will offer unique store windows for Spanish manufacturers. However, more marketing expertise is required if many goods are to "stand on their own feet" and not sold for relabelling in other lands—as with olive oil sent to Italy. Openings exist for foreigners able to help Spanish firms in the setting up of distribution networks North of the Pyrenees. Companies are beginning to leap this traditional mountain barrier—oil companies are building gas stations in France, retailers and banks are crossing into Portugal, Basque steel companies are buying distribution networks, notably in France.

The peseta's 25 percent appreciation against other EC currencies in the 1985–89 period hit exports, yet the Bank of Spain has resolutely opposed devaluation. Spain's integration into the new Europe is best shown by the breakdown of trade: 65 percent with the rest of the EC (France absorbs 27 percent, West Germany 19 percent, Britain 17 percent, Italy 16 percent). The US and Latin America have lost ground, while Japan moves up.

TRANSPORTATION AND COMMUNICATIONS

New investment, as well as inter-regional connections are at risk if the national transport system—and the telecommunications network—are not raised to EC standards. Public investment in infrastructure rose sharply in 1990 to more than seven billion dollars, while Telefonica, the telephone monopoly, is earmarking five billion dollars a year until 1994 to improve the network, including digitalization and business services.

Roadworks are a priority and half the seven billion dollars in 1990 went on expressways, such as the extension of the highway along the Mediterranean coast to Jaen in the south, and on improvements and additions to ring roads around Madrid, Barcelona, Seville, Valencia, and Malaga. The five-year, national highway plan to 1991 will cost one trillion pesetas and will add 2,250 miles (3,600 kilometers) of modern roads, long demanded by road haulers and tourists—tourism has been stagnating partly because of poor roads. The M30 ring road around Madrid will help link the new business parks to the capital. A second ring road will provide a connection between northern Madrid, scene of the latest office development, and the airport, with its new exhibition grounds.

The next largest chunk of public money will go to the State railway, Renfe, which has a two trillion investment program until 2001. Under this plan, rolling stock is being ordered from foreign manufacturers. Lines leading to Madrid's dormitory towns in Castille are being modernized and, last but not least, the country's first-ever, ultra high-speed train line is being laid between Madrid and Seville that will cut travelling time by three hours. Hopefully, the service will be ready for the opening of the Seville Fair in April, 1992. The Prime Minister and many of his closest colleagues come from Seville so the line, and an expressway south, have some powerful supporters. The railway, which is being designed according to the continental narrow-gauge system, is going to be serviced by 24 high-speed, TGV-style trains from Alsthom, of France, and will be completely State-financed. Another part of the deal was for Alsthom to take over loss-making Spanish rolling stock manufacturers. The French agreed, as they had mounted a high-level sales campaign to sell the trains, with President Mitterrand adopting the role of chief salesman in discussions with Premier Gonzalez. The rising cost of the Madrid-Seville line, however, has made the government balk at paying the full cost of a planned Madrid-Barcelona-Perpignan high-speed line that may be ready by around 1996. The financing here would be shared by a consortium of State and private companies. An extension of this line to Milan in north Italy has run into trouble with environmental groups in southern France. But all these improvements should lead to a sharp rise in passenger and freight traffic by rail.

Billions of pesetas of public money have been set aside for work at the airports of Madrid, Barcelona, Malaga, and Seville, with the latter the most in need of a rapid extension. In the longterm, Madrid's capacity is to be tripled at a cost of 200 billion pesetas ($2 billion).

A new plant at Tres Cantos, near Madrid, which will make transmission equipment and central office switches is one of AT&T's major "weapons" for the Single Europe. It will strengthen the American giant's position in Spain and will be used as an export center with up to 80 percent of production destined for other countries. AT&T is targeting Spain and Italy in Europe. Both countries need to expand their telecommunications networks fast to be competitive. The Spanish plant is a joint venture between AT&T Network Systems Espana, in which AT&T has a 51 percent stake, and Amper, the Spanish telephone and key set manufacturer closely linked to the national phone company, Telefonica. Spain is set for fast telecoms growth hopefully before the Olympics in Barcelona and the World Exposition in Seville. The market could well double by 1994. AT&T is taking on Sweden's Ericsson and France's Alcatel in Spain, but is spending big to challenge these well-established rivals—a $200 million investment in adapting its switching system to meet Spanish network standards. It's not only costly, but also a major technological challenge for AT&T is having to produce new software. Whereas the switch can be used by any US Bell company, it has to be adapted to different signalling, tones and billing in different European countries. There's a crying need throughout the land for more telephones and fax machines. The hall lined with telephone booths inside the Telefonica building in Madrid conveys a false impression. The telephone monopoly had a waiting list at the beginning of 1990 of some 530,000, rising by at least 15 percent a year. And many of those with telephones could hardly hear those at the other end. Telefonica's charges for international calls are way above the rest of Europe. A three-year crash program is underway with Telefonica digging up the nation's streets and throwing money at the problem—five billion dollars a year, including $800 million in 1990 for the Barcelona network. Switching equipment is being bought from AT&T Network Systems, Alcatel-Standard Electrica and Intelsa-LM Ericsson. Progress has been made at Telefonica under new management, but Spain still lags in Europe—12 million lines in service for its 39 million people, compared with 25 million lines in France for $56 million. The glass fiber lines are being laid as fast as possible, but for the moment, as they used to say in France, half the nation is waiting for the dial tone, while the other half waits for the telephone.

MANAGEMENT AND WORKFORCE

Spain has the fifth largest population in the EC after Germany, Italy, France, and Britain, with latest projections indicating a rise in the total population to 39.7 million in 1992 and 40.8 million in the year 2000. The economically "active"—with or without jobs—are put at 14.6 million (two men to every woman), and the number actually employed at 12.4 million, some two million more than in the mid-1980s. Farther back, in the 1960s and up to 1978, the birth rate was very high and the death rate somewhat lower. The baby boomers of that time are now coming onto the job market. There's now a "baby slump," and Spain, the European leader in the Franco years when a large family was a patriotic duty, has dropped to 1.5 children per woman, in statistical terms. So, in ten to fifteen years' time, Spain will share with many other European countries the problem of having a larger number of inhabitants who are pensionable and inactive. The breakdown shows that a quarter of the population is under 25. Many of the jobless are to be found in this bracket and among women aspiring to work. Women, in fact, outnumber men in Spain— 19.8 million to 19.2 million. The government has an ambitious job-training program, and there are funds available from the European Community. The programs are not yet sufficiently adapted to the needs of the 2.7 million unemployed, the changing technology, the specific regional needs— site workers, for example, in Andalusia for the World's Fair and the regional development associated with this massive undertaking. The will is there, but better coordination is required between labor, employers, and unions. The sums allocated are impressive, and the European Community Social Fund plans to allot $3.5 billion to Spain up to 1992–93, and most of this will be spent in the less-favored of Spain's 17 autonomous regions. The government says that of those who have been trained, half secured jobs in their chosen field, notably the transport and food industries. Unemployment, the highest in the EC and the OECD, has been falling, and the most encouraging figure has been the 430,000 new jobs found for the young in 1989. The sectors where most jobs are now being created are construction and those related to education and research. The services sector, however, is by far the biggest employer, providing just over half of all jobs, with industry supplying a quarter. Agriculture (15 percent) and construction (eight percent) are down the line. Then there's the public sector, which absorbs 16 percent of the workforce and provides 40 percent of new jobs.

But the problems remain daunting. For example, one in three is unemployed in the traditionally farming region of Andalusia, while one young man in two is out of work in the industrial Basque region in the northwest. But most of the job hunters are women, with only a third of the would-be economically active female population in work, one of the lowest proportions within the European Community. Women, for the moment, are concentrated in the less-skilled occupations—and are drawn, more than men, into Spain's large black economy.

Relations have been strained between the Socialist government, the employers organization, the CEOE, and the trade unions, of which the most important are the Communist Confederation of Workers Commissions (CCOO) and the socialist General Workers Union (UGT). The UGT has distanced itself from the government, and both unions once called a one-day general strike once that was seconded by some eight million Spaniards. At the center of discontent has been the government's introduction of temporary work contracts lasting six months to three years, and part-time work contracts for women. Labor claims that employment has thus become precarious. One quarter of all state employees in Spain now hold temporary contracts of some kind with even more in the private sector. The unions also worry that companies are using temporary workers to replace more expensive ones, and not to expand the workforce. On their side, employers argue that labor laws still have rigid aspects. For instance, they claim, it can cost more to fire a 34-year-old worker than to retire one aged 54. Employers in Madrid reckon that it costs a company almost twice as much to fire a worker than the European norm. In 1990, employers were furious when the unions were allowed to oversee temporary work contracts to ensure that no legal abuses were committed. This is a union "right" in other EC countries.

Following an example set by Italy, the Gonzalez government wants to establish an employment, wages, and productivity pact with unions and employers until 1993, one that will guarantee Spain's competitiveness in the Single Market. Consensus has been hard to achieve, for unions were winning wage increases above the government-proposed ceiling of 7.5 percent. Now, the government is seeking a 5.8 percent limit.

Despite this general trend towards higher wages, annual increases in private sector productivity, more than twice the OECD average, have been reducing real unit costs. The OECD forecasts a further 1.2 percent increase in productivity in the private sector. A recent study by a West German bank also claims that Spanish manufacturing costs per hour are 54 percent of West Germany's and about the same as Britain's, after hefty Spanish social security contributions are deducted. In fact, European television documentaries often show the wide difference in wages and lifestyles between Volkswagen workers in West Germany and Spain. However, the shadow of cheap East European manufacturing is now less threatening to Spain. Spanish wages are still considered by most employers to be the lowest in the EC, after Greek and Portuguese wages.

The growth in the economy has created bottlenecks and shortages higher up the scale—engineers, especially telecommunications engineers, skilled construction staff, and managers. In top management, Spain is winning better marks. More of the "best and brightest" are going to business schools such as Barcelona's ESADE. The best brains are shunning the ministries for the private sector. Young ex-Treasury officials who know the government "system" are worth their weight in gold to banks and to a wide range of companies. Members of the elite *cuerpos del estado*, or State corps, are switching for big salaries to Spanish and foreign companies along Madrid's showpiece avenue, Paseo de la Castellana. The most notable is Mario Conde, head of the Banesto bank with its broad stakes in industry. One leading consultant said that these men would later run the future pan-European Spanish companies. These are virtually non-existent, but he felt they would arrive in the late 1990s, just as the new, pan-European Italian companies appeared on the scene in the 1980s.

REAL ESTATE

Madrid's office market has been squeezed by the small army of incoming banks and financial companies, leading to the quick letting of the latest skyscraper. Tighter zoning laws in the sought-after central area have added to pressure on prices. Agents Jones Lang and Wootton have let a converted mansion on a coveted, downtown site for 5,200 pesetas a square meter per month. The 46-story Torre Picasso office tower in the northern part of the city let at 4,200 pesetas, but since then the "5,000 barrier" has been pierced. The Picasso building went mainly to building and property firms, media and financial groups. It has shops and restaurants for the new business class (one restaurant boasts a *menu especial yupis*). There is old and new money along the big business arteries of Madrid. Both categories are beginning to tire of paying high prices on and off the Paseo de la Castellana, the Fifth Avenue or Champs Elysées of Madrid. These companies—and government offices—are moving out to the north and to the northeast and northwest. Prices there are half, while buildings are accessible by the capital's new ring roads. Business parks are flowering near the universities; one is Las Rozas, 12 miles from the city, which offers offices and headquarters buildings. The same facilities exist at the Technological Park of Madrid, one of a series planned by the regional authority, the Community of Madrid. Similar developments are to found near the airport, and to the south. The acute shortage is in the 200 to 300 square meter bracket. Prices, heavy traffic and recent tough laws on selling or dividing central residential buildings are forcing decentralization, and returning some sanity to an overheated market, stoked by local and foreign developers. Rents for some industrial developments have trebled in five years. There's shortage too in the "high tech" market, so active elsewhere in Europe. Spanish builders have limited experience in providing "business space." The big electronics companies are finding their own solutions with their own buildings. Barcelona is 25 to 30 percent cheaper than Madrid and offers good prospects for the future. Bilbao and Valencia are also developing as modern business centers (the former has a long tradition of heavy industry) and rents are considerably cheaper than in the capital. Extremely generous grants become increasingly available with every kilometer from Madrid.

S P O T L I G H T

• *Construction* •

Long the locomotive of the economy, the Spanish construction industry is today strong enough to survive a turndown in the number of tourists. There will be no repeat of 1974 when the oil crisis sent the industry reeling. It made up in both orders and job levels in the late 1980s, and is confident, despite the worrying 1989 and 1990 tourist figures. The world's second most popular tourist destination (after the US), Spain saw total receipts fall four percent in 1989 to $16 billion, and in some areas the number of visitors was down 20 percent. The 1990 season was 6.5 percent lower. In addition, builders are finding it harder to obtain State subsidies and other underpinnings. The State Secretariat for Tourism, the State-run Banco Hipotecaria, the economy ministry, and the private banks all want quality projects. Quantity is out. Still, the level of support remains high, given the importance of the sector, and some big, multi-billion pesetas schemes—the Anheuser Busch complex on Costa Dorada, NE Spain, and the Magic Mountain amusement park at Malaga, for example—get a quarter of the 30 billion peseta ($300 mil-

continued

lion) cost. Other four to five billion peseta projects, notably in Andalusia for the 1992 Expo will be backed. The contractors federation, Seopan, is optimistic that road and hydraulic contracts will make up for any lost hotels. Anyway, Barcelona and Seville will both need many, many thousands more hotel beds for their moments of glory in 1992.

• *Advertising* •

The supermarket boom and the import boom have created the largely foreign-owned advertising industry boom, too. Spending on advertising has doubled in three years to more than $6 billion and could grow at 20 to 30 percent a year. Spain is now the fifth market in the EC, after Britain, West Germany, France, and Italy, but could move up the table, despite the credit squeeze and the dampening of the economy. It's certainly the fastest-growing and the latest clients are the new mega-banks engaged in a vicious, interest rate war to attract savers. Signs all over Madrid promise up to 14 percent interest to depositors. The big British, other European, and US advertising firms—J. Walter Thompson, Saatchi & Saatchi, Leo Burnett, France's SCA and BDDP, HDM, Bassat, Ogilvy and Mather, Belier WCRS Espana—are following in the wake of the major international investors in the Spanish economy. Young Spaniards' taste for things foreign is creating new markets—imported beer, for example. However, the cost of any decent campaign is several million dollars. The government itself now spends heavily on advertising, as do most banks and financial houses. New, privately-owned TV channels will provide new—and expensive—means of communicating the message. Media buying is becoming all important. It's a long way from the epoch when Franco's censors had to approve all ads before they were shown on the only channel—in black and white.

• *Getting To Know the Capital* •

Madrid and its suburbs sprawl over the Castilian plain. Business Madrid is compact, though, concentrated in the center, with many government ministries housed in tower blocks to the north. Madrid boasts one of the tallest office buildings in Europe, the 46-story Torre Picasso, the new symbol of business, yet is still a charming mixture architecturally of ancient and modern, and socially of dynamism and courtliness.

Madrid has good bus and subway systems. The subway is called the Metro. Most business visitors will find taxis easier and faster, however, if they are not familiar with the city's layout. Taxis are cheap by European standards, drivers do not expect a tip, and many speak English or understand even a mangled version of Spanish street names. Taxis are white with a diagonal red line. They display a green light when they are free, and by the rear window is a meter that, by law, must show the driver's duty hours.

EUROCITY BARCELONA

Preparations for the 1992 summer Olympic Games plus the strong presence of foreign investors in the surrounding Catalonian countryside have done much to satisfy Barcelona's ambition to be regarded as a Eurocity of stature and an international center for trade and manufacturing, as well as the stage for the world's finest athletes.

The ancient capital of Catalonia, its 3.5 million inhabitants squeezed into the space between mountains and sea, has been a vast construction site for two years as it has added sports facilities, highways and hotels, while improving El Prat airport, and urban telecommunications. It has seen a massive, $4 billion renewal program spurred by the Olympics. The city hopes to move on from the Games to become one of the great business and cultural centers of Southern Europe.

Barcelona's proximity to France, its window on the Mediterranean and, above all, its dynamism and work ethic have helped Catalonia as a whole to become the leading industrial center in Spain. It has attracted up to 30 percent of all foreign investment in the country and the Japanese, who are major investors, cite the mentality and motivation of the Catalan workforce. This sentiment is one with which French and Germans agree. Barcelona is more than a place of hard work. Its people, and the Catalans in general, are proud of their specific culture, language, and lifestyle. They are beginning to lose their complex *vis-à-vis* Madrid and have managed to wring more concessions and favors than any of the other autonomous Spanish regions. Figures tell part of the success story which continues despite increased competition for foreign investment from Madrid and Andalucia. Some 16 percent of Spain's population lives in Catalonia, but the region is responsible for a fifth of the nation's gross domestic product and 27 percent of industry. The other part of the story is the manner of living. Barcelona's pulse beats on the Ramblas, the tree-lined boulevard running from the Plaza Catalunya with its banks and trading companies down to the port. This is the place for strolling and talking, much of it in the Catalan language, now taught in all schools. Nearby is the expanse of the Plaza San Jaume with city hall and the Generalitat, the legislative assembly, one of the most powerful regional parliaments in Europe, let alone Spain. Catalonia, as its inhabitants like to say, is both nationalistic and patriotic, but the key word is autonomy under the long leadership of doctor-turned-politician Jordi Pujol, president of the Generalitat, controlled by a conservative coalition, the *Convergeencia i Union*. He supports the Socialist government of Felipe Gonzalez in Madrid and this pays off for Catalonia.

Barcelona mixes dynamism with a dose of disorder. This has given rise to the question as to whether it will be ready for the 16,000 athletes and their trainers, 5,000 newsmen, 7,000 television presenters and technicians, 2,000 referees, and half a million visitors staying for the duration of the Games.

There was an unhappy precedent in 1989 with the inauguration of the Montjuic Stadium when King Juan Carlos's car was stuck in a traffic jam, work on the stadium was not complete, and spectators were drenched in rain. The bad publicity led to a redoubling of efforts to cut red tape and complete all the infrastructure projects, notably the Olympic village, an ambitious scheme which has been designed for athletes but also for later use as apartments, high-rise offices, and as a hotel and conference center.

Barcelona's city authorities, private companies, the Generalitat and central government have pulled together. Part of the work has involved bulldozing rundown districts, warehouses and railway lines cluttering the city's sea front. Coastal highways and ring roads, in addition to the modernized airport, will be big pluses for Barcelona's future as a major business city within the Single Market. Among new hotels are a Hilton and a Ramada, but not all the planned hotels will be built on time. Some 7000 rooms are to be added to the present 15,000, well short of Olympic needs. Prices at existing establishments have risen sharply to $180 for a double at two and three-star hotels and a whopping $420 at the Ritz. Prices are expected to soar during the Olympic period.

Barcelona, city of Dali, Miro, and Picasso (the latter bequeathed many of his works to the Picasso museum) is also famous for its turn-of-the century modernist architecture, some of the most splendid in Europe. The city plays a leading role in an organization of Eurocities which promotes Europe's "second cities."

Through the Office of Foreign Trade and Investment, city and region have attracted numerous foreign firms, notably Japanese companies such as Sony, whose Catalonia video and color tv plant in Barcelona won the Sony plant of the year prize two years ago, Hitachi, Honda, Kao Corp., Matsushita, Mitsubishi, Sharpe, Sanyo with an R & D center, and Yoshida. In all the Japanese have created 17,000 jobs. Other investors form an impressive roll call—Americans Culligan and Hewlett Packard and others in the pipeline; Benetton; Volkswagen through its ownership of Seat; Bayer, Ciba-Geigy, Henkel, Hoechst, Montefibre, and Sandoz among chemical concerns, plus Nestlé and Danone in food.

The region's growth has slowed since the heady rate of 5.6 percent in 1988 and some sectors, notably textiles, have been hit. Nevertheless, Catalonia has managed to woo foreigners because of its skills and not through the kind of subsidies available in Spain's poorer regions where grants range up to 70 percent of startup costs.

Barcelona's port is another selling point. It is Spain's busiest with one of the largest container terminals in the Mediterranean. A wide variety of goods—some 50 million tons—pass through the miles of wharves with their 300 cranes and specialized handling equipment.

The key organization for would-be investors is the Center for Information and Promotion of Business (CIPEM), a branch of the autonomous government:

Avgda Diagonal
Barcelona
Tel: 215-8582 and 215-7178.

:::::: OPPORTUNITIES IN THE REGIONS ::::::

On a map of the Directorate General for Regional Economic Incentives in Madrid, large areas of Spain are colored brown, indicating 50 percent subsidies of new manufacturing investment. (Ministerio de Economia y Hacienda, Direccion General de Incentivos Economicos Regionales, Paseo de la Castellana 147, 28046 Madrid, Spain Tel: 34-1-571-4412). This map is an essential tool for potential investors, and there are even some areas of Spain colored purple, indicating 75 percent grants. The Directorate has carefully mapped the entire country, although the investor will notice some white zones which do not qualify for subsidies, as they are traditional and successful industrial and commercial areas: the Madrid region, for example; Catalonia around Barcelona; the area farther south along the Mediterranean coast around Valencia and Alicante; and, of course, the industrial heartlands of the Basque country, near Bilbao, and those around Vitoria and Pamplona. The lowest subsidies—up to 20 percent—are for so-called Special Areas (ZE); the higher for Declining Industrial Areas (ZID) and Economic Promotion Areas (ZPE), the last-named being the regions with the lowest levels of economic activity and income. The Directorate states that "while respecting EC regulations," especially those regarding "particularly susceptible, or controlled, areas," such as iron and steel, shipbuilding, textiles, synthetic fibers, fish, and food processing, subsidies are granted for high-tech extraction and processing, some food and aquaculture sectors covered by Royal Decree, industrial support services and those which need better commercial structures, as well as specific installations for tourism linked to an area's development.

Investments have to be in the specifically-designated areas to receive these often highly-generous grants (high tech in rural Andalusia, for example, or a brand new industry in the northwestern tip of the country facing the Atlantic). They must involve new fixed assets of 15 million pesetas or more; involve 30 percent self financing—and of course, create the maximum of jobs to dent unemployment, running 26 percent in Andalusia.

The "1992 effect" is most tangible in Andalusia, where Seville is hosting the world's fair to commemorate the 500th anniversary of Christopher Columbus setting sail for the New World. This will mean $6.6 billion of public money for the fair and its surroundings, in addition to billions poured into the region in recent years by foreigners. And in Barcelona for the Olympics massive public spending will be added to other heavy investment in Catalonia. Any specialist at any member of the Big Eight accountants in Madrid, or Barcelona, will explain the breakdown of the highly significant flow of EC funds from Brussels. Investors can benefit through links with Spanish companies, particularly in tapping the European Development Fund and R&D programs; the aid of the central administration, acting through the 1987 regional incentives law; and regional governments' incentives running parallel to those of Madrid. The government has ranked the less-developed regions, in order of need, as Andalusia, Castilla-Leon, Galicia, Castilla-La Mancha, Extremedura, the Canaries, Asturias, Murcia. The regions themselves are increasingly active in their efforts to attract foreign investment and some have built technological parks, notably Andalusia, Asturias, Cataluna, Castilla-Leon, Madrid, and Valencia.

Catalonia, the Basque Country, and the Canaries have permanent delegations outside Spain. The Catalans have their office in New York, while all regions are represented in Brussels.

The business newcomer to Spain must also take heed of the changing—and tightening—legal and accounting systems. This already voluminous arsenal will be completed by application decrees and regulations and, in the course of coming years, by a body of doctrine and standards. The aim has been to harmonize national legislation with European Directives on accounting and corporate matters. The context of the financial markets has also been transformed by the entry into force of a 1988 law of modernization, but the key reform is the law on business practice (the July 25, 1989 law) which covers the

Commercial Code, the Commercial Register (Registro Mercantil), for accounting, company audits, disclosure of accounting information, public and private limited companies and limited partnerships. For example, all businesses must keep legal records...the annual financial statements should be standardized...groups must prepare annual consolidated financial statements with notes...and more. Over at the stock exchange, the Comision Nacional des Mercado de Valores, a Spanish SEC, has been formed and the stockbrokers profession revamped. All highly ambitious and all safeguards for the inward-investor.

Andalusia

The Exposition in Seville (100 participating countries, 20 million visitors) has made Andalusia, at the southern tip of the European Community, the magnet for massive investment. Funds are pouring in from various EC funds (EC Madrid office: Calle de Serrano 41, 5A Planta, Madrid 1. Tel: 34-1-435-1700. Fax: 34-1-276-0387), which will be spent on both agriculture and industry thoughout the eight provinces. Money is coming from Madrid, too, particularly for the new express train which will be the umbilical cord between the capital of the country and the capital of the largest of Spain's 17 autonomous regions. Matadors, flamenco and the spirit of Carmen survive in beautiful, romantic Seville, now emerging as a modern Eurocity after centuries of faded glory, scruffiness, and incompetence. There's a new dream—call it high-tech—accompanied by considerable ambition to make money. High-tech has already been injected into farming which is becoming increasingly sophisticated with high-yielding fruit and vegetable crops, plus tobacco and cotton. The land is rich, the sunshine perpetual and the Dutch were the first with modern methods. Andalusia is set to become one of the most highly-competitive farming regions in Europe and for that reason produce will not be allowed to flood the EC until 1996. Real estate investment in the area remains high, although government and local junta (regional authority) are being more selective in grants for hotel and leisure projects as part of the campaign to raise the quality of Spanish tourism. Another development is retirement homes. For example, Six Flags, of the US, is building apartments, villas, hotels, and golf courses in Marbella; Ryokuchui Home, of Japan, has plans for apartments and hotels in Almeria. Andalusia seems destined to become a major retirement area for the well-to-do from northern Europe and Japan. Already, there are some 300,000 foreigners living all or part of the year in Andalusia, in addition to more than a million tourists a year.

Most of the several billion dollars in funds is destined for adjacent projects to be used after the Fair closes on October 12, 1992, and to provide a hoped-for 200,000 new jobs. Long-term policy is to transform the once sleepy, inward-looking—and often backward area—into something resembling the European California heralded in the wilder passages of local propaganda. Andalusia is growing at 5.5 percent, two points higher than the rest of Spain. Industry is expanding at 10 percent a year and represents 19.5 percent of regional GDP. The service sector is now 60 percent of this GDP. Big names are investing in the Fair itself—Fuji, Rank Xerox, Fujitsu, Alcatel, Siemens, IBM, and Philips Iberica. Elsewhere, the growth areas are metalworking and precision machining with General Motors in Cadiz, one of the main centers of activity. Land Rover Santana and CASA, the State aircraft and aerospace company, are expanding operations in Andalusia, while chemicals and electronics are on the move.

Andalusia is also the site for technology parks. The main one is the Andalusia Technology Park at Malaga (Malaga Tel: 289924. Fax: 285695, or consultants Marcial Echenique & Compania, Madrid, or Trumpington, Cambridge, UK). The park lies within an area designated by the EC as a priority zone for development. Investors are eligible for subsidies up to 50 percent. The Andalusia Development Agency offers advice and money: venture capital and loans, tax and social security concessions, guarantees and subsidies on investment and interest rates. The Japanese have already seen the possibilities. Key Address: Instituto de Fomento de Andalucia, Avda San Francisco Javier 15, 3A, 41005 Sevilla, Spain. Tel: 466-1711. Fax: 466-0360. Next to Cadiz there is a plan for a huge new town-new resort-new science park.

SUCCESS STORIES

MOUNTLEIGH

Mountleigh, an Anglo-American property group, which in Britain focuses on real estate, is trying to demonstrate in Spain that real estate and clothes retailing can successfully go hand in hand. The group calls Spain "one of the most exciting economies in Europe," stating that in the all-important area of spending power, more than one-third of the country's 39 million people are between 18 and 40, the so-called affluent age group. Then there's what retailers call concentrated wealth, namely 27 million Spaniards living in 57 major towns and cities.

Three years ago, Mountleigh bought Galerias Preciados, Spain's second largest and then loss-making clothes chain, for just over 30 billion pesetas, or $275 million. It was the fifth change of ownership since 1979—the owner before Mountleigh was the Venezuelan retailer Diego Cisneros who sold to the Anglo-Americans for four times what he paid in 1984. But the new owners are not complaining. Indeed, such has been the appreciation of property values in Spain, that the GP chain, now numbering 30 stores, is today worth $600 million as real estate. So Mountleigh has doubled its money just on that front. However, contrary to many expectations, the group also seems infected by the retailing virus. It has announced 15 billion pesetas in investment between now and 1995, remodelling existing stores and opening new ones in both Spain and Portugal. Just after this announcement, Mountleigh opened a new, five billion pesetas store in the busy Madrid suburb of Leganes. Another sign of a long-term investment was the decision to float 55 percent of the company on the revitalized Madrid stock exchange. Additionally, part of the capital will be placed with the 7,500 employees, whose morale has suffered with the many management changes, plus, it must be said, 1,800 layoffs by the new owners. Nonetheless, GP cannot seek a quotation on the exchange until it has posted profits for three successive years. The first such year, after several lossmakers, came under the new management—four billion pesetas profit on sales of 85 billion. Debts have been cleared by selling 14 properties to a Mountleigh subsidiary for 30 billion. To placate the unions, the British-American management has promised no more segmenting of the business. Prior to the pledge, the company had signed a concession with Ivarte, one of Spain's biggest electrical goods retailers, now owned by British Home Products, to run the domestic appliances outlets. Similar franchise agreements on maternity and childwear, underwear, and furniture were made with the British retailers, Mothercare, Marks & Spencer, and Habitat. Meanwhile, GP sold a majority of its credit offshoot to the French bank, Credit Agricole, which has joined the already impressive French banking and insurance presence in Madrid. The British haulers, National Carriers, have signed to manage Galerias' distribution throughout the Iberian peninsula. But, will the British and Americans succeed in selling the necessary quantities of clothes? It's not easy, for the Spanish-owned El Corte Ingles chain remains number one and goes from strength to strength. Its sales are six times those of GP and it has model relations with its 40,000 workforce, partly through profit-sharing and share distribution—the route GP will have to follow.

CARREFOUR

Renault and Citroen manufacture cars in Spain. The French are also well entrenched in tourism, as well as the financial services sector. One of the most impressive investments is in food retailing. Carrefour, France's and one of the world's leading supermarket chains ($15 billion annual sales), has linked with the March group, of Spain, a banking and industrial giant with three billion dollars a year in turnover. The French bought Hipermercados Pryca from March and, in return, one of the March group's holding companies bought nearly five percent of Carrefour and acquired a seat on the board. The rarity of the development stems from the fact that since Spain's EC membership, very few Spanish companies have reacted to the multiple acquisition of Spanish concerns by foreigners by making international investment themselves. Battery maker, Tudor, is the notable exception becoming number two in Europe through takeovers in Scandinavia and Germany. The ratio between foreign purchases in Spain and Spanish purchases beyond the frontiers is almost ten to one. Carrefour is one of 1,600 French companies registered in Spain, compared with 250 Spanish firms in France. The French retailing giant with its 124 supermarkets worldwide and 217 other shops, is not the only French company to have targeted Spain's food retailing sector: number two in Spain is now Saudisa-Continente (16 supermarkets), owned three-quarters by Promodes, of France, and a quarter by Banco Bilbao Vizcaya, one of the country's largest banks. Third-ranking is Alcampo (12 stores), now an affiliate of France's Auchan. These three French retailers together control 75 percent of Spanish supermarket foods sales. The nearest local challenger, Hipercor (El Corte Ingles group) has a mere twelfth of the market. So much French investment in a single area is a calculated gamble, yet analysts of the market reckon there is more room for growth in Spain in supermarket sales than in any other EC country. Why? Because, such sales represent little more than a quarter of total food sales, whereas elsewhere in the EC—in France, for example—they are over 40 percent. The argument here is the same heard elsewhere—Spain is less saturated.

ELECTROLUX

Swedish trade and investment in Spain has been faster than to any other EC country since Spain's membership, with Belgium the rival in the property sector. This interest reflects the concern about the implications for third countries of the EC's single deregulated market. Unlike more northern EC markets, such as Britain, which have reached saturation point for many of the products made by Electrolux, Spain's market is under-developed. On top of this, labor costs are cheaper than anywhere else in the EC, except Greece and Portugal. Although the Swedish company has been making vacuum cleaners in Spain since the 1920s, it has gone into white goods much more recently, investing ten billion pesetas over the past three years. The world leader in the field, it has adopted the strategy of buying controlling stakes in Spanish companies rather than setting up its own plants. This is obviously less expensive, while the companies acquired have a market presence and infrastructure. The Swedes want these majority-controlled companies to form part of their international planning. Electrolux has basically been buying market shares, and in the white goods sector it now has one-third of the total Spanish market. The fruit of this investment is a brand new holding company, Electrolux Holding SA, which comprises 15 companies, with 67 billion pesetas in annual sales, profits of 3.5 billion pesetas, and 5,000 workers. A quarter of the output is exported, principally to the rest of the EC, but also to North Africa and Latin America, two areas of Spanish influence. Electrolux in Spain has Unidad Hermetica, which produces three and a half million compressors a year for refrigerators; Ibelsa, which makes the whole range of white goods, including cookers, for large, industrial installations (both acquired when Electrolux took over Italy's failing white goods group, Zanussi); Corbero, maker of microwave ovens and cookers, and Domar, manufacturer of the popular New Pol washing machines. That is far from the end of expansion. Electrolux is going to double investment over the coming four to five years to 20 billion pesetas, but this time in new areas: services related to the detection, prevention, and correction of atmospheric pollution and other environmental problems, such as water cleansing and waste disposal; and a second new area for Spain—integrated house management services, from the installation of cooking and washing equipment to house security, even gardening.

Jane Monahan

Madrid with its surroundings today holds five million people, making it Europe's third-largest metropolis. This means a new, high standard of living for many, a new sheen on the city's looks, but also the problems, notably expensive housing and the scourge of drugs, that exist in other big European cities. Property prices in the city's prime areas have trebled since 1985, and there is a shortage both of offices and hotel rooms. Compared with other EC countries, fewer houses or apartments are available for rent, not just in Madrid, but also in the whole of Spain. Surveys show that while 58 percent of buildings in West Germany, and 38 percent of those in France have been rented at one time or another, the figure for Spain is a mere 11 percent. For the moment, one can still see mountains across an empty plain when standing atop a Madrid building. Now the plains increasingly are becoming suburbs.

However, the same studies show rents to be about the lowest in the EC, with the obvious exceptions of the downtown areas of Madrid and Barcelona. Average rent, in one recent study, was $230 a month, with only just over one percent of people paying more than $500 a month. The government is planning to make it easier for tenants to rent for short terms, thus introducing greater flexibility into the Madrid housing market. Prosperity has brought bumper-to-bumper traffic to Madrid while the noise level is among the highest in Europe. Pollution, too, is bad, with little or no control over coal and oil burning or the incineration of rubbish. City and industry will have to improve their acts. So why does Madrid earn so many column inches in the media? Well, the contemporary effervescence of the city is light years from the repressive gloom of the Franco era—and the often worrisome times after Franco. The city has beautiful parks. One anti-pollution effort is succeeding, the clean-up of the River Manzanares where the first "reborn" fish have appeared. The city also is now one of Europe's most important art capitals and will house the Thyssen collection of masterpieces which will be the counterpoint to Spain's leading museum, the Prado. The Teatro Real is reverting to opera, while the new National Auditorium is on the European and international circuits for the best concerts, conductors, and orchestras. Film-making is alive. Fashion flourishes. The old city, near the Plaza Mayor and the flea market, is being restored. Next to Barajas Airport, a brand new conference and exhibition center, the Campo de la Naciones, is being built to herald Madrid's new vocation as an international services center. The national airline, Iberia, is combining high profits with superb service, including its front-running business lounges.

Madrid has shed much of its old provincialism. Yet this has happened without the Madrilenos opting for anywhere less hectic. Most of those who could leave say there's no place like the capital. Why? They cite its vitality, even the degree of anarchy.

THE LEADERS

TOP 20 COMPANIES (1989)

		(Millions of pesetas)	
		Sales	*Profits*
(1)	Repsol	926,283	55,944
(2)	Telefonica	612,536	62,845
(3)	El Corte Ingles	475,283	18,619
(4)	Endesa	457,502	61,670
(5)	Tabacalera	443,443	9,777
(6)	SEAT	384,110	1,172
(7)	Fasa Renault	382,224	11,747
(8)	Cepsa	363,242	12,429
(9)	General Motors	352,159	27,895
(10)	Iberia	334,806	24,256
(11)	Ford Espana	290,586	—

(12)	Hidroelectrica	257,080	20,770
(13)	Iberduero	252,751	26,026
(14)	Union Electrica	202,732	10,417
(15)	Pryca	202,000	7,056
(16)	Citroen Hispana	187,695	13,746
(17)	IBM	187,090	21,396
(18)	Hypermercados Continente	186,813	—
(19)	Rio Tinto	181,976	5,272
(20)	Peugeot Talbot	176,534	17,480

(Source: Mercado magazine/Price Waterhouse)

TOP 20 BANKS

		(Millions of pesetas) Turnover
(1)	BBV	576,654
(2)	Banesto	355,751
(3)	Hispano Americano	329,076
(4)	Central	328,454
(5)	Exterior	292,221
(6)	Santander	276,127
(7)	La Caixa	274,637
(8)	Caja de Madrid	172,796
(9)	Popular Espanol	156,527
(10)	Caja de Barcelona	107,153
(11)	Urquijo Union	92,588
(12)	Bankinter	87,327
(13)	Catalana	85,525
(14)	Sabadell	82,683
(15)	Atlantico	67,691
(16)	Pastor	67,179
(17)	Caja de Cataluna	66,987
(18)	Ibercaja	59,988
(19)	Caja de Galicia	50,623
(20)	Caja de Mediterraneo	49,598

(Source: Mercado magazine/Price Waterhouse)
Recent mergers, notably between Banco Central and Banco Hispano Americano, resulted in 1991
in the following, unofficial ranking: (1) Central Hispanoamericano; (2) Corporacion Bancaria

de Espana; (3) Banco Bilbao Vizcaya; (4) La Caixa; (5) Banco Santander; (6) Banesto; (7) Caja Madrid; and (8) Banco Popular.

TOP 10 INSURANCE COMPANIES

		(Millions of pesetas) Turnover
(1)	Euroseguros	260,624
(2)	Rentcaixa	229,894
(3)	Vida Caixa	224,773
(4)	Union El Fenix	105,229
(5)	Banco Vitalicio	67,829
(6)	Caser	62,546
(7)	La Estrella	55,065
(8)	Mapfre Mutualidad	43,512
(9)	Mapfre Mutua Patronal	37,400
(10)	Mutua Automovilista	35,221

(Source: Mercado magazine/Price Waterhouse)

KEY CONTACTS

USEFUL MADRID TELEPHONE NUMBERS

Trade and Commercial Information

European Community: 34-1-435-1700
Stock Exchange: 34-1-521-4790
Convention Bureau: 34-1-463-6334
Commerce, State Secretariat: 34-1-458-8664
Directorate, Regional Incentives: 34-1-571-4412
Economy, State Secretariat: 34-1-468-2000

Government Offices

Labor: 34-1-253-6000
Industry, Energy: 34-1-458-8010
Transport: 34-1-456-1144

Madrid Community

Employment: 34-1-410-5092
Industry, Energy: 34-1-402-5150
Labor, Commerce: 34-1-419-8048
Technology Park: 34-1-803-3550
High Council, Chambers of Commerce: 34-1-275-2303
IMADE (Foreign Investment): 34-1-410-2063
Madrid Chamber of Commerce: 34-1-429-3193
Sepes (Cost Price Land): 34-1-456-5015

Embassies

Member Nations
Belgium: 34-1-401-9558
Britain: 34-1-419-0200
Denmark: 34-1-431-8445
France: 34-1-435-5560
Germany: 34-1-419-9100
Greece: 34-1-411-3345
Ireland: 34-1-276-3500
Italy: 34-1-402-5436
Netherlands: 34-1-458-2100
Portugal: 34-1-261-7800

Others
Algeria: 34-1-411-6065
Argentina: 34-1-442-4500
Austria: 34-1-456-5315
Bolivia: 34-1-270-9858
Brazil: 34-1-431-1225
Canada: 34-1-431-4300
Chile: 34-1-431-9160
China: 34-1-413-4889
Costa Rica: 34-1-441-6767
Cuba: 34-1-458-2500
Ecuador: 34-1-262-7215

Egypt: 34-1-401-9600
El Salvador: 34-1-262-8002
Finland: 34-1-419-6172
Guatemala: 34-1-457-7827
Honduras: 34-1-279-0251
India: 34-1-413-6161
Indonesia: 34-1-458-0668
Japan: 34-1-262-5546
Korea: 34-1-410-0439
Libya: 34-1-458-0458
Mexico: 34-1-456-1263
Morocco: 34-1-458-0950
Norway: 34-1-401-6262
Pakistan: 34-1-431-5441
Panama: 34-1-276-2747
Paraguay: 34-1-435-8858
Soviet Union: 34-1-262-2264
Sweden: 34-1-419-7550
Tunisia: 34-1-447-3508
United States: 34-1-577-4000
Uruguay: 34-1-248-7035
Venezuela: 34-1-455-8455
Yugoslavia: 34-1-262-4710

USEFUL BARCELONA/CATALONIA TELEPHONE NUMBERS

Government Offices

CIDEM (Business Development Center): 34-3-215-8582/215-7178
  (CIDEM, New York: (212-755-8830)
Commerce Department: 34-3-237-9045
Economy and Finance: 34-3-302-5020
Industry and Energy: 34-3-237-3645

Chambers of Commerce

Member Nations
Belgium: 34-3-237-9464
Britain: 34-3-317-3220
France: 34-3-317-6738
Germany: 34-3-218-8262
Italy: 34-3-318-5999
Netherlands: 34-3-217-5985
Portugal: 34-3-318-5200

Others
Council of Chambers of
  Commerce: 34-3-319-2412
Barcelona: 34-3-219-1300
United States: 34-3-321-8195

Consulates

Member Nations
Belgium: 34-3-318-9899
Britain: 34-3-322-2151
Denmark: 34-3-310-2091
France: 34-3-209-6722
Germany: 34-3-218-4750
Greece: 34-3-246-2290
Ireland: 34-3-330-9652
Italy: 34-3-215-1654

Luxembourg: 34-3-237-3701
Netherlands: 34-3-217-3358
Portugal: 34-3-318-8150

Others
America: 34-3-319-9550
Canada: 34-3-209-0634
Japan: 34-3-310-2097

USEFUL SEVILLE/ANDALUCIA TELEPHONE NUMBERS

Trade and Commercial Information

Instituto de Fomento de Andalucia: 34-954-466-1711

Consulates

Member Nations
Belgium: 34-954-677061
Britain: 34-954-228875
Denmark: 34-954-611489
France: 34-954-222896
Germany: 34-954-477811
Greece: 34-954-419000

Italy: 34-954-227774
Netherlands: 34-954-228750
Portugal: 34-954-231150

Others
United States: 34-954-231885

INDEX